Ethics and Economics

This textbook applies economic ethics to evaluate the free market system and enables students to examine the impact of free markets using the three main ethical approaches: utilitarianism, principle-based ethics and virtue ethics.

Ethics and Economics systematically links empirical research to these ethical questions, with a focus on the core topics of happiness, inequality and virtues. Each chapter offers a recommended further reading list. The final chapter provides a practical method for applying the different ethical approaches to morally evaluate an economic policy proposal and an example of the methodology being applied to a real-life policy.

This book will give students a clear theoretical and methodological toolkit for analyzing the ethics of market policies, making it a valuable resource for courses on economic ethics and economic philosophy.

Johan Graafland (1960) has been a full professor of economics, business and ethics at Tilburg University, the Netherlands, since 2000 and is a fellow of the Tilburg Sustainability Center.

"With this book, Graafland provides both an excellent introduction to ethics-and-economics and an innovative exploration of the effect of free markets on happiness and inequality, grounded in moral philosophy and economic theory and supplemented by a wealth of real-world data. This is truly a landmark achievement that is certain to be an indispensable resource for scholars, teachers, and students for years to come."

—Mark D. White, Chair and Professor, Department of Philosophy,
College of Staten Island/CUNY, and editor of
The Oxford Handbook of Ethics and Economics

Ethics and Economics

An Introduction to Free Markets, Equality and Happiness

Johan Graafland

Routledge
Taylor & Francis Group
LONDON AND NEW YORK

TILBURG ◆ UNIVERSITY

First published 2022
by Routledge
2 Park Square, Milton Park, Abingdon, Oxon OX14 4RN

and by Routledge
605 Third Avenue, New York, NY 10158

Routledge is an imprint of the Taylor & Francis Group, an informa business

British Library Cataloguing-in-Publication Data
A catalogue record for this book is available from the British Library

Library of Congress Cataloging-in-Publication Data
Names: Graafland, J. J., author.
Title: Ethics and economics : an introduction to free markets, equality and
    happiness / Johan Graafland.
Description: 1 Edition. | New York : Routledge, 2021. | Includes
    bibliographical references and index.
Subjects: LCSH: Economics—Moral and ethical aspects. |
    Utilitarianism—Moral and ethical aspects. | Free enterprise—Moral
    and ethical aspects. | Equality. | Social justice. | Virtue. | Conduct of life.
Classification: LCC HB72 .G723 2021 (print) | LCC HB72 (ebook) |
    DDC 174/.4—dc23
LC record available at https://lccn.loc.gov/2021006038
LC ebook record available at https://lccn.loc.gov/2021006039

ISBN: 978-1-032-02098-3 (hbk)
ISBN: 978-1-032-02062-4 (pbk)
ISBN: 978-1-003-18183-5 (ebk)

DOI: 10.4324/9781003181835

Typeset in Minion
by Apex CoVantage, LLC

Access the Support Material: www.routledge.com/9781032020624

Contents

Figures

Tables

Boxes

Author biography

Johan Graafland (1960) is a full professor of economics, business and ethics at Tilburg University, the Netherlands, since 2000 and is a fellow of the Tilburg Sustainability Center. He is a member of the economics department at the faculty of Economics and Business Administration, philosophy department at the Faculty of Humanities and theology department at Tilburg University. He studied economics at Erasmus University Rotterdam and theology at Utrecht University. His research focuses on economic ethics, business ethics, corporate social responsibility and the relationship between economics and religion. From 2017 until 2021 Johan Graafland led a large multidisciplinary research of a consortium of Tilburg University, Radboud University, Erasmus University and the Vrije Universiteit on the research project 'What Good Markets Are Good For'. He has published seven books and about 70 articles in peer-reviewed journals. He teaches the courses 'Philosophy of Economics and Economic Ethics', 'History of Economic Thought', 'Christianity in Dialogue with Social Economic World' and 'Corporate Social Responsibility' at Tilburg University. His work has attracted over 2,500 ISI citations.

Preface

Since the seventies of the twentieth century, governments have pursued a free market policy of deregulation and privatization. This free market system has generated welfare and economic growth, particularly in emerging countries like China and India. However, increasing income inequalities, depletion of the natural environment, the financial crisis in 2008 and the current COVID crisis have led to an intense debate about the advantages and disadvantages of free market institutions. This calls into question to what extent one should favor free markets as a means to increase well-being.

This book aims to contribute to this debate by focusing on three interrelated research topics, which are generally considered of importance when studying the consequences of free markets: happiness, (in)equality and virtues/virtuousness. The first part of the book evaluates free market institutions from a happiness point of view by relating three influential economic perspectives to the ethical theory of utilitarianism. In economic theory, the notion that freely operating markets are conducive to utility (i.e. happiness) is well established. In fact, it can be understood as one of the central tenets of economics, dating back to Adam Smith's *Wealth of Nations*. However, this does not automatically imply that free markets foster human happiness (and quality of life in a broader sense). In this part of the book, we introduce utilitarianism; review neoliberalism, neoclassical and Keynesian perspectives on free markets; and present empirical evidence on the impact of free market institutions on welfare, happiness and quality of life.

The second part of the book considers free markets from the principle-based perspectives of the ethics of rights and justice. Free market institutions have been defended from a negative rights ethics and capitalist justice viewpoint. However, during the last decades, inequality in wealth and income has been on the rise in both Western and non-Western market economies. This has induced a commonly shared feeling of uneasiness about the current worldwide economic order and doubts about its distributive justness. After introducing some key ethical theories on rights and justice, this part of the book provides empirical evidence that nuances the debate on free markets and justice by showing that some free market institutions increase and others decrease income inequality.

In the third part of the book we discuss the relationship between free market institutions, virtuousness of the market actors and happiness with the help of virtue ethics. In the literature, two main debates have attracted the attention of economists and philosophers.

First, there is a long and ongoing dispute over whether free market institutions encourage or discourage virtues. According to the 'doux commerce thesis', free markets nurture virtues such as honesty. The antithesis is the 'self-destruction thesis', which states that free market institutions favor a cultural learning process that is inimical to the virtues needed for well-functioning markets. The second debate, related to but distinguished from the first debate, concerns the effect of virtuousness on human or societal happiness. In classical virtue ethics, practicing virtues enables people to become happy. In contrast, Mandeville argued in his *Fable of the Bees* that the practice of private virtues leads to societal disaster and therefore, ultimately, to human unhappiness. His idea is that without vices, a nation will not prosper. In this part of the book, we introduce virtue ethics and will review different views on both debates and present empirical evidence that helps to settle them.

The book will be used as the main textbook in a course on economic ethics. Books educating students to systematically link the ethics of economics to recent empirical research in economics on free market institutions are rare. In this book I confront the three main ethical approaches – utilitarianism, principle-based ethics and virtue ethics – with current economic literature on the effects of market institutions. I do so by focusing on three core topics: happiness, inequality and virtues. The book concludes with a practical method for applying these three ethical approaches to the moral evaluation of concrete economic policy proposals that aim to improve market institutions. The aim of the book is, thus, to provide the reader insights and tools for applying various ethical theories to the evaluation of market policies, taking into account recent insights of economic research into the effects of free market institutions.

At the start of this book I want to thank my colleagues from the research project 'What Good Markets Are Good For' (see www.moralmarkets.org), in particular Lans Bovenberg, Reyer Gerlagh, Bjorn Lous, Niels Noorderhaven, Tom Wells and Harmen Verbruggen who co-authored some of the scientific articles that I used in this book. I also want to thank Govert Buijs, Eefje de Gelder and Ilse Oosterlaken with whom I managed the research in this project. I want to thank Templeton World Charity Foundation, Inc., for providing me financial assistance for the research project that allowed me to devote a substantial part of my time on research in the relationship between free market institutions, virtues and human flourishing during 2017–2020.

Gouda January 2021
The Netherlands

1

Introduction

1.1 ECONOMIC ETHICS

What is ethics?

Ethics is the study of morality. But what is morality? Velasquez (1998) gives the following definition: "Morality concerns the standards that an individual or a group has about what is right and wrong" (Velasquez, 1998: 8). Moral standards are imperative in nature and may imply moral duties. They do not refer primarily to what people actually do or how the world is, but rather what people ought to do, how the world should be.

Besides moral standards there are many non-moral normative standards, e.g. standards in successful marketing of products. Moral standards differ from non-moral standards in several aspects. First, as already noted earlier, moral standards are prescriptive statements. They are action-guiding imperatives that do not describe states of affairs but what people ought to do. Second, we feel that moral standards should overrule other, non-moral standards. Even if it is in our personal interest to cheat at a certain moment, moral standards tell us that we should not do so. A third and related characteristic is that moral standards should be impartial. That means that moral standards are evaluated from a point of view that goes beyond the interests of a particular individual or group to a universal standpoint in which everyone's interests are impartially counted. Morality sets rules for everyone's conduct. A moral judgment must, for any person who accepts the judgment, apply to all relevantly similar circumstances. Fourth, moral standards deal with issues that have serious consequences for the welfare of human beings. This criterion focuses on the moral content. Moral action guides have some reference to the welfare of others or human flourishing, or are at least concerned with serious harm and benefit to other persons.

Moral standards include the values (or ideals) we place on the kinds of objects we believe are morally right or wrong, as well as the norms we have about the kinds of actions we believe are right or wrong. Values concern ends or ideals that persons pursue and give content to how they define the good life. They are sustainable convictions of persons about what makes certain acts or a certain way of life valuable. Examples of moral values are freedom, respect for other people and justice. Values can be both intrinsic and extrinsic in nature. One intrinsically values something when one values it in itself, that is, apart from valuing anything else. Extrinsic values are values that are merely good as a means to something else. Money, for example, is for most people only extrinsically valuable: it is usually valued not for the sake of having stacks of money, but because the money can be used to purchase goods and services that have intrinsic value (Beauchamp, 1982). Extrinsic values are therefore also called instrumental values.

DOI: 10.4324/9781003181835-1

Norms are the rules or conventions that should be followed up in order to realize moral values. They relate to values as means relate to ends. If norms do not serve any value, they are meaningless. On the other hand, without norms, values remain unattainable.[1] Norms give an answer to the question: What should we do? For example, in order to respect a person, one should not offend other persons. Other examples of norms are: Don't cheat; don't steal. Whereas values are rather global in nature and hold in most situations, moral norms are often dependent on the context of the situation. For example, whereas in a democratic political system politicians respect the general public by being transparent about their decisions, a doctor respects his or her patient by being confidential. Furthermore, whereas values motivate persons, norms regulate the behavior. They are often structured as 'Thou shall . . .' or 'Thou shall not . . .'. Besides moral norms, behavior can also be regulated by social norms (etiquette) or legal norms (De Beer and den Hoed, 2004). All three types of norms oblige to a certain type of behavior. Moral norms judge behavior as good and evil, legal norms as legal or illegal and social norms as proper or improper. Often the three types of norms overlap. For example, stealing is bad, illegal and improper. As argued earlier, the moral dimension is in most cases of greater importance than law or etiquette. Laws are often grounded in certain moral convictions that have led legislators to enact them.

Moral dilemmas

A moral dilemma can be seen as a conflict between different moral standards, including values (Anderson, 1993), ideals (Railton, 1996) and duties (Brink, 1996; Donagan, 1996). In order to classify dilemmas according to the standards that generate them, we draw a distinction between two types of standards: moral standards and practical standards. Examples of practical standards include, for example, profitability, self-interest and pride. Dilemmas, conceived of as a conflict between different standards, can therefore be divided into four categories, as shown in Table 1.1.

A dilemma arising from a conflict between two moral standards is classified as a moral dilemma. Situations in which these dilemmas occur are particularly challenging, because one has to weight two important standards. A dilemma that arises from a conflict between a moral standard and a practical standard is classified as a motivational dilemma. This dilemma confronts an individual with the problem of moral motivation: what motivates people to act in accordance with their moral standards (Crisp, 1998). A dilemma that results from a conflict between two practical standards is classified as a practical dilemma. A wide range of practical dilemmas are conceivable, from the dilemma of deciding on the color of the new company vehicles to the dilemma of deciding what amount of money should be invested in the next year.

TABLE 1.1
Classification of dilemmas

	Moral standard	Practical standard
Moral standard	Moral dilemma	Motivational dilemma
Practical standard	Motivational dilemma	Practical dilemma

Economics

Economics is the study of the economy. The neoclassical definition of economics is often based on the definition offered by Robbins (1935) in his famous book *Essays on the Nature and Significance of Economic Science*. He defines economics as "the science which studies human behavior as a relationship between ends and scarce means which have alternative uses" (Robbins, 1935: 16). The core element of this definition is scarcity: if a person would have ample time and ample means, all ends can be realized and the agent does not have to economize. Robbins argues that economics is not only concerned with material production and consumption. The domain of economics exists in all aspects of human behavior in circumstances of scarcity. Any human act has an economic aspect insofar as persons must make a choice between scarce material and/or non-material means.

Positive and normative statements

Whereas economics is a social science that engages in a descriptive study of the economy that attempts to describe or explain the economy without reaching conclusions about what ought to be done, ethics is a normative study that attempts to reach normative conclusions about what things are good or bad. The task of economics is to provide knowledge of 'what is' that can be used to make correct predictions about the consequences of any change in circumstances. Like other sciences, economics helps us to understand the world and to act within the world. Any economic policy conclusion necessarily rests on economic predictions about the consequences of doing one thing rather than another.

The conclusions of positive economics are therefore immediately relevant to questions of what ought to be done and how any given goal can be attained (Friedman, 1953). But any policy advice does not only relate to facts but also to values. Indeed, economic policy advice about what policy makers should do is derived from these two elements: a value statement that prescribes the goal of economic policy (e.g. what desired state of affairs we aim at) and a description of how different policies affect the economy and to what extent they help realize this desired state of affairs:

1 Value statement: the government should foster goal x
2 Positive statement: application of economic policy instrument y will improve the realization of goal x
3 Policy conclusion: the government should apply policy instrument y

The first statement is derived from normative theory that is concerned with values and says what ought to be, the second statement is derived from positive theory that describes facts and the third statement is derived from the combination of positive theory and normative theory.

According to Friedman (1953), differences about economic policy derive predominantly from different predictions about the economic consequences of taking action (statement 2) rather than from fundamental differences in values (statement 1). An obvious example is minimum wage legislation. Most economists would probably agree to the goal of diminishing poverty for people at the lower end of the labor market. However, they do not agree whether minimum wages will contribute to this goal. Whereas some argue that higher minimum wages will diminish poverty by raising the wages at the lower end of the labor market, others believe (predict) that higher legal minimum wages increase poverty by increasing unemployment.

Economic ethics

The application of ethics to a certain field is to be distinguished from general normative ethics. General normative ethics is the philosophical attempt to formulate and defend basic moral principles. Parts I to III of the book describe several general normative ethical principles: utilitarianism, duty ethics, rights ethics, justice ethics, virtue ethics and care ethics. These principles can be applied to a range of fields. The application or further specification of moral action guides to a certain field is commonly referred to as applied ethics. Examples are medical ethics, engineering ethics and journalistic ethics. This book is about economic ethics. Economic ethics reflect on the moral standards that apply to economic phenomena. Economic ethics thus has the same domain as economics. However, the perspective from which economic phenomena are studied differs: whereas economics explains the relationships between economic phenomena, economic ethics evaluates them from a moral point of view.

Kouwenhoven (1981) distinguishes between two strands of economic ethics: micro- and macroeconomic ethics. Microeconomic ethics encompasses both individuals and individual households and businesses and evaluates the actions of these individual entities given the economic structures or institutions. How should the individual economic agent behave on the market? The macroeconomic ethics considers the morality of economic structures. Does the economic order respect ethical standards? This book is mainly about macroeconomic ethics, because it will evaluate the institution of the market. However, the distinction between micro- and macroeconomic ethics is not very sharp. Macroeconomic ethics cannot do without microeconomic ethics: the evaluation of the institution of the market often reverts to the micro-ethical roots, i.e. the way how individuals should behave. On the other hand, microeconomic ethics can also not be studied in isolation from macroeconomic institutions. The microeconomic ethics should take account of the moral incentives from economic structures on individual behavior. For example, if competition is fierce, companies that engage in (costly forms of) corporate social responsibility (CSR) may see their costs increase and risk losses in market shares that might eventually result in bankruptcy. Fierce competition therefore can be a mitigating factor that lessens a company's moral responsibility depending on how serious the wrong is.

Macroeconomic ethics belongs to the broader category of social ethics. The domain of social ethics is the morality of the societal relationships and structures. It studies the collective decisions of groups (families, action groups, states) and the structural relations (social systems) that connect these groups. In Part II we discuss several social philosophers such as Rawls and Nozick. Since our interest is mainly in economic ethics (and not in other applications of social ethics), we will pay particular attention to those parts of social philosophy that are useful to evaluate the institution of the market. Likewise, microeconomic ethics belongs to the broader category of individual ethics that studies the individuals as the subject of ethical considerations and actions, often in direct relations with other individuals.

1.2 DEFENSE AND CRITIQUE OF FREE MARKETS

In this book we apply economic ethics to evaluate the free market system. The free market system is an economic system in which the economic decisions and the pricing of goods and services are guided solely by the interactions of individual citizens and businesses (Voigt and Kiwit, 1998), that means, free from government regulations. Markets are regulated by institutions that shape and regulate the coordination of economic behavior of persons and enterprises in the marketplace. Institutions can be defined as "systems of established and prevalent social rules that structure social interactions" (Hodgson, 2006: 2). Kostova (1997) distinguishes three types of institutions: regulatory, normative and cognitive. Regulative elements include rules, sanctions and regulations which tend to codify socially accepted behavior and promote certain types of behavior and restrict others, such as government regulations. Normative elements are values, social norms, beliefs and assumptions about human nature and human behavior that are socially shared. Cognitive elements include cognitive structures and social knowledge shared by people in a given country that shape inferential sets that people use when selecting and interpreting information.

In this book, we particularly focus on regulative institutions. The regulative institutions that shape the free market system can be characterized by the concept of economic freedom. Economic freedom means that individuals are free to use, exchange or give their property to another as long as their actions do not violate property rights of others (see also Chapter 4). Economic freedom implies low taxes (and hence small size of government); protection of individual property rights; absence of restrictions on free trade; and no government interference in credit, labor and product markets. In a free market system, government intervention is thus limited to providing legally secured property rights and acquisition procedures.

Traditional defense of the free market system

The most well-known moral defenses of the free market system go back to John Locke and Adam Smith. John Locke, an English political philosopher (1632–1704), based the market system on a theory of moral rights. The two rights that free markets are supposed to respect are the right to freedom and the right to private property. John Locke derives these basic rights from a state of nature, as if there were no governments. In this state, each man would be equal to all others and perfectly free of any constraints other than the moral principles that God gave to humanity, according to Locke. For Locke, reason teaches that these moral principles hold that no one ought to harm another in his life, health, liberty or possessions. Each has a right to liberty and a right of ownership over his own body, his own labor and the products of his labor. In this state of nature, individuals are, however, in constant danger of being harmed by others. Consequently, individuals have an incentive to create a government whose primary purpose is to provide protection of their natural rights. Since the citizen consents to government only with an intention to preserve himself, his liberty and his property, the power of the government may never extend beyond what is needed to preserve these rights, according to Locke. The government is not allowed to intervene in economic transactions that individuals voluntarily conclude on the market.

The second major moral defense of the free market system rests on the utilitarian argument that market institutions will produce greater benefits than any other institution that coordinates the demand and supply of goods, like central planning by the government or the unpaid economy in which people offer services to each other for free. This utilitarian defense of markets has been developed by Adam Smith (1723–1790). At the beginning of the capitalist era when Adam Smith published his famous book *An Inquiry into the Nature and Causes of the Wealth of Nations* (1776), the economic policy was mercantilist. In the mercantile system, markets were highly regulated by the government. The deregulation of the market economy in combination with the industrial revolution stimulated economic growth after 1800. In Great Britain, real wages doubled between 1800 and 1850 and doubled again between 1850 and 1900. The gains in liberty of personal choice – in a more varied diet, new beverages, new skills – increased accordingly (Novak, 1982). One of the reasons why the market stimulates economic growth is that it allows a high specialization between different industries and companies. In the first chapter of *The Wealth of Nations* Adam Smith illustrates the advantages of the division of labor by the example of a pin factory. A worker not specialized in this business could scarcely make 20 pins in a day. By dividing the work into a number of eight distinct operations, a group of ten workers can make 48,000 pins in a day. This great increase in productivity results from specialization – allowing the increase of dexterity of every workman and saving time, which is lost in passing from one species of work to another – and the invention of specialized machines which facilitate labor. This division of labor is, however, only possible if people can efficiently trade the products they make. The market offers an efficient mechanism for exchanging the products produced by specialized units. First, in a free competitive market, the price will tend to what Smith calls the natural price. The commodity is then sold for what it is worth, namely for what it really costs the person who brings it to the market. Competition forces producers to supply what consumers want in the most productive way and at the lowest price. If they set their price higher than competitors do, they will lose market shares. Second, competition will also efficiently allocate the resources of the economy (capital and labor) among the various industries of a society. If consumer preferences change, the sales of some products will decline and the business supplying these products will lose market shares and see their price fall. As a result, their profitability will fall, and some firms will close their operations and move to market segments that show a rise in demand and an increase in profitability. In this way, the flexible price mechanism takes care of an allocation of capital and labor that optimally fits the demand for goods and thus contributes to maximizing total welfare.

An interesting aspect of Smith's theory is that this optimal situation is realized by self-interested actors. Motivated by their own micro-goals of maximum utility or maximum profits, consumers and producers carry out plans that simultaneously serve the macro-goal of maximal economic utility of the society at large. As Smith states:

> He (the businessman) generally, indeed, neither intends to promote the public interest, nor knows how much he is promoting it . . . he intends only his own gain, and he is in this, as in many other cases, led by an *invisible hand* to promote an end which was no part of his intention. . . . By pursuing his own interest he frequently promotes that of the society more effectually than when he really intends to promote it.
>
> (Smith, 2000 [1776]: IV.ii.9)

This citation reflects the theory of the unintended consequences: although the businessman intends to serve his own interest, the consequence of his action also serves the interests of his customers and the community. Adam Smith uses the invisible hand as a metaphor for the idea that if people interact freely, the pursuit of their self-interest is not incompatible with serving the common good (Peil, 1995).

Later, other economists supplemented Smith's market theory by arguing that it is impossible for the government or any human to allocate resources with the same efficiency. They simply never can have enough information nor calculate fast enough to coordinate in an efficient way the millions of transactions that take place every day in a complex economy.[2] In a market economy, the price signals on the thousands of sub-markets that are linked to each other do this job. In this way, the market economizes on the information that people require. The only information individual consumers or producers need to have about the rest of the economy to adjust their behavior in an efficient way is conveyed through prices. Hence, an efficient outcome can be accomplished by decentralized, voluntary transactions among people, each of whom has only a tiny portion of the requisite information.

Economic objections

Many economists still defend the free market system. But this position has also been criticized on several economic grounds. For example, the assumption that the market economy will force prices down to their lowest levels only holds in case of perfect competition between a great number of producers. In reality, there are many market imperfections that distort the operating of the market. For example, companies have an incentive to reduce competition in order to raise their profitability, for example, by merging or price agreements.[3] Therefore, in reality many industries and markets are characterized by monopolies or oligopolies, in which a few companies compete with each other with no free entry for other firms. In these markets, firms have the power to set prices higher than the production costs. In order to remedy the efforts of companies to reduce competition, a government must pursue an active anti-trust policy, for example, by only allowing mergers if certain conditions are met.

Another important market imperfection is the existence of so-called external effects. External effects are costs or benefits from a decision which are not borne by the decision-maker and cannot be charged to him or her because of a missing market. In free markets, all microeconomic agents will base their plans on the individual costs and benefits and not consider these side effects of their operations. For example, when travelers use their car, they produce more CO_2 emissions. However, their individual contribution is so small that they will not consider this negative effect on the environment when deciding about going by train or by car. But if all travelers make the same consideration and choose to go by car, the total negative impact on the environment is considerable. In free markets, consumers or producers do not have to pay a price for pollution. As a result, they will not economize on the scarce resource of a good environment. This causes social waste and lack of unsustainable economic development.

Furthermore, well-functioning markets assume that individuals are rational. However, in reality the rationality of people is bounded (Conlisk, 1996; Rabin, 1998). Conflicting interests that change over time will make it difficult to make a consistent choice. Individual preferences for commodities and services are not just given and can be an object of manipulation. Furthermore, people have limited cognitive ability to solve the complex problem of choosing an optimal consumption bundle that maximizes their utility. These bounds in rationality create another market imperfection that yields inefficient economic outcomes in a free market context.

Ethical objections

The criticism on the defense of the free market system is not only inspired by the existence of market imperfections; there are several other objections against the defense of free operation of market which are more moral in nature.

First, from a justice ethical point of view, it is sometimes argued that the free market system allows large inequalities. A person's consumer power will be proportionate to the amount of labor he possesses. Those individuals who have accumulated a great deal of wealth and who have access to education and training will be able to accumulate even more wealth. As a result, without government intervention, the gap between the rich and the poor will widen until large disparities of wealth emerge.

Second, Locke takes the assumption that people have rights to liberty and property as self-evident, but this assumption is unproven. Markets only respect certain negative rights. For example, buyers and sellers are free to enter or leave the market. They are not forced to buy or sell anything other than what they freely consent to. Free markets thus embody the negative rights of freedom of consent and freedom from coercion. However, even if human beings have a natural right to liberty and property, it does not follow that these rights override all other rights. The negative right to liberty, for example, may conflict with someone else's positive right to food or medical care. If a person has a positive right to food, other people may have the moral duty to refrain from certain actions that reduce the supply of food and cause starvation. These positive rights are also explicitly recognized in the United Nations' declaration of human rights, which expands the negative 'natural rights' of Locke to positive rights to food, clothing, housing and medical care. It is not clear why the negative right to liberty should be overriding.

Third, from a virtue ethical point of view, it can be argued that free markets ignore the demands of caring. The dominant attention to efficiency may foster character traits that maximize individual economic well-being, but may neglect character traits associated with building personal relationships with others that foster trust. The virtues of loyalty, kindness and caring tend to diminish, while the vices of being greedy, self-seeking and calculating are encouraged. This will crowd out the community and ultimately the happiness of individuals partaking in the community.

Our view on the free market thus depends both on our economic views about how the free market contributes to important moral standards and on our moral views about which ethical standards should prevail. Also policy advice of economists is based on economic analysis as well as on ethical values.

1.3   PURPOSE AND PLAN OF THE BOOK[4]

The primary aim of this text is to introduce the reader to the application of economic ethics to the evaluation of the market. The reader will gain insight into the characteristics of three major ethical theories that can be used to evaluate the market economy. A secondary aim of this book is to give an overview of empirical research into the impacts of free market institutions on important ethical goals, e.g. happiness, justice and virtues. These economic insights provide background knowledge that contribute to a nuanced ethical evaluation of market institutions.

The book thus researches three main questions. The first question concerns the effect of market institutions on happiness. This is the subject of Part I. Chapter 2 discusses the ethical theory of utilitarianism. Compared to the other ethical standards, utilitarianism is most aligned to economic thought. Chapter 2 describes three characteristics of utilitarianism: consequentialism, welfarism and sum ranking. This is followed by a discussion of some philosophical problems in consequentialism, welfarism and sum ranking and how utilitarianism has responded to these problems.

Economists have endorsed these characteristics of utilitarianism except sum ranking, because of some methodological problems of the interpersonal comparison of utilities. If the utility of different individuals cannot be compared, how can one say anything about the total sum of utilities generated by an action or policy? Economists have answered this question by developing Pareto optimality as welfare criterion. Chapter 3 considers three different economic paradigms of the market economy that propose different roles of government regulation, as well as social responsibility of companies. It examines the theorems of welfare economics, discusses the conditions of a perfect market and identifies several types of market imperfections that reduce the efficiency of the market.

Chapter 4 presents recent research on the relationship between a free market economy and happiness. One of the main arguments in favor of markets is the creation of welfare. Whether the free market system fosters happiness in society should be settled by empirical research. Chapter 4 presents an overview of empirical research of the influence of free market institutions as measured by economic freedom on economic growth, life satisfaction, human development and quality of life.

The second theme is how market institutions relate to principles of rights and justice. This is the subject of Part II. Many condemn neoliberal globalization of the free market system on grounds of injustice, but this may lack a nuanced view on the causes of worldwide poverty and the role of globalization. To contribute to this debate, we investigate the concepts of rights and (distributive) justice. Liberal authors in particular have developed a rights ethic to argue that the free market is best suited to respect the individual right to freedom. Moral rights correlate with moral duties. Chapter 5 gives an exposition of deontological ethics that includes duty and rights ethics. We distinguish negative and positive rights ethics. The ethics of negative rights hold that the individual has the right to freedom and the right to private property. These are so-called negative rights because they protect a person from the coercion of other human beings. The last section discusses positive rights ethics that argue that real freedom also requires positive rights, such as a right to a minimum subsistence level of welfare.

Chapter 6 describes justice ethics. The free operation of markets may increase inequalities in income. This implies that the free market, from a justice point of view, may need correction. In Chapter 6 we explain the nature of justice. After a short introduction to the concept of justice, we describe the neo-Kantian theory of John Rawls. This is followed by an analysis of the libertarian rights–based theory of justice. Chapter 6 concludes with an overview of several criteria for distributive justice. Next, we turn in Chapter 7 to empirical evidence that the free market system increases or decreases poverty and inequality within countries and between countries.

Ethics is not only about applying certain principles such as principles of distributive justice. It is also concerned with character formation or virtues. Market competition is often accused of stimulating vices, like greed, envy and materialism. The third question that we discuss in Part III therefore considers whether free market institutions enforce or crowd out virtues. Virtue ethics views the cultivation of certain traits of character as one of morality's primary functions, because these virtues enable people to live a good life. Chapter 8 starts with a discussion of the virtue ethics of Aristotle, Adam Smith and some modern philosophers. This is followed by a discussion of the ethics of care, which is related to virtue ethics and stresses the care for relatives.

In Chapter 9 we analyze the views of Adam Smith, the father of economics, on the relationships between markets and virtues. It seems that Adam Smith largely sided with the view that free market institutions encourage virtues and that virtues increase human happiness. However, closer inspection shows that Smith was also aware that market institutions can have destructive effects. Another debate concerns the effect of virtues on human or societal happiness. According to the classical virtue ethics of Aristotle, virtues enable people to become happy. As a virtue ethicist, Adam Smith believed that virtues enhance human and societal happiness. He wholeheartedly disagreed with Mandeville's Fable of the Bees, where Mandeville argued that the practice of private virtues leads to a societal disaster.

Chapter 10 analyzes modern economic research on the interaction between virtues and the operation of the free market. The debate on the influence of markets on virtues has focused on two opposite hypotheses: the doux commerce thesis and the self-destruction thesis. Whereas the doux commerce hypothesis assumes that capitalism polishes human manners, the self-destruction hypothesis holds that capitalism erodes the moral foundation of society. In this chapter we will research for which type of virtues the doux commerce or self-destruction thesis is likely to hold. Then we analyze the role of virtues in economic outcomes in game theory and empirical research on the influence of virtues on happiness. This chapter closes with an analysis of the moderating role of virtues in the relationship between free market economies and human flourishing. We describe several empirical studies that support the thesis that the influence of free markets on human flourishing is conditional on virtues.

Chapter 11 connects the theories of Parts I, II and III to two broad philosophical approaches: liberalism and communitarianism. Each approach embodies a certain set of descriptive convictions (beliefs) and normative convictions (values). Liberalism rests on two pillars: individual sovereignty and rationalism. Chapter 11 characterizes liberalism as the philosophical approach that encompasses utilitarianism, the ethics of duty, rights ethics and the ethics of justice. Next, it discusses the communitarian approach, which criticizes the individualistic basis of the liberal tradition. According to this approach, liberalism has an impoverished view of the self, because it is grounded in an attenuated view of the self as an unencumbered self, a self not defined in terms of its relationships to others. Communitarian authors tend to criticize the core assumptions underlying the traditional defense of the free market and stress the alternative assumptions like bounded rationality and the interdependency of agents.

Chapter 12 concludes with a discussion of the priority of the different ethical criteria and offers a decision model to apply and integrate different ethical standards to concrete cases.

NOTES

1   Besides values and norms, one can distinguish virtues. Virtues are personal character traits that enable a person to realize certain values. Examples are patience, attentiveness, concern, humility, honesty, integrity and self-control (see more on virtues in Part III).

2   Also Smith argues that the individual businessman can judge much better than any statesman or lawgiver how to produce, because he is more familiar with the local situation.

3   Also Smith was aware of this market imperfection, as is shown by the following citation: "People of the same trade seldom meet together, even for merriment and diversion, but the conversation ends in a conspiracy against the public, or in some contrivance to raise prices. It is impossible to prevent such meetings, by any law. . . . But though the law cannot hinder people of the same trade from sometimes assembling together, it ought to do nothing to facilitate such assemblies" (Smith, 2000 [1776]: I.x.c.27).

4   Some parts of Chapters 1–3, 5–6, 8–9, and 11–12 were previously published in Graafland, J.J. (2007), *Economics, Ethics, and the Market. Introduction and applications,* London: Routledge. Parts of Section 12.3 and 12.4 were previously published in Graafland, J.J. (2010), *The Market, Happiness, and Solidarity. A Christian Perspective.* London: Routledge.

Recommended literature

Beauchamp, T.L. (1982) *Philosophical Ethics, an Introduction to Moral Philosophy,* New York: McGraw-Hill Inc.

Friedman, M. (1953) *Essays in Positive Economics,* Chicago: University of Chicago Press.

Hodgson, G.M. (2006) 'What are institutions?', *Journal of Economic Issues,* XL(1): 1–25.

Robbins, L. (1935) *An Essay on the Nature and Significance of Economic Science,* Second edition, London: MacMillan and Co.

Smith, Adam (1776) *Inquiry into the Nature and Causes of the Wealth of Nations,* New York: Prometheus Books.

Part I

Free markets, welfare
and happiness

2

Utilitarianism

2.1 CHARACTERISTICS OF UTILITARIANISM

The basic principle of utilitarianism is 'the greatest happiness of the greatest number'. Or, more formally: an action is right if and only if the sum total of utilities produced by that act is greater than the sum total of utilities produced by any other act the agent could have performed in its place.

Utilitarianism as a principle can be seen to be a combination of three elementary requirements (Sen, 1987):

Consequentialism

Utilitarianism is a consequentialist ethical theory. Consequentialism asserts that actions, choices or policies must be judged exclusively in terms of the resulting, or consequent, effects, rather than by any intrinsic features they may have. Outcome, not process, matters. Consequentialism specifies a particular structure for ethics. First, one needs to decide what is intrinsically valuable. Then one assesses actions, policies and institutions in terms of their consequences or contribution to these valuable goals. If the consequences of an action or policy are better than those of any alternative policy, consequentialism states that this policy is morally obligatory.

In order to clarify consequentialism, think about how a consequentialist would approach the question of punishing criminal activities. An example is the construction sector in the Netherlands. In November 2001, a TV program showed that many large Dutch construction companies participated in illegal price fixing. Should these companies fully compensate the clients for the harm due to the rise in prices induced by the illegal price agreements? In a consequential argument, the entire focus will be on the consequences of a policy of punishing construction companies. Will the fines deter companies from illegal price fixing in the future? What if many construction companies are not able to pay these fines and go bankrupt? But the question whether they *deserve* to pay compensation will not be taken into account.

Since the consequences of an action are almost always uncertain, most utilitarians do not express their view in terms of the actual but rather the expected outcomes of actions. The expected outcome of an action is calculated by multiplying the value of the outcome by the probability of its occurring.

DOI: 10.4324/9781003181835-3

Welfarism

But what are valuable goals? What is intrinsically good? A utilitarian is a consequentialist who says that what is good is welfare.[1] Welfarism requires that the goodness of a state of affairs be a function only of the utility or welfare obtained by individuals in that state. It excludes all non-utility aspects of the situation.

But what is utility or welfare? In this respect, there are different varieties of utilitarianism. Some take welfare to be some mental state like happiness or pleasure. This is expressed by the slogan of Jeremy Bentham who invented utilitarianism: 'the greatest happiness of the greatest number'. Bentham argued that two 'sovereign masters', pleasure and pain, regulate all human behavior and that all human experience might theoretically be measured in terms of these basic units (pleasure ranking as + and pain as –). Bentham claimed that pleasure is a kind of sensation, common to all those experiences described as enjoyable or as contributing to the value of a life to the person living it. Likewise, pain refers to all those experiences which people find objectionable. Since all pleasures and all pains are structurally similar sensations, it should be possible to calculate a net sum total of utility. This theory is called hedonism. Thus, in principle, qualitative differences of experience could be reduced to standard units of pleasure/pain, and Bentham gave some simple rules for their measurement. This would imply that if the quantity of pleasure experienced during a circus performance is equal to the pleasure from reading a poem, a circus performance is as good as a poem.

Bentham applies a monistic concept of utility by assuming that all values can be measured on the same scale of pleasure minus pain. In reaction to the accusation that utilitarianism is a philosophy worthy of pigs, John Stuart Mill (1871) distinguished higher pleasures (such as the pleasures of the intellect and moral sentiments) that are qualitatively different from the lower pleasures such as eating. For Mill, one cannot conclude that a satisfied pig is happier than an unsatisfied human being. The comparison of the human happiness to that of beasts is felt as degrading, precisely because a beast's pleasures do not satisfy a human being's conception of happiness. It is the higher faculties that give man their sense of dignity. No intelligent human being would consent to be a fool. No person of feeling and conscience would like to be selfish and base, even if they would be persuaded that the fool or the rascal is better satisfied with his lot than they are with theirs. As Mill (1871: Section 2.6) states: "It is better to be a human being dissatisfied than a pig satisfied". Finally, Mill believes that the verdict on which of two pleasures has the highest quality is up to those who are competently acquainted with both, or, if they differ, that of the majority among them. The greatest happiness principle therefore is the greatest balance of pleasures over pain, both in quantity and quality. The quality and the rule of measuring it against quantity is to be assessed by competent judges.

The utilitarianism of Bentham offers a substantive theory of utility or welfare. A substantive theory of well-being says which things are intrinsically good for people. Economists are reluctant to make assumptions about what is good or bad for people and propose an alternative definition of utility. They prefer individual sovereignty. Individual sovereignty implies that individuals are the best judges of their own welfare. Any assessment of individual welfare should be based on a person's own judgment. It rejects paternalism, the notion that a third party may know better than the individuals themselves what serves their interests. Let individuals decide by themselves what is good and what is wrong, because they are best informed about their own circumstances. Utility is then equated to the satisfaction of actual preferences that individuals happen to have. Preferences are priorities of persons between different things. They are derived from the underlying values of the person and depend on how much he or she is interested in different goods or services. This means that economists prefer a formal theory of welfare instead of a substantive theory. Formal theories specify how one finds out which things are intrinsically good for people, but do not specify what those things are (Hausman and McPherson, 1996). Utility is a formal attribute, a common denominator, according to which all specific quests for satisfaction can be ranked. What is intrinsically valuable is what each individual prefers to obtain.

As economists are mostly concerned with explaining and predicting economic behavior, taking the satisfaction of actual preferences as a measure for welfare is a logical choice. However, as we will see, defining the good as the satisfaction of actual preferences can be criticized from a philosophical point of view, which renders this criterion less useful for normative evaluations.

Sum ranking

Although individualistic experiences of pleasure and pain (in substantial theory) or valuations (in formal theory) form the only basis for evaluating an action or policy, utilitarianism is not an egoistic ethical theory. The fundamental thesis of utilitarianism is that one should do whatever maximizes the total sum of utilities. Actions and policies should be evaluated on the basis of the benefits and the costs they will impose on the society as a whole, giving equal weight to everyone's interests. Hence, as between his own happiness and that of all others, utilitarianism requires one to be as strictly impartial as a disinterested and benevolent spectator. As Mill (1871: Section 2.18) states: "To do as one would be done by, and to love one's neighbor as oneself, constitute the ideal perfection of utilitarian morality".[2] Maximizing total welfare means that the marginal utility of different persons should be equalized. Assuming declining marginal utility from income (i.e. the increase in utility from an increase in income by one unit), utilitarianism implies that income should be redistributed until the marginal utility from additional income is equal for all persons.

Singer (1972) illustrates the social implications of utilitarianism by considering the moral duty with respect to giving money for funds that help refugees. Assuming that suffering and death from lack of food, shelter and medical care are bad, he argues that if it is in our power to prevent this from happening, without thereby sacrificing anything of comparable moral importance, we ought morally to do it. It is clear that if we would act upon this principle, our world would fundamentally change. Nevertheless, that is what utilitarianism implies. It makes no moral difference whether the person I can help is a neighbor's child or a Syrian whose name I do not know. If we accept impartiality and equality, we cannot discriminate against someone merely because he is far away from us. Nor does the principle make a distinction between cases in which I am the only person who could possibly do anything and cases in which I am just one among millions in the same position. Otherwise, this would imply, for example, that I am less obliged to help a refugee if, on looking around, I see other people are doing nothing too. Numbers do not reduce obligation. From the utilitarian principle it follows that I ought to give as much as possible up to the point at which by giving more one would begin to cause more suffering for oneself and one's dependent than one would prevent for the receiver of the gift. Charity is in this strict utilitarian reasoning not a supererogatory act, but a moral duty: we ought to give the money to lift the need of the poor, and it is wrong not to do so.

Under some conditions utilitarianism therefore implies a high degree of equality in income between different persons. If a rich man experiences a smaller increase in utility from one additional Euro than a poor man (i.e. if utility is degressively related to income), the egalitarian principle of equalizing incomes (see Chapter 6) is consistent with the utilitarian principle. In that case, the total welfare is maximized if all citizens receive an equal income. However, this consistency between the egalitarian principle and the utilitarian principle only holds if the institution producing this result (like the tax and social benefit system) does not have a negative impact on the efforts of the economic agents. In particular, the obligation to pay taxes may take away the incentive to work and therefore reduce the total welfare. If these negative incentive effects are taken into account, the utilitarian principle will generally imply a less extreme distribution rule than the egalitarian principle. Also Singer (1972) admits that there is a limit to the extent that Western societies should help the poor:

> If we gave away, say, 40 per cent of our GNP, we would slow down our economy so much that in absolute terms we would be giving less than if we gave 25 per cent of the much larger GNP that we would have if we limited our contribution to this smaller percentage.
>
> (Singer, 1972: 36)

2.2 COST–BENEFIT ANALYSIS

In order to estimate the total welfare gain from an action, utilitarianism requires that utilities can be measured and that utilities of different persons can be added. There are, however, several problems in making interpersonal comparisons of welfare. Economists often argue that preferences are subjective and difficult to test. In addition, there are conceptual problems in making interpersonal comparisons of preference satisfaction. How is one to compare how well-satisfied the preferences of different people are? One possibility is to make judgments by imagining how well-off one would be if one had the preferences of other persons. Hausman and McPherson (1996) argue, however, that it is impossible to separate the utility effect of the action considered and the preference satisfaction from other factors related to the person whose shoes one puts on.

In ordinary life we do, however, habitually make interpersonal utility comparisons, for example, when distributing presents among friends or members of a family, and we do not think that such comparisons are pointless. However, it seems that exact quantification is problematic. Instead of cardinal comparisons, we make ordinal comparisons in which we order which effect dominates but nothing more than that. Thus it might be reasonable to say that John will get more satisfaction from a bicycle than Susan from a doll's house, but rather artificial to contend that John will get ten units of utility and Susan will get nine (Self, 1975).

Although in simple cases in which a very limited number of individuals are affected, ordinal utility comparison may be possible, one requires cardinal comparison if many individuals are involved.[3] In order to solve the lack of comparability of utilities of different people if many individuals are involved, Kaldor and Hicks proposed a compensation test that tests whether the winners (those whose utility increases by a certain policy) might be able to overcompensate the losers (those whose utility decreases). For each policy, one could ask the winners how much they would like to pay (so-called willingness to pay) for this policy and ask the losers how much compensation they need to receive to compensate for their loss of utility caused by this policy. In this way, we avoid invoking interpersonal utility comparisons, as people themselves decide how much they value the effects of different policies on their utility. After summing up the stated prices for all who are affected by the policies under consideration, the policy with the largest net benefit is best.

This proposal is the basis for cost–benefit analysis. The compensation test introduces a kind of interpersonal utility comparison by relating it to the price individuals are willing to pay for a certain measure. Cost–benefit analysis is thus often viewed as the practical way to implement utilitarianism to decisions related to market issues and regulation policies of the government.

Cost–benefit analysis can be illustrated by examples concerning the airplane sector, which exhibits many externalities related to key decisions with respect to the location of air fields, the safety of the airplanes and their crews, etc. A very simple application is given by Michael Kinsley. He describes the case of sloppy practices of ValuJet. Regulators shut down this discount airline after a crash on 11 May 1996 in Florida that killed 110 people. The *Washington Post* declared in an editorial comment that the public needs evidence that the government is insisting on the highest safety standards possible. Michael Kinsley doubted this conclusion, however. The law of diminishing returns implies that any additional amount of money put into safety will yield a smaller amount of utility, and at some point it will reduce total welfare if alternative uses have a higher return. This indicates that you should stop investing in the safety of airplanes well short of the highest possible standards. Kinsley illustrates his arguments by a simple cost–benefit analysis on the back of an envelope. First, he notes that discount airlines have lowered ticket prices by an average of $54. The standard statistic on airline safety is that you could fly once a day, every day, for 21,000 years before dying in an airplane crash. Kinsley supposes that flying discount makes it ten times more likely that you die in a crash. In that case, the probability of an accident increases by $1/2,100 * 365 - 1/21,000 * 365 = 1/855,000$. Is it worth to pay the extra $54 to avoid the additional risk? Kinsley does not think so. If saving $54 only increases the probability of losing your life by $1/855,000$, the implicit price of your life is $54 * 855,000 = 46 million. That is a very high price. If you value your life less than this high price, then you would like to choose the lower safety level.

This example shows the basic procedure of cost–benefit analysis. If we have to decide whether to do A or not, the rule is: do A if the benefits exceed those of the next best alternative course of action; if not, don't. For this purpose, assign numerical values to costs and benefits and arrive at decisions by adding them up and accepting those projects with the greatest net benefits. This requires several steps. First, investigate the relevant alternatives. Second, trace the consequences of these alternatives and who are affected by these consequences. Third, determine the numerical valuation of these consequences by these individuals. For this, cost–benefit analysis relies on the valuation of individuals by asking what they would be willing to pay to acquire the benefits or to avoid the costs generated by the action. The fourth step is to deduce the change in the total social welfare by adding up the changes in individual welfare. The best policy maximizes the sum of the 'willingness to pay' scales of all affected individuals.

Cost–benefit analysis is often applied to aspects of policies for which a market does not exist. It imitates the market by measuring the values of goods by individuals' willingness to pay as a monetary metric for utility. One method for attributing prices to non-market goods is to ask people directly what they would be willing to pay for them if the goods were marketed. However, one can worry whether people will express their true preference in this way. One problem is that the preferences can depend on the way questions are framed. For example, the expressed preference for environmental protection varies significantly according to whether people are asked how much they would be willing to pay for a good that they do not own or how much they would demand in compensation to give up a good that they do own. Instead of actually asking people for their willingness to pay for a certain policy, the prices are usually derived from studies of market transactions in which individuals trade off commodified versions of these goods against money. For example, the supposedly higher wages people accept for working at hazardous jobs is used to measure the cash value people are thought to implicitly place on their own lives. In daily life we constantly put implicit prices on all kind of values. Apart from the fact that it is in practice costly to ask people how much they would pay or how much compensation they require, economists consider this market information to be more reliable in revealing the authentic individual preferences than valuations expressed in questionnaires or public debate, because the latter may be biased by strategic considerations. In accordance with the theory of revealed preference, they attempt to define preference in terms of real choices. Choosing x when one might have had y at a lower cost reveals a preference for x over y. However, it should be noted that very often this type of implicit price shows a very large range, because people often make these implicit valuations unconsciously of the implications which economists derive from them. In order for wage differentials to reveal the implicit price of a risk of death, workers must be aware of the levels of risk they face, they must be free to choose different jobs with different risk levels and they must be satisfied with their compensation for the level of risk they have accepted. These are rather strong assumptions, and it is a rare situation in which they are all well justified (MacLean, 1994). This reduces the usefulness of implicit prices as an objective basis for these calculations.

Apart from measurement problems, there are other several problems with cost–benefit analysis. Although in theory the benefits from a policy could be shared by reallocating some of them to the losers, in reality this compensation is often not effectuated. Why should the mere possibility of compensating the losers be adequate to establish a social improvement if the compensation is not, in fact, to be paid? If the losers include the worst off and the most miserable in society, there is little consolation to be got from being told that it is possible to be fully compensated, but no actual plan to do so exists (see also Section 2.3).

2.3 PROBLEMS WITH UTILITARIANISM

There are several difficulties with utilitarianism and cost–benefit analysis. We categorize these problems according to the three characteristics of utilitarianism mentioned in Section 2.1: consequentialism, welfarism and sum ranking (see Table 2.1).

Problems of consequentialism

As only consequences matter, utilitarianism is unable to deal with moral issues that relate to rights. In the utilitarian approach, rights are viewed as merely instrumental to achieving other goods, in particular, utilities. No intrinsic importance is attached to the fulfillment of

TABLE 2.1
Problems of utilitarianism

Consequentialism	Welfarism	Sum ranking
No intrinsic value of rights	Happiness is not the only valuable thing	Value-free interpersonal comparison of utilities impossible
No consideration of intentions	Utility does not adequately represent well-being	No distributive justice
Disregards retributive justice	Problem of incommensurability	How to count future generations?
Consequences are difficult to predict	Immoral preferences	How to determine the number of people?
	Non-rational preferences	How to count animals?
	No community valuation	Over-demandingness

rights. Utilitarianism can therefore imply that certain actions are morally right when in fact they violate people's rights. One of the most basic rights is the right to freedom (for the ethics of rights, see Chapter 5). Freedom may be valued because it assists achievement: selecting a certain option without having alternative options is normally valued less than selecting the same option (with the same consequences) when one is free to select many other options. But respect of rights is also intrinsically valuable. For example, on utilitarian grounds it could be defendable to withhold medical treatment of old, sick people in the Netherlands and reallocate the money for the expensive medical treatment for these people to the medical treatment of young, sick African citizens who will experience a lifetime utility gain. However, from a rights perspective, this would be a violation of the right to life and health care. These rights set absolute side-constraints that cannot be overruled by consequential reasons and within which a social choice is to be made by excluding certain alternatives. To give a more extreme example (Sen, 1982): The utilitarian will accept the torture of an innocent person if the torturer gains more than the tortured loses. Must we then support the torture? A rights ethics would say: no. The right to personal liberty of the tortured may not be violated on grounds of the net consequences for the torturer and tortured.

Another criticism of consequentialism is that it does not consider the intentions of the person performing the act, only the consequences of his act. The moral value of an action of the businessman in Smith's text who is motivated by self-interest does not differ from that of the action of a businessman who intrinsically intends to contribute to society, if the effects of the actions of both businessmen on societal welfare are equal. The importance of intentions for a moral evaluation of actions is most clearly stated by Immanuel Kant (see Chapter 5). In his view an action is morally good only if the intention of the person who performed the action is good (the so-called 'Gesinnungsethik'). The outcome of that action does not matter.

A third problem is that consequentialism abstracts from considerations of retributive justice. Retributive justice refers to the just imposition of punishments upon those who do wrong. Utilitarianism only considers future consequences; it does not look back to the past. Hence, utilitarianism would suggest setting the penalty for a crime at the least point where any greater penalty would cause more additional unhappiness for the criminal than would reduce the unhappiness of the victim, plus the happiness of the potential victims of the crimes deterred by the additional increase in punishment. If the criminal would experience high psychological, social and emotional costs of being apprehended and if the deterrence effect were negligible, this might result in a penalty well below the retributive level that compensates the harm done to the victim in the past. This shows that utilitarianism disregards that justice be done to the victims by punishing the criminals for their harmful behavior towards them.

A final problem is that consequences of an action, and hence the costs and benefits it generates, are difficult to predict and subject to different degrees of uncertainty. Take, for example, the probability of an accident when deciding about the regulation of the airplane sector. In the example described earlier, Michael Kinsley just makes an assumption about the increase in the probability of crashes when flying with a discount airline. Indeed, it is difficult to predict the probability of disasters because of the incidental character and the complexity of factors that cause such an accident. Moreover, as explained in Section 2.2, it is difficult to measure the value of the effects on the utility of people. As a result, the benefits and costs of an action cannot be adequately measured. By adding these uncertain outcomes to the costs of other aspects, the utilitarian calculus mixes together relatively 'hard' and very 'soft' figures within a single equation. The uncertainty involved with the prediction of possible consequences of a policy strongly diminishes the value of utilitarianism as an ethical standard compared to other ethical standards.

Problems of welfarism

Utilitarianism cannot only be criticized because of unethical implications of consequentialism, but also because of problems from considering utility or welfare as the sole type of good consequences. Most of these problems are particularly relevant for the formal theory of welfare that equates utility to the satisfaction of the actual preferences of individuals.

A first problem with welfarism is that happiness is not the only relevant argument in an evaluation of an action or policy. A person may value promotion of certain things, even if they do not advance his happiness (Sen, 1987). MacLean (1994) gives two examples. The first example concerns an antique Russian samovar that he himself owns. It is a family heirloom that goes back several generations on his mother's side. MacLean actually does not particularly like it. In fact, he is stuck with it. But because his mother passed it on to him, he would never sell it. The second example concerns rescue missions undertaken on the battlefield to retrieve the corpses of slain soldiers. Great risks are sometimes taken in such missions. It is clear that the benefit of retrieving corpses does not outweigh the costs of soldiers who die while trying to save them. Apparently, soldiers who do so do not think in these terms. Indeed, a commitment to one's family or one's friends can sometimes be a severe burden and exact a heavy personal toll.[4]

A second criticism on (especially the formal variant of) welfarism is that utility (defined as preference satisfaction) does not adequately represent well-being. Desire fulfillment depends on the circumstances of the agent. A homeless beggar may manage to suppress intense suffering because of a cheerful and resilient temperament, but that does not imply that a corresponding small value should be attached to the loss of his house because of his survival strategy. In a welfarist calculus, the fact of his homelessness should play no part, because of the easier desire fulfillment of the beggar. This utility-based narrow vision of well-being makes utilitarianism fundamentally inadequate as a basis for evaluating actions and economic policies. Judging well-being by the mental metric of desire fulfillment can become biased if the mental reactions reflect defeatist compromises with the harsh reality. Deprived people may come to terms with their predicaments and lose the courage to desire a better life by the necessity of survival. Discontent is replaced by acceptance, hopeless rebellion by conformist quiet and suffering and anger by cheerful endurance. Sen (1984) illustrates this argument by the outcomes of a survey in India in 1944, the year just after the Great Bengal Famine. Among the categories of people surveyed in this post-famine year there were many widows and widowers. Although the position of women in terms of nutrition was particularly bad, only 2.5% of widows confided that they were ill or in indifferent health (against 48.5% of the widowers). Quiet acceptance of deprivation and bad fate had affected the scale of dissatisfaction generated, and the utilitarian calculus gives sanctity to that distortion. This particular problem of the influence of contingent circumstances on the metric of utility shows the insufficient depth of desire fulfillment in judging a person's well-being. If one has to get away from this mental reaction view of deprivation, one must look at deprivation in terms of some other metric than preference satisfaction. Valuation of well-being requires a more direct method of assessing the value of the consequences than preference satisfaction.

A third criticism is that welfarism assumes that different values are reducible to one basic value, namely utility. This criticism only holds for the monistic variants of utilitarianism (hedonism and cost–benefit analysis). Monism means that the value of every action can be measured in terms of one dimension, because there is just one good. Hence, we can compare various actions and determine which action generates the most value. In other words, welfarism assumes commensurability of values. Commensurability states simply that an agent can *compare* all values. Suppose two options x and y must be evaluated in terms of two values A and B. One option (x) ranks higher in terms of value A, whereas the other option (y) values higher in terms of value B. Commensurability requires that one be able to weigh up value A and B and to decide on balance which alternative, x or y, is superior to the other. Values are, however, often incommensurable in nature, relating to several generic incomparable goods rather than only a single one (see more on this in Section 3.3). Cost–benefit analysis is unable to deal with these qualitatively different ways of valuation. Self (1975) argues that to many people it seems wrong or even impious to set a monetary value upon all sorts of phenomena that are not normally so valued. Consider a solitary monk who devotes all his time to either prayer and contemplation or growing his own food. The cost–benefit analyst will say that the opportunity cost to the monk of an extra hour spent in prayer is equal to the price of the food thereby foregone. But the monk is unlikely to see the issue in this way. He more probably views prayer and contemplation as the purpose of his life and will see the necessity to grow food as only a constraint upon this goal. The value that a person places upon his or her goals can therefore not be inferred from the resources that he or she devotes to them. The discontinuity between different values, which supports norms that prohibit certain trade-offs between them, plays no part in the cost–benefit analysis. Incommensurability therefore casts doubt on the assumption of cost–benefit analysis that the value of certain states can be accounted through cash equivalents. Cost–benefit analysis assumes that goods are substitutable with any alternative commodity. However, some benefits and costs are not tradable or substitutable. Some goods, such as endangered species, may be valued as unique and irreplaceable higher goods. Also the samovar of MacLean is not for sale. Hence, we have no information on its price. This is especially true for human life. Kant famously proclaimed that rational human beings have dignity and that whatever has dignity is "above all price, and therefore admits of no equivalent". This implies that the safety of human lives cannot be traded against money.[5] For freedom, life, health and beauty, there is no objective measure.[6]

A fourth problem with the formal theory of welfare arises if individuals have morally unacceptable preferences according to, say, standard group norms (Beauchamp, 1982). For example, a person's strong sexual preference may be to rape young children, but this preference is morally intolerable. Utilitarianism based purely on subjective preferences is satisfactory, then, only if a range of acceptable values can be formulated, where acceptability is agent-neutral and thus not a matter of preferences. This is inconsistent with a pure preference approach, because that approach logically ties human values to preferences, which are by their nature not agent-neutral.

Fifth, relying on actual preferences or 'willingness to pay' scales assumes that individuals are rational. However, rationality is a rather strong assumption (see also Section 3.3). People may prefer something that is bad for them because of ignorance. Moreover, other parties can manipulate the preferences of people (for example, by advertisements). Other people only want things precisely because they cannot have them. The importance of social identity and relative economic status may also lead individuals to significantly underestimate the full social benefits of public goods and non-market environmental services. In order to value preferences for a certain state, one should therefore know the reasons why people prefer this state. Cost–benefit analysis is only responsive to given wants without evaluating the reasons people have for wanting the goods in question.

A related point is that one can doubt whether individual preferences should be the sole base for evaluating social welfare. The individual does not create his autonomy and rationality by himself, but receives them from his community. Only if communal relationships are good can individuals develop their capacities. From a communitarian perspective one could therefore defend that community goals rather than individual goals should be the criterion to judge the desirability of a certain policy (see also Chapter 11).

Problems of sum ranking

Utilitarianism assumes interpersonal welfare comparisons. As discussed earlier, the extent of desire fulfillment depends on the circumstances of the agent. As a result, the utilities that different actions have for different people are difficult to compare. The cost–benefit analysis hoped to avoid invoking interpersonal utility comparisons by using willingness to pay. However, cost–benefit analysis is not free from distributional commitments. If income is equally distributed, it is reasonable to value the prices of all individuals equally, regardless of whose they are. But if income or wealth is not equally distributed, the preferences of those with larger incomes will carry more weight than the preferences of those with smaller incomes, because the rich people are more prepared and able to pay a high price for improving their utility than poor people. Also Sen (1987) argues that it is difficult to compare the desire fulfillment of different persons, since the extent of desire fulfillment depends on the circumstances of the agent. Questions of the total social welfare effect will therefore become entwined with questions of justice. A person who has had a life of misfortune, with very little opportunities, and consequently little hope for improvement, may be more easily reconciled to deprivations than others reared in more fortunate and affluent circumstances. As a consequence, the deprived person may take much more pleasure in small mercies and also be trained to suppress intensive suffering from the necessity of continuing survival. But according to Sen (1984), it would be ethically mistaken to attach a higher value to a small reduction in the consumption of a spoiled child than to a large reduction in consumption of a poor child that is used to survive in times of hunger. He argues that the most blatant forms of inequalities and exploitations survive in the world through making allies out of the deprived and the exploited. Thus, cost–benefit analysis will reproduce the inequality of the status quo in its results. To prevent this outcome, cost–benefit analyses sometimes use equivalence scales that correct for differences in the value of one unit of money for different groups of people. For example, we may need to value the poor person's price more highly than the rich person's price by multiplying the first with a factor $s > 1$. But how large should s be? That is a normative choice. Hence, the cost–benefit analysis cannot remain neutral on distributive questions.

Utilitarianism can therefore also go wrong when it defends a measure that imposes such unequal incomes that it is clearly immoral and offends against justice. Take, for example, a large reduction of social assistance. This may generate several positive effects on the economy and decrease unemployment (Graafland et al., 2001). As a result, some unemployed will find a job and improve their position. Also other members of the working population will benefit because taxes and social premiums will decline. Hence, aggregate utility might rise. Still, there will be a group of unemployed that is not able to benefit from the rise in employment, while their income (which was already low) will decline with the reduction in unemployment benefits.

A fourth question is to what extent the utility analysis should take account of future generations of human beings who are unable to express their preferences. Should the utility calculus be extended to all those who are not yet born? If so, how should we represent their interests in the utility calculus? Many projects in society have very long-term effects. Take, for example, the storage of nuclear waste or the use of oil reserves. If all future generations are taken into account, then it might lead to the outcome that our generation must sacrifice much of its welfare. Therefore, utilitarians have mostly claimed that these future consequences should be discounted (given less weight) proportionate to their distance in the future. But how high should the discount rate be? According to Pigou, present preferences of people are fundamentally selfish and express themselves in a very strong time preference. For this reason, he argues that the state should represent the interests of future generations:

> But there is wide agreement that the State should protect the interests of the future in some degree against the effects or our irrational discounting and of our preference for ourselves over our descendants. . . . It is the clear duty of government, which is the trustee for unborn generations as well as for its present citizens, to watch over, and, if need be, by legislative enactment to defend the exhaustible natural resources of the country from rash and reckless spoliation.
>
> (cited in Van Liedekerke, 2000: 83)

This so-called super-responsibility argument (the government has responsibility not merely to the current generation but also to future generations) provides a reason why the social rate of discount used in cost–benefit analysis should be lower than the private rate of discount. But how high should the social rate of discount be? That is a question that utilitarianism cannot answer.

A fifth problem of the summing up of utilities that emerges, for instance, when one considers the implications of utilitarianism for future generations, is that utilitarianism becomes notoriously inept with decisions that affect the number of people. Maximizing the total happiness of all living beings requires continuing to add persons so long as their net utility is positive and is sufficient to counterbalance the loss in utility their presence in the world causes to others. The population should be encouraged to grow indefinitely no matter how low the average utility of persons may fall so long as total utility increases. In order to avoid this implication, utilitarian ethicists sometimes propose to maximize the average utility per person instead of total utility. However, maximizing average utility also leads to absurd conclusions. For example, it would imply that I should not have a child if its happiness will be lower than the existing average. Another implication is that it is allowed to kill poor people painlessly, in the night, provided one did not first announce it. Because, once the person is dead, he does not count anymore and average utility might rise. Of course, one could argue that the possibility of being killed generates fear to other people who are still living. But do we forbid murder only to prevent feelings of worry on the part of potential victims (Nozick, 1974)?

A sixth problem is how to include the utility of animals or other elements of non-human reality that cannot communicate their preferences. Most people believe that there is something morally wrong about inflicting suffering on animals needlessly. One could argue that once animals exist, they, too, may have claims to certain treatments. The utilitarian criterion should then be: maximize the total utility of all living beings (Singer, 2009). But how can we estimate the utility of animals? Animals cannot communicate how much they value certain states. Of course, one could try to estimate the happiness or pain of animals and attach a weight to the net benefit of animals in the total sum of utilities. However, this method invokes many problems. How should one weigh the pain of an animal (or of different types of animals) as compared to the pain of a human being? Should the life of 1,000 cows count more than the life of one human being? May we inflict some suffering on a person to avoid a (slightly) greater suffering of an animal? It seems that utilitarianism cannot provide a satisfactory answer to these questions.

A final problem of sum ranking is over-demandingness. Utilitarianism requires that, other things being equal, a certain utility should matter to me equally, whether it is to be experienced by me, a friend or a relative of mine or a complete stranger. This implies that utilitarianism becomes very demanding, especially if other people are not living up to the moral duties implied by utilitarianism.[7] For example, if other parents do not give presents to their children (or are not able to do so), sum ranking implies that it is my duty to reallocate part of my budget for presents for my own children in favor of the welfare of these children. However, normally we consider our responsibility for our own children different from our responsibility for children of other parents. The legitimacy of giving a present to one's own children cannot therefore only be evaluated in terms of the welfare gains received by these children in comparison to the welfare gains other children would experience when getting the same amount of resources. This point is stressed by the ethical theory of care (see Chapter 8). Another example to illustrate this point is that of famine relief. If others are not making any contribution, utilitarianism might imply that I am obligated to surrender all of my spare time and money in order to save as many lives as possible. According to Williams (1981), utilitarianism may then threaten my personal integrity. This has become known as 'the integrity objection' (Crisp, 1998). Williams believes that people have certain ground projects that are so central and important to their lives that they should not be required to give them up just because the utilitarian calculation happens to come out that way. To a significant degree the ground projects give meaning to a person's life and constitute his or her character. If they have to give up their ground projects, they will lose their personal integrity.

2.4 ADAPTATIONS OF UTILITARIANISM

In response to all these problems, some philosophers have adapted utilitarianism in order to reduce its disadvantages. In this section we describe some of these responses.

Diminishing the problems of consequentialism: rule utilitarianism

In order to prevent problems with rights, utilitarianism has developed an alternative version of utilitarianism, the so-called rule utilitarianism. The basic idea of this alternative is that utilitarianism can only be applied to rules (like the rule that you should keep your promise), not to concrete actions in a particular situation (so-called act utilitarianism). Rules are justified when they are rules that maximize utility if there is general acceptance of this rule. Thus, rule utilitarianism is the view that the right action is that which is in accord with that set of rules which, if generally or universally accepted, would maximize utility. Restricting utilitarianism to rules only will ensure that the protection of rights and justice will be more taken into consideration. Another advantage of rule utilitarianism is that it is less time consuming. For practicing act utilitarianism, utilitarians would have to spend vast amounts of time to calculate the benefits and costs of the various courses of action open to them and the probabilities related to each. Applying utilitarianism only to rules saves time. Moreover, it also benefits from past experiences, because knowledge of the most efficient rules of morality emerges gradually. Only in cases of conflict between different rules is it requisite that one should employ act utilitarianism to decide what to do (Crisp, 1998).

However, it is easy to see that rule utilitarianism is not sufficient. Rules that allow exceptions will generally produce more utility than rules that do not allow any exceptions, because the rule can operate as an inefficient constraint. Rule utilitarianism will have to accept this rule. However, then we are back in the situation of act utilitarianism, because for every concrete act we should have to determine whether the exception is allowed.

Reduction of the problems of welfarism: extra welfarism and capability approach

Besides utilitarianism, there are also several other consequentialist theories that are non-utilitarian. These so-called extra-welfaristic theories take the good consequences to be things other than welfare or the satisfaction of preferences. An example is the capability approach offered by Sen (1984, 1987).[8] Whereas standard utilitarianism judges an action entirely by the goodness of its consequences on welfare and ignores everything else, Sen argues for a consequentialism, which sees consequences in very broad terms, including the value of freedom or the disvalue of violated rights. This broadening of consequentialism shows that Sen is prepared to compromise on welfarism. Indeed, welfare is not necessarily the only goal of an agent; people may value objectives other than maximizing one's own welfare. Happiness or desire fulfillment represents only one aspect of human existence. Sen develops a view of consequential evaluation in which capabilities that foster freedom play a more important role than happiness. Capability reflects what a person can do. A person's freedom depends on being able to perform functions that require certain capabilities. For example, literacy is a capability which allows the function of reading. Social policy should focus on fostering capabilities that help achieve these functions. Another example described by Sen (1983) is a bicycle. Having a bike gives a person the capability to move to a certain place, which he may not be able to do without the bike. Hence, there is a sequence from having a commodity (the bike), to capability (being able to move), to function (moving). Whereas utilitarianism only takes account of the utility produced by having a bike, Sen's extra-welfarism focuses on the capability that the entitlement to a bike generates. The utility from the bike does not provide the right standard. A person that obtains a bike but is spoiled and not satisfied with a particular bike still has a higher standard of living, although the satisfaction of desires maybe does not increase. Also the ownership of the bike does not yield a good standard, because it does not guarantee the freedom of the owner. A handicapped person cannot use a bike and needs another means of transportation in order to obtain the capability of moving. This illustrates that the conversion of commodities into capabilities varies enormously with a number of parameters, like age, sex, health, social relations, class background, education and ideology. Ultimately, the process of economic development should be concerned with what people can or cannot do, whether they are able to read and write and communicate and whether they can participate in the activities of the community.

A good example of the relevance of extra-welfarism is the health sector. It is commonly held that health, not utility, is the most relevant outcome for conducting normative analysis of health policies. In order to measure health, extra-welfarists use more objective criteria in terms of capacities that people need to attain desired states. With this emphasis on need (rather than wants), extra-welfarism has affinity with those philosophers who give a central place in normative analysis to meeting *basic needs*. But then we cannot neglect the question of what needs should be met in order to live a good life. Because of the reluctance of economists to include normative elements in their analysis, economists have generally rejected the distinction between mere wants and needs.

Extra-welfarism also diminishes the problem of immoral or non-rational preferences, as policies that improve capabilities and meet basic needs are less susceptible to the problem of immoral or non-rational preferences. Furthermore, it reduces the neglect of respect of rights in consequentialism, because of its focus on capabilities to meet freedom rights. Also the problems of interpersonal comparison are moderated. The focus on needs instead of wants, as proposed by extra-welfarism, is more convincing when interpersonal comparisons must be made than the valuation of more sophisticated types of experience. Governments can more easily tell what people need than what will satisfy their preferences, because the variety in needs is not as large as the variety in wants.

Other responses to the problems of sum ranking

A response that tries to solve the problem of over-demandingness of utilitarianism is to incorporate an agent-related prerogative by allowing one to devote more energy and attention to one's own interests (Scheffler, 1994). For example, one is allowed to assign n times more weight to one's own interests than to the interests of others. Bosma (2013) criticizes this solution for two reasons. First, it is unlikely that all interests would qualify for this. If somebody has a trivial interest, it seems odd to allow him to assign more weight to that. Thus, it would be desirable to make some qualifications regarding the interests that are allowed to play a part in the agent-centered prerogative. Second, even by introducing the agent-related prerogative, the objection from integrity still holds. If there is appalling poverty in the world, the poverty might be that great that even if you sacrifice everything, it is not resolved. Then, assigning more weight to your own interests will not take away over-demandingness. Scheffler could only save his defense against the objection from integrity by assigning an enormous value to n, with the likely result that the prerogative will collapse into egoism, which is something Scheffler would find undesirable.

2.5 CONCLUSION

From the objections of Section 2.3, it can be concluded that utilitarianism does not give a fully satisfactory theoretical account of our moral intuitions. Utilitarianism and cost–benefit analysis have several problems that can only be solved by explicit normative reference to what can be considered to be good or bad.

Still, utilitarianism has some profound advantages and has great practical value. For one thing, it fits with the way a lot of people make up their mind, namely by looking at the beneficial and harmful consequences of a particular action. It also fits with the value of efficiency. With respect to the problem of measurement, the strong assumptions of utilitarianism can be relaxed when such measurements are impossible. From a pragmatic point of view, utilitarianism merely requires a systematic overview of the benefits and costs.

Utilitarianism can further be improved by applying extra-welfarist approaches, like that of Sen that tries to avoid the criticism from a perspective of rights and justice by broadening the concept of welfare but remains consequentialist in nature. Extra-welfarist approaches have the additional advantage that they can avoid the problem of immoral or irrational preferences and are less vulnerable to the criticism on sum ranking.

NOTES

1 Consequentialist moral theories are not committed to the utilitarian concept of goodness. A non-utilitarian consequentialist might regard other goals than welfare as valuable.

2 Mill makes this remark to invalidate the claim that utilitarianism is godless. In the golden rule of Jesus, he reads the complete spirit of the ethics of utility. In 2:22 he states: "If it be true that God desires, above all things, the happiness of his creatures, utility is profoundly religious".

3 An *ordinal* utility function represents the order of an individual's preferences. One could assign numbers to each row in the ordering, but the relative magnitude of these numbers has no meaning in an ordinal ordering. In *cardinal* utility functions, one can assign numbers to utility differences that reflect the exact different valuation in a quantitative way. Cardinal rankings therefore allow more precise comparisons of combinations of options.

4 The importance of commitments illustrates a related problem of welfarism. This is the so-called paradox of hedonism. This paradox states that constantly aiming at your own happiness will lead you to regard all your actions and all other people as having only instrumental value. This will, however, interfere in serious ways with achieving real happiness, because happiness comes to those who can form commitments. That means they can engage themselves in projects because the objects or goals of those projects are valued in themselves, as ends (MacLean, 1994). A person does not throw himself into personal commitments with the idea that he will monitor the costs and benefits from time to time, but with the faith that this is the right thing to do. If we would constantly reflect on the happiness we get from a commitment, this could diminish or even destroy its value.

5 Walzer lists 14 major items that are not considered legitimate material for exchange. These include marriage, basic freedoms and divine grace. See Etzioni (1988: 81).

6   Here is a connection with the criticism on consequentialism, because valuations related to rights are generally considered to be non-tradable with values related to individual utility and effectively restrict the choice set for a utilitarian utility calculus.

7   Another reason for over-demandingness is that utilitarianism makes one as responsible for things that one fails to prevent (for example, the dying of other people as a consequence of famine which could be prevented by giving aid) as for things one brings about oneself (killing another person).

8   Another example of extra-welfarism is the concept of *primary social goods* used by Rawls. See Chapter 6.

Recommended literature

Hausman, D.M. and McPherson, M.S. (1996) *Economic Analysis and Moral Philosophy*, Cambridge: Cambridge University Press.

Mill, J.S. (1871) *Utilitarianism*, Oxford: Oxford University Press.

Sen, A. (1984) *Resources, Values and Development*, Oxford: Blackwell.

Sen, A. (1987) *On Ethics and Economics*, Oxford: Blackwell.

Singer, P. (1972) 'Famine, affluence and morality', *Philosophy and Public Affairs*, 3: 229–243.

Three economic perspectives on the 'good' market system[1]

The 1980s and 1990s saw a revival of the popularity of capitalism. The decline of the USSR not only proved that socialist planned economies are less efficient than capitalist economies, but it has also shown that the freedom of choice by individuals is much smaller in these socialist economies. Moreover, one can doubt whether a socialist system really brings more equality between citizens. These moral advantages of the market system – welfare, freedom of choice and justice – depend crucially on the competitive nature of the system. If firms collude and use their power to drive out competitors with unfair practices, the market ceases to be efficient and fair and will restrict people's freedom.

The notion that freely operating markets are conducive to social welfare is well-established in economics. In fact, it can be understood as one of the central tenets of economics, which dates back to Adam Smith's *Wealth of Nations*. It is also generally acknowledged that free markets cannot operate in a vacuum, but rather must be backed and facilitated by the government. Here, the question of both the appropriateness and the extent of governmental intervention in a market economy engenders a broad spectrum of opinions and political practices, which, in turn, are manifested in concrete practices. There is an expansive field of research investigating so-called varieties of capitalism (Hall and Soskice, 2001). Hall and Soskice's classification of Liberal Market Economies (LME) and Coordinated Market Economies (CME) is well-known. Hall and Gingerich (2009) subsequently added the category of Mixed Market Economies (MME) to this dichotomy by combining features of LMEs and CMEs. Witt et al. (2018) proposed nine main types of political economies, covering 94% of global gross domestic product (GDP). Their taxonomy comprises geographically differentiated economic systems with distinct characteristics, which serves as the foundation for their theorization about the implications of these different systems for economic and political performance.

Against this background, a perennial debate in economics is what should be left up to the market, and in what circumstances, as well as to what extent, governments should intervene to ensure the well-being of their citizens. In this chapter, we distinguish between three different economic perspectives on what role the government should play in market processes. First, at one end of the spectrum, we examine the free market perspective, according to which the smaller and less interventionist a government is, the less likely the freedom of economic agents to pursue their own trade-offs, and preferences will be substituted by governmental decision-making. From the free market perspective, markets require

DOI: 10.4324/9781003181835-4

as a *condition sine qua non* solid foundations, such as property rights, contract security, legal certainty and protection against aggression. This has to be guaranteed by a minimal state. Second, there is the perfectly competitive market perspective, or shortly, the perfect market perspective. In this perspective, the ideal of economic policy is a perfectly competitive market economy. A free market with a minimal state is not a well-functioning (perfect) market per se, and, as such, it is the responsibility of the government to intervene and correct for market failures (Sandmo, 2011). Some of the most important of these failures are positive and negative external effects, as well as the lack of competition that inhibits a well-functioning and market-clearing price mechanism. Third, at the other end of the spectrum, the welfare-state model accords the government a leading role, namely in terms of managing effective demand and providing social security to smooth the sharp edges of the free market.

The three perspectives are inspired by, and indeed, have their lineage in, three distinct theoretical systems, as well as their attendant policy recommendations and accompanying market institutions. These distinct schools of economic thought about the balance between the market and governments are the neoliberal, neoclassical and Keynesian perspectives. Clearly, all three of these perspectives strive for the economic betterment of people, albeit in different ways. The question can be posed: Which particular composition of market institutions constitutes a 'good' market? Of course, this question cannot be settled by pure positivistic economic analysis alone, as it is intertwined with moral considerations and political ideologies. According to the free market perspective, a good market respects individual freedom as an end in itself (see Chapter 5) and generates a variety of positive social and economic goals, including greater per capita wealth, poverty elimination and human development. In the perfect market perspective, the criterion for a good market is based on Pareto optimality, which is closely related to the criterion of good in utilitarianism (see Section 3.2). Conversely, the welfare-state perspective is predicated on the notion of inclusive economic growth. According to Keynes, his general theory should provide for full employment and "reduce [the] arbitrary and inequitable distribution of wealth and income" (Keynes, 1936, 1973: 372).

This chapter takes recourse to these three different schools of economic thought to describe the three perspectives, namely (1) the free market perspective of the neoliberal school, (2) the perfect market perspective of the neoclassical school and (3) the welfare-state perspective of the Keynesian school.

3.1 THE FREE MARKET PERSPECTIVE OF NEOLIBERALISM

Neoliberalism is a rather vague and often highly contested concept. Thorsen (2009) purports that neoliberalism is a loose set of ideas pertaining to how the relationship between the government, individuals and the market ought to be organized, which, in turn, links to a heterogeneous set of political theories. In one of the first titles referring to the concept (Cros, 1950), neoliberalism is described as the political ideology of neo-Austrian theorists, who aimed to reinvigorate the classical liberalism of Locke and Smith (Ryan, 1993). Ver Eecke (1982) defined neoliberalism as a particular kind of liberalism, which is marked by a deep-seated commitment to laissez-faire economic policies. As well as neo-Austrians such as Mises, Hayek and Schumpeter, it also refers to monetarists and other economists, such as Friedman (1962), who defend 'free markets'.

View on economic development

Notwithstanding the diversity of its usage in political theory, neoliberalism does have a clear view on economic institutions. Specifically, it proposes that human well-being can best be advanced by liberating individual entrepreneurial freedoms and skills within an institutional framework characterized by strong private property rights, free markets and free trade (Harvey, 2005). In the field of international trade, free exchange rates and free trade are favored.

In the free market perspective of the neoliberal school of economic thought (Schumpeter, Hayek, Friedman) economic growth does not result from price competition, but rather from the competition in introducing new consumer goods, new technologies, sources of supply and new types of organization structures. This kind of competition commands a decisive cost or quality advantage that strikes not at the margins of the profits and outputs of the existing firms – like price competition – but at their formation and their very lives. Entrepreneurs play a dominant role as inspirators and organizers of technological innovation. According to Schumpeter (1976), the fundamental impulse that sets and keeps the capitalist engine in motion is the new consumer goods, new methods of production or transportation, new markets and new forms of industrial organization that capitalist enterprise generates, rather than competition over who can offer the lowest price at any given point in time. There is a constant process of renewal that revolutionizes the economic structure from within. Schumpeter uses the term creative destruction to describe this process and considers this the core of capitalism. Such (monopolistic and oligopolistic) competition is not only more common than perfect competition, but it is also believed to be much more effective in terms of expanding output in the long term and reducing prices. In contrast, perfect competition solely yields short-term wealth creation (as a result of lower prices) and, as such, is inferior insofar as it limits the potential of a company to engage in a long-term strategy of price and process development. The high profits that oligopolistic structures allow provide a strong incentive to a small group of market leaders that introduce new and successful products that replace other products. This type of competition disciplines before it attacks because the businessman feels himself in a competitive situation even if he is alone in his field, because of the constant threat that another company will introduce a new product or technique that makes his product superfluous.

Role of government

The organization of the free market economy through voluntary exchange presupposes a legal framework capable of ensuring that one person cannot coerce another, that contracts are enforced and that the meaning of property rights is defined, interpreted appropriately and enforced when needed. The entrepreneurs must be sure that they will be the one to pick the fruit of their labor. This requires a well-developed system of property rights, low taxes and a frugal system of social assistance. These aforementioned matters should be guaranteed by the government, because "the role of government is just considered to be something that the market cannot do for itself, namely, to determine, arbitrate, and enforce the rules of the game" (Friedman, 1962: 27). In addition to this, the government must provide military, police and courts as public goods.

The government should refrain from intervening in the economic sphere via macroeconomic policy, industrial policy or price and wage policy. The government must simply guarantee the quality and integrity of money, as opposed to adopting monetary or budgetary policies to stabilize the economy. Active regulation is considered to be counterproductive, because the government has limited information and no incentive to take advantage of the available opportunities. "Competition must be seen as a process in which people acquire and communicate knowledge; to treat it as if all this knowledge were available to any one person at the outset is to make nonsense of it" (Hayek, 1979: 68). According to Hayek, we can never have complete knowledge of the circumstances, neither at the individual or societal level. Hence, decisions should be decentralized as much as possible to people who know the circumstances and can foresee the requisite changes, which can then be anticipated with the available resources.

Even in the sphere of public goods provision and the correction of market imperfections (externalities), government action should be limited, because of both the high likelihood of government failure and the distortions it creates in the market process. Stigler (1971) forcefully argued that regulation is wanted by industry and is designed and operated primarily for its benefit. In many cases, the government is simply unable to correct recognized market failures (Harvey, 2005). The argument here is that such failures stem from, among other things, asymmetric information, failing to put the public interest first (instead prioritizing the interests of various lobby groups), self-seeking bureaucrats and a lack of human and financial resources.

Also competition policy is criticized. Hayek does not reject monopolies or oligopolies and profits that are made if they have been lawfully created.

> It is evidently neither desirable nor possible that every commodity or service that is significantly different from others should be produced by a large number of producers, or that there should always be a large number of producers capable of producing any particular thing at the same cost.
> (Hayek, 1979: 66)

Regarding monopolies, Hayek argues:

> Where the source of a monopoly position is a unique skill. (. . .) There is no more an argument in justice, or a moral case, against such a monopoly making a monopoly profit than there is against anyone who decides that he will work no more than he finds worth his while.
> (Hayek, 1979: 72)

It is permissible for companies to charge higher prices for products than the cost price. The profits that are made stimulate the innovation of products and services. However, monopoly positions may not be used to keep other companies out of the market.

> Where "market power" consists in a power of preventing others from serving the customers better (. . .) it is true that even the power over prices, etc. may confer upon a monopolist the power of influencing the market behavior or others in a manner which protects him against unwelcome competition. We will see that in such cases there is indeed a strong argument for preventing him from doing so. . . . What is harmful is not the existence of monopolies that are due to greater efficiency or to the control of particular limited resources, but the ability of some monopolies

to protect and preserve their monopolistic position after the original cause or their superiority has disappeared.

(Hayek, 1979: 84, 86)

Hayek also rejects the protection of monopoly positions through tariffs and patents. With this, governments encourage powerful monopoly positions. Governments should only take measures in a general sense so that market forces are promoted.

Also Friedman is skeptical about government intervention. Friedman initially allowed slightly more room for government intervention than Hayek if markets are missing or if the marketing of products through markets is associated with exceptionally high costs. Friedman was originally a strong advocate of anti-competition policy by the government to promote competition. But in his later years, Friedman turned against government intervention in the market and turned away from active anti-competition policy by governments.

> When I started in this business, as a believer in competition, I was a great supporter of antitrust laws; I thought enforcing them was one of the few desirable things that the government could do to promote more competition. But as I watched what actually happened, I saw that, instead of promoting competition, antitrust laws tended to do exactly the opposite, because they tended, like so many government activities, to be taken over by the people they were supposed to regulate and control. And so over time I have gradually come to the conclusion that antitrust laws do more harm than good and that we would be better off if we didn't have them at all.

(Friedman, 1999: 7)

Just like Hayek, Friedman believes, however, that the government is essential for determining the rules of the game and enforcing them. The organization of the free market through voluntary exchange presupposes a legal framework that ensures that one person cannot coerce over another person, the enforcement of contracts, the definition of the meaning of property rights and the interpretation and enforcement of these rights and the determination of a monetary system. The aforementioned matters should be guaranteed by the government because the market cannot do this itself. "The role of government is just considered to be something that the market cannot do for itself, namely, to determine, arbitrate, and enforce the rules of the game" (Friedman, 1962: 31).

Finally, proponents of free market economics espouse that in their preferred market form, there is simply no place for a social safety net, except at a bare minimum, and income redistribution policies. In contradistinction to the government, economic agents are assumed to be knowledgeable and sufficiently rational to make their own trade-offs at the right time and take care of themselves. The adoption of a minimal state would thus foster an environment in which markets would flow by themselves completely undisturbed in such a way that would deliver the desired welfare-enhancing outcomes, while, simultaneously, guaranteeing individual rights and freedoms (Chang, 2014).

3.2   THE PERFECT MARKET PERSPECTIVE OF THE NEOCLASSICAL SCHOOL

Neoclassical economics dominates the mainstream of economic science. The ideal in neoclassical economics (Marshall, 1920; Pigou, 1932) is the perfect market that is free from market imperfections. In this perspective, the basis of economic growth is a well-functioning price mechanism that coordinates the decisions of various economic subjects (CPB, 1992). The price mechanism leads to equilibrium between supply and demand in the various markets. The level of prosperity depends on the available production factors (natural resources, quantity and quality of the labor supply and size of capital stock) and the state of technology. The level of saving determines the growth of the capital stock. Research and development (R&D) and investments in human capital are also major growth-determining factors, which derive from the optimal choices of companies and households. As a result of free trade, countries specialize in products that they have a comparative advantage in, while international trade provides opportunities for exploiting economies of scale (Baldwin, 1992).

The criterion for good: Pareto optimality

We have learned from Chapter 1 that when economists advice policy makers to use the market mechanism to coordinate economic behavior, they somehow must combine descriptive statements with a prescriptive or normative statement about the goal of economic policy to arrive at this policy conclusion. For this normative framework, neoclassical economists do not use utilitarianism. Although they generally endorse consequentialism and (formal) welfarism, they reject sum ranking because of the problems with interpersonal comparison of utilities. If utilitarianism is not acceptable for economists, on what normative criterion do neoclassical economists base their preference for perfect markets? Neoclassical economists have answered this question by developing Pareto optimality as a criterion for right and wrong.

The Pareto criterion is an efficiency norm and a central piece in welfare theory. It deals exclusively with efficiency in utilities, defined as the satisfaction of preferences. Before explaining Pareto optimality, we first define Pareto improvement: a measure generates a Pareto improvement if it makes one or more people in society better off (i.e. reach a more preferred state) without making anyone worse off. Pareto optimality will then exist if no further changes of this kind are possible. This criterion requires only a very modest ethical principle. Virtually everybody would agree that it is a morally good thing to make (some) people better off, other things being equal. Hausman (1992) calls this the ethical principle of minimal benevolence.

Like utilitarianism, the Pareto criterion assumes consequentialism and welfarism. Unlike utilitarianism, the Pareto criterion does not require interpersonal utility comparison. Although this seems to be an advantage, the price of giving up interpersonal utility comparison seems to be very high. In particular, because of this restriction, the applicability of the Pareto criterion seems to be very restricted because true Pareto improvements are extremely rare in reality. The Pareto criterion is therefore strongly biased to the status quo. In almost all real-life situations, an action or policy measure will affect the utility of some people in a negative way. There is no such thing as a free lunch. Institutional changes usually involve both winners and losers. In rejecting any possibility of interpersonal comparison, economists may safeguard the technical purity of their analysis, but also throw away the baby with the bath water. For most people would not be interested in economics at all if they did not think it had some relevance to aggregate human welfare (Self, 1975).

Theoretical foundation of the ideal of perfect market: welfare theorems

The ideal of the perfect market has been theoretically based on welfare theory. The so-called first welfare theorem has shown that any perfectly competitive market equilibrium is Pareto optimal. As long as producers and consumers act as price takers and there is a market for every commodity, the equilibrium allocation of resources is Pareto-efficient.

At first sight, the ethical content of this welfare theorem seems rather modest, because the criterion of Pareto optimality is a very limited way of evaluating a social state. This criterion only focuses on efficiency and does not consider the fairness of the outcome of perfect markets. An outcome can be Pareto optimal with some people in extreme misery and others wallowing in luxury if the miserable cannot be made better off without cutting into the luxury of the rich. However, welfare theory also provided a second theorem that gives an answer to this moral criticism. This second welfare theorem states that every Pareto optimum can be obtained as a competitive general equilibrium given some distribution of initial endowments to economic agents. This means that no Pareto-optimal outcome is unattainable as a competitive equilibrium, including those that fit with ideas of social justice. The optimal allocation of welfare can be obtained by shifting initial endowments before people enter the market, for example, by special forms of taxes (lump-sum taxes) or by education. For example, Varian (1974) proposes to let agents acquire at birth (or upon reaching maturity) an initial endowment of an equal share of society's resources. Upon death, each agent's property reverts to the state to be distributed equally to new generations. Next, agents can transfer ownership of goods and services only through the market mechanism. Under such a competitive market arrangement, the resulting allocation will be both efficient and fair. Thus, concerns about justice do not necessarily require interference with market transactions. Because of this result of the second welfare theorem, economists have felt free to analyze only questions of efficiency, leaving questions of a fair distribution of resources to the political process.

The argument that neoclassical economists use when defending the ideal of perfect markets can now be divided in the following steps (Hausman, 1992):

1 Suppose that one accepts that individual well-being can be identified with the satisfaction of actual preferences
2 And that one accepts the moral principle of Pareto optimality that, other things being equal, it is morally good if (at least) one person is better off
   From these premises and the definition of Pareto optimality, one can derive that Pareto improvements are moral improvements and that Pareto optima are morally desirable. From the first theorem of welfare theory we further know that
3 Competitive equilibriums are Pareto efficient
   Hence, we can conclude that competitive equilibriums are morally good and that market failures are morally bad, were it not that a Pareto improvement that leads to distributional injustice is not morally desirable. It is here that the second welfare theorem is important, which states that
4 All Pareto-efficient states of affairs can be obtained as competitive general equilibriums given the right initial distribution of endowments to individuals

Combining these four premises, neoclassical economists conclude that perfectly competitive economies are morally desirable and market failures are morally bad and that adjusting the initial distribution of financial and human endowments can satisfy all other moral concerns. Since the principle of Pareto optimality is only a modest ethical require-ment, it seems that positive economic reasoning very easily bridges the gap to normative theories. This explains why economists feel that they speak with moral authority when they favor a commitment to the ideal of perfect competition, without the trouble of doing moral philosophy (Hausman, 1992).

Still, the welfare theorems share several implicit premises that are open to consider-able doubt. First, since the Pareto criterion combines consequentialism and welfarism, it is subject to the moral criticisms on these characteristics discussed in Chapter 2. Second, the second welfare theorem does not always meet the Pareto criterion. Even if people are taxed after their death (as proposed by Varian (1974)), the tax will lower their utility if they attach an intrinsic value to the welfare position of their children (or other people who inherit their wealth). Also institutional reforms designed to obtain perfect competi-tion may be inconsistent with the Pareto criterion. For instance, if a monopoly position is eliminated, the purchasing power of those who consume the product of the monopolist will increase, but obviously the income of the monopolist will decline. Therefore, such a reform is not a Pareto improvement (Van de Klundert, 1999). The second welfare theo-rem is therefore incoherent with the principles that underpin the first welfare theorem. A third difficulty in applying this result to economic policy arises from the fact that it seems politically very difficult to redistribute resources among people by non-distorting taxes like lump-sum transfers. This would require radical redistributions of the owner-ship of means of production before the market would be allowed to do the rest. However, any system that relates the redistribution of financial and human capital to the wealth or income actually earned by individuals will distort the market mechanism and take away the optimal welfare effect of markets. In the absence of costless, lump-sum transfers in the real world, efficiency and distributional concerns obviously cannot be separated. Finally, a practical difficulty in applying this result of welfare theory in public action arises from the fact that the information needed to calculate the required initial distribu-tion of endowments is very hard to get, because one does not know the individual capa-bilities beforehand.

Conditions for perfect competition

Welfare theory illustrates, at an abstract level, Adam Smith's famous invisible hand the-orem. Namely, that people pursuing their own ends in competitive markets promote an important social goal – economic welfare – which they do not actually have any intention of promoting and which they may not even understand. But what are the conditions for a per-fectly competitive market? Any economic textbook lists the following features that perfect competition requires (Velasquez, 1998):

1 No external parties, such as the government, regulate the price, quantity or quality of the goods traded on the market.
2 There are so many independent traders on each side of the market, none of whom is large in relation to total industry sales, that no one can significantly influence the market price and overall industry output. This requires that there be no barriers to entry or exit from the market. All buyers and sellers can freely and immediately enter or leave the market.

There are no impediments across firms in the mobility of resources into, around and out of a particular industry.

3 All the firms in the industry produce standardized or homogenous goods, which are perfectly substitutable in the eyes of consumers. The goods are so similar to each other that no one cares with whom he trades. Homogeneity in goods contributes to the establishment of a uniform price for the product. Producers will be unable to sell their product for a higher price than competitors if the products are viewed as interchangeable, because consumers will always purchase from the lower-priced source.

4 Transparency of the market: the traders have perfect knowledge of prices, quantity and quality of all goods being traded to make the correct economic decisions.

5 The costs and benefits of producing or using the exchanged goods are borne entirely by those buying or selling the goods and not by any other external parties. This requires that there be markets for all goods and services and that there are no externalities and no interdependencies among people's utility functions.

6 The traders are rational. They are utility maximizers and try to get as much as possible for as little as possible.

In addition to these conditions, neoclassical economics agrees with the neoliberals that a competitive market needs an enforceable private property system and an underlying system of contracts that allows traders to transfer ownership.

No industry completely fulfils all the conditions for perfect competition (Greenwald and Stiglitz, 1986). From the conditions of perfect markets, we can identify six types of market imperfections. First, if the government intervenes in the market by regulating the price, quantity or quality of the goods traded on the market, this creates market imperfections.[2]

Second, there is always an inherent tendency for individual companies in free markets to try to prevent market competition from other firms, for example, through mergers or through agreements between a few oligopolists. Because a highly concentrated oligopoly has a relatively small number of firms, it is relatively easy for the managers of these firms to meet secretly and join forces and act as a unit. By agreeing to set their prices at the same levels and to restrict their output accordingly, the oligopolists can function much like a monopolist. As explicit agreements may be punished by anti-trust agencies, cooperation between oligopolistic companies most often takes place by unspoken or tacit agreements. This happens when the managers of the major firms in an oligopoly learn from experience that competition is not in their interest, as price cutting will always be followed by other companies, yielding a lower profit for all. Each firm may then come to the conclusion that they will all benefit if they follow a price change of one of them, mostly the so-called price leader, knowing that all other firms will also follow.

Third, many real-world markets seem to be incompatible with product homogeneity. If products are not homogeneous but the industry faces unrestricted entry and exit, the market features monopolistic competition. Product differentiation may reflect real differences among products (in function, design or quality), or it may be based only on the belief that there are differences (by advertising or brand names). Because of the monopolistic power, firms will charge a price that is higher than the marginal cost and produce too little. In her book *No Logo* Klein (2002) shows that international companies like Coca-Cola, Nike, Levi, Benetton, Apple, Disney and Starbucks consciously try to increase the heterogeneity in products by selling a brand rather than a product and connecting their brands to lifestyles by lifestyle marketing. This increases the market imperfection of heterogeneity in product by branding.

Fourth, as information is costly, virtually every commercial transaction is subject to limited information. When information is costly, consumers are not fully informed and lack either knowledge of the prices different firms charge or the quality of the products they sell, or both. Imperfect information often goes together with informational asymmetry (when one party to a transaction has more information to the transaction than the other party does). This may allow the better-informed party to exploit the less informed party by manipulating the quantity, quality or price in a way that is not easily detectable to the latter.

Fifth, an important market imperfection is externalities. An externality can be described as a cost or benefit from some decision which is not borne by the decision-maker and cannot be charged to him or her because of a missing market. A well-known example of external effects is pollution. Clean water and air are public goods. Public goods have two characteristics: non-rival consumption and non-exclusion. A good is non-rival in consumption if, with a given level of production, consumption by one person need not diminish the quantity consumed by others. A second characteristic of public goods is non-exclusion. Non-exclusion means that confining a good's benefits (once produced) to selected persons is impossible or prohibitively costly. Pure public goods are goods from the enjoyment of the benefits of which others cannot be excluded. Non-rivalry in consumption and the impossibility of excluding consumers generate the problem of how to prevent free riding, that is enjoying the public good but not contributing to its provision. Free riding is rational at the micro-level, but it hinders the ability of private markets to cater efficiently to the demand for a public good. Externalities also result from side effects of economic activities, for example, when the consumption of one household affects the level of satisfaction of other households. These side effects of ordinary economic activities are called external benefits when the effects are positive and external costs when they are negative. An example is the externality caused by communicable diseases. An action taken by one person, like keeping a safe distance from others or immunizing oneself against a communicable disease, generates direct health benefits for other individuals. If people trade off their personal cost of this action against their own personal benefit and do not take into account the benefits for other people, they will spend less effort than is optimal from a social point of view.

Finally, market imperfections arise if people are not fully rational. Rationality requires that three conditions are met (Hausman, 1992). First, individuals always choose the alternative that yields the highest utility to them (defined as satisfaction of preferences). The second condition for rationality is that a person has a rational belief about the likely consequences of his actions. This means, for example, that people should use all available past information to form optimal expectations and not make systematic prediction errors. Third, individuals are able to rank the utility obtained from all available alternatives in a consistent way. Otherwise stated, individuals have a rational set of preferences. A set of preferences is rational if it meets three sub-requirements: transitivity, completeness (also called commensurability) and continuity. Transitivity means that if for all options x, y and z, an agent prefers x to y and y to z, the agent must prefer x to z. Completeness (or commensurability) states simply that an agent can compare all options. An agent's set of preferences is complete if for all options x and y, either the agent prefers x to y or y to x, or the agent is indifferent between x and y. Continuity means that, at some point, the marginal value of two alternative goods is equal. Economists often argue that the claim that one value is incomparably higher than another only means that it is much more valuable than the other.

The actual behavior of human agents often diverts from rational behavior and is subject to bounded rationality. First, people do not have consistent preferences over time. People choose means largely on the basis of emotions and only secondarily on the basis of logical-empirical considerations. Conclusions reached by rational deliberations may be overridden by strong emotional impulses (Selten, 1999). Second, people may not be rational if they lack the cognitive abilities. Due to deliberation costs, people use heuristics or rules of thumb, which fail to accommodate the full logic of a decision, and make systematic errors. Rabin (1998) gives several examples of this phenomenon. First, according to a bias called 'the law of small numbers', people derive too much certainty from a limited number of experiences and make false inferences about causality and, hence, about the possible consequences of their choices. Second, once people have formed an idea about how reality works, they are often very inattentive to new information that contradicts their idea (so-called hypothesis-based filtering of information). On the basis of our hypothetical beliefs, we filter new information and ignore relevant information that contradicts our beliefs. Third, hindsight bias causes people to exaggerate the degree to which their beliefs before an informative event is similar to their current beliefs. People are prone toward overconfidence in their judgments relative to evidence. Fourth, people often systematically mispredict the well-being from future experiences, for example, because they do not take into account the choice's effect on future utilities through changing reference levels through habit formation. A final example is the so-called framing effect. This means that two logically equivalent statements of a problem lead decision-makers to choose different options if the equivalence is untransparent. The explanation is that because of our bounded rationality, the presentation of a choice may draw our attention to different aspects of a problem. Many other systematic biases have been found to be built into people's cognitive apparatus. In contrast to the standard neoclassical assumption that people behave rationally, people are to be better viewed as commanding varying degrees of rationality.

Third, the valuations of people may be incommensurable, that means, two goods cannot be ranked on one scale. In such cases, there is no guarantee that either choice will make better sense of one's valuations than the other. Preferences are discontinuous if there exists a hierarchy in values implying that two values are not exchangeable at all. Money, commodities and sensual pleasures are often seen as not comparable on the same scale as values like human life, friendship, freedom and human rights. Social norms often prohibit the trade-off between these higher and lower goods. According to Anderson (1993), incommensurability is more common than commensurability. There may be three reasons for incommensurability. First, there is a great diversity of worthwhile values or standards that cannot be compared, like beauty, friendship, knowledge and pleasure. Take, for example, music and knowledge. Bach and Darwin were each highly successful in their own ways of being brilliant. But it is silly to claim that if Darwin had achieved some brilliant insights into genetic theory as well as evolution, he would thereby have exceeded Bach in brilliance. The more a given scale of value encompasses very different, categorically unranked ways of meeting it, the more scope there is for incommensurability. Second, people care about things and people in different ways, such as loving, respecting, using, tolerating and honoring. Beautiful things are worthy of appreciation, rational beings of respect, sentient beings of consideration, virtuous ones of admiration, convenient things of use. These different modes of valuation are often incompatible. Comparative value judgments using scales are therefore limited to specific dimensions of welfare. Third, the valuation of a good is dependent on the social context. We make ourselves different kinds of persons through participating in different kinds of social relations. No single preference ranking can explain a person's choices across all of his social roles. When a parent sets aside his child's demand for attention in order to deal with a client's need, it typically makes a big difference for the valuation of this act, whether the parent is acting in his role as parent or in his role as businessperson at that time. And this, in turn, typically depends upon whether he is at home or at work.

The role of the government

In the perfect market perspective, the role of the government is modest and strictly limited to the production of pure public goods (such as defense, infrastructure and justice) and combating market imperfections. It is well established in neoclassical economics that markets can fail. If markets are imperfect, there are options for government regulations that improve the efficiency of the market (Greenwald and Stiglitz, 1986). For example, both at the international and the national levels, governments try to restrict market power by anti-trust policies. Besides anti-trust statutes, policy makers also rely on price regulation to deal with monopolies. Furthermore, in order to prevent a lack of information or informational asymmetry, the government may pursue policies that improve the transparency of the market.

To prevent externalities, the government may define and enforce clear and appropriate property rights that motivate the economic agents to internalize the external effects. Marshall, who is widely credited with inventing the concept of external effects (Sandmo, 2011), suggested that one ought to tax negative externalities and use the revenue to subsidize positive externalities (Marshall, 1920: 472–473). Subsequently, Pigou (1932) elaborated on the difference between social and private marginal costs and benefits deriving from external effects, as well as showing that competitive markets can produce inefficient levels of output. According to Pigou, the principal welfare task of governments is to equalize private and social marginal costs and benefits via taxes and subsidies associated with legal regulation.

There is no place for governments to implement active labor market policies or provide collective social insurance within the neoclassical perspective, because humans are assumed to be rational and capable of making their own choices. Neoclassical economists, for example, posit that unemployment, or, at the very least, some degree of unemployment, is voluntary and a structural feature of equilibrium (Boyer and Smith, 2001). Nevertheless, the government may opt to correct the income distribution that results in market equilibrium in order to assist those who are unable to earn a sufficient income. This is a political decision that depends on the political trade-off between efficiency and equity.

3.3   THE WELFARE STATE PERSPECTIVE OF THE KEYNESIAN SCHOOL

The third perspective is grounded in the thought of Keynes and Beveridge. Keynes (1936) argued that the future is fundamentally uncertain, which, in turn, provides space for fluctuations in expectations (animal spirits) that are both self-fulfilling and cumulative. If companies face a decline in the demand of product and dismiss employees, the purchasing power of the employees will fall, and this may enforce the decline in the demand of products. This may result in a recession and unemployment for quite some time. Markets are not self-correcting (Blaug, 1978). These uncertainties and fluctuations also negatively affect long-term economic growth as a result of its detrimental effects on human and physical capital formation (Blanchard and Fischer, 1992). Consequently, the atomistic pursuit of private interest may fail to engender stable economic development.

In order to achieve economic development, some degree of cooperation and coordination by the government is instead required. The Keynesian theory of persistent disequilibria supports an important role for national and international macroeconomic stabilization policy. To prevent an economic crisis like in the early thirties of the twentieth century, John Maynard Keynes therefore stressed the government should pursue active anti-cyclical policies and support employment creation. Notwithstanding the rational expectation revolution in the 1970s, stabilization policy is still an important aspect of the international and national economic order. A recent example of stabilization policy was the government response to the credit crisis in 2008. All Western governments and many non-Western countries initiated major government programs, including tax cuts and lowering interest rates, to stop the sudden fall of the demand in goods and services in order to restore trust. A similar response has been seen in 2020 following the COVID-19 crisis.

To reduce uncertainty, market regulations, industrial policies and coordinated decision-making in strategic projects with potential long-term gains for national welfare are required. In the field of international trade, the desire to reduce uncertainty leads to the preference for government-controlled exchange rates and trade policies (quotas, import tariffs, qualitative restrictions, export subsidies, R&D subsidies for emerging industries) as a means of correcting potentially myopic entrepreneurs or protecting against a volatile global market or aggressive foreign competition.[3]

Although Keynes observed the curse of unemployment, he was not initially interested in social policy. The major breakthrough in welfare-state economics came with the publication of the Beveridge report in 1942. Beveridge sought and received assistance from Keynes, subsequently becoming a convert of Keynesianism, despite rejecting his plea for protectionism. Keynes supported Beveridge's plan to extend social security benefits and contributions to the entire population, although he was concerned about the budgetary implications of doing so. In a letter to Beveridge on 14 October 1942, Keynes referred to Beveridge's plan as a grand document and hoped that its key components would be adopted (Marcuzzo, 2010: 202).[4] In the welfare-state perspective, there is a potentially extensive role for the government to correct the myopia of economic agents (Brue and Grant, 2007; Berggren and Bjørnskov, 2019). The government may, depending on the political constellation, also wish to correct the outcome of free market processes out of a desire for greater equality in income distribution. The ideology of the welfare state is predicated on the notion that in order to advance individual freedom, the state must adopt an active role in implementing social reform. This motivates a broad range of welfare-state policies in health care, social insurance and assistance, housing, public transportation, minimum wage legislation and the redistribution of income through a progressive tax system. The principal objectives of a welfare state are to boost living standards and reduce inequality (Marcuzzo, 2010). This implies, for example, that government regulations that aim to correct gender inequities in the labor market via the introduction of gendered welfare-state provisions are justified (Terjesen et al., 2015).

3.4 OVERVIEW

Table 3.1 summarizes the policy preferences of the three schools of thought with respect to specific indicators of government institutions.

The free market perspective has been operationalized in Gwartney et al.'s (1996) concept of economic freedom, along with being defined in measurable indicators by the Fraser Institute's Economic Freedom of the World Index (Fraser-EFW index). According to this definition, individuals have economic freedom when property rights are secure and when they are free to use, exchange or give their property to another, provided their actions do not violate the identical rights of others. Friedman, among others, was involved in the creation of this index. This index consists of several indicators which are grouped into five sub-constructs of economic freedom. The first construct concerns the size of the government (low general government consumption spending, low transfers and subsidies, no government enterprises and investment and low top marginal tax rate). The second sub-index relates to the design of the legal system, paying special attention to the rule of law, protection of property rights, enforcement of contracts, independent judiciary and an impartial court system. The third element of economic freedom expresses a sound monetary policy, so that citizens can rely on a hard currency (low money growth, low standard deviation of inflation, low inflation in the most recent year, freedom of citizens to own foreign currency bank accounts) that protects their personal wealth and prevents governments from lowering the real value of government debt through expansionary monetary policy. The fourth sub-index relates to the freedom to exchange goods and services internationally, indicated by the absence of tariffs, quotas, hidden administrative restraints and exchange rate and capital controls. Finally, the fifth sub-index measures the degree to which governments interfere in markets and focuses on regulatory restraints that limit the freedom of exchange in credit, labor and product markets.

The perfect market perspective supports the notion of economic freedom espoused by the free market school, insofar as its adherents believe that the market is largely able to self-regulate. It also stresses the need for protecting property rights, sound monetary policy and free trade. However, in contrast to the free market perspective, neoclassical economists argue that the government has a vital role to play in correcting market imperfections. For example, the government should prevent collusion by active anti-trust policy and correct for positive externalities (e.g. by financing public goods such as education that create positive externalities) and negative externalities (for example, via environmental regulation). This implies that neoclassical economists adopt an intermediate stance vis-à-vis government regulation.

TABLE 3.1
Market institutions preferred by different economic schools

— From less to more government intervention →			
Schools	Free market	Perfect market	
		Welfare state	Welfare state
Institutions	Economic freedom	Regulations that reduce market imperfections	Regulations that ensure reasonable equality

Like the perfect market school, the welfare-state school fully supports the importance of rule of law (protection of property rights). But when it comes to the other dimensions of economic freedom, the welfare-state school lies at the opposite end of the spectrum in comparison to the free market perspective. First, the welfare-state perspective endorses institutions that redistribute income and therefore supports a progressive tax system. This implies that the welfare-state perspective opposes a small government (which includes a marginal income tax rate as a measure of the progressivity of the tax system). Furthermore, whereas free market economists believe that government intervention in labor markets should be minimal, welfare-state economists see it as essential that governments provide social insurance and assistance, as well as applying a progressive income tax. Similarly to the neoclassical school, it stresses the need for active anti-trust policy, education policies and environmental regulation, but when it comes to labor market regulation, their view on structuring labor markets is contrary to both the neoclassical and neoliberal position that higher levels of labor market regulation are ultimately inefficient, particularly the regulations in the Fraser Institute's measurement that shield insiders from competition from outsiders (e.g. hiring and firing regulations and mandated cost of worker dismissal) (Lindbeck and Snower, 1986, 1987; Flanagan, 1988; Blanchflower et al., 1990).

NOTES

1   Some parts of the introduction and sections 3.1, 3.3 and 3.4 were previously published in Graafland and Verbruggen (2021).
2   However, government regulations may also aim to reduce one or more of the other market imperfections (see later).
3   At the Economic Advisory Council's Committee of Economists, Keynes made a plea for protectionism to reduce unemployment (Marcuzzo, 2010).
4   The welfare state also came to be embraced by the post-Keynesian school at the initiation of Joan Robinson.

Recommended literature

Friedman, M. (1962) *Capitalism and Freedom*, Chicago: University of Chicago Press.
Hausman, D.M. (1992) *The Inexact and Separate Science of Economics*, Cambridge: Cambridge University Press.
Hayek, F.A. (1979) *Law, Legislation and Liberty: A New Statement of the Principles of Justice and Political Economy*, Vol. 3, London: Routledge and Kegan Paul Ltd.
Keynes, J.M. (1936, 1973) *The General Theory of Employment, Interest and Money*, The Royal Economic Society, London: MacMillan Press.

4

Free markets, welfare and happiness

Empirical research

Since the 1970s, increased living standards enabled social scientists to reconsider the importance of directing policies towards economic growth. In 1974, Richard Easterlin published his famous research that showed that while income per capita had been steadily growing, self-reported happiness had been stable over the period 1946–1970 in the United States. This suggests that 'money does not buy happiness' and hence calls for a reorientation of the importance of policies directed towards economic growth. Not only scientists but also politicians have begun to think about the importance of happiness. For example, in July 2011, the United Nations' General Assembly adopted a resolution to make happiness a development indicator.

This chapter analyzes free market institutions from a utilitarian or happiness point of view. Market institutions stimulate mankind to exploit their talents and motivate man to economic activities that are favorable to the happiness of all. However, whether free market institutions increase happiness in society has not been proven theoretically and should be settled by empirical research. Welfare theory has only proven that perfect markets are efficient in the sense of Pareto optimality (see Chapter 3). In this chapter, we first discuss the cross-country relationship between free markets (measured by economic freedom) and income per capita. Then we deal with the question of whether income increases happiness (as measured by subjective well-being). In Section 4.3 we analyze the relationship between free market institutions and happiness. Fourth, we analyze the effect of economic freedom on dimensions of quality of life other than subjective well-being. In the last section, we compare the explanatory power of the neoliberal, neoclassical and Keynesian schools in describing human development.

4.1 FREE MARKETS AND INCOME

The causes of economic growth are manifold. Landes (1998) describes in his historical study *The Wealth and Poverty of Nations: Why Some Are So Rich and Some So Poor* the multiple causes of economic growth. For example, natural circumstances have a great impact on wealth. A warm, clammy climate hampers hard work and threatens human health by parasites. Drought and desertification prevent agriculture. Disasters (floods, earthquakes, cyclones, etc.) may cause many casualties and destroy the infrastructure. Still, geographic

DOI: 10.4324/9781003181835-5

circumstances are not decisive. Their role can be diminished by science and technology. Major conditions for the development of science and technology are good political structures and stable and honest governance. Also other factors have proven to be of great importance, such as culture (entrepreneurial spirit and the Jewish-Christian respect for labor, Calvinistic frugality and industry, linear time perspective), the absence of destructive wars, the separation of church and state, the institutionalization of science and research, and military power.

In this section, we are particularly interested in the relationship between free market institutions and income or economic growth. In literature, free market institutions have been operationalized by the concept of economic freedom. Economic freedom is an important concept in the neoliberal thinking of Hayek and Friedman There are various indices that quantify the economic freedom of a large number of countries in the world.[1] The most commonly used index is the Index of Economic Freedom as published by the Fraser Institute (see section 3.4).

One of the main mechanisms through which the various aspects of economic freedom may increase life satisfaction is that they stimulate income per capita. A small government and low taxes can lead to a more efficient allocation of resources (Graafland and Compen, 2015). A good legal system that secures property rights and contracts provides incentives for innovation, as the protection of property rights ensures that entrepreneurs can reap the fruit of their labor (Nyström, 2008). Property rights ensure that the gains from the trade flow to the investor, which stimulates investments. Moreover, the enforcement of contracts makes it easier to access credit markets, which also fosters investment (Farhadi et al., 2015). Stable prices due to sound monetary policy can reduce uncertainty and foster entrepreneurship (Bjørnskov and Foss, 2008), while trade openness can provide opportunities for economies of scale and facilitate exchange of knowledge (Lucas, 2000). Government regulation may take insufficient account of economic dynamics and cause market rigidity (Friedman, 1999). Various empirical studies have indeed shown economic freedom is positively related to economic growth or income per capita (De Haan et al., 2006; Justesen, 2008; Hall et al., 2010; Azman-Saini et al., 2010; Farhadi et al., 2015; Murphy, 2016; Bennett et al., 2017; Spruk and Kešeljević, 2018).

In literature, particularly the second aspect of economic freedom has received much attention in this regard, as research indicates that the protection of property rights is significantly positively related to income per capita (Rodrik et al., 2002; Blume and Voigt, 2006). On a sample of 120 countries, Graafland and Compen (2015) test how each of the five dimensions of economic freedom affect income per capita. They find that only the rule of law significantly increases income per capita – all other indices do not significantly improve welfare. This finding is robust if one uses indices of economic freedom from the Heritage Foundation instead of the Fraser Institute. When splitting the sample in rich and poor countries, they find that the positive relationship between income per capita and the quality of the legal system and protection of private property holds for both poor and rich countries.

4.2   DOES MORE INCOME MAKE US HAPPIER?

Happiness is often measured by subjective well-being indicators. Subjective well-being can refer to an overall evaluation of life, as well as to positive or negative feelings.

Among life evaluation standards, life satisfaction is one of the most prominent ones. It provides a comprehensive appraisal of life as it is in comparison to how life should be (Veenhoven, 2000).

Empirical research gives a mixed picture of the relationship between income per capita and life satisfaction. A path-breaking work was a paper of Richard Easterlin in the mid-1970s. Using data from a broad range of Western and developing countries, Easterlin (1974) established three findings. First, in any given country at a given time, wealthy persons report a higher subjective well-being (SWB) than do poor persons. Consumption of elementary goods, like being well fed, clothed and housed, is essential for well-being. These goods have an incontrovertible positive impact on human well-being, not only for biological reasons but also for social reasons. In such a situation, a general rise in prosperity reducing starvation and hunger increases well-being. A second finding of Easterlin is that the life satisfaction of a typical member of a Western society typically remained substantially unchanged during a period of rapid economic growth. Third, he examined the relationship between average SWB and average income for different countries in a cross-section and found that there was no correlation between these variables. Apparently, the SWB of a citizen of a nation is not tied to that nation's material prosperity.[2]

The first finding of Easterlin is largely confirmed by later research. Stevenson and Wolfers (2008) have found a positive correlation between subjective well-being and income at the micro-level. Income is also important, because it provides opportunities for human development by education. Furthermore, income may affect life satisfaction by reducing unemployment. As documented in many studies, unemployment has a strong detrimental effect on life satisfaction (Frey and Stutzer, 2000; Di Tella et al., 2001).

Also the second finding has been supported by later research. Based on a range of data for the United States, nine European countries and Japan, a rise in the incomes of all has not affected happiness at all (Kenny, 1999). In the United States, happiness peaked in the 1950s and has never recovered since then (Schor, 1997). Record levels of consumer debt burden Americans. Their incomes, it would appear, are insufficient to support the lifestyles to which they aspire. In Japan, reported happiness remained at almost the same level between 1958 and 1988, whereas Japanese income per capita in constant dollars climbed from $2,436 to $13,153 (Kenny, 1999).

The third finding of Easterlin appeared to be less robust. Schor (1997) cites cross-sectional research to the relationship between income and various measures of self-reported happiness. Both within countries and across countries, income and subjective well-being are usually positively and significantly correlated. But except for the poor and low-income individuals, the measured effects are rather modest. In more prosperous societies, diminishing returns set in so that SWB is relatively unaffected by further economic growth. An increase in one's income is important for all people, but more so for people living in poorer nations than in the richer ones (Deaton, 2008). Fischer (2008) argued that the Easterlin Paradox is an illusion based on a misspecification of wealth. Easterlin et al. (2011) and Di Tella and MacCulloch (2010) admit that income positively influences life satisfaction, but its significance disappears in the long run (i.e. ten years). Due to habit formation, higher levels of income per capita do not cause higher levels of subjective well-being over longer periods of time. Hence, they conclude that the effects of increases in income per capita on subjective well-being are not permanent, but still are relatively long-lasting.

Why does income hardly increase happiness in rich countries?

Notwithstanding the human capacities for improving fate and for extracting enjoyment from natural resources by art, labor and industry, most philosophers think that the human being will not be able to create a paradise in which all needs can be satisfied. The common situation of society will remain one of *(moderate) scarcity*. According to Hume, there will always be insufficient means to meet all the desires and necessities of all people (Claassen, 2004). Why is that? And why would that still be true?

This question can also be asked in another way. In the last 50 years, the Western world has become very rich. Still, working hours have not declined during this period. Instead, all economic progress has been channeled towards the production of more output and more consumption. Whereas it was widely believed in the thirties (including Keynes) that we would have by now been experiencing abundant leisure, our society is full of stress. Why is this the case?

Several arguments can explain the persistence of scarcity. A first explanation for the continuing restless economic growth is the insatiability of demand because people get used to higher levels of consumption (habit formation). Schor (1997) mentions an interesting outcome of a 1979 survey for the United States that showed that only 5% of the employees wanted to reduce current income in exchange for free time, but that 85% of the respondents preferred the option of trading future pay increases for more leisure. Yet over the next decade, almost no employees got that result. Instead, they got more income (and in many cases, longer hours). Yet by the end of the 1980s, a majority was still expressing satisfaction with their current hours. Schor explains this outcome by changing preferences. Rather than getting what they want (the standard neoclassical story), people end up wanting what they have already got (more working hours and more money). The new level of consumption sets a new standard for the reference level of consumption in the future. Therefore, any positive satisfaction from a discretionary consumption is quickly dissipated. New goods, originally experienced as luxurious and contributing to welfare, become part of the things people are used to. Only the loss of them is experienced as painful. This creates a positive bias in spending: human beings are continually seeking new luxuries, whereas, at the same time, they are unwilling to give up old ones (Schor, 1997). Many empirical studies show consumption patterns are subject to habit formation (Brekke and Howarth, 2002; Layard, 2003). The satisfaction from an increase in incomes is largely temporary, because people get used to the higher consumption level (Clark, 1999). The reference level of consumption that people feel they minimally need is for two-thirds related to the rise in their real income (Layard, 2003). So the happiness from more income is crowded out after some time by a rise in the reference level of needs.

A second explanation of persistent scarcity is supply-induced demand. In a capitalist system, companies can only be successful if they continuously realize competitive advantages by innovation in products or production patterns that reduce costs or increase productivity. In order to sell the increased production, it is necessary that new needs are created among consumers by marketing strategies. The primary function of commercial advertisements is to sell a product to prospective buyers. It creates desires in consumers for the sole purpose of absorbing industrial output. The replacement of consumer sovereignty by producer sovereignty calls into question the whole rationale of economic growth in the interest of want satisfaction. Product innovation indubitably increases the satisfaction of customers, but it also may create artificial needs. Continuous product development, spurious model changes and planned obsolescence may be undesirable from the point of view of the customer. Were goods made to last, were they reliable and sturdy, they would require less frequent replacement and would narrow the market for the output of the firm.

A third explanation of persistent scarcity is the social phenomenon that people relate their satisfaction from consumption to the consumption level of others rather than to their own consumption level only. Many prominent economists in the past, including Adam Smith, John Stuart Mill, Karl Marx, Alfred Marshall, Thorstein Veblen and John Maynard Keynes, acknowledged that standards of decency are socially determined: "the Greeks and Romans lived ... very comfortably though they had no linen" but "in the present time, though the greater part of Europe, a creditable day-laborer would be ashamed to appear in public without a linen shirt" (Smith, 2000 [1776]: 541). In his 1899 classic *The Theory of Leisure* Thorstein Veblen argues that consumption is mainly important not for the intrinsic functionality of products to satisfy material needs, but for its social symbolism. This explains also why advertisements mostly do not focus on the usefulness of products, but on the social message that the product signals about the owner of the product (Tieleman, 1989). The relevant question is not: 'What does the product do for me?', but rather: 'What does the product tell about me?' Rich people signal their status by luxury goods (Heilbronner, 1986). In Veblen's world, individuals of all classes emulate those directly above, and so consumption patterns trickle down through society, from rich to the various layers of the middle class and eventually to the poor. Empirical economic research confirmed the role of social interaction in the creation of new needs. For example, Solnick and Hemenway (1998) and Carlsson et al. (2007) found that students prefer a lower income if others get less than them over a situation where they get a higher income while others get more than them. In economics this phenomenon has become known as the idea of 'keeping up with the Joneses' (Alessie and Kapteyn, 1991).

René Girard, a French philosopher, also has stressed the social context of the satisfaction of goods in his book *Mensonge Romantique et Vérité Romanesque* (1961) but in a somewhat different way than Smith and Veblen. According to Girard, individuals want certain goods or services only because other people want these goods or services. The value an individual attaches to a certain good is derived from the value he or she supposes other people attach to this good. He calls this type of desire 'mimetic', because individuals copy the wants of other individuals. Mimesis is a central human characteristic that enables individuals to learn from other persons. However, mimesis is not only peaceful. It signifies that the other person is not only a model for defining our own wants but also the competitor in obtaining the desired good. Therefore, mimetic wants can also generate envy, rivalry and resentment. According to Girard, the particular choice of the good that becomes popular is random and not related to the intrinsic qualities of the good to satisfy certain material needs. This, too, implies that needs in our society are always floating. If we base our material desire only on what other persons possess, then there will never be an end to our needs, because the satisfaction is not derived from the consumption of the intrinsic aspects of the good. This results in a very low valuation and respect for the material reality itself, including the means and environmental resources that are required to produce the consumer goods. A good only continues to satisfy the social needs as long as other individuals have not obtained the good yet. The needs are not anchored anymore in the reality of what people actually need to live (Tieleman, 1991; Goudzwaard and De Lange, 1995).

Another interesting account of the relative value of consumption growth because of social interaction has been given by Fred Hirsch (1977). He distinguishes between private goods and goods that confer status, which he calls positional goods. The satisfaction derived from private goods is independent of the consumption level of others. In contrast, the satisfaction from positional goods is purely relative and only present if others cannot enjoy the good. A very interesting aspect of Hirsch's theory is the thesis that the demand for private goods diminishes when people become richer, whereas the demand for positional goods increases with wealth. Economic growth therefore goes together with increasing competition for positional goods. Since only a few people are able to acquire positional goods, this kind of competition generates frustration among those who do not succeed in the competition. The higher the share of positional competition, the lower the satisfaction economic growth will generate.

A fourth reason for persistent scarcity is the inherent tendency of the free market system to crowd out public goods through negative external effects. Policy makers believe that these negative externalities will only diminish if economic growth continues. Economic growth provides the necessary means for social policies that invest in public goods, save the environment and preserve cultural treasures and all other kinds of public goods. Therefore, economic growth remains priority one in economic policy.

A final explanation of persistence in scarcity is concerned with power as a means to guarantee safety. According to the philosopher Hobbes, the need for power is based on people's restless fear of loss of control and finally of death. One can only be saved from violence by others if one has sufficient power over them. Knowledge, richness, status and military means are all means to gain power. But just as status goods, power is a relative good. If others get richer, one also needs more economic means in order to maintain the power balance. Economic growth in order to gain or maintain power and secure one's freedom or safety is therefore endless.

Towards a stationary state?

John Stuart Mill hoped in his *Principles of Political Economy* (1848) that economic growth would be a transitory phase that, although necessary to relieve material scarcity, would set the stage for a better social state: "The best state for human nature is that in which, while no one is poor, no one desires to be richer, nor has any reason to fear being thrust back, by the efforts of others to push themselves forward".[3] His analysis extended to a concern over the links between population growth, economic activity and environmental quality, and he sincerely hoped that, for the sake of posterity, people will be content to be stationary, long before the exhaustion of the earthly resources would compel them to it.

John Maynard Keynes predicted in 1930 in his essay *Economic Possibilities for Our Grandchildren* that the technological development and the resulting economic growth would indeed eventually lead to a happy and satisfied society. At that time he expected that in about 100 years the economic problem would be definitely solved. Thanks to the economic growth, humanity would be able to spend its energy on non-economic purposes. He stated:

> I see us free, therefore, to return to some of the most sure and certain principles of religion and traditional virtue – that avarice is a vice, . . . and the love of money is detestable, that those walk

most truly in the paths of virtue and sane wisdom who take least thought for the morrow. We shall once more value ends above means and prefer the good to the useful.

(cited in Goudzwaard, 1976: 167)

Only for the meantime, as long as this happy stage of history is not attained, Keynes thought that money and vices like egotism and avarice serve the human purpose: "For only they can lead us out of the tunnel of economic necessity into daylight" (Goudzwaard, 1976: 167). However, the analysis in this chapter casts doubt on the realism of this prediction.

4.3   FREE MARKETS AND HAPPINESS

In Sections 4.1 and 4.2, we have shown that free market institutions, as measured by economic freedom, have a positive influence on income per capita, whereas income per capita has a positive, although decreasing, impact on life satisfaction. One would therefore expect that economic freedom and life satisfaction are positively related. This has been confirmed by a number of empirical studies (Ovaska and Takashima, 2006; Gropper et al., 2011; Hafer and Belasen, 2012; Gehring, 2013).

Theoretically, there are indeed several reasons why the various aspects of economic freedom may foster life satisfaction, but there are also reasons to expect that the influence of each of them on life satisfaction may vary. First, a large government may decrease people's life satisfaction, because when a government spends relatively more than individuals, households and businesses, this reduces economic freedom, as personal choice is effectively substituted by government decision-making. Bjørnskov et al. (2007) find that the share of very satisfied people decreases with higher government consumption, while government capital formation and social spending have no significant impact. However, Ott (2010) estimates that it is not the size of the government that affects life satisfaction, but rather the quality of governance.

Second, the rule of law will not only stimulate life satisfaction by raising income but also by fostering entrepreneurship. This will increase average life satisfaction, according to Benz and Frey (2003), who show that entrepreneurs are relatively more satisfied with their lives than employees. More generally, one may expect that the effectiveness of the judiciary and the enforceability of contracts will affect life satisfaction directly, because fair and predictable rules form the basis for economic and social interaction.

Also the third element of the index of economic freedom, i.e. access to sound money, is essential for doing business, because a hard currency will prevent inflation. Inflation erodes the value of property held in monetary instruments. When governments finance their expenditures by creating money, in effect, they are expropriating the property and violating the economic freedom of their citizens. Di Tella et al. (2001) indeed find that inflation has a significant negative effect on subjective well-being. Inflation, particularly when it is unanticipated, creates uncertainty about the future and may therefore reduce life satisfaction. Furthermore, Bjørnskov and Foss (2008) show that higher levels of 'sound money' also significantly promote entrepreneurial activity.

The fourth aspect of economic freedom, i.e. free international trade, may contribute to life satisfaction by stimulating economic growth, because open economies benefit more from the knowledge that is available in other parts of the world than do closed economies (Lucas, 2000). As foreign trade leads to specialization in areas of comparative advantage, it will ultimately increase welfare (Bjørnskov et al., 2007). Still, the empirical evidence is mixed. For example, Helliwell and Huang (2008) do not find any significant relationship between trade openness and life satisfaction. However, according to Tsai (2009), the length of the experience of openness is decisive. Countries that have been open for a long time show a higher life satisfaction than closed countries, whereas countries shifting from a closed to an open policy did not fare better than closed countries. Still, Tsai (2009) also concludes that trade openness, although having a positive influence on life satisfaction, is only of secondary importance, as it enhances subjective well-being only slightly.

It is less evident that the fifth aspect of economic freedom, i.e. no government regulation, will increase life satisfaction, because government regulation may provide security to citizens and limit market imperfections. Particularly anti-trust policy may be important in order to provide sufficient conditions that free markets operate efficiently. However, others doubt the efficiency of government regulation, because, as argued by Friedman (1999), anti-trust laws tend to be taken over by the people they were supposed to regulate and control.

Recent empirical research

Table 4.1 reports the results of the multiple regression analysis of the five sub-dimensions of economic freedom, income per capita and life satisfaction of Graafland and Compen (2015) on a sample of 120 countries.

The data for life satisfaction stem from self-reports on an identical survey question, defined as 'All things considered, how satisfied are you with your life as a whole these days?' measured on an 11-step scale ranging from dissatisfied (0) to satisfied (10).[4] The data for economic freedom are taken from the Fraser Institute and the Heritage Foundation.[5]

Table 4.1 shows that life satisfaction is significantly related to (the logarithm of) income per capita. Using the economic freedom indices of the Fraser Institute, none of the economic freedom indicators has a significant direct effect on life satisfaction, but for the estimations with economic freedom indices of the Heritage Foundation, small size of the government

TABLE 4.1
Life satisfaction and economic freedom: estimation results

	Fraser Institute			Heritage Foundation		
	1	*2*	*3*	*5*	*6*	*7*
	Life satisfaction		*Ln income per capita*	*Life satisfaction*		*Ln income per capita*
Small size of the government	−0.05	−0.14*	−0.12	−0.11*	−0.15*	−0.08
Legal system	0.15	0.53***	0.56***	−0.02	0.32**	0.45**
Sound money	0.01	0.17*	0.18			
Freedom to trade	−0.03	0.07	0.14	−0.04	−0.08	−0.06
No regulation	0.03	−0.09	−0.17	0.18	0.32*	0.13
(ln) Income per capita	0.71***			0.78**		
Radj²	0.78	0.67	0.73	0.78	0.63	0.70

*: $p < 0.05$; **: $p < 0.01$; ***: $p < 0.001$; unstandardized coefficients. Controlled for various control variables, see Graafland and Compen (2015).

TABLE 4.2
Indirect effects of economic freedom on life satisfaction through income per capita

Small size of the government	Legal system	Sound money	Freedom to trade	No regulation
	Economic Freedom Fraser Institute			
−0.09	0.40*	0.14*	0.10	−0.12
	Economic Freedom Heritage Foundation			
−0.06	0.35*		−0.05	0.10

* $p < 0.05$.

has a significantly negative direct effect on life satisfaction. If we drop income per capita, small government size has a negative effect for both economic freedom indices. The rule of law also becomes significant. The last column indicates that this is partly due to mediation by income per capita, which is shown to be significantly related to the quality of the legal system. For the other indices, the results depend on which indices for economic freedom are used. Using the ratings of the Fraser Institute, sound money also becomes significant, whereas for the ratings of the Heritage Foundation, low regulation becomes significant.

Table 4.2 reports the significance of the indirect effects of the indices of economic freedom on life satisfaction through income per capita. If we employ the economic freedom indices of the Fraser Institute, the rule of law and sound money are significantly positively mediated by income per capita. If the indices of the Heritage Foundation are used, only the rule of law is significantly positively mediated by gross domestic product (GDP) per capita.[6]

4.4 FREE MARKETS AND QUALITY OF LIFE[7]

Most previous research on economic institutions has used GDP per capita as a measure of good economic performance. Undoubtedly, GDP per capita does provide relevant information about the quality of life in a given country. Indeed, improved living standards not only provide a direct indication of material dimensions of well-being, but they are also an important pre-condition for other types of well-being, such as the level of health and leisure time (Ruseski and Maresova, 2014) and life satisfaction (Di Tella et al., 2003). Whereas economists for a long time focused on income per capita as an indicator of well-being, they increasingly acknowledge its limitations as an indicator of what human beings value in life (Stiglitz et al., 2009). For example, high income does not guarantee respect of human freedom rights (Bennett et al., 2016); it does not track changes in the quality of products; does not take account of depreciation of capital and the degradation in the quality of the natural environment (due to negative externalities); has difficulties in measuring the quality of government-provided services; does not isolate defensive consumption that has no direct benefit; and is only related to wealth in the long term (dependent on the savings ratio). Furthermore, income per capita does not capture non-market household production, informal economic activity, leisure and other non-material aspects of quality of life.

Some of the limitations of income per capita as an indicator of well-being are reduced by using subjective well-being. The greatest strength of subjective well-being measures is their simplicity: relying on people's own judgments is a convenient shortcut and potentially provides a natural way to aggregate various experiences in a manner that reflects people's satisfaction with their own preferences. However, subjective well-being measures lack a more objective estimation of well-being dimensions, such as physical capital, human capital, environmental capital (i.e. natural resources, biodiversity, climate) and social capital. If the subjective valuation is based on irrational considerations (e.g. types of preference satisfaction that harm the individual's happiness), its usefulness as a measurement of well-being diminishes. Other weaknesses are that life satisfaction reports can be influenced by situational factors, may be dependent on temperament or may be influenced by social expectations. Finally, the importance of subjective well-being as an attribute of the quality of life may vary across individuals and nations (Diener and Suh, 1997)

Drawing upon recommendations made by Stiglitz et al. (2009), the Organisation for Economic Co-operation and Development (OECD) constructed a so-called 'Better Life Index' (BLI) which complements income and life satisfaction with nine other dimensions of well-being or quality of life: housing, jobs, community, education, civic engagement, environment, health, work–life balance and safety (Mizobuchi, 2014). This approach gives prominence to people's objective conditions and the opportunities available to them (Sen, 1984; Nussbaum, 2011). The OECD BLI is a recent holistic approach to measuring these dimensions of well-being across different countries (Durand, 2015; Peiró-Palomino and Picazo-Tadeo, 2018; Balestra et al., 2018).[8]

Economic freedom may also have a favorable effect on these other dimensions of quality of life. Nikolaev (2014) analyzed the relationship between economic freedom and all the sub-dimensions of well-being distinguished in the BLI for 34 OECD countries and found a positive correlation for almost all aspects. These results tended to be consistent across genders and income classes, although some differences were found.

These findings are supported by studies that addressed the influence of economic freedom on one of the dimensions of quality of life (other than income per capita and life satisfaction mentioned earlier). First, Campbell et al. (2008) found that economic freedom improves a state's well-being and it therefore becomes a more attractive place to live. Furthermore, as economic freedom has been found to increase income and income has been shown to correlate with health (Benzeval and Judge, 2001; Frijters et al., 2005), it is not surprising that some studies have found economic freedom is also positively related to better health. Stroup (2007) has shown that an increase in economic freedom will not only lead to greater prosperity but also to choices by individuals that enable them to live longer, healthier lives. Other studies have argued that economic freedom encourages education (Schofer and Meyer, 2005; Stroup, 2007; Aixalá and Fabro, 2009; King et al., 2012; Feldmann, 2017). Secure property rights, a low level of taxation and monetary stability protect economic agents from expropriation and create an incentive to invest in human capital. They also enhance the gains from economic exchange, incentivizing individuals to maximize the return on their human capital. Through education, economic freedom may also raise civic participation. Milligan et al. (2004) found that education is positively linked to the quantity and to the quality of citizens' involvement in the electoral process. OECD (2000) likewise found that educated people show more active political participation.

Economic freedom has also been found to be positively related to environmental quality. Baughn et al. (2007) and Hartmann and Uhlenbruck (2015) found a positive link between economic freedom and the corporate environmental responsibility of companies. The reason could be that economic freedom stimulates entrepreneurial solutions to problems such as global warming and environmental protection. Protection of property rights encourages companies to make future-oriented investments in environmental performance, as there is more certainty that they will benefit from the returns to these investments. Better protection of property rights also implies that there is less scope for harming others' interests by pollution (Stroup, 2003) which may help overcome the tragedy of the commons. Furthermore, in societies with low levels of economic freedom, people and companies may perceive that the government is in charge of social welfare and define their own environmental responsibilities very narrowly. Stroup (2003) found, however, that economic freedom is only negatively related to air pollution levels (i.e. sulfur oxides, oxides of nitrogen, visible particulates, and carbon dioxide) per dollar of GDP when a country has a relatively low level of economic freedom. This would indicate that economic freedom and the environmental quality of a country are unrelated for countries with high economic freedom. Graafland (2019a) found that small size of government and freedom from government regulation decrease rather than increase corporate environmental responsibility. The test results are robust for the type of economic freedom data (Fraser Institute or Heritage Foundation) used. This would suggest that the effect of economic freedom on corporate environmental responsibility of companies is ambiguous and dependent on the type of economic freedom.

Whereas the explorative research by Nikolaev (2014) indicated a positive relationship between economic freedom and well-being as measured by the OECD BLI, his findings seem to identify one exception, namely work–life balance. Indeed, whereas free markets foster industry, entrepreneurship and the intrinsic motivation to work (Kreps, 1997; Maitland, 1997), the downside of the work incentives of free market economies might be that markets encourage a commitment to working that distorts private life. Research by Reynolds and Renzulli (2005) has shown, for example, that entrepreneurship causes considerable interference between private life and work. Block et al. (2018) also found that entrepreneurs experience a poorer work–life balance, since being one's own boss makes one work harder than salaried employment (McCloskey, 2006). Furthermore, due to competition, firms have a strong interest in their employees working long hours in order to get as much as possible from them (Schor, 1993). As a result, people may find themselves working many hours per week at the expense of other important commitments in their lives, such as family relationships, for a financial reward that, if they thought about it, they might realize they do not really need. Free trade (one of the dimensions of economic freedom) can also distort work–life balance. Due to constant organizational changes in response to the dynamics of the world market, individuals feel more pressure and experience more demanding working practices (White et al., 2003; Lewis, 2003; Guest, 2002). However, there are also arguments to expect a positive relationship between economic freedom and work–life balance. Economic freedom enables people to enjoy more leisure because of an increase in income. Most leisure activities require purchasing power to finance the costs incurred by these activities, such as equipment, membership fees, travel cost and the like. People with more purchasing power are better able to afford these costs. As economic freedom increases income per capita, it might therefore encourage more leisure and time for personal care. This is supported by empirical research by Ruseski and Maresova (2014) that shows participation in sports to increase with economic freedom (as well as to decline with hours worked and full-time employment status). They explain this relationship by pointing out that countries with high economic freedom have more market-driven economies that supply more of the facilities, equipment and instruction required for individuals to be physically active.

Finally, economic freedom might also be negatively related to community. Economic freedom assumes personal autonomy (i.e. a state of individual freedom from external authority) and self-reliance (i.e. individuals are solely responsible for their own well-being) and has a close kinship to classical and neoliberalism (Bozeman, 2007). Arikan (2011) found that low government spending correlates with individualism, whereas Mayda and Rodrik (2005) report that people's preferences with regard to freer trade are negatively related to values concerning neighborhood attachment. However, the empirical evidence is ambiguous. The correlation analysis between economic freedom and the community dimension of the BLI of the OECD by Nikolaev (2014) showed a positive relationship. A possible explanation is that a higher internal locus of control tends to make people more socially active (Nikolaev and Bennett, 2016). Furthermore, as economic freedom increases generalized trust (see Chapter 10), it may also encourage people to participate in community life. The relationship between economic freedom and community is therefore likely to be ambiguous.

4.5   TESTING THE THREE PERSPECTIVES ON THE 'GOOD' MARKET SYSTEM

We close this chapter by presenting recent explorative results on the relationship between human development and market institutions of Graafland and Verbruggen (2021). The issue of what composition of market institutions constitutes a 'good' market has received renewed attention in recent years due, in part, to a nascent awareness that the traditional form of capitalism, that is, the free market perspective, may in fact undermine the good life (Skidelsky and Skidelsky, 2012). Graafland and Verbruggen set out to empirically test the performance of the three alternative economic perspectives discussed in Chapter 3. They defined 'good' markets as those markets that foster human development. They used the definition of human development delineated in the human development index (HDI). The HDI captures three essential components of human development: a long and healthy life, access to knowledge and a decent standard of living (Nikolaev, 2014). Because of the inclusion of information on health and education, the HDI provides a more complete measure of overall development than GDP per capita (Özcan and Bjørnskov, 2011). Through recourse to Sen's (1984) capability approach, the HDI attempts to track people's capacity to exercise their freedom in the pursuit of a better life. Although the HDI does not account for other important dimensions of human life, it is nevertheless the best measure in terms of both allowing for a comparison of a large number of countries over a long period of time (Nikolaev, 2014) and being a better predictor of the good life as measured by the OECD BLI than GDP per capita.[9]

Table 4.3 reports the results of the multiple regression analysis. The overall level of economic freedom and government size does not affect human development or one of its underlying dimensions. These results thus do not support the free market perspective. Conversely, expenditure on publicly financed education (as a percentage of GDP) significantly increases human development and its sub-dimension, education, which supports the perfect market and welfare-state perspectives on good markets (see section 3.4). Furthermore, regulation of labor markets significantly decreases human development, as well as the three underlying dimensions of the HDI. Consequently, this finding does not support the welfare-state perspective. Finally, gender regulation slightly increases human development, which provides support for the welfare-state perspective.

Columns 4 and 5 show that environmental pollution reduces life expectancy, while environmental regulations by the government significantly reduce environmental pollution. This suggests that environmental regulations improve the third dimension of human

TABLE 4.3
Three perspectives on "good markets": estimation results[a]

	1	2	3	4	5	6
	HDI	Income	Education	Life expectancy	Environmental pollution	
Economic freedom	−0.05	−0.09	−0.10	−0.16	−0.10	0.22
(Small) size of government	−0.01	−0.03	0.00	−0.08	−0.03	
Public education expenditure	0.04[+]	0.09	0.22*	0.08	−0.01	
Environmental pollution	−0.10*	−0.26*	−0.17	−0.48**		
Environmental regulation					−0.10*	−0.17**
Labor regulation	−0.10***	−0.20***	−0.38***	−0.21***	0.05	
Gender regulation	0.01**	0.02	0.04**	0.02	−0.01	
R^2	0.30	0.57	0.47	0.51	0.03	0.06

[a] $+ p < 0.10$; $* p < 0.05$; $** p < 0.01$; $*** p < 0.001$. Robust standard errors. Controlled for control variables.

development, namely life expectancy. This finding once again supports the perfect market and welfare-state perspectives on good markets, while providing no support for the free market view. If Graafland and Verbruggen take out the size of government, public education expenditure and labor regulation, then the number of observations increases from 216 to 403, which, in turn, increases the significance of environmental regulation.

Overall, Graafland and Verbruggen conclude that the estimation results tend to support the perfect market perspective on good markets more than the welfare-state view because of the negative effect of regulation of labor markets, although the significant, but small, positive effect of gender regulation lends support for the welfare-state perspective. The free market perspective is not supported either, as indicated by the lack of significance of overall economic freedom, the significant positive effect of public education and gender regulation and the indirect positive effect of environmental regulation on life expectancy.

The policy recommendation of the neoclassical school that governments should correct market failures to produce socially optimal outcomes is clearly substantiated by this study, particularly in relation to the public financing of education, which is also endorsed by Keynesian thinking and environmental regulation. The first correction creates a positive externality and cannot be viewed in isolation from a flexible labor market. A well-educated, mobile labor force, supported by post-initial education and retraining programs is conducive to human development and flourishing. The second correction refers to the internalization of environmental externalities through regulation. Developing a healthier and sustainable living environment is a policy recommendation that requires no further substantiation.

Interestingly, Graafland and Verbruggen also found a positive relationship between human development and regulation of board gender quotas. National welfare states play an integral role in determining women's economic activities, labor market participation and occupational opportunities (Terjesen et al., 2015). The positive effect of legal gender board quotas suggests that in countries that currently lack this type of regulation, women's talents are being underutilized at the decision-making level, especially at the top level. This is problematic because the literature has demonstrated that gender diversity increases innovation (Miller and del Carmen Triana, 2009). This finding is supported by our results, which show that greater levels of gender equality increase income, as well as education and health.

NOTES

1   There are four indices that quantify economic freedom: (1) the Fraser Institute, (2) the Heritage Foundation, (3) the Freedom House and (4) the Scully and Slottje measure. The majority of researchers use the Fraser Institute's index in economic growth studies, as this index covers the largest number of years (Doucouliagos, 2005: 369).

2   For Adam Smith, the material welfare that free market institutions cause increases societal happiness, as is witnessed by the following citations from The Wealth of Nations (WN) "No society can surely be flourishing and happy, of which the far greater part of the members are poor and miserable" (WN, I, viii.36). However, Smith was also skeptical about the happiness that money can buy (Bréban, 2014): "In the most glittering and exalted situation that our idle fancy can hold out to us, the pleasures from which we propose to derive our real happiness, are almost always the same with those which, in our actual, though humble station, we have at all times at hand, and in our power" (TMS, III, iii, 31). The rich do not tend to be much happier than the poor in commercial society, according to Smith, because they both enjoy liberty and security under the law (Rasmussen, 2006). Although fortune plays a role in attaining happiness, probably the most important reason for Smith that free market institutions contribute to human happiness is that they tend to provide people with a greater degree of liberty and security (Paganelli, 2010): "Commerce and manufactures gradually introduced order and good government, and with them, the liberty and security of individuals. This, though it has been the least observed, is by far the most important of all their effects" (WN, III iv.4).

3   Book IV, Chapter VI.

4   One can question whether the meaning of life satisfaction varies in different cultures. Helliwell et al. (2009) find, however, that despite cultural differences, people value the same (relatively small) set of variables in comparable ways across the globe. Also Veenhoven (2000) and Diener and Suh (2002) argue that aggregate SWB scores can be meaningfully compared across cultures.

5   It should be noted that the measurement of institutional characteristics is inherently difficult (Dawson, 1998). Although the quantitative indicators of the Index of Economic Freedom of the Fraser Institute are based on data (published by the World Bank, International Monetary Foundation [IMF] and other statistical offices), qualitative data are often based on questionnaires and therefore contain elements of subjective evaluation (Tsai, 2009).

6   It is important to note that the results might be influenced by reverse causality, as socioeconomic circumstances may influence a country's adoption of the institutions of economic freedom (Berggren, 1999). Economists have tried solving these problems by using instrumental variables (Tabellini, 2010), but the exclusion restriction remains problematic. We should therefore be careful with deriving policy implications from these empirical studies.

7   Part of this section was published in Graafland (2019b).

8   See https://stats.oecd.org/index.aspx?DataSetCode=BLI for a detailed description of the underlying indicators of the BLI.

9   Alongside the overall Index of Economic Freedom, they used two sub-dimensions of this index to measure government size and government regulation of the labor market. The Fraser-EFW sub-index for government size includes (1) government consumption as a percentage of total consumption, (2) transfers and subsidies as a percentage of GDP, (3) government investment as a percentage of total investment, (4) top marginal income (payroll) tax rate and (5) state ownership (the degree to which the state owns and controls capital (including land) in the industrial, agricultural and service sectors). The larger the government size, the lower the Fraser-EFW sub-index for small government, as government expenditure and income distort economic freedom. The Fraser-EFW index 'Labor Market Regulation' comprises a number of sub-components characteristic of a sheltered labor market: minimum wage, hiring and firing regulations, centralized collective bargaining, hours regulations, mandated cost of worker dismissal and conscription. Public education refers to government expenditure on education as a percentage of GDP of the World Bank. Environmental regulation is measured by the OECD environmental policy stringency index, defined as the degree to which a government's environmental policies put a price on polluting and environmentally harmful behaviors. Environmental pollution is measured by emissions of air pollutants (in thousands of tons) per capita. Gender regulation is measured by the share of female board members in the board that is minimally legally required (Terjesen et al., 2015).

Recommended literature

Easterlin, R. (1974) 'Does economic growth improve the human lot?', in: P. David and M. Reder (eds.) *Nations and Households in Economic Growth: Essays in Honor of Moses Abramowitz*, New York: Academic Press, 89–125.

Girard, R. (1961) *Mensonge romantique et vérité romansesque* (De romantische leugen en de romaneske waarheid), Kampen: Kok.

Hirsch, F. (1977) *Social Limits to Growth*, London: Routledge and Kegan Paul.

Keynes, J.M. (1930) *Economic Possibilities for Our Grandchildren*. In: Essays in Persuasion (New York: Harcourt Brace, 1932), 358–373.

Mill, J.S. (1848/1994) *Principles of Political Economy*, Oxford: Oxford University Press.

Skidelsky, R. and Skidelsky, E. (2012) *How Much Is Enough: The Love of Money, and the Case for the Good Life*, London: Allen Lane.

Part II

Free markets, rights and inequality

5

The ethics of duties and rights

In Part I we have evaluated the market from the perspective of utilitarianism. If the market meets certain conditions, it generates an optimal social welfare for the society. From this perspective, the market economy is often defended as the most efficient mechanism to coordinate the demands and supplies of goods in the economy. Pro-market institutions are therefore often defended on utilitarian grounds.

One of the criticisms of utilitarianism concerns its consequentialism in combination with its sum ranking. As argued in Chapter 2, utilitarianism may yield conclusions that we feel are unethical. For example, utilitarianism may demand to take the life of some individual persons in order to improve the life of many other people. In order to prevent this unethical outcome of the utilitarian calculation, there are several ethical theories that do not take the consequences as a basis for evaluating the moral value of a certain act or policy, but consider intrinsic aspects of the act. These ethical theories are non-consequentialist in nature and based on deontological theory developed by Immanuel Kant.

In this chapter we investigate three alternative elaborations of deontological theory. First, Section 1 explains the basic difference between consequentialist ethical theories and deontological theories. In Section 2 we consider the deontological ethical theory of duties of Kant. In Section 3 we discuss the libertarian theory of rights, which goes back to the theory of natural rights developed by John Locke. We discuss the contemporary defense of libertarianism by Robert Nozick and illustrate the libertarian view by Friedrich Hayek's view on free markets and Milton Friedman's defense of the shareholder model. Section 4 deals with positive rights, including human rights, and discusses some implications for corporate social responsibility.

5.1 CONSEQUENTIALIST VERSUS DEONTOLOGICAL ETHICAL THEORIES

In Chapter 2 we described consequentialism as one of the characteristics of utilitarianism. Consequentialism asserts that actions, choices or policies must be judged exclusively in terms of the resulting, or consequent, effects, rather than by any intrinsic features they may have. In utilitarianism, the satisfaction of any desire has some value in itself that must be taken into account in calculating the total sum of utilities. Thus, if a person takes a certain pleasure in torturing another person, then the satisfaction of both persons should be weighed. Only if the negative consequences for the victim dominate the positive pleasure of the wrongdoer is the act rejected by utilitarianism.

DOI: 10.4324/9781003181835-7

In contrast, deontological theories judge that actions or policy measures must be right or wrong for reasons other than only their good consequences. The most famous deontological theory is the ethics of duty developed by Immanuel Kant (see later). His approach is labeled 'deontological' because the Greek word 'deon' means duty or obligation. In this approach an act is only right if it conforms to the relevant moral obligation. Keeping a promise or respecting the rights of others is right, because it is a moral duty, whether or not such an action maximizes utility (Beauchamp, 1982). Moral standards exist independently of the consequences that actions have. In the example of torture: an individual who derives pleasure from torturing another person has no claim whatsoever to his enjoyment, because one has a moral duty not to torture others. Torturing is wrong in itself. Deontological theories thus put limits on which satisfactions have value (Rawls, 1999a: 27). In this way they provide keys that prevent some problems of consequentialism discussed in Chapter 2, like no intrinsic values of rights, no retributive justice, uncertainty of predicted consequences and no consideration of intentions.

An example that illustrates how consequential reasoning leads to different moral judgments than deontological reasoning is the use of medical knowledge obtained by experiments during World War II of German doctors with prisoners, who died as a result of these experiments. In a consequentialist framework, once this knowledge exists, one should use it for developing medicines that can cure people. Although this knowledge has been acquired at the expense of the lives of prisoners, consequentialism accepts the use of it because these prisoners are already dead. Now only the future counts. In a deontological framework, one can question whether one is morally allowed to use this knowledge because it has been obtained in an immoral way through killing innocent people. Not the future outcomes count, but the moral value of the act itself. Because the right to freedom of prisoners has been violated, using this knowledge may be immoral. Consequentialism gives little consideration to the past. It thus disregards retributive justice.

Since deontological theories focus on the acts rather than on the consequences, the moral judgment of deontological reasoning is not more or less dependent on uncertain consequences in the future. Whether certain acts violate the rights of certain people can be more easily ascertained and is often subject to less uncertainty than whether these acts maximize the future utility of all who are influenced by these acts.

Many deontologists (although not all) often combine deontological ethics with 'Gesinnungsethik' that emphasizes that the moral value of actions follows from the intention of the person who acts.[1] For example, in order to ascertain the badness of manslaughter, consequentialist reasoning only considers the consequence of the homicide, the death of a person. Gesinnungsethik will also take into account the motive of the homicide. If the person willingly intended to kill the person, the action is considered to be worse than if the killing was not intended and happened by accident.

Furthermore, it should be noted that deontological theories do not disregard consequences completely. As Rawls (1999a) argues, all ethical doctrines take consequences into account in judging the rightness of an action or institution. But deontological theories do not consider maximizing the good consequences to be the sole standard. Also Johnson (2001) argues that consequentialist and deontological reasoning are not mutually exclusive. He illustrates his argument by the right to privacy. Privacy is valuable for various consequentialist reasons, such as the promotion of happiness by keeping secret intimate facts about oneself from the prying eyes or ears of others. Yet it is also defended by deontological reasons, because privacy contributes to the respect of the individual dignity. Whereas consequentialist reasoning is mostly forward-looking (what does personal privacy contribute to future well-being?), deontological reasoning is often backward looking (what should be done to the violation of existing rights?).

5.2   ETHICS OF DUTY OF KANT

Deontologists have identified many different principles to judge the moral value of a policy or act. The most prominent deontologist is Immanuel Kant. Many other philosophers, like Robert Nozick and John Rawls (see later), have developed their theories on a Kantian basis. In this section, we describe the ethics of duty of Kant.

Intentions instead of consequences (*Gesinnungsethik*)

Kant defends *Gesinnungsethik*. An action is morally right, according to Kant, only if the person performing it is motivated by a good will. Only a good will is good in itself – all other human virtues are conditional: "It is completely impossible to consider something as unconditionally good in the world or outside the world, except a good will" (Kant, 1997: 35). A good will is not good because of its ability to realize good consequences, but only good because it wants to do good. Suppose that a person with a good will is not able to realize what she or he intends to do, because of bad luck or a lack of natural gifts. Despite the greatest efforts (the good intention may not be limited to good wishes but should express itself in doing all that is in one's power), the person does not produce any good consequences. In that case, the good will would still shine as a jewel, according to Kant, and have a high value on its own. Lack of good results or an increase in utility does not reduce the moral value of the good intention.

An act is morally wrong if it is not motivated by a good will. Loyalty, courage, sympathy or any other laudable virtue is, in most cases, good, but these virtues can become very harmful if used by a bad will. The courage of a criminal person makes this person even more dangerous and detestable than without this virtue. This also holds for several aspects of happiness, like power, richness, honor and even health, because without a good will, these gifts can result in recklessness, unless there is a good will that corrects the impact of these goods on the mood and resulting actions of a person. According to Kant, a good will is therefore a necessary condition in order to deserve to be happy.

What does Kant mean by a 'good will'? Essentially, he means the action is done from a sense of duty and nothing else. Only if a person acts from a sense of duty – independent whether she or he enjoys the act or not – she or he performs a moral act which is motivated by a good will. An act that is done from the motive of self-interest has no moral value. For example, if a baker sells good bread for a fair price, he serves the consumer. But if this act is not done from the intention to fulfil the duty of serving the customer, but rather from the self-interested motive to make more profit, the act is without moral value (note the contrast with utilitarianism). Even if an act is motivated by sympathy and by the inner pleasure from contributing to the happiness of others, the act has no real moral value in Kant's view. Although such acts are lovable, they are not done because of the duty to contribute to the happiness of others. In contrast, suppose that a person has lost all pleasure from helping others and is insensitive to the needs of others, for example, because of a great personal sorrow, but still is prepared to assist others purely from a sense of duty, although it does not produce any pleasure to himself or herself, then this act has really a moral value. As an illustration, Kant mentions a text from the Bible where Jesus calls his audience to love their enemies.

The categorical imperative

But what is our duty? Kant defines duty as the necessity of an act motivated by respect for the moral law. For an act to be morally good, the act must not only be in accordance with the moral law but also done with the intention to obey the moral law. Otherwise, the conformity of the act with the moral law will only be accidental: if acts are not motivated by the intention to obey the moral law, they will normally divert from the moral law.

In order to determine what the moral law is, Kant proposes the so-called 'categorical imperative'.[2] Kant expresses the categorical imperative in several ways, but attention has centered on two definitions. The first formulation of the categorical imperative is:

> I ought never to act except in such a way that I can also will that my maxim should become a universal law.
>
> (Kant, 1997: 48)

The maxim is the subjective principle on which I want to act. A universal law is an objective principle that all reasonable beings would act on if the ratio would completely control their will. The first formulation of the categorical imperative then requires that the principle or reason upon which we act should be one that we can with consistency wish all other people to act upon. Is it a principle that can be applied in a universal law? This is the test of universalizability.

An example given by Kant is the duty to keep your promise. In particular, he asks whether we may make a promise that we do not intend to keep in case of difficult circumstances. A prudent man would accept making false promises, provided that the probability of losing the trust of others is low. If the probability of personal harm is high, the prudent man will conclude that he should keep his promises. In either case, the subjective principle on which one acts is the care for possible negative consequences for one's own interest. However, this maxim is not universalizable. The whole point of promises is that they are kept. If everyone were free to make false promises in difficult circumstances, then the practice of promise making would lose all purpose, because one would have no reason to believe promises anymore (Chryssides and Kaler, 1993). Nobody would believe that promises are held and only laugh at such void expressions of intention. We cannot, with consistency, want a general law that would allow making promises without the intention to keep them, because then promises will hold out to exist. Therefore, the maxim of the prudent man is not universalizable. A moral person will argue that he should keep his promises, even if not keeping them would not harm him at all.

Another way of testing whether an action or norm meets the categorical imperative is the test of reversibility. In order to apply this test, we can ask ourselves: How would I like it if another did to me what I have done to him or her? How would I like it if I was in his or her place? Kant gives the example of the duty to help other persons who are in great need. Is it allowed to dismiss this duty by arguing that one is only obligated not to hurt other persons? As Adam Smith argues, the latter duty of justice (interpreted as a sacred regard not to hurt the happiness of the other, see Chapter 8) is much more important for the subsistence of society than a positive willingness to help. Kant argues, however, that acting on the maxim that one does not have to be concerned about the need of others and does not have to help them if one does not want to is not universalizable. For a person who argues in this way will be inconsistent, because in situations where she or he needs herself or himself the assistance and love of other, she or he would probably argue in another way. This test also makes clear that breaking promises is not allowed, because we ourselves do not appreciate it when other people do not keep their promises made to us, simply because it would harm their self-interest to keep their promise.

Kant's first formulation of the categorical imperative is purely formal. The categorical imperative adds nothing to the content of a norm. It only requires that norms be universalizable. It offers the form that any rule must have in order to be an acceptable rule of morality (Beauchamp, 1982). In particular, it tests the consistency of the norm. According to Kant, the test of universalizability is much easier to apply than consequentialist reasoning that tries to estimate some (uncertain) consequences of an act in order to find out what we ought to do. To be universalizable, a norm must only be without contradiction. Indeed, one of the clearest cases of immoral actions is when a person seeks a special exemption for himself or herself, while expecting others to obey the rule.

However, one can doubt whether universalizability is a necessary and sufficient condition for determining the moral acceptability of an action or norm. MacIntyre (1985) argues that many trivial immoral maxims also pass Kant's formal test of consistency. For example, the norm: 'Let everyone except me be treated as a means' may be immoral, but it is not inconsistent, because there is no inconsistency in willing a universe of egotists, all of whom live by this maxim. It would be inconvenient for each if everyone lived by this maxim, but it would not be impossible.

Besides the first formulation of the categorical imperative, Kant has also given a second formulation that is less formal. The basis for this second formulation is that anything with a reasonable will has absolute value and serves as a ground for universal laws. As Kant states:

> Now I say: the human being and in general every reasonable being exists as an end in itself, not just as a means for arbitrary use by this or that will, but should in all his acts, either directed at himself or directed at other reasonable beings, at the same time be treated as an end.
>
> (Kant, 1997: 83, my translation)

From this statement follows the second formulation of the categorical imperative:

> Act in such a way that you always treat humanity, both in your own person and in any other, never simply as a means, but always at the same time as an end.
>
> (Kant, 1997: 84)

This formulation clearly does have a moral content and is similar to what we would call 'respect for persons'. It implies that each human being should be treated as a being whose existence as a free rational person should be promoted. For Kant this means two things: (1) respecting each person's freedom by treating people only as they have freely consented to be treated beforehand and (2) developing each person's capacity to freely choose for himself or herself the aims he or she will pursue (Velasquez, 1998).

Kant illustrates the second formulation of the categorical imperative by the same examples that he uses for the first formulation. For example, a person facing great problems who makes a promise to another person that he does not intend to hold uses the person only as an instrument to solve his or her own problems. She or he does not treat the other person as an end, because the other person will never voluntarily agree with a promise not intended to be kept. For the second example of helping needy persons, Kant argues that a positive attitude to humanity as an end in itself implies that everybody should strive at promoting the purposes of others insofar that is possible to him.

Sometimes it is said that Kant is arguing that we should never treat another as a means to our ends. However, this interpretation is too strict. Kant only argues that we must not treat another exclusively as a means to our ends. For example, we may hire a person to perform a job that serves our own interest as long as we respect the dignity to which every person is entitled to at all times. This means we must not exploit other persons in a way that completely disregards their personhood. The ground for the dignity of the human being is the autonomy of the reasonable will. The dignity of human life has no equivalent. The law-making will determines the value of all other things and has therefore an unconditional unique value. Kant therefore argues that human life cannot be valued by a market price.

Prima facie duties and all things considered duties

One of the problems of Kant's ethics of duties is that it does not provide a solution when a person faces conflicting duties in a concrete situation. For example, suppose that a company has promised its employees lifetime employment, but only can do so by infringing on some environmental laws. Which duty should be limited in favor of the other? In order to solve this problem, moral philosophers have come to regard all obligations not as absolute standards but as strong moral demands that may be validly overridden when they compete with other obligations. For this purpose, some philosophers introduce a distinction between prima facie obligations and actual obligations. A prima facie duty is an obligation that presumes fulfillment unless it conflicts on a particular occasion with a stronger obligation. It is a duty conditional on not being overridden by competing duties. The actual duty is the most important duty that is determined by an examination of the priority of the competing prima facie obligations and selecting the duty that produces the greatest balance of right over wrong (the so-called all things considered duty). One must intuit as best as one can which potential duty has the greater weight in the case of two conflicting obligations (Donagan, 1996; Marcus, 1996). You have only the duty to act in accordance with the duty with the highest weight. If the two conflicting obligations have equal weight, one must choose arbitrarily. Only obligations that are undefeated and defeat all competing obligations constitute all things considered duties.

5.3   NEGATIVE RIGHTS ETHICS: LIBERTARIANISM

There is a second tradition in deontological thinking that can be seen as complementary to Kantian deontologism, namely the ethics of rights. Rights correlate with duties. Moral rights identify interests that individuals must be left free to pursue as they autonomously choose; this freedom must not be subordinated to the interests of others. That is what both formulations of Kant's imperative require. The connection between the ethics of rights and the ethics of duties of Kant is therefore very strong. To infringe upon people's human rights is to fail to treat them as ends in themselves. When there is a right to be respected, there is generally also a moral duty to respect that right. Whereas a duty concerns morality from the point of view of the person that performs an action, a right concerns morality from the point of view of people on the receiving end of the action (Chryssides and Kaler, 1993).

Perfect and imperfect duties

A direct relationship between duties and rights is, however, not always obvious. Some duties do not correlate with rights. For example, Kant would argue that we have a duty to be kind, benevolent and generous. But arguably, people do not have a right to demand this of us. Kant classifies this kind of duty as imperfect duties (White, 2004, 2007). Imperfect duties are duties that do not correspond to the rights of others. The agent has some discretion in deciding when and in relation to whom to discharge the obligation. These duties mostly concern positive duties. That means, the duty demands that you do something for others, not that you refrain from doing something. An example is to make a donation to a non-governmental organization to fight absolute poverty in developing countries. This kind of duty cannot be enforced legally. The law cannot specify precisely in what way one is to act and how much one is to do. The poor do not have a corresponding right on the assistance of the rich. Imperfect duties are usually derived from the second formulation of the categorical imperative, which instructs us to consider the ends of others as our own. Since there is some latitude in performing imperfect duties, they can be interpreted as moral preferences that can be traded off against other preferences. In an economic model, they can be included as arguments in the utility function. An example is a utility function in which you can trade off spending your money on toys for your own children with giving a donation to Save the Children that helps children in great need due to poverty, conflicts and great disasters.

Besides imperfect duties, Kant distinguishes perfect duties. With perfect duties there is generally a corresponding right. A perfect duty is one that permits no exception in the interest of inclination. These duties mostly concern actions that you should refrain from, so-called negative duties. Perfect duties can normally be enforced by the law. They correspond to rights of the person to whom you have a duty. The duty not to murder, for example, is a perfect duty that corresponds with the right to life. Another example is the duty not to steal, which corresponds to the right to private property. Clearly, these perfect duties are more important than imperfect duties. They bind everyone all the time. Perfect duties can be easily derived from the first categorical imperative. It is impossible to want everybody stealing. Because it is a perfect duty, this duty has higher priority than merely satisfaction of personal preferences. Perfect duties take precedence over all inclinations and all imperfect duties and can therefore not be included in the utility function as preferences. In an economic model they should therefore be included as constraints that limit the solution and cannot be traded off.[3] So, one is free to pursue one's own ends, as long as one acts within the constraints given by the perfect duties.

Negative rights and free markets

In the libertarian tradition, the rights ethics has resulted in a defense of the market that is based on so-called negative rights. Negative rights are rights that impose a duty on other persons not to interfere in certain activities of the person who holds a given right. They require other people merely to refrain from acting in certain ways – to do nothing that violates the rights. In contrast, a positive right imposes a duty on other persons to provide the holder of the positive right with what she or he needs to freely pursue her or his interests (Velasquez, 1998). They require other people to act positively – to do something.

Free markets are supposed to preserve the negative rights to freedom and to private property. The right to freedom is preserved insofar as markets enable each individual to voluntarily exchange goods with others free from the coercive power of others, including the government. The right to private property is preserved insofar as each individual is free to decide what will be done with what he or she owns without interference from others.

This defense of the free market system based on the negative rights to freedom and private property is still popular. After a short review of the historical background of the negative rights of freedom and property in the thinking of John Locke, we discuss three representative authors. First, we present the theory of entitlement of Robert Nozick. Next, we describe an application of libertarian thought by Friedrich Hayek on the economic tasks of the government. Lastly we describe Milton Friedman's view on the task of enterprises in a market economy. In Chapter 6 we explain the implications of libertarianism for justice by discussing the entitlement theory of Nozick and his objections against the welfare state in more detail.

John Locke

As noted in Chapter 1, the defense of the free market system based on individual rights goes back to the thinking of John Locke. The two rights that free markets are supposed to protect are the right to freedom and the right to private property. Locke assumed these rights are 'natural' or 'human' rights. In particular, Locke believes that God has given the earth to the community of mankind. The natural law is directed to the peace and survival of humanity. The people are His property, and they should preserve their lives to His glory. The natural law does not only prescribe to preserve one's own life (suicide is not allowed), but one must also do as much as possible to maintain the rest of humanity.

The right to keep safe your life implies a right to the resources that are required, like food and drink. For this purpose, the earth and its produce are given to humanity as a community. Initially, nobody had an exclusive private right to property. However, although the earth is a common property of humanity, the yields of the earth must be appropriated in order to enable individual persons to sustain their lives. Locke relates the individual appropriation to the labor of people. Each person has a right to liberty and a right to ownership over his own body, his own labor and the products of his labor (Achterhuis, 1988).[4] If people take an unowned object from nature and mix it with their labor, it becomes their property because it is the labor that generates 99% of the added value of a good. For this appropriation of produce from the common property of the community, a person does not need the consent of others. If people would have to ask permission from the community for every property that they obtain by mixing their labor with the nature, people would die, notwithstanding the natural abundance of resources created by God.

However, this private right to property is, according to Locke, subject to one proviso, namely that there be enough and as good left in common for others.[5] This Lockean proviso is meant to ensure that the situation of others is not worsened. Someone who appropriates an unowned thing and whose appropriation would worsen the situation of others (by no longer being able to use freely what they previously could) does not violate the proviso, provided she or he compensates the others so that their situation is not thereby worsened. Unless the person does compensate these others, the appropriation will violate the proviso of the principle of justice in acquisition (see Chapter 6) and will be an illegitimate one (Nozick, 1974: 178). This is implied by the natural law. Each person has the right to sustain his or her life. The private property right of Locke is therefore embedded in the original inclusive concept of common property of all people. Private property is never allowed to become an absolute right that can be used to exclude others completely. People have a right to survive.

In Locke's state of nature, people live in perfect freedom within the bounds of the law of nature. These bounds of the law of nature require that no one harms another's right to life, health, liberty or possessions. Although people have a legitimate right to liberty and private property, they cannot be sure that others respect their negative rights. Some people transgress these bounds, and in response people may defend themselves against such invaders of rights and claim retribution proportionate to the harm done by the transgression. However, men who judge their own case will give themselves the benefit of the doubt and tend to overestimate the harm they have suffered. People are inclined to apply the natural law to their own advantage. Moreover, in a state of nature a person may lack the power to enforce her rights and to exact compensation. No authority can judge in an impartial way, satisfying all parties in the conflict, or be effectively able to terminate the conflict. For these inconveniences of the state of nature, all people voluntarily decide to conclude a social contract that constitutes a civil government as the proper remedy.

Although Locke's proviso was designed to preserve the life of others, his concept of property rights does not prevent strong inequalities in property. As any yields of one's labor belong to one's property and as people have different productivity, there are no principal limitations to inequalities in income or wealth. By hard work, assiduity and economy and sustained by good health and intellect, a class of fortunate people succeeds in obtaining the means of production, whereas others are forced to sell their labor in order to keep alive. It should be noted that Locke did not intend to develop a theory of property rights that would enable the rise of large inequalities as a result of absolute private property rights. His proviso intended to prevent that the poor would lack the opportunity to earn a living income. However, the possibility of unlimited increases in wealth by the fortunate threatened the practical realization of this ideal. Moreover, Locke interpreted the proviso also in a more loosely sense by assuming that the labor of the fortunate will also benefit other people, because it increases the total produce (Achterhuis, 1988: 86). This theory was especially useful for the colonization of America. By relating property to labor, all Europeans who started to cultivate land were assigned property rights. Hunting and just collecting wild produce without laboring the land does not generate property rights, according to Locke. Hence, because the original population of America, the Indians, did not mix their labor with the unused land, America was an unowned country ready to be appropriated by the white Europeans.

Locke's proviso and sustainability

In environmental economics, the proviso of Locke is used as a capital constraint that secures sustainable development (van Geesbergen et al., 2020). Environmental economics combines traditional work in the field of welfare economics and the theory of economic growth with more recent perspectives from the philosophy of sustainable development. The Brundtland Commission (1987: 43) has defined sustainable development as follows: "Sustainable development is development that meets the needs of the present without compromising the ability of future generations to meet their own needs". A core element of this definition is the balancing of intergenerational justice and economic growth. The duty of the current generation with regard to sustainable development poses the problem of the time discount. According to Pearce and Turner (1990), economic analyses tend to undervalue future revenues and expenses. At a societal level, the assessment must be discounted over time with the social discount rate. This deviates from the discount rate on the market, which reflects decisions related to individual preferences. By contrast, social discount rates reflect public interests. Pearce and Turner point out that determining the social discount rate can be difficult under conditions of imperfect market forces; there is theoretically no unambiguous answer to the question as to what social discount rate should be selected. Because of the indeterminacy of the discount rate, Pearce and Turner propose a capital restriction that tries to do justice to the ethical obligation of the present generation to compensate the future generation for any reduction in their access to easily extracted and conveniently located natural resources due to the activities of the current generation. The restriction requires that the total capital stock should increase in per capita terms over time (Pearce, 2002). This stock is made up of human-made capital, human capital (knowledge, skills), natural or environmental capital and social capital. From this condition, intergenerational rules of conduct can be derived that ensure that each generation bequeaths to the next generation a capital endowment no less than the one it has now. Pearce and Turner (1990) believe that this sustainability condition meets the intergenerational equity objective and that their sustainability principle is general enough to both encompass the environmental ethical concerns of consequentialist philosophy and meet the intergenerational equity objective. After all, the duty to ensure that "there [will] be enough and as good left in common for others" is fulfilled. In this way a (qualitative) duty from outside, the deontological Lockean proviso, is converted into an economic (quantitative) principle.

Robert Nozick: the minimal state

Robert Nozick (1974) builds on Locke's theory of rights and claims that the only basic right that every individual possesses is the negative right to be free from the coercion of other human beings. Nozick argues that this basic right is consistent with the Kantian principle that individuals are ends and not merely means. They may not be sacrificed or used for achieving other ends without their consent (Nozick, 1974: 31–33). Nozick then goes on to argue that the negative right to freedom from the coercion of others implies that people must be left free to do what they want with their own labor. This in turn implies that people must be left free to acquire property, to use it in whatever way they wish and to exchange it with others in free markets. No one is entitled to force persons to bear the costs that benefit other persons for the sake of the overall social good. To use a person in this way does not sufficiently respect that she or he is a separate person.

In order to secure the property rights, Nozick – just like Locke – pleads for a minimal state, limited to the functions of protecting the citizens against force, theft and fraud and ensuring the enforcement of contracts.[6] Nozick argues that this minimal state will arise in a natural and voluntary way. In order to protect their rights and secure compensation and effective termination of conflicts in case of transgression of their rights, groups of individuals may join and form mutual protection associations and turn over the decision power about conflicts to this association. In order to be accepted as just, the association would have to be thought neutral and upright. If two groups form different associations and these agencies fight each other in case of conflicts between members of these different groups, the two agencies will again have an incentive to avoid these costly conflicts and agree to set up some third judge or association to which they can turn when their respective judgments differ. Thus emerges one unified judicial system of which all local agencies are components. Although the dominant agency is not entitled to force local agencies to cooperate, it does occupy a unique position by virtue of its power and receives de facto a monopoly on the use of force, because it can offer its customers a guarantee that no other agencies can match. Its power provides the possibility to determine what is just. Hence, out of a state of nature, pressed by spontaneous groupings, division of labor and economies of scale, there arises a kind of minimal state from the self-interested and rational actions of persons in a Lockean state of nature (Nozick, 1974: 16–17).

Nozick's theory is deontological in nature. In his view, the right to individual freedom sets an absolute side-constraint on government intervention. He rejects utilitarianism, because it does not properly take rights and their non-violation into account. Thus, the government is not allowed to correct market inefficiencies if all those who are affected by them do not voluntarily agree upon the measures the government takes for this purpose.

One of the criticisms of Nozick's theory and the defense of the minimal state is that many actions are not really voluntary if the weak party faces severely limited options, with all the others being much worse than the one she or he chooses. A poor child in India is not free to reject performing labor in miserable circumstances if it would starve otherwise. According to Nozick, whether one's action is voluntary depends on what limits one's alternatives. If facts of nature do so, the actions are voluntary. However, other people also perform actions that limit one's available opportunities. But in those cases, one's action remains voluntary, provided that others do have the right to act as they did. This implies, for example, that for a person who has only two options – working in miserable circumstances or starving – because the choices and actions of all other people do not add up to provide this person with another option, the choice to work is voluntary if all other persons acted voluntarily and within their rights (Nozick, 1974: 263).

Libertarian paternalism and nudging

The negative rights ethics implies that any government intervention that limits the freedom of individuals should be rejected. This includes government policies that are paternalistic. Paternalism can be defined as the limitation of the autonomy of a person, in which the person who limits autonomy appeals exclusively to grounds of protection for the person whose autonomy is limited (Beauchamp, 1982). According to libertarianism, such paternalism violates individual rights and unduly restricts free choice. Nozick finds any paternalistic power of the state or any class of individuals in a position of authority unacceptable, because the rightful authority resides in the individual who is controlled.

Behavioral economics has, however, shown that people often lack full rationality (see Chapter 3). Their decisions are subject to several biases (e.g. anchoring, overconfidence, loss aversion, status quo bias, framing, etc.). Bounded rationality presents a major challenge to the market organization of society. This has led to an approach in economics that is called libertarian paternalism (Thaler and Sunstein, 2008). Libertarian paternalism claims that widespread 'nudging' is needed to channel people away from bad choices and toward good ones. The libertarian aspect of this approach lies in its insistence that, in general, people should be free to do what they like. The paternalistic aspect lies in the claim that it is legitimate to try to influence people's behavior in order to make their lives or community life better, by nudges. A nudge is any aspect of the choice architecture (i.e. the context in which people make decisions) that alters people's behavior in a predictable way without forbidding any options or significantly changing their economic incentives. So-called pro-self nudges aim at steering people's behavior in a private welfare-promoting direction, whereas pro-social nudges aim at steering people's behavior such as to promote public goods. Different types of nudges can be considered, varying from selecting smart default options, providing feedback to decisions, helping people understand the mapping from choice to their welfare, structuring complex choices or providing incentives that induce people to make smarter choices.

Ardent libertarians believe, however, that nudges infringe on the autonomy of an individual (Barton and Grüne-Yanoff, 2015). These libertarians are more concerned about liberty than about welfare. They prefer that people make their own choices rather than being nudged. People have the right to make wrong decisions. Only nudges that merely provide people with the information necessary to make an informed choice may be acceptable to them. Another criticism is that a policy maker does not know the preferences of nudgees. Even if a nudge steers some people to act more according to their own preferences, it may force other people in a direction opposite to their preferences, as preferences are heterogeneous. For example, some people may prefer to eat unhealthy but tasty food over healthy food, or smoke willingly, even when taking into account the risks involved. Third, a nudge may become manipulative if the nudgee is not informed about the nudge and its target. Another worry is that once we accept modest libertarian paternalism, more intrusive interventions may follow (slippery slope). Fifth, pro-social nudges may require others to pay something for the program that organizes the nudge.

In response to this criticism, three conditions have been proposed to guarantee that (pro-self) nudges are compatible with autonomy and freedom. First, the nudging policy should intend to facilitate the nudgee's pursuit of her own goal. Second, it should have an acceptably low opt-out cost, so that people can easily adopt their own course of action and freedom of choice is retained. Third, it should satisfy conditions of publicity and transparency. The condition of publicity means that the government may only use a nudging policy if it is able and willing to defend this policy publicly to its citizens. This condition might prevent treating citizens as tools for manipulation, that means, merely as means, not as ends. Finally, it should be noted that in many cases, some kind of nudge is inevitable. For example, not changing the choice architecture also directs people into a certain direction. Furthermore, if choices are hard and the options are complex and numerous, people may prefer that they are not compelled to make all choices themselves. Lastly, for pro-social nudges it could be argued that if the people who need the help improve their decisions, it may reduce the societal costs (for example, lower health costs) from which all who contribute to the costs of the nudging policy may also benefit.

Friedrich Hayek on individual freedom[7]

The ideas of individual freedom and minimal interventions by governments have gained much influence on economic policy in Western Europe and America since the eighties through the rise of neoliberal economic thought. Thatcher and Reagan, among others, were major proponents of neoliberal thinking, and also other European countries implemented liberalization and privatization policies in line with neoliberalism.

For the Austrian economist and political philosopher Hayek, the individuality of man is a central principle. Hayek regards individual freedom as a value in itself and as a moral principle of political action. As a result, an important role is assigned to individual freedom and human responsibility. In *The Constitution of Liberty*, Hayek describes individual freedom as "that condition of being in which coercion or some by others is reduced as much as possible in society" (Hayek, 1960: 57). Freedom means that people have the ability to act in accordance with their own decisions and plans.

According to Hayek, individual freedom cannot be detached from individual responsibility. However, Hayek emphasizes that individual responsibility does not mean that we are responsible for the consequences of our actions for others. "The main function of the belief in individual responsibility is to make use of our own knowledge and capacities to achieve the full in achieving our ends" (Hayek, 1960: 143). Individuals should take responsibility in order to better achieve their own goals. For economic freedom, this means that the freedom of our economic activity inevitably also carries the risk and the responsibility of that right (Hayek, 1944). According to Hayek, there can be no collective responsibility in a free society unless all individuals in a group know themselves individually responsible for the responsibility in question. Altruism in a general sense is a meaningless concept according to Hayek. Nobody can take care of other people in general. The individual ultimately determines who he or she cares for or who he or she does not help (Hayek, 1944). According to Hayek, if this right is violated, the dignity of man is not respected and the concept of freedom in such a society cannot really be known.

With the notion of individuality, Hayek fights in particular the increasing collectivism of the 1950s, in which a central, planned organization of society should realize social goals, usually vaguely described as general welfare or prosperity. Hayek is of the opinion, however, that the general interest of a society cannot be established: "the general welfare at which a government ought to aim cannot consist of the sum of particular satisfactions of the several individuals for the simple reason that neither those nor all the circumstances determining them can be known to government or anybody else" (Hayek, 1976: 2). Governments must focus on the conditions that make spontaneous organization possible in which individuals can use their knowledge for their own goals. According to Hayek, coercion by the government must therefore be limited to providing legal frameworks so that social order can develop, the so-called rule of law. The rule of law is primarily about the form, but not about the content, of laws. In all its actions, the government should commit itself to rules that have been established and announced in advance, which makes it possible to predict with fairly great precision how the government will use the coercive forces at its disposal in certain circumstances. In this way, everyone is free, within the known rules of the game, to pursue one's personal purposes in the certainty that the powers of the government will not be used to destroy the activities of the individual. The notion of justice plays an important role in this. "The guiding principle will always be that justice, i.e. the generally applicable rule, must prevail over the particular (. . .) desire" (Hayek, 1976: 41).

Milton Friedman's defense of the shareholder model

Friedman (1962) also prefers voluntary coordination via the market, whereby a transaction is concluded voluntarily and where both parties benefit from the transaction. According to Friedman, the government is a threat to human freedom. In his book *Capitalism and Freedom*, he argues for limiting the power of the state. Exchange should be achieved without coercion. According to Friedman, the impersonal nature of the market creates a separation between economic activities and political beliefs and therefore protects against discrimination within the economic domain. For example, if a person buys a loaf of bread, she or he does not know whether the wheat with which the bread is baked was cultivated by a communist or a republican farmer.

Libertarianism does not only limit the regulating tasks of governments but also reduces the scope for corporate social responsibility as a means to reduce market imperfections. This can be illustrated by a well-known application of the libertarian argument (that in an ideal free market no individual can coerce any other) by Milton Friedman (1970) on corporate social responsibility. In a famous article in the *New York Times Magazine*, he argues that the only social responsibility of the company is to increase profits. According to this so-called shareholder model, managers of the firm should serve in the best possible way the interests of shareholders, using the resources of the corporation to increase the wealth of the latter by seeking profits.[8]

In his article Friedman gives several arguments for his view. The first argument is that only people can have responsibilities. Therefore, only businessmen – individual proprietors or corporate executives – are to be responsible. The business as a whole cannot be said to have a responsibility.

The second argument is that managers are agents of the shareholders in the business they work for and should respect their property rights. The responsibility of managers is to conduct the business in accordance with the desires of the shareholders. The task that the executive must perform is normally straightforward and described in the voluntary contractual arrangements between the company and the executives. According to Friedman, this will generally be to make as much money as possible. Only in their private lives can executives take up more responsibilities and, for example, devote part of their income to causes they consider worthy. In that case, they are spending their own income, not that of the owner of the company. Of course, some owners may have a different objective than profit making. For example, a group of persons may establish a corporation for other purposes, like a hospital or a school. But if an owner wants to spend part of the company's profits on social goals, she or he is spending her or his own money and not someone else's.

A third argument of Friedman against corporate social responsibility is that the cost involved with taking social responsibility implies a tax on shareholders, customers or workers. This would imply that political mechanisms would interfere with economic mechanisms. If an executive decides to pursue other goals than maximal profits, for example, by making expenditures on reducing pollution beyond the amount that maximizes profits or is required by the law, the profit and the value of the shares will decline and so will the returns to stockholders. Moreover, insofar as such actions raise the price for customers, the executive is spending the customers' money. Also the interests of employees may be harmed insofar as the additional costs diminish the firm's capacity to pay attractive wages. In this way the executive reduces the freedom of the stakeholders. The executive in effect imposes a tax on the income of these stakeholders and also decides how to spend the revenues of this tax. In this way, the manager adopts political functions without any democratic basis. These political functions belong to the government. Whereas in politics we have a system of checks and balances, such a system is for the most part lacking in business. What it amounts to is that an executive who has apparently failed to persuade a majority of his fellow citizens to vote for the measures that she or he likes is seeking to attain by undemocratic procedures what she or he cannot attain by democratic procedures. According to Friedman, these stakeholders can better decide on their own how much of their own money they want to contribute to social goals.

Finally, Friedman shares Adam Smith's skepticism about the benefits that can be expected from 'those who affected to trade for the public good'. People pursuing their own self-interest best serve the common good.

Friedman does not argue, however, that the company should not pay any attention to social goals at all. There are two exceptions. First, if the pursuing of social goals also raises the profitability of the company, Friedman recognizes that it would be inconsistent to call on corporate executives to refrain from these actions. However, Friedman has little respect for companies that use corporate social responsibility purely as a means for window dressing and disdains such tactics. Another possibility is that the government requires such actions. Indeed, according to Friedman, it is the responsibility of the government to decide in a democratic way which social goals have to be served. Business must conform to the basic rules of society as embodied in law and ethical custom (which means without deception or fraud). But assigning responsibility for the common good to corporate executives mixes the economic and the political mechanism in an undesirable way.

The latter point shows that Friedman potentially allows a large role to the government. In this respect, Friedman's view on the role of government differs significantly from the libertarian theory of Nozick, who rejects any violation of the (negative) right to freedom by government decisions to foster social goals. Fundamental to Friedman's criticism on corporate social responsibility is that corporate social responsibility gives managers more opportunities to influence public issues than others (Dubbink, 2005). This is in contrast to the democratic principle that all citizens have an equal right to influence decisions that are intended to influence the public good. The only institution that guarantees citizens equal influence on decision-making is the state. Therefore, it follows that, according to Friedman, all decisions that affect the public good should be taken by the state. Although the intention of Friedman is to safeguard the (negative) right to freedom of others by subjecting all decisions that affect fellow citizens to the control of the democratically elected government, he runs the risk of a strong state that is allowed to enforce positive rights as well. Since many individual decisions have public effects (by positive or negative externalities), this severely limits the private freedom.

5.4   POSITIVE RIGHTS ETHICS

Although the libertarian tradition builds on the Kantian principle of respect for other persons, this approach is often criticized because respect of the freedom of one person will generally impose constraints on the freedom of other persons. Allowing one kind of freedom to one group therefore entails restrictions to other kinds of freedom for other groups (Velasquez, 1998). Indeed, as also Sen (1984) notes, ensuring the negative freedom sometimes requires positive actions. If the violation of negative freedom is to be avoided, many positive actions in pursuit of negative freedom are required. For example, one has the moral duty to prevent a murderer from killing another person if one has the possibility to do so. A demand for physical security is not normally a demand simply to be left alone, but a demand to be protected against harm. One does not only have a duty to refrain from killing another person oneself but is also under some obligation to consider how others can be stopped from molesting other people if the state fails to provide effective protection. It even may be right to infringe on a third person's property rights – for example, by using a car without the permission of its owner in order to prevent the murder – to bring about the prevention of a more serious violation of the negative freedom of someone else. In any imperfect society enjoyment of the right to physical security will depend to some extent upon protection against those who do choose to violate it. It is impossible to protect any-one's right to physical security without taking a wide range of positive actions. The protec-tion necessitates police forces, criminal courts, penitentiaries, schools for training policy, lawyers and guards. Taxes are needed to support this system for the prevention, detection and punishment of violations of the right to physical security. Valuing negative freedom therefore has some positive implications.

Another criticism of libertarianism is that the concept of freedom is too narrow. In particular, besides coercion by others, lack of freedom will occur if a person has insufficient power, skill, opportunity or resources to act (lack of real freedom) or if one is psychologi-cally impaired in a way that prevents controlling one's own actions (lack of autonomy). Real freedom or 'well-being freedom' is a central notion in the writings of Sen and relates the freedom of an act to the availability of certain basic capacities (see the theory on extra-welfarism in Chapter 2). Autonomy or self-governance is a central theme in the theory of Buchanan and is primarily related to the psychological state of the individual. Autonomy presumes the capability to make choices that promote one's own well-being. These other aspects of freedom – real freedom and autonomy – are complementary to freedom defined as an absence of coercion. Indeed, in order to be able to perform a certain act, a person must not be hindered by others, but must also have the basic capacities or resources that are required and must have the control over her or his own rational authentic will to execute this act.

The basic right to subsistence

Real freedom and the exercise of certain capacities require some minimal resources. This means that positive rights belong among the rights with the highest priority. This thesis is defended by Shue (1996). A positive right implies that some other people make some arrangements so that one will still be able to enjoy the right if it is not within one's own power to arrange on one's own to enjoy the substance of the right. It is not enough that no one is violating the negative right to freedom.

In his account of the concept of rights, Shue introduces the concept of a basic right, which he defines as a right that is essential to the enjoyment of other rights. When a right is genuinely basic, any attempt to enjoy any other right by sacrificing the basic right would be self-defeating. For example, if people have a right to free association, they should also have the basic right to physical security. No one can fully enjoy any right if someone else can credibly threaten him with murder, rape or beating when he tries to enjoy the alleged right. One cannot enjoy free association if one is vulnerable to physical violence by other people. Basic rights therefore need to be established securely before other non-basic rights can be secured.

Shue also classifies the right to minimal subsistence as a basic right. By minimal subsistence – or economic security – Shue means a minimal cleanliness of air and water, adequate food, adequate clothing, adequate shelter and minimal preventive public health care. The basic idea is to have available for consumption what is needed for a decent chance at a reasonable healthy and active life of more or less normal length, barring tragic interventions (Shue, 1996: 23). Of course, many complications arise when one wants to specify more exactly what is necessary for subsistence. At one extreme, a right to subsistence would not mean that people dying of cancer should receive an expensive treatment. But it would also not count as adequate a diet that produces a life expectancy of 35 years and a constant fight against illness and hunger. Just as with the right to physical security, no one can fully enjoy any other right if one lacks the essentials for a reasonable healthy and active life. Deficiencies in the means of life that cause malnutrition or severe and irreversible brain damage, for example, can effectively prevent the exercise of any right requiring clear thought. The right to subsistence may even be more basic than the right to physical security, because people who lack protection can fight back against their attackers or flee, but people who lack subsistence and are sick are utterly helpless.

Correlative duties

Respect of real freedom and autonomy thus implies that people should also have positive rights to an adequate standard of living, including a minimum level of health care and education. These positive rights are, for example, explicitly recognized in the United Nations' declaration of human rights, which expands the negative 'natural rights' distinguished by Locke (and other negative rights like the rights to freedom of expression, belief and association) to positive rights to food, clothing, housing, education and medical care. That means that if some people are not able to provide themselves with an adequate standard of living, other people have the duty to do so. This may sometimes require that the government places limits to the use of property and imposes compulsory taxes when these are needed to care for those who are not able to support themselves.

Frequently it is assumed that subsistence rights do not imply correlative duties because subsistence rights are positive rights and secondary to negative rights. However, rights to subsistence are considerably more complex than simply positive. In many cases these rights merely require the provision of opportunities for supporting oneself. The request is not to be supported, but to be allowed to be self-supporting on the basis of one's own hard work. Moreover, in practice it is very difficult to distinguish between positive and negative rights. Shue (1996) gives an example of a peasant in a developing country who concludes a contract with an international company to grow flowers for export instead of black beans for the local market. The contract also offers the opportunity to borrow capital for investing in equipment that would enable the peasant to dismiss four local workers. The dismissal of the laborers causes hardship for their families, which is even enforced by the increasing price of beans on the local market caused by the reduction in the supply of beans. According to Nozick (1974), both the peasant and the international company act within their (negative) rights. However, according to Shue, where subsistence depends upon tight supplies of essential commodities (like food), a switch in land use can have an indirect but predictable and devastating effect on other people's ability to survive. Amidst a scarcity of food, the decision to grow flowers can cause malnutrition and death for others. This suggests that the Lockean proviso should also hold for transactions of property (and not merely for acquisition of unowned things).

From the basic right to subsistence, Shue derives three types of perfect duties: (1) the duty to avoid depriving – one should not eliminate a person's only available means of subsistence; (2) the duty to protect from deprivation the only available means of subsistence by other people; (3) and the duty to aid the deprived by providing for the subsistence of those unable to provide for their own (Shue, 1996: 53). The first duty is the most 'negative' or passive kind of duty, but may also require that one does not perform actions that have foreseeable depriving consequences for others (like in the case of the peasant described earlier). The second duty is related to the maintenance of the first duty: if everyone could be counted upon voluntarily to fulfill duties to avoid, duties to protect would be largely unnecessary. But in an imperfect world not everybody will fulfill the first duty. Thus, it will also be necessary that some individuals or institutions enforce the duty to protect. In many cases the harm to the victims may even be entirely unintended and the product of the joint workings of individual actions, no one of which by itself caused the harm. This does not mean that no one is responsible. Rather, there is a collective responsibility to construct institutions that provide the second type of duty. In cases where individual restraint would be too much to ask or individuals lack the information and comprehension necessary to foresee the consequences of their transfers, the duty to protect includes the design of laws and institutions. These institutions can either imply prohibitions of certain actions or incentives to stimulate individuals to internalize the externalities of their actions. If both duties to avoid and to protect are not lived up, the third duty arises of assisting people who have lost the last available means of subsistence.

Positive rights and the stakeholder model

Besides this implication for the role of the government, the difference between the libertarian approach of negative rights and a broader Kantian approach that also recognizes positive rights also has implications for corporate social responsibility. This is argued in an interesting article of Evan and Freeman (1988) in which they plead for a stakeholder model of the modern corporation. In the stakeholder model, managers should aim at creating value for all stakeholders of the firm. Stakeholders are those groups who have a stake in or claim on the firm. Besides shareholders, the group of stakeholders includes, for example, suppliers, customers, employees, competitors and the community at large. According to Evan and Freeman, the second formulation of the categorical imperative requires that each of these stakeholder groups has a moral right not to be just treated as a means to some end (maximization of the shareholder value) but as an end in themselves. This means that the property rights of shareholders are not absolute, especially when they conflict with important rights of other stakeholders. Property rights are not a license to ignore Kant's principle of respect for persons. Just as stockholders have a right to certain actions by management, so do other stakeholders. The management of the company should balance the multiple claims of conflicting stakeholders.[9]

On basis of these Kantian notions, Evan and Freeman propose several management principles. The first management principle states that the corporation should be managed for the benefit of its stakeholders. The rights of these groups must be ensured. This implies, for example, that stakeholders have a right to participate in corporate decisions that substantially affect their welfare or involve their being used as a means to another end. The second management principle is that the management bears a fiduciary relationship to the stakeholders and that it must act in the interest of all stakeholders. This implies that the management must act to ensure the survival of the firm if that requires the safeguarding of the long-term stakes of each group. The reason for paying returns to shareholders is therefore not primarily because they own the firm: the real reason is that their support is necessary for the survival of the firm and that they have a legitimate claim on the firm, like all other stakeholders do.

NOTES

1   The combination of *Gesinnungsethik* and deontology is most obvious for Kant (see Section 5.2). A deontologist who does not apply *Gesinnungsethik* is Nozick (see Section 5.3). There are also examples of *Gesinnungsethik* in combination with virtue ethics (rather than deontological ethics) such as Aristotle and Adam Smith (see Chapter 8).

2   An imperative is a formulation of a command. It is a prescriptive statement. It describes the relationship between the moral law and the will of a person that is not necessarily in accordance with the moral law. Categorical means 'unconditional': the imperative holds independently from whether it serves some other goal. Kant contrasts categorical imperatives with hypothetical imperatives that command acts purely as a means for other goals. Hypothetical imperatives therefore cease to hold if we give up these goals.

3   An example is a budget constraint in a microeconomic model of household behavior that does not allow stealing. For example, in a consumption model, the agent aims to maximize $u = u(c, l)$ subject to a budget constraint $c = (W * (t - l) + O) / pc$, where u is utility, c is consumption, l is leisure, W is wage rate, t is total time, O is other income and pc is the price of consumption. The budget constraint does not include stealing from others as a source of income.

4   Christman (1998) argues that Locke's argument is based, in effect, on two distinct arguments. In the first version, the fact of self-ownership plays the crucial role: when one mixes some object with one's own labor, the object cannot be expropriated anymore without violating the right on the fruits of one's own labor. Alternatively, one can interpret Locke's argument as resting on the natural right to liberty, that means the right to act in ways that do not violate others' rights. The argument is then that if one takes any action, such as appropriation of unowned material, then one has a natural right to engage in that action.

5   Besides, Locke required a second proviso, namely that the goods in question do not spoil while in the possession of the owner (Christman, 1998).

6   Adam Smith argued for a slightly more extensive state. In his theory the state has three duties: (1) protecting the society from the violence and invasion of other independent societies; (2) protecting each member of the society from the injustice or oppression of every other member of it (mainly by impartial jurisdiction); and (3) erecting and maintaining of certain public institutions (education) and public works (infrastructure). See *Wealth of Nations*, book V.

7   This section is based on Hayek (1944) and Chapter 3 of Oosterhuis-Blok (2020).

8   Hayek expresses a similar view on the purpose of companies as Friedman. The goal of companies is, according to Hayek, "the long-run maximization of the return on capital placed under their control" (Hayek, 1960: 300), while complying with the law and prevailing morality. Hayek disputes that companies must act in the public interest. The public interest "would turn corporations from institutions serving the expressed needs of individual men into institutions determining which endeavors of individual people should serve" (Hayek, 1960: 305).

9   Insofar as stakeholder management increases rather than diminishes profitability, there is no difference between the shareholder and stakeholder model from a consequentialist point of view. From a Kantian point of view, the moral value still differs, however, if the respect for stakeholders is intrinsically (treating them as ends in themselves) and not extrinsically motivated (the real motive being profit maximization).

Recommended literature

Evan, W.M. and Freeman, R.E. (1988) 'A stakeholder theory of the modern corporation: Kantian capitalism', in: T.L. Beauchamp and N. Bowie (eds.) *Ethical Theory and Business*, Englewood Cliffs: Prentice Hall, 75–84.

Friedman, M. (1962) *Capitalism and Freedom*, Chicago: University of Chicago Press.

Friedman, M. (1970) 'The social responsibility of business is to increase its profits', *The New York Times Magazine*: 13 September.

Hayek, F.A. (1944) *The Road to Serfdom*, London: Routledge & Sons.

Hayek, F.A. (1960) *The Constitution of Liberty*, Chicago: The University of Chicago Press.

Kant, I. (1997) *Grundlegung zur Metaphysik der Sitten*, trans. T. Mertens, Amsterdam: Boom.

Nozick, R. (1974) *Anarchy, State and Utopia*, New York: Basic Books.

Pearce, D.W. and Turner, R.K. (1990) *Economics of Natural Resources and the Environment*, Harlow: Pearson Education Ltd.

Rawls, J. (1999a) *A Theory of Justice*, Revised edition, Boston: Harvard University Press.

Shue, H. (1996) *Basic Rights: Subsistence, Affluence and U.S. Foreign Policy*, Second edition, Princeton, NJ: Princeton University Press.

6

The ethics of justice

The ethics of duty and rights limit the scope for the utilitarian calculus of maximizing the total sum of utilities. In our Western society, the protection of the individual is generally considered to have a higher priority than the maximization of the interests of the majority. Duties, rights, and welfare represent incommensurable values that cannot be put on one par. This implies that favorable consequences for welfare may not overrule a violation of duties and rights. In order to safeguard these values, Western societies have introduced to greater or lesser degrees institutions that limit the scope for competition to such a point that these basic rights are respected.

Still, one can wonder whether duties and rights ethics provide a sufficient basis for morally evaluating the market system. If the market process does respect individual rights but still results in a highly uneven income distribution, does this outcome really meet all our intuitions of fairness or distributive justice? For example, is it fair that Jack Welch of General Electric earned as much as 15,000 employees of General Electric in Mexico? The ethics of duties does not help us in providing a satisfying answer to these questions. Indeed, although Kant teaches us to respect people, his theory does not tell us how conflicting legitimate rights of different persons should be resolved, nor what the relative importance of their interests is.

Also on a macroeconomic scale, one can question the fairness of market outcomes. In an interesting historical overview of factors explaining the divergence in wealth between rich and poor countries, Landes (1998) notes that since the Western industrial revolution, the gap between the average income per capita of the richest country and the poorest country has nominally increased from about 5:1 in 1750 to 400:1 in 2000 and in real terms to 56:1. This might indicate that the capitalist market system benefits the Western countries more than the poor countries. Are these differences between rich and poor countries morally defendable?

In order to evaluate market institutions from a justice point of view, we need a clear concept of justice. In this chapter we investigate how justice can be defined. First, we discuss the nature of justice. Section 2 describes the theory of John Rawls and discusses some implications for the role of the government. Next, we consider the procedural justice proposed by Robert Nozick. He argues that the criterion of justice does not relate to outcomes, but only to the process that produces these outcomes. In his view, any distribution is just as long as individuals can freely choose when transacting goods on the market. Section 4 introduces the principle of meritocracy. Section 5 then presents an overview

DOI: 10.4324/9781003181835-8

and discusses several other conceptions of distributive justice, including socialist justice and capitalist justice.

6.1   THE CONCEPT OF JUSTICE

The ethics of justice is highly intertwined with the ethics of duties and rights. It is considered unjust to break faith with any one by violating an engagement or to deprive any one of her personal liberty, her property or any other thing which belongs to her by law. The question of how goods should be distributed is therefore very much connected to one's view on the right to private property. Conversely, what rights citizens ought to be afforded over their property – what ownership structure ought to be adopted for particular owners – is a matter covered by principles of justice and just social institutions. Both rights and justice theories are deontological and judge the goodness of an action by applying other criteria than only its consequences.

Although rights and justice are highly connected (as we will also see when discussing the theories of Rawls and Nozick in Sections 6.2 and 6.3), the focus of both theories is distinctive. Whereas the ethic of rights is mainly concerned with the protection of vital interests of the individual against possible threats by other people or the state and is non-comparative in nature, the ethics of justice focuses on balancing the interests of different people. It provides comparative principles to determine what one person deserves in relation to the claims of other persons. Such comparative principles become necessary when various persons have conflicting rights in a concrete situation. For example, if poor people in developing countries are deprived of the means of subsistence and their national governments neglect the duty to protect these citizens, there arises a positive right to aid from rich countries, which conflicts with the property rights of the rich people in the affluent countries. Which right should have priority in such cases? In order to answer this question, we must compare the subsistence right of the poor with the property right of the rich.

The formal principle of justice (traditionally attributed to Aristotle) is that equals should be treated equally and unequals unequally. Or more precisely:

> Individuals who are similar in all respects relevant to the kind of treatment in question should be given similar benefits and burdens, even if they are dissimilar in other irrelevant respects; and individuals who are dissimilar in a relevant respect ought to be treated dissimilarly, in proportion to their dissimilarity.
>
> (Velasquez, 1998: 105)

This principle is formal, because it does not specify the standards that are relevant for judging whether individuals are equal or unequal. For example, when judging the similarity between Jack Welch and one of the Mexican employees of General Electric, one normally considers the gender of Welch and the Mexican employee to be an irrelevant standard to discriminate between the income of Jack Welch and the employee's income in a morally valid way.

The remainder of this chapter discusses two alternative theories of justice of John Rawls and Robert Nozick. In both theories the concepts of rights and justice are highly connected. In Section 6.4 we discuss the justice theory of meritocracy. In Section 6.5 we discuss in greater detail different concepts of distributive justice. Justice as a virtue will return in Chapter 8 where we discuss the virtue ethics of Aristotle and Adam Smith.

6.2   THE THEORY OF JUSTICE OF RAWLS

A neo-Kantian theory that helps us to evaluate market institutions from a moral point of view is the theory of justice of John Rawls. John Rawls (1999a) has provided a comprehensive theory that draws several notions of justice together into a logical whole. Rawls's theory is especially interesting, as his principles are designed to evaluate the major cooperative institutional arrangements like the political constitution and the institution of the market.

We first discuss his famous book, *A Theory of Justice*. In this book Rawls only deals with the justice within nations. He only wants to develop a reasonable concept of justice for the basic structure of the society isolated from other societies.[1] In his later book, *The Law of Peoples* that we discuss later, he extends his theory to justice between nations.

A fair procedure for deriving principles of justice

John Rawls presents his theory as a challenge to utilitarianism, partly because he believes that utilitarianism cannot provide a satisfactory account of the basic rights and liberties of citizens as free and equal persons, and partly because utilitarianism has long dominated the philosophical tradition and continues to do so. The task, as he sees it, is to advocate an alternative ethical theory capable of grounding principles of justice. A shared concept of justice is of great importance for society and establishes the bonds of civic friendship.

For this purpose, Rawls developed a hypothetical social-contract procedure to determine what principles a group of persons would choose under two conditions:

Original position after a veil of ignorance
The persons who will conclude the social contract are in an original position in which they have no information about the position they will have themselves in the real world, but only general information. They are behind a veil of ignorance: each person is ignorant of his or her particular situation in society and does not know to which generation she or he belongs or the personal preferences or plan of life that she or he will have. Hence, they will also be ignorant of the consequent advantages or disadvantages from the principles upon which they agree. There are no limitations on general information, that is, on general laws and theories. Society is perceived as a cooperative venture that is marked by a conflict, as well as by an identity of interests. There is an identity of interest, since social cooperation generates benefits for all on top of benefits achieved if they would not cooperate. There is a conflict of interest, because any person wants to obtain the largest share possible of the benefits created by cooperation. Rawls also assumes the economic conditions can be characterized by circumstances of moderate scarcity. That means natural and other resources are not so abundant that schemes of cooperation become superfluous, nor are conditions so harsh that cooperation is not possible at all (Rawls, 1999a: 110).

The idea of the original position is to set up a fair procedure so that any principles to assign rights and distribute benefits agreed upon in this position will be just. The original position is a purely hypothetical situation. Nothing resembling it need ever take place. The hypothetical nature of this original position invites the question: Why should we take any interest in the normative principles derived from this position? Rawls answers this question by noting that the original position embodies several conditions that it seems reasonable to impose on arguments for principles of justice. Thus it seems reasonable that (1) no person should be advantaged or disadvantaged by natural fortune or social circumstances in the choice of principles. It should be impossible to tailor principles to the circumstances of one's own case. For example, if a man knew that he would be wealthy, he might find it rational to advance the principle that various taxes for welfare measures be counted unjust; if he knew he would be poor, he would most likely propose the contrary principle. Also the particular inclinations and persons' preferences should not affect the principles adopted. Hence, because of the veil of ignorance, the original position is defined so that each person chooses impartially; (2) it seems reasonable to suppose that the persons in the original position are equal. All have the same rights in the procedure for choosing principles; (3) all persons should agree with the principles. As each person is unaware of the differences between the parties, everyone is equally situated and will be convinced by the same arguments. Because of the equal situation of all persons, the agreement on the principles selected in the original position will be unanimous. Note that this implies that the principles that the imaginary persons in the original position will accept will pass the test of reversibility and universalizability required by the categorical imperative of Kant.

Self-interested rationality

The persons in the original position are mutually disinterested and rational. The concept of rationality means that agents take the most effective means to a given ends. However, as Rawls assumes that they do not know their own situation (including their personal preferences and conception of the good), how can these persons decide which principles of justice are most to their advantage? For this purpose, Rawls introduces the notion of primary social goods. Primary social goods are social goods that every rational man is presumed to want. These goods have a use whatever a person's particular personal aims or plan of life. Rawls gives the following examples of primary social goods: rights, liberties, opportunities, income and wealth and self-respect.[2] Rational persons in the original position are assumed to prefer more primary social goods rather than less. They know that in general they must try to protect their liberties, widen their opportunities and enlarge their means for promoting their particular aims, whatever these may be.[3]

Furthermore, Rawls assumes that rational persons do not suffer from envy. Men have their own plan of life and are mutually disinterested in the primary social goods obtained by others. They are not moved by affection or rancor. They only try to win for themselves the highest index of primary social goods, since this enables them to satisfy their preferences most effectively, whatever they turn out to be. Although Rawls acknowledges that people sometimes value the interests of others, the postulate of mutual disinterest in the original position is made to ensure that the principles of justice do not depend upon strong assumptions and avoid any controversial ethical elements. A theory of justice should not presuppose extensive ties of natural sentiments, but only incorporate weak and widely shared conditions.

Rawls's three principles of justice

Rawls argues that under these two conditions, people will unanimously agree to three fundamental principles of justice to resolve social distribution conflicts.

The principle of equal liberty

This principle requires that each person be permitted to have an equal right to the most extensive scheme of equal basic liberties compatible with a similar liberty for others.

Important among these are political liberty (the right to vote and to hold public office) and freedom of speech and assembly; liberty of conscience and freedom of thought; freedom of the person, which includes freedom from psychological oppression and physical assault; the right to hold personal property; and freedom from arbitrary arrest and seizure. Each citizen's liberties must be protected from invasion by others and must be equal to those of others (Rawls, 1999a: 53). Since the liberties may be limited when they clash with one another, none of these liberties is absolute.

It is remarkable that Rawls does not mention the basic right to minimal subsistence stressed by Shue (1996) (see Section 5.4). According to Shue, Western liberalism has a blind spot for severe economic need. It should be noted, however, that Rawls developed his theory to derive a concept of justice for one society in a situation of moderate scarcity and isolated from other societies. The assumption of moderate scarcity has the effect of assuming that everyone's subsistence is taken care of. In a later book, Rawls deals more explicitly with justice between nations and mentions means to subsistence and security as a basic right to live.[4]

Once the principle of equal basic liberties is assured, inequalities in primary social goods (in particular wealth and income) are to be allowed, provided that two other principles hold.

The principle of fair equality of opportunity
This principle holds that inequalities are attached to offices and positions open to all under conditions of fair equality of opportunity. This principle expresses the conviction that if some places were not open on a basis fair to all, those kept out would be right in feeling unjustly treated, not only because they would be excluded from some external rewards, but, even more important, because they would be hindered to realize their potential and to develop self-esteem. The principle of fair equality of opportunity means that no person should be granted social benefits on the basis of undeserved advantaging properties. Assuming that there is a distribution of natural assets (health, intelligence, etc.), those who are at the same level of ability and talent, and have the same willingness to use them, should have the same prospects of success regardless of their initial place in the social system. The positions should not only be open in a formal sense, but all should have a fair chance of attaining them. This means that the influence of social contingencies and natural fortune should be mitigated. In our knowledge economy this requires, for example, that each person must have free access to training and education.

The difference principle
This principle requires that inequalities be to the greatest benefit of everyone, thus including the least advantaged group. The difference principle is perfectly satisfied where the institutional framework leads to an outcome wherein the least advantaged receive the maximum primary social goods in comparison to alternative institutional frameworks. Figure 6.1 illustrates this for a society that only consists of two groups of persons, a more productive (x) and a less productive (y).

In Figure 6.1, the point O, the origin, represents the hypothetical state in which all primary social goods are distributed equally, for example, because the government taxes all income with a 100% income tax rate and redistributes the income equally between both persons. X and Y represent the goods acquired by x and y, respectively. The curve represents the primary social goods obtained by x and y under different policies. If the government would increase inequality by reducing the tax rate, the primary social good of x will increase. Up to some point of inequality, also the goods of y, the least advantaged person, will rise as the

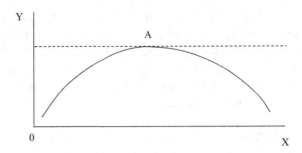

FIGURE 6.1 The difference principle

economy flourishes. The difference principle is perfectly satisfied when the curve is just tangent to the highest indifference curve of the least advantaged person (point A). Beyond this point, an increase in inequality due to a further decrease of the income tax rate will benefit the primary social good of x but harm that of y.

Note that if the principle is perfectly fulfilled, the distribution of primary social goods is compatible with Pareto optimality, for it is impossible to make anyone better off without making another worse off. On the other hand, not every Pareto optimal distribution is consistent with the difference principle. In particular, if the primary social goods are distributed at the right of point A in Figure 6.1, the difference principle requires that primary social goods be redistributed from the most favored to the least favored group of persons, whereas the Pareto principle would not allow such redistribution.[5]

The difference principle assumes that a productive society will incorporate inequalities, but that steps will be taken to improve the position of the most needy members of the society. However, Rawls rejects radical egalitarianism in which primary social goods should be completely equalized on the ground that if there are inequalities that render everyone better off in comparison to initial equality, these inequalities would be desirable. The higher benefits of those receiving a larger share of primary social goods are just if (and only if) they improve the primary social goods of the least advantaged members of society. No matter how some persons may gain from inequalities in primary social goods (wealth and income), there is no gain from the standpoint of the difference principle unless the others (including the least advantaged) gain also.

Strong and weak difference principle

Although Rawls does not discuss it in his own book, in later literature, strong and weak versions of the difference principle have been distinguished. In the strong variant the difference principle rules out any inequality that does not improve the position of the worst off: an inequality that does not maximally improve the prospects of the worst off is unjust. One of the objections against this strong difference principle is the leveling-down argument of Parfit (1998), which argues that the strong version of the difference principle does not allow the better off to improve even if it does not harm the least well off. Rather than letting some people have more goods than others, the quest for equality throws away goods that cannot be evenly divided. In other words, if there is no way to share or redistribute the benefits that improve the situation of the better off without making others worse, the strong interpretation of the difference principle forgoes these benefits (Arneson, 2007). Some philosophers consider this highly counterintuitive (Murphy, 1998; Arneson, 2002; Crisp, 2003).

In the weak variant, the difference principle rules out any inequality that worsens the position of the worst off. An inequality that does not worsen the prospects of the worst off can be just. The weak variant is consistent with the lexical difference principle. The lexical difference principle directs us to maximize the prospects of the worst-off group, and then, subject to this constraint, maximize the prospects of the next worst-off group, and so on until the prospects of the best-off group are maximized. So, inequalities are fine as long as they do not hurt the worst off or, if the worst-off category is unaffected, the worst-off category but one, etc.

Intergenerational justice

The theory of justice of Rawls has also been applied to intergenerational justice. To determine a just way of distributing resources between generations, Rawls suggests that the members of each generation should put themselves in the original position with the veil of ignorance. That means that without knowing what generation they belong to. In this position, they have to ascertain how much they would set aside for their children by asking themselves what they believe themselves entitled to claim of their own parents. The outcome of this reasoning is, according to Rawls, that justice demands of us that we hand to the next generation a situation no worse than we received from the generation before us. This idea is similar to the famous definition of sustainable development used by the so-called Brundtland committee in 1987 (43): "to meet the needs of the present without compromising the ability of future generations to meet their own needs" and also similar to the Lockean proviso (see Chapter 5).

One of the questions that arises, however, is whether the current generation should actually save for future generations, if that would mean that the social primary goods of future generations is better than that of current generations. The difference principle would reject this behavior, as it requires to maximize the social primary goods of the least advantaged generation. Some philosophers find this counterintuitive, and this criticism is similar to the criticism of the weak difference principle in the sense that it allows benefits to the least advantaged generation to trump benefits of future generations.

Serial order between principles of justice

The principles of justice are to be arranged in a serial order with the first principle prior to the second principle, and the second principle should have priority over the third principle.

The first ordering means that infringements on the basic equal liberties protected by the first principle cannot be justified or compensated for by greater social and economic advantages. These basic liberties may only be limited when they clash with one another. Thus, a certain hierarchy of interests moves the persons in the original position. Assuming a situation of moderate scarcity (that needs and material wants are fulfilled to a certain degree), the contract partners give precedence to liberty. The acquisition of means that enable them to advance the other desires and ends has a subordinate place. Another argument for the priority of basic equal liberties is that inequalities in basic rights are more harmful to the self-respect of persons than social and economic differences. Social and economic differ-ences are not likely to generate the degree of animosity and hardships arising from political and civic inequality and cultural and ethnic discrimination, according to Rawls.

The priority of the principle of fair equality of opportunity over the difference principle can be argued by the conviction that if some places were not open on a basis fair to all, those kept out would be right in feeling unjustly treated even if they benefited from the greater efforts of those who were allowed to hold them. One should therefore hold positions acces-sible to all and then, subject to this constraint, arrange social and economic inequalities so that everyone benefits.

Furthermore, it should be noted that Rawls's principles leave much room for personal responsibility. Rawls's theory shows this, among other things, from the fact that the prin-ciple of equal opportunities has priority over the difference principle. Strictly speaking, a situation may even arise in which the priority of the principle of equal opportunities leaves no more resources for the application of the difference principle (Van Parijs, 2003). Even if the government has already devoted many resources to promoting equal opportunities, for example, through education, Rawls's hierarchy requires that additional collective resources be used for this as well, as long as it has a positive effect on equal opportunities. There will then be no resources to promote the income of the least advantaged according to the differ-ence principle. Moreover, the difference principle itself also leaves a lot of room for personal responsibility and does not neglect people's autonomy and corresponding self-responsibility. The reason is that the difference principle intends to maximize the expected primary social goods of a representative person of the least-favored group. So it is not about improving the position of the actually perceived poorest people, but about the position within the group of least favored people who are potentially within their reach, with their own efforts. This means that the difference principle places considerable emphasis on personal responsibility and ambition and is less egalitarian for individual cases.

Defense of the principles of justice

Rawls gives several reasons to defend his principles of justice. First, it can be argued that the principles will be *rational* in the eyes of the persons in the original position. To clarify this argument, Rawls refers to the maximin criterion. When evaluating a set of alternative policies, the maximin rule only focuses on the people with the worst position and then selects the policy that maximizes their position. In other words, it maximizes the worst outcome.[6] The maximin rule is generally understood as a suitable guide for choices under great uncertainty marked by certain features. According to Rawls, the original position has these features to a very high degree. First, the parties in the original position have very little knowledge of probabilities because of the veil of ignorance and therefore prefer the maxi-min solution rather than maximizing the expected average (in accordance with the prin-ciple of average utility in utilitarianism, see Chapter 2). The parties would prefer to secure their liberties straightway rather than have them depend upon uncertain and speculative actuarial calculations. Persons care very much about their basic liberties. It is not worth-while for them to take a chance for the sake of further advantages when this involves risks of losing something that is very important to them. The parties will not wish to jeopardize the minimum of basic liberties for the sake of greater economic or social advantages. Moreover, by adopting the difference principle, they ensure that even the primary social goods of the least advantaged will be as high as possible. In contrast, utilitarianism does not exclude serious infractions of liberty – like slavery or serfdom – for the sake of greater social benefits.

Second, the principles of justice reflect considerations of the principle of redress. This is the principle that undeserved inequalities call for redress, like inequalities of birth and natural endowments. This type of inequality is undeserved from a moral point of view, according to Rawls, because no one deserves a greater natural capacity nor merits a more favorable starting place in society. The superior character that enables us to develop our capacities depends in good part upon fortunate family and social circumstances in early life, for which we can claim no credit. Therefore, they should somehow be compensated for. This characteristic follows directly from the procedure of deriving the principles of justice from the hypothetical contract in the original position and the assumption of the veil of ignorance, which is just made to make principles of justice independent from contingent and arbitrary circumstances (see earlier). The difference principle achieves some of the intent of the principle of redress by allocating resources to improve the long-term expectation of the least favored and by letting the more fortunate compensate in return for their undeserved advantages.

The difference principle can additionally be defended by the argument that it is in accordance with reciprocity. Everyone's well-being depends upon the cooperation with others. Without cooperation, no one could have a satisfactory life, according to Rawls (Rawls, 1999a: 13). The division of advantages should therefore be such as to draw forth the willing cooperation of everyone taking part in it, including the least advantaged. The least advantaged should not complain about others receiving more, because they receive more in the unequal system than they would in an equal one. The difference principle seems also fair to the better endowed, because they recognize that the well-being of each depends on social cooperation and that they can expect others to collaborate with them only if the terms of distribution are reasonable. They regard themselves as already compensated for by the advantages to which no one (including themselves) had a prior claim (in the original position). This shows that Rawls's defense of the difference principle rests on reciprocity between the better and the least advantaged. It is a principle of mutual benefit (Rawls, 1999a: 88). This is also clear from Figure 6.1: society should try to reach point A, where a harmony of social interests is achieved and no one can gain more without making another person less well off. Only reciprocal advantages are allowed.

A further merit of the difference principle according to Rawls is that it provides an interpretation of the principle of fraternity. Normally the ideal of fraternity is thought to involve ties of sentiment and feeling between persons. For members of a wider society, this is unrealistic. Yet the difference principle seems to correspond to another meaning of fraternity, namely a kind of social solidarity understood as not wanting to have greater advantages unless this is to the benefit of others as well. Just like members of a family, who commonly also do not wish to gain unless other members of the family also benefit.

Contrast with utilitarianism

As already noted, Rawls developed his theory as an alternative for utilitarianism. Utilitarianism implies that a society is rightly ordered, and therefore just, when its major institutions are arranged so as to achieve the greatest net balance of satisfaction summed over all the individuals belonging to it (see Chapter 2). Just as it is rational for one man to maximize the fulfillment of his desires, so it is right for a society to maximize the net balance of satisfaction taken over all of its members. It does not matter how this sum of satisfactions is distributed among individuals any more than it matters how one man distributes his satisfactions over time. It is then a natural way to adopt for society as a whole the principle of rational choice for one man.

Rawls's theory contrasts in several aspects with utilitarianism. First, Rawls distinguishes between the claims of rights and liberties and the desirability of increasing social welfare and gives priority to the first. In utilitarianism, rights and justice have only a subordinate validity as secondary rules that arise from the fact that there is greater social utility in following these rules. In contrast, Rawls's theory of justice as fairness is deontological. The principles of moral rights and justice put limits on which satisfactions have value. Thus, if man takes a certain pleasure in discriminating others, he will understand that he has no claim to this enjoyment. The concept of the right is prior to the good. Another reason why Rawls's theory is deontological is that he does not interpret the right as maximizing the good. If one could speak of maximizing something, the focus would be more on the primary social goods of the least advantaged persons.

Implications for the role of government

In Rawls's view, the market system may be consistent with equal liberties and fair equality of opportunity if it is backed by some requisite background institutions. Rawls has four types of governmental branches in mind (Rawls, 1999a: 242–251). First, the allocative branch that aims at preserving the competition and preventing the formation of unreasonable market power.[7] Second, the stabilization branch that strives to bring about reasonably full employment in the sense that those who want to work can find a job. These two branches together establish the efficiency of the market economy.[8] Third, the transfer branch that takes needs into account and guarantees a certain level of well-being. The difference principle implies a decent distribution of income and wealth. All citizens must be assured the all-purpose means necessary for them to take intelligent and effective advantage of their basic freedoms. Basic health care should be assured for all citizens. Finally, there is a distribution branch. Its task is to preserve an approximate justice in distributive shares by means of taxation and the necessary adjustments in the rights of property. For example, inheritance and gift taxes set restrictions on bequests and in this way gradually and continually correct the distribution of wealth. This prevents concentrations of power and may therefore help to preserve the fair value of equal (political) liberty and fair equality of opportunity in the long run. When inequalities in wealth exceed a certain limit, the younger generations will not have similar chances of education, and the openness of fortunate positions and offices may decline. The political liberty likewise will tend to lose its value if economic power becomes highly concentrated. Furthermore, income or expenditure taxation may be required, enabling the government to provide public goods and to finance the transfer payments necessary to satisfy the difference principle.

How these different branches are balanced will vary with the political conception in a country. All Western economies accept some minimum positive rights and, hence, some redistribution by the government to guarantee a minimum living wage. Indeed, it is believed that it is in the mutual interest of all citizens that the state and its subsidiary levels of government should provide a safety net of welfare. The degree of redistribution and the resulting importance of the role of the government depend, however, on the preferences of fairness of the citizens. For example, in the United States citizens are more willing to accept a 'winner takes it all' economy than in Europe. Accordingly, the US system mainly reflects libertarian values. Although minimum wage legislation and minimum welfare programs exist, the minimum level is relatively much lower than in European countries, whereas the access to health and educational provisions is much more based on private purchasing power. In the European society the socialist notion of distribution according to needs and abilities has received relatively more priority. This is partly due to the perception of Europeans that differences in welfare cannot be fully traced back to differences in effort: whereas 71% of the American people believe that poverty can be overcome by personal effort, only 40% of Europeans agree with this belief. The majority believes that income is more determined by luck (Van de Klundert, 2005). Americans believe that if someone is poor, it is their own fault, because in their view Americans live in an open and fair society with equal opportunities.[9]

Box 6.1   Anglo-Saxon versus Rhineland model

The Anglo-Saxon model (so-called because it is supposedly practiced in English-speaking countries such as the UK and the United States) best characterizes a free market economy with low levels of regulation, taxes and government expenditures. The main role of government is to secure private property rights. Government intervention or regulation is kept at a minimum, because it is believed to be more harmful than beneficial to the economy. Equity markets are the primary source of funding for companies in Anglo-Saxon countries (direct finance). The organization of companies is subservient to the interests of the stockholders (shareholder model). In order to stimulate directors of companies to act in the interests of shareholders, companies apply reward systems that link the director's income to parameters related to shareholders' interests (Hall and Soskice, 2001). The influence of labor unions is limited (Boyer, 1995). Senior management has control over the firm, including the freedom to hire and fire. This results in a highly fluid labor market. The focus is on respecting the individual rights of employees rather than on cooperating with unions as social partners. Trade negotiations take place at the local or firm level.

The Rhineland model (so-called because it is most visibly practiced in Germany) also assumes a large role for free market operation, but the primacy of private property is more limited than in the Anglo-Saxon model by government and other institutions. The government is allowed to actively regulate the economy with respect to all kind of social matters by environmental protection, education policy and other social policies (minimum wages, social insurance, health care and pensions). Labor unions have a strong position as social partners that is supported by legal provisions that facilitate collective agreements. The company is not only subservient to the interests of the shareholders but takes into account the interests of other stakeholders as well (employees, clients, suppliers and society at large) (stakeholder model). The board of directors should not strive at short-term profitability, but rather at long-term continuity. Companies are often controlled by stable owners who are well informed about their company and have a long-term commitment to the firms they control.

Similar differences between the American and European cultures can be detected when we consider corporate social responsibility of companies. Whereas the American Anglo-Saxon model emphasizes the property rights of shareholders, the European Rhineland model stresses the respect for stakeholder values. In European countries, employees do not favor excessive chief executive officer (CEO) compensation, as they value fairness and wage compression. They require a more 'responsible' attitude from their boss. Moreover, because of the stronger position of unions, they can more easily communicate their views towards management. In this way, the principles that lie at the basis of the European corporate governance model lower CEO compensation.

The law of peoples

As stated in the introduction of this section, Rawls developed his theory of justice for the basic structure of a society isolated from other societies. In a more recent book, *The Law of Peoples,* he developed a political concept of right and justice that applies to the principles and norms of international practice. His concept is limited to well-ordered societies and does not include outlaw states or societies burdened by extremely unfavorable conditions. Using the idea of the original position a second time, with the parties now understood to be the representatives of peoples, Rawls derives the content of the principles of global justice. The representatives partaking in the hypothetical contract are again subjected to a veil of ignorance adjusted for the case at hand: they do not know, for example, the size of the territory or the population, the relative strength of the people whose fundamental interests they represent, the extent of their natural resources or the level of their economic development. Just as reasonable citizens in domestic society offer to cooperate on fair terms with other citizens, so reasonable peoples offer fair terms of cooperation to other peoples. The criterion of reciprocity applies to the law of peoples in the same way as it does to the principles of justice for a society.

Rawls argues that the hypothetical contract between the representatives of peoples will yield eight principles of justice among peoples (Rawls, 1999b: 37): (1) people are free and independent, and their freedom and independency are to be respected by other people; (2) people are to observe treaties and undertakings; (3) people are equal and are parties to the agreements that bind them; (4) people are to observe a duty of non-intervention; (5) people have the right of self-defense, but no right to instigate war for reasons other than self-defense; (6) people are to honor human rights; (7) people are to observe certain specified restrictions in the conduct of war; (8) people have a duty to assist other people living under unfavorable conditions that prevent their having a just or decent political and social regime.

For the purpose of this book, we are especially interested in the sixth and eighth principles. Just as Shue (1996), Rawls means by basic rights roughly those rights that must be met if citizens are to be in a position to take advantage of their rights, liberties and opportunities of their society. Among the human rights Rawls counts the right to liberty (including freedom from slavery, serfdom and forced occupation and, to a sufficient measure, liberty of conscience to ensure freedom of religion and thought), to personal property, to formal equality (similar cases be treated similarly) and the right to life (to the means of subsistence and security, see also Shue (1996: 65)). The last aspect of the sixth principle is connected to the eighth principle. Well-ordered societies have a duty to assist societies burdened by a lack of favorable political and cultural traditions, human capital and material and technological resources needed to be well-ordered themselves. Once a burdened society achieves the goal of becoming a well-ordered society, further assistance is not required, even though the now well-ordered society may still be relatively poor.

In addition to agreeing to the principles that define the basic equality of all people, the parties will formulate guidelines for setting up cooperative organizations and agree to standards of fairness of trade, as well as certain provisions for mutual assistance. Thus, rational representatives of people will set up international organizations such as the World Trade Organization (WTO), World Bank and International Monetary Fund (IMF). Suppose, for example, that a free competitive market trading scheme is to everyone's mutual advantage in the longer run and that larger nations with the wealthier economies will not attempt to monopolize the market. The veil of ignorance then holds that all representatives would agree to fair standards of trade to keep the market free and competitive.

What does the law of people imply for distributive justice between peoples? Here Rawls draws a parallel with the difference principle for domestic societies. However, the concept of the difference principle in the *Law of Peoples* differs from the concept described in the *Theory of Justice*. In the *Theory of Justice*, the difference principle requires that inequalities be arranged to the greatest benefit of the least advantaged. However, in the *Law of Peoples* the content of the principle is that the least advantaged have sufficient all-purpose means to make effective use of their freedoms and to lead worthwhile lives. When that situation exists, there is no further need to narrow the gap between the rich and the poor. Similarly, for international relations between peoples, the duty of assistance is satisfied if all people have a well-ordered society. It does not matter how great the gap between rich and poor may be. Rawls thus rejects an unqualified global egalitarian principle. The role of the duty of assistance is to assist burdened societies to become full members of the society of peoples and to be able to determine the path of their own future for themselves. It is a principle of transition. The duty to assist ceases once this target is reached.

Rawls's concept of global distributional justice shows that he does not believe in the cosmopolitical view that considers all individuals equal, worldwide, without regard for the societies in which they live. Suppose, for example, two different societies have internally just institutions that each meet the difference principle domestically, but the worst-off representative person in the first society is worse off than the worst-off representative person in the other society. Then the cosmopolitical view would prefer assistance from the second society to improve the lot of the worst-off representative person in the first society, whereas Rawls would not.

6.3   THE ENTITLEMENT THEORY OF NOZICK

Although Rawls provides an elegant integration of several notions of rights and justice, his theory has also been criticized, especially by libertarian philosophers. Robert Nozick published his book *Anarchy, State and Utopia* some years after the first edition of *A Theory of Justice*. He spends a lot of attention on Rawls's theory of justice. He acknowledges that Rawls's book is the most powerful, systematic work in political and moral philosophy since the writings of John Stuart Mill. Political philosophers must either work with Rawls or explain why not. Nozick does not neglect this latter task and gives illuminating criticism on Rawls. In this section we first describe Nozick's own theory on justice. Next, we present his arguments against redistribution and his other criticism on Rawls's theory of justice. We end with some critical notes on Nozick's theory.

Procedural justice: the entitlement theory

The rights ethics of Nozick discussed in Chapter 5 have direct implications for his view on justice. Nozick refers to his theory as an 'entitlement theory' of justice, because the protection of the fundamental rights or entitlements of the citizens is the cornerstone of his theory. In particular, by making the right to individual freedom and voluntary consent an overriding principle, Nozick's theory implies that no particular way of distributing goods can be said to be just or unjust apart from the free choices that individuals make. There is no pattern of just distribution independent of free market procedures for acquiring unowned property without violating the right of others. The government is not allowed to tax income in order to finance social programs without the voluntary consent of individuals. What everybody gets, one gets from others who give to her or him voluntarily in exchange for something, or as a gift. A libertarian therefore insists on a system in which, for example, individuals privately and voluntarily purchase health care insurance. This entirely voluntary system is preferable because no one should have his property coercively extracted by the state in order to benefit someone else. In Nozick's theory, the use of a tax code to effect social goals such as alleviating poverty or saving lives through advanced medical technology is based on what a majority prefers rather than on what justice demands (Beauchamp, 1982).

Justice consists, according to the entitlement theory of Nozick, in an unhindered operation of just procedures, not in the production of just outcomes (such as an equal distribution of resources). If the process is legitimate, then the outcome will also be acceptable. In particular, Nozick presents three procedural principles that should hold: justice in acquisition, justice in transfer and justice in rectification. Justice in acquisition concerns the appropriation of unheld things. A person who acquires a holding in accordance with the principle of justice in acquisition is entitled to that holding. For example, in the theory of John Locke a person obtains a property right in an unowned object if the person mixes his labor with it, provided that there be enough and as good left in common for others. Thus a person discovering a water hole in the desert may not appropriate it if it is the only water hole. An intermediate case is a person discovering that a certain substance, which no one else likes to have, effectively treats a certain disease and appropriates the total supply. She does not harm the others. Yet it is likely that in the absence of her invention, sometime later someone else would have come up with it. This suggests that the property right in this case should be temporary (like patents). Justice in transfer concerns the processes through which a person transfers holdings to another. The transfer is just if both parties voluntarily agree to the transfer. Under this topic come voluntary exchanges and gifts. A person who acquires a holding in accordance with the principle of justice in transfer from someone else entitled to the holding is herself entitled to that holding. Justice in rectification concerns the rectification of injustice in holdings as a result of violations of the first two principles, for example, as a result of stealing. This principle uses historical information about previous situations and injustices done to them and of information about what would have occurred if the injustice had not taken place to determine what should be done to rectify the injustices.

This procedural theory of justice implies that justice in distribution can only be determined by a historical account of the property rights: whether a distribution is just depends upon how it came about. Nozick gives the following example.

> If some persons are in prison for murder, we do not say that to assess the justice of distribution in the society we must look only at what this person has . . . at the current time. We think it relevant to ask whether someone did something so that he deserved to be punished, deserved to have a lower share.
>
> (Nozick, 1974: 154)

The historical principle of Nozick contrasts with end-result principles that only look at who ends up with what and judge the justice of the distribution in terms of some other principle (like distribution according to needs or how hard a person tries, see Section 6.4), without considering how the distribution came about. The principle of entitlement is not patterned in this way. The property that a person obtains can result from receiving their marginal product, but also by winning a gamble, receiving gifts from foundations, finding things and so on. All these properties are just if they are obtained in accordance with the principles of justice in acquisition, transfer or rectification.

Ignoring acquisition and rectification, Nozick summarizes his entitlement theory with the following words:

> From each what he chooses to do, to each according to what he makes for himself (perhaps with the contracted aid of others) and what others choose to do for him and choose to give him of what they've been given previously and haven't yet expended or transferred.
>
> (Nozick, 1974: 160)

As a further simplification he gives: "From each as they choose, to each as they are chosen" (Nozick, 1974: 160).

Arguments against redistribution

Whereas a minimal state that secures the negative rights of liberty and property is justified (see Section 5.3), Nozick rejects any more extensive state. According to the entitlement theory of justice, there is no argument for a more extensive state based on distributive justice (except if all citizens voluntarily agree to it).[10] Nozick gives several reasons for rejecting any redistribution of properties (except those required to finance the minimal state) on the basis of principles of fairness other than the entitlement theory.

The most important reason for rejecting redistribution is, according to Nozick, that being forced to pay taxes that can be transferred to more needy persons violates people's property rights. Because of the tax, you have to work more hours to obtain the same net amount of income. Nozick therefore interprets the tax system as a system of forced labor. When others decide what you are to do, they become part-owner of you. It gives them a property right to you.

Another argument against redistribution is that such a system implies that one can obtain a claim without being involved in a transaction. Suppose, for example, that D1 is a just distribution and some people voluntarily transfer some of their resources to the richest person (for example, by buying software from Microsoft), yielding distribution D2 that is less equal (Bill Gates having become richer), then a third party (the poor) can complain and demand compensation. In Nozick's view this is ridiculous, because these third parties were not involved in the transactions and still have their legitimate shares. For what reason could such a transfer give rise to a claim by the third party that distribution D2 is unjust?

This example also invokes another point of criticism, namely that any substantial distributive principle of justice that defines justice in terms of end results of distribution (like distribution to need, see Section 6.4) requires continuous interference with people's lives. Any just distribution (according to the preferred end result) is continually transformed into unjust distributions, because the likelihood is small that any actual voluntary transfer or exchange fits the pattern favored by the end-state principle. Therefore, the government should continuously intervene in order to restore the end state required by the substantial distributive principle. Hayek (1960) voiced a similar criticism. He argued that the only equality that is compatible with freedom is the purely formal equality of all citizens before the law. The state should not try to create a level playing field by providing equal or even compensatory opportunities, as providing all an equal prospect for success would necessitate state coercion.

A fourth argument against redistribution through (income) taxation is that it favors persons who prefer a lot of leisure and therefore earn a relatively low income in comparison to persons whose happiness requires a lot of material goods or services. Why should persons who work many hours because they prefer an expensive car contribute more to aid the needy than persons who prefer to have more time for their children?

A fifth argument against redistribution is that it may be motivated by envy. According to Nozick, people have great ingenuity in rationalizing their emotions by arguments of justice. Often we evaluate how well off we are by comparing ourselves with others. Inequalities in income or position rankle so much because of the feeling that they are undeserved and therefore make the least well off feel less worthy. If people feel inferior because they do poorly, then redistribution may reduce their feelings of inferiority. However, according to Nozick, self-esteem is based on differentiating characteristics. If wealth or income is equalized, the society may come to agree that some other dimension is more important, like aesthetic attractiveness or intelligence, to differentiate yourself from others. Then the phenomenon might repeat itself (if possible). Therefore, envy may not decrease by equalizing incomes. On the contrary, as the number of differentiating dimensions of life diminishes when some of them are equalized, people have to compete on a smaller number of dimensions. Assuming that people especially value those dimensions where they perform very well, reducing the number of dimensions will make less people able to gain self-esteem. The most promising way for a society to avoid differences in self-esteem is therefore a high diversity of differentiating dimensions.[11]

The only reason why redistribution may be helpful, according to Nozick, is that principles of distributive justice may work as rough rules of thumb that contribute to the realization of the principle of rectification of injustice if historical information is lacking. The least well-off group in the society might have the highest probability of being the (descendants of) victims of injustice who are owed compensation by those who benefited from the injustices. In that case, redistributing income from the well off to the least well off may approximate the result of rectifying injustices.

Other criticism on Rawls

In his book *Anarchy, State and Utopia* Nozick presents some more specific criticisms on the details of Rawls's theory of justice.

The first point of criticism is that Rawls bases his principles on the notion that they define an appropriate distribution of the benefits and burdens of social cooperation (Rawls, 1999a: 4). Nozick notes that this problem might be conceived of in two alternative ways: (1) How is the total benefit to be allocated? Or (2) How is the incremental amount due to social cooperation – the difference between the total benefit and the sum of what each individual gets acting separately – to be allocated? Rawls does not distinguish between these two formulations, but implicitly opts for the first formulation because he applies his principles of justice to the total sum of benefit. Nozick argues, however, that the principles of distributional justice only hold for the second type of benefits due to the cooperation. All persons who cooperate together often explicitly agree to share the additional benefits from their cooperation. But in the case of non-cooperation, each individual deserves what he gets by his own efforts according to the entitlement theory. If Rawls's principles of justice would hold for the total sum of benefits, the well-off persons would refuse to cooperate with the less well off, because entering into such social cooperation would seriously worsen their position. Only if one can prove that the non-cooperative benefits are so small in comparison to any benefits from cooperation may one apply Rawls's principles to society at large. According to Nozick, this is highly unlikely. Only if things fell from heaven like manna – and no manna would fall unless all agreed to a particular distribution and somehow the quantity varied depending on the distribution – would the difference principle make sense according to Nozick (Nozick, 1974: 198).

Rawls rejects the entitlement theory because it permits distributive shares to be influenced by natural abilities and talents. The existing distribution of income and wealth is the cumulative effect of prior distributions of such natural assets, which are arbitrary from a moral point of view, as they have been developed over time by social circumstances and such contingencies as accident and good fortune (Rawls, 1999a: 63). The totality of natural assets is therefore viewed as a collective asset, with no one having differential claims. However, according to Nozick, persons also have a choice of freedom to develop their abilities. Why is that left out? Maybe Rawls would argue that such choices are also the products of factors outside the person's control, like the family in which she or he was raised, which is also arbitrary from a moral point of view according to Rawls. Nozick criticizes this view by noting that this is a risky line of defending Rawls's theory (which otherwise stresses so much the role of individual choices), because it would reject the autonomy and the corresponding responsibility of a person. It would imply that any action of a person should be attributed to certain sorts of external factors.

Another point of criticism is that Rawls assumes that the individuals in the original position would choose principles that focus on groups rather than on individuals and that the principles only apply to the basic institutional structure of the society rather than to every concrete situation. Why would the persons in the original position refrain from applying the difference principle to individuals? We may think that correct principles of justice are universally applicable. Principles that fail for micro-situations cannot be correct. Rawls does not give an adequate motivation for this. Yet it is clear that applying the difference principle to individuals yields implausible results. As an example, Nozick refers to the operation of the difference principle of Rawls in a family.

> Should a family devote its resources to maximizing the position of its least well-off child, holding back the other children or only using resources for their development if they will contribute to maximizing the position of their least fortunate brother or sister? Surely not.
>
> (Nozick, 1974: 167)

In the wider society, application of the difference principle to individuals instead of groups would reduce questions of evaluating social institutions to the issue of how the unhappiest fares. Although the welfare of the least advantaged does play an important role, focusing only on this group seems to be too one-sided.

A fourth point of criticism is that it remains unclear whether Rawls's arguments for the three principles of justice are made by people in the original position or by people living in the actual world. For example, when Rawls states that the least advantaged have no reason to complain, one can hardly imagine that he argues from the position of a person in the original position, for in that position the person is agreeing to the difference principle. He knows he has no reason to complain later, because he himself rationally chooses for the difference principle in the original position. Nozick therefore assumes that Rawls addresses himself here to individuals outside the original position, to the least advantaged here and now, to convince them that the difference principle is fair and wants to tell them that the inequalities work out to their advantage. Rawls does not say: you have gambled and you lost. He also wants a consideration apart from the original position that will convince the least advantaged person that his position in the unequal society is just (Rawls, 1999a: 197). One can therefore question why Rawls uses the construal of the original position to derive this principle.

Criticism on libertarianism

From Nozick's criticisms on Rawls's theory one may conclude that Rawls's theory, however ingenious, provides no fully plausible account of the principles of justice. However, Nozick's theory can also be criticized for accepting only negative rights. Indeed, it is remarkable that Nozick does not deal with the question whether the negative right to freedom should always have priority. Nowhere in his book does he consider whether a rich person has the moral obligation to help a poor starving person, because the positive right to life may have priority over the negative right of private property in certain circumstances. More generally, one can doubt whether the deontological approach of Nozick is satisfactory if the consequences are disastrous. The exercise of rights in market situations may have terrible consequences. Many famines have taken place in the past with no overall decline of food availability, reflecting a sharp failure of the entitlement theory of Nozick (Sen, 1984). The famines occurred precisely because of shifts in entitlements resulting from exercises of rights that are legitimate from a legal point of view. One can question whether an unhindered operation of the procedures proposed by Nozick is still morally acceptable if it results in starvation and famine. Why should rules of ownership have absolute priority over life-and-death questions? If one would accept a moral obligation to prevent starvation, the whole entitlement theory should be reconsidered. Once trade-offs based on consequentialist evaluation are accepted, the door is open for taking a less rigid view than Nozick and for rejecting assessment by just procedures only.

Another point of criticism made by Varian (1974) is that Nozick provides no acceptable analysis of how the initial endowments of the agents are to be determined. Whereas Nozick believes that a free market economy is a reasonable way to achieve justice in transfers, the first part – how agents come to acquire legitimate holdings – is left largely unanalyzed. Since Nozick's theory does not allow any redistribution, a just initial distribution of endowments is of relatively high importance. In particular, there are two problems with the operation of justice in acquisition. The first problem is that little has been unowned for the last few hundred years. The unfortunate people who are born at this late date have nothing left to appropriate, while the descendants of the original appropriators live in wealth. A second problem is that the acquisition of entitlements is subject to a great deal of randomness. Although Rawls may be worrying too much about the fact that natural assets are distributed randomly, it seems unreasonable to disregard it completely. Nozick proposes no mechanism to correct for any kind of randomness. If there are large random components that move a society to an unequal final allocation that are arbitrary from a moral point of view, it is unreasonable to attach a great moral significance to the outcomes of such a process. According to Varian (1974), it is totally unacceptable if the initial endowments of wealth were randomly determined centuries ago.

A third problem with Nozick's theory is that justice in rectification is hard to realize. Some of the property rights held today can trace their lineage back to forceful appropriation in the past, like the wrongful appropriation of the American land from the Indians. Nozick would argue that unjust transfers should be rectified according to his principle of justice in rectification by asking what would have happened if injustices had not occurred. But this is highly impractical. How would we have to determine the current distribution of entitlements if the past injustice to the Indians had not occurred?

6.4 MERITOCRACY

Meritocracy distributes benefits according to moral desert. This principle states that each person should obtain that which she or he deserves. Central to the meritocratic ethics is the idea that economic goods are vested in individual people on the basis of talent, effort and achievement and not based on factors beyond their control. The principle is therefore closely related to the principle of equal opportunities of Rawls, which distributes the better positions in society in accordance with talent and ability.

Traditional versions of meritocracy prescribe that the merits include moral and civic virtue. In a more technocratic version of meritocracy, this link between merit and moral virtue is severed. Rather, it then simply assumes that the merit is equal to the value of people's contribution to the economy, i.e. the market value of the goods and services they sell. This is also called capitalist justice. Capitalist justice distributes benefits according to the value of the contribution that the individual makes (see also Section 6.5). Provided that markets operate within a fair system of equal opportunity and are not distorted by market imperfections, they give people what they deserve. For competitive markets, one's market value is a good measure of one's contribution to society.

In distributing jobs between different people, meritocracy has several advantages (Sandel, 2020). First, it enhances efficiency, as it selects people on the basis of their competence.

Second, meritocracy is fair, because it does not discriminate against the most qualified applicant, for example, by basing the selection on racial, religious or sexist prejudice. Third, rewarding merit supports freedom, as it puts one's destiny in one's own hand and does not make success dependent on forces beyond one's control. Fourth, it strengthens personal responsibility for one's own choices and life. It respects people's capacity to think and act for themselves. One's fate is not fixed, but is to oneself to decide. Those who work hard and play by the rules should be able to rise as far as their talents will take them. This enforces human agency. Lastly, a meritocratic society is inspiring as it makes people proud of their achievements. All get what they deserve, as success is the result of one's own doing, something that one has earned through talent and hard work.

Sandel (2020) argued, however, that these advantages come with a high price. If the successful people deserve their success, it also means that those who are left behind deserve their fate as well. If you are poor in a society that does not reward merit, as in feudal society, you would not be burdened by the idea that you were responsible for your poverty, but in a meritocratic society you are. It denigrates the losers and erodes the dignity of their work, and this creates humiliation and resentment among them. According to Sandel, this sentiment is at the heart of the populist uprising against elites in the United States and in Europe and has weakened democratic societies. Second, meritocracy obscures that those who prevail are indebted to others in many ways. It diminishes the awareness of contingency of their fortune and that their talents are (at least partly) a matter of luck. It banishes all sense of fortune, gift or grace and generates arrogance among the winners. Third, meritocracy erodes solidarity with those who have not been that lucky. If unsuccessful people are themselves responsible for their own fate, they do not deserve and should not expect help from their more successful fellow citizens. Only those who are needy through no fault of their own have a claim on the community's help. Fourth, by stressing human agency, it places a heavy burden on young people by demanding strenuous effort in the competition for the favorable positions in society. The hyper-competitive selection mechanisms of prestigious universities induce prosperous parents to boost the credentials of their children, leading to high-stress, anxiety-ridden years in education that harm a student's mental health. Fifth, it may increase inequality. Since the seventies, when meritocracy became popular in the United States, income inequality has been on the rise. Hence, meritocracy has not proven to be a remedy for inequality; rather it provides a justification of inequality. Whereas the ratio of income of CEOs of major American companies and income of the average worker has substantially increased since 1979, the median income of American males stagnated, creating frustration among the average worker. Traditionally, Americans accepted high income inequality because they believed in the American dream that anyone who works hard can escape the lower ranks in society. This would make inequality matter less, as no one is consigned to the lower class. But contrary to this perception, research has shown that upward mobility is actually lower in the United States than in Europe.

Both libertarians and liberal democrats have criticized meritocratic ethics. For example, Hayek (1960) rejected the idea that economic rewards reflect people's merit, because the value of the goods and services one offers to the market is contingent on supply and demand conditions, and therefore a matter of luck. Also Sandel (2020) considers that one's market value cannot be equated to one's merit, as it is simply reflecting the degree of satisfaction of desires people happen to express on the marketplace. One's contribution should be measured, instead, in terms of the moral importance of the ends they serve. Rawls also acknowledged the morally arbitrary value of talents. Effort is not solely due to personal choice, but rather contingent, depending on family and social circumstances. Rawls therefore added his difference principle to the principle of equal opportunity in this theory of justice, which requires the winners to share their rewards with the less fortunate. However, according to Sandel, Rawls's rejection of meritocracy did not prevent meritocratic hubris, as Rawls admitted inequalities that meet the principles of fair equality of opportunity and the difference principle. Therefore, wealthy CEOs could justify their high reward by arguing that this creates the necessary incentive to work to the advantage of the least advantaged. This justification can easily shape an attitude of meritocratic arrogance.

6.5 DISTRIBUTIVE JUSTICE: AN OVERVIEW OF CRITERIA

In Chapters 2, 5 and the previous sections of Chapter 6 we have discussed several ethical theories. In this section, we provide an overview of the implications of these theories for questions of distributive justice. Distributive justice is concerned with the fair allocation of resources among diverse members of a community. In all cases where different people put forth conflicting claims or property rights, which cannot be satisfied simultaneously, questions of distributive justice arise. The formal principle of justice requires that equals should be treated equally and unequals should be treated unequal in proportion to the degree in which they are unequal. This is an evident principle, but the difficulty starts with the question: When are people equal and when are they unequal? Which criteria should be applied to compare different persons? As illustrated by Table 6.1, there are several possibilities ranging from absolute egalitarianism that stresses equality in income to the libertarian principle that gives priority to individual freedom.

Absolute egalitarianism holds that all people are equal in all aspects. There are no relevant differences that justify unequal treatment. This principle implies an equal share in the benefits

TABLE 6.1
Standards for distributional justice

	Standard	Description
1	Absolute egalitarianism	Everybody has an equal income
2	Difference principle of Rawls	Inequalities are allowed up to the point where the least advantaged get the most
3	Socialist justice of Marx	People get in accordance to needs, and people should contribute in accordance with ability
4	Capability principle of Sen	People who need more to develop capabilities get more
5	Utilitarianism of Bentham	Maximize total utility
6	Equal opportunities principle of Rawls	Positions are open to all under conditions of fair equality of opportunity
7	Capitalist justice:	Distribution according to contribution
	a Effort	a Distribution according to effort of individuals
	b Productivity	b Distribution according to productivity of individuals
	c Market price	c Distribution according to perfect market mechanism
8	Entitlement theory of Nozick	Distribution by free transactions: from each as they choose, to each as they are chosen

and burdens. An application of egalitarianism is the voting right in politics. It was only during the previous century that men and women received equal voting rights. An example of an economic application is a strict communist system in which each person obtains an equal income (absolute egalitarianism). Such a system requires that all incomes be taxed for 100% and that the revenues of the tax are completely equally distributed to all by a central authority.

An absolute communistic system of income distribution may, however, be very harmful for the economy. If everyone receives the same income, the lazy person will earn as much as the industrious person. Hence, there will be no incentive to work. A less extreme variant of egalitarianism is the difference principle of Rawls that acknowledges that allowing some inequalities will benefit all people, including the least advantaged. The difference principle requires that the primary social goods of the worst-off group be maximized.

The Rawlsian difference principle is, however, insensitive to special needs, such as of the disabled, the old or the ill. These groups may be unable to produce anything worthwhile and at the same time need more income than healthy persons to obtain a similar level of well-being. Therefore, we also need distribution mechanisms that take needs as a norm. In particular, the socialist justice principle of Marx argues that the benefits should be distributed according to people's needs, but the burdens should be distributed according to people's ability (Velasquez, 1998). Sen (1981) notes that differences of needs can also arise from climatic conditions (such as clothing and shelter), urbanization (such as pollution effects), work performed (such as calories or other nutrients) or even body size. To judge equality only in terms of availability of primary social goods, as by the difference principle of Rawls, disregards the relevance of these other factors.

A theory that is closely related to the approach of meeting needs is the extra-welfaristic capability theory of Sen (1984). His theory does not concentrate on utility or on the availability of primary goods, but on the realization of certain powers or basic capabilities (see Chapter 2). The cripple's entitlement to more income arises in this view from the deprivation of his ability to move unless he happens to have more income or more specialized goods (for example, vehicles for the disabled).[12] There are, however, some specific differences between a needs approach and Sen's capability approach. First, in the socialist needs approach the needs are defined in terms of commodities. Particular goods and services are required to achieve certain results, even though it is acknowledged that different persons need different commodities to satisfy their needs. However, the relation between commodities and capabilities may be a many-one correspondence, with the same capabilities being achievable by more than one particular bundle of commodities. For example, different combinations of food and health services may produce the same level of nutrition. Second, the commodity requirement for specific capabilities may be dependent on the social context. For example, in a poor country the resources or commodities needed to participate in the standard activities of the community may be more limited than in a rich country. This has not merely the consequence that absolute deprivation in capabilities may take the form of relative deprivation in terms of commodities and incomes but also that the need of commodities is not absolutely specifiable. Sen acknowledges, however, that the application of his extra-welfarism has practical problems. For example, how can we measure the extent of power fulfillment, and what capabilities count as primary? A third difference is that 'needs' is a more passive concept than capability. The concept of capability therefore links more naturally with positive freedom. A final difference is that the needs approach tends to focus on basic needs, i.e. on a minimum quantity of particular goods. This may lead to a softening of the opposition to inequality when the average level of welfare increases. Equality of capabilities is not prejudiced by the special concern with basic needs and can be used for judging justice at any level of development.

In contrast to egalitarianism, Sen's extra-welfarism does not exclude sum ranking and is therefore more aligned with utilitarianism. In contrast to Sen's focus on capabilities, utilitarianism is about the maximization of the total amount of happiness or desire fulfillment. As illustrated by the discussion in Chapter 2, utilitarianism does not exclude a high degree of equality, because the utilitarian criterion of maximizing total utility prescribes that income should be redistributed until the marginal utility of all persons is equalized. As Singer (1972) argues, this may imply a substantial redistribution from rich to poor countries.

The next principle, the principle of equal opportunities proposed by John Rawls, does not focus on outcomes, but on opportunities. Although this principle is more liberal in nature, it is still closely related to socialism, because the principle of equal opportunity requires that the influence of social contingencies and natural fortune should be mitigated. This may require, for example, affirmative action to rectify the effects of past discrimination. For example, if jobs are not distributed in accordance with criteria like ability, effort and contribution but also according to irrelevant criteria like race and sex, affirmative action is required, bringing about equal opportunities for groups that are disadvantaged in the assignment of jobs.

Capitalist justice ('technocratic' meritocracy) distributes benefits according to the value of the contribution that the individual makes. Thus, when a person has performed labor on some property, he or she has engaged in an activity that either displays some sort of human excellence (such as working hard) or confers a needed benefit on surrounding others (like making an object they want to buy) (Christman, 1998). Thus, if a worker adds value to the lives of others in some permissible way and without being required to do so, that person deserves a fitting benefit. There are several ways of measuring this value. If a person works together with other persons within a company, one aspect of the contribution is the work effort of a person. However, this approach encounters several problems like problems of measurement of work effort and a lack of compensatory justice if people work hard but not in a productive way. For this reason, it might be better to relate the contribution to the productivity of the person.[13] This criterion of justice is consistent with Locke's property concept, that each person has a right to ownership over his own body, his own labor and the products of his labor. However, just as with work effort, it is often difficult to determine the exact productivity of workers, especially if their work is complementary to the work of others. The third approach, the market mechanism, determines one's contribution on basis of the market price of the worker. In a perfect market each factor of production will be paid its marginal product. That is, the wage rate of a certain kind of labor will be equal to the difference between the value of the output produced by the total labor used by a profit-maximizing firm minus the value of output produced using one less unit of that kind of labor. Similarly, the owner of a particular part of land or capital equipment will be paid according to the marginal contribution of their production factor to the production process.

The total income reaped by an owner of production factors is the product of the price of the goods and labor he holds and the amount of his endowment of that factor. The market approach only works well for a market in which market imperfections are not present. If there are market imperfections, this approach is less reliable and the fair remuneration is highly indeterminate.

Box 6.2   Equality in the health care sector

Hurley (2000) illustrates some of the distribution rules for the health sector. In the case of egalitarianism, one can argue that the relevant equality principle is equality of health. Given that health care is consumed to produce health, it follows that an equitable allocation of health care is that which gives rise to an equal distribution of health. The problem of this way of defining fairness in health care is that health care is not the only determinant of health. Balancing differences in other determinants of health might therefore imply a highly uneven distribution in health care. Even then it is not expected that health care alone can lead to an equal distribution of health.

An alternative and often-heard standard for health care is equality of access. Access can be defined as 'freedom or ability to obtain or make use of'. Equal access, then, implies that everyone in society is equally able to obtain or make use of health care. It is linked to the notion of equal opportunity or fair chance. Sometimes, equal access to a good is defined as a situation in which individuals face the same price for health care. An alternative definition of equal access to a good is a situation in which everyone is able to consume the same quantity of the good. This means that everybody is allowed to spend an identical amount of money on health care.

The most common way of distributing health care is the socialist way, distribution by need. One of the problems of this distribution rule is how to define need. There are several alternative options here. The first equates need for health care with ill health and the degree of need with the severity of illness. Those who are most severely ill have the greatest need. This definition, however, ignores the fact that there may be no effective treatments for some types of ill health. If there is no effective treatment, there is no need for health care. The second definition of need is more consequentialist and centers on effectiveness. It argues that a need can be defined only with respect to a specific objective that the community endorses as worthwhile. A need, then, only exists if there is a treatment that has been proved to be effective in achieving this objective.

The most liberal principle of justice is the entitlement theory of Nozick. As explained in Section 6.3, Nozick does not accept any end-result principle. Justice only consists of an unhindered operation of the just procedures of justice in acquisition, transfer and rectification. His theory therefore also differs from the capitalist principle of income in accordance with contribution. For example, Nozick also accepts voluntary transactions that do not allocate income according to merit, for example, by inheritance or gifts, provided that these transactions are voluntary.

Finally, we note that Table 6.1 abstracts from agent-relative principles of the ethics of care to be discussed in Chapter 8. The special responsibility that a person feels for his or her family or friends may influence the goodness of a certain distribution. For example, one may argue that it is right that one gives a toy to one's own child although egalitarian principles or utilitarian principles would demand she or he gives it to a child in the street or living in another country. This argument can be based on the notion that parents have a special duty to their own child because of the relationship. Sen (1981) calls this class of agent-relative obligations 'relational obligations'. These agent-relative duties do not only concern ties of kinship or affection but also other relationships like political relationships and relationships resulting from past events (for example, because of a promise which binds you to a certain person).

NOTES

1 Another restriction is that Rawls primarily considers a well-ordered society where everyone is presumed to act justly. The reason is that such an ideal theory is the only way to start in order to analyze more complex and realistic situations of individuals only partly complying with the principles of justice.

2 Besides, Rawls distinguishes other primary goods such as health, vigor and intelligence. These are natural goods, because their possession is not so directly under control of society.

3 Another advantage of only considering the distribution of primary social goods is that the problems of interpersonal comparison are not as large as for the satisfaction of preferences. See also Chapter 2.

4 See the last part of this section.

5 Note further that whereas utilitarianism should investigate all consequences for all people, Rawls's difference principle only requires comparison of the primary social goods for the least advantaged for different alternatives. This greatly simplifies the selection of the most favorable alternative.

6 Suppose one can choose between m alternatives Xm which can yield n possibilities for social primary goods (Xm,n), then the maximin rule is to select Xm that satisfies max (min (Xm,n)).

7 In Rawls (1999b: 50) Rawls also pleads for public financing of elections in order to ensure that officials are sufficiently independent of particular social and economic interests.

8 In Rawls (1999b: 50) Rawls also argues for the government as employer of last resort, because the lack of a sense of long-term security and of the opportunity of meaningful work is destructive not only of the citizens' self-respect but also of their sense that they are members of society.

9 According to Galbraith (1992), this is one of the characteristics of a culture of a self-complacency, where the content majority strongly rejects public expenditure to social assistance, housing, public education and any other redistributive policy measures that require high taxes and violate the right to private property. The content majority also opposes active government policies that safeguard the long-term interests of society, because they believe the government is inefficient, inexpert and arrogant (the bureaucratic syndrome).

10 Also, other social goals like reduction of poverty, meaningful work and workers' control over labor conditions may be realized only by voluntary actions of those who are involved, according to Nozick. If all prefer reduction of poverty, meaningful work situations and worker-controlled factories provided that the others do also, they can jointly contract to give resources to realize these goals. Making this contract contingent upon the others' giving may prevent free-rider problems. But Nozick rejects imposing one's view on all those workers who would choose to achieve other ends (Nozick, 1974: 267–268).

11 Plato and Aristotle already argued that equality stimulates envy because people particularly envy those who are most similar to them. A nice example of this psychological phenomenon is given by Mandeville: a person who has to walk envies a person with a small carriage with four horses more than a person with a large carriage with six horses. Also Hobbes argued that in a society of equals there will be an endless rivalry, dispute and eventually war and that inequality would solve this fight of all to all.

12 Sen (1984: 320) thinks that there are good reasons to assume that Rawls also – contrary to what Rawls states – is really after something like capabilities instead of primary social goods, because Rawls puts the focus on primary goods by discussing what these goods enable people to do.

13 The criticism of Marx on capitalism can also be based on capitalist justice. In his theory of unpaid labor surplus, Marx argued that capitalists have the power to pay workers only a subsistence wage, i.e. what it takes to keep them alive and working. The workers do not receive the full value of what they contribute to the product. The difference creates surplus value or profit to the capitalist. According to Marx, the capitalist's power to exploit the workers is due to his ownership of the means of production.

Recommended literature

Beauchamp, T.L. (1982) *Philosophical Ethics, an Introduction to Moral Philosophy*, New York: McGraw-Hill Inc.

Nozick, R. (1974) *Anarchy, State and Utopia*, New York: Basic Books.

Rawls, J. (1999a) *A Theory of Justice*, Revised edition, Boston: Harvard University Press.

Rawls, J. (1999b) *The Law of Peoples: With 'The Idea of Public Reason Revisited'*, Boston: Harvard University Press.

Sandel, M.J. (2020) *The Tyranny of Merit: What's Become of the Common Good?* London: Penguin Books.

Sen, A. (1984) *Resources, Values and Development*, Oxford: Blackwell.

Varian, H.R. (1974) 'Distributive justice, welfare economics, and the theory of fairness', *Philosophy and Public Affairs*, 4: 223–247.

Velasquez, M.G. (1998) *Business Ethics: Concepts and Cases*, Fourth edition, Upper Saddle River, NJ: Prentice Hall.

7

Free markets, rights and inequality

Empirical research

In this chapter we review empirical research into the relationship between markets, rights and justice. First, we consider the relationship between free market institutions and respect of negative rights and capitalist justice. Second, we consider the relationship between free market institutions and positive rights. In the third and fourth sections, we deal with the question of whether economic freedom increases income inequality within countries and between countries. In the last section we consider the effects of income inequality on trust and happiness, which is important for the evaluation of free markets from a utilitarian point of view.

7.1 FREE MARKETS, NEGATIVE RIGHTS AND CAPITALIST JUSTICE

Free market institutions seem logically coherent with the protection of negative rights to freedom and with capitalist justice. If an economic order transforms from a collective planning economy towards a free capitalist economy, property rights and the principle of moral desert will be more respected.

However, complete liberalization or privatization may also threaten the respect of negative rights, even if the government secures private property rights. If the government abstains from active competition policy, market imperfections may increase that violate the negative right to freedom in transactions. If companies have the freedom to reduce transparency in order to shield their output from competition, the freedom of choice of the consumer is diminished. Market imperfections also reduce the principle of moral desert. If companies acquire economic power by successfully limiting market entrance, prices will go up, enabling companies to get more than their effort or productivity justifies.

Also fierce competition in free international markets can obstruct respect of negative rights, because it may induce companies to do business with undemocratic governments. Trade enables these undemocratic and oppressive regimes to continue ruling their country by selling the country's resources. According to Pogge (2001), any group controlling a preponderance of the means of coercion within a country is internationally recognized as the legitimate government of this country. The international order confers upon it the privilege freely to do economic transactions (borrowing, selling resources). The economic freedom

DOI: 10.4324/9781003181835-9

helps such governments stay in power. The international economic order thus indirectly contributes to the violation of negative rights in these countries.

7.2   FREE MARKETS AND POSITIVE RIGHTS

Free market institutions are, however, more often criticized because of a lack of respect of positive rights. The number of people living below certain poverty lines, so-called absolute poverty where household income is too low to meet basic needs of life including food, shelter, safe drinking water, etc., is used as approximations of the respect of the positive right to subsistence.

The globalization of the world economy during the last decade has been accompanied by a decline in poverty. From 1880 to 2015 the share of people living below the poverty line of $1 per day declined from more than 80% to less than 10%. During the last decades, poverty particularly substantially declined in East Asia. An example is China. After the gradual transformation to a market system since 1978, the number of people living in poverty (below $1 per day) declined from 634 million in 1981 to 212 million in 2001 (World Bank, 2006), and in 2020 China claimed to have completely banned absolute poverty. In Africa, the absolute number of poor people remained high, but as a percentage of population, the statistics also show a modest decline, particularly after 1999. However, these trends are not only due to the rise of free markets. The analysis of the impact of markets on poverty is hindered by the fact that pure market liberalization seldom takes place. China grew because it allowed more private initiative but flouted many other rules of the free market (Rodrik, 2002).

Still, empirical studies broadly support the view that trade liberalization will be poverty alleviating in the long run and on average (Winters et al., 2004). Winters et al. distinguish several channels. First, trade liberalization will stimulate economic growth, and economic growth tends to decrease absolute poverty. Trade liberalization also fosters productivity growth. Although the effect on poverty reduction is uncertain, productivity growth is seen as a necessary part of any viable poverty reduction strategy for the long term. The empirical evidence for other channels through which trade liberalization may reduce poverty – through more economic stability, through price reduction of consumer goods, through the creation and destruction of markets, through the creation of employment or increase in wages, through more government revenue – is, however, not unambiguous and highly dependent on local institutions and complementing policies of the government. There is quite a lot of evidence that poorer households may be less able than richer ones to protect themselves against adverse effects from more trade liberalization or to take advantage of new opportunities created by openness. Therefore, there is an important role for additional policies to provide social protection and to enhance the ability of poorer households to benefit from new opportunities.

This analysis is supported by Table 7.1 that relates the share of people living in absolute poverty to various dimensions of economic freedom and gross domestic product (GDP) per capita (Graafland, 2017). The estimation results in column 1 show that the quality of the legal system and free trade have a strong positive effect on GDP per capita. The other dimensions of economic freedom are not found to significantly affect income per capita. Columns 2 to 3 show a regression analysis into the relationship between GDP per capita and the share of people living in absolute poverty while controlling for income inequality. The share of people in absolute poverty in a country is significantly negatively related to GDP per capita,

TABLE 7.1
Economic freedom and absolute poverty: estimation results[a]

	1	2	3	4
	Ln GDP per capita	Share of people in absolute poverty		
		Poor	Middle	Rich
Ln GDP per capita		−0.71***	−0.48**	−0.24
Fiscal freedom	0.04			
Rule of law	0.60***			
Sound money	−0.02			
Free trade	0.40***			
Low regulation	−0.11			
Gini		0.23	0.47**	−0.04
R^2	0.65	0.57	0.35	0.19
Number of countries	103	38	39	33

[a] Standardized coefficients; * $p <0.05$; ** $p <0.01$; *** $p <0.001$. Controlled for various control variables. For more details, see Graafland (2017).

particularly in poor countries. Combining these results with the results in column 1, the implication is that improving the rule of law and freedom to trade reduces absolute poverty in developing countries.[1]

7.3 FREE MARKETS AND INCOME INEQUALITY WITHIN COUNTRIES[2]

Equality can be based on income, wealth, consumption or any other reasonable proxy for well-being (such as job opportunities and social security). Most of the empirical research focuses on inequality of annual income, because data for other types of inequality are less available and less measurable (Verme, 2011; Piketty, 2014). Income inequality is also important for many other dimensions of human well-being (e.g. education, health, etc.). In this section we therefore focus on income inequality within countries.

Break down of Kuznets curve

According to the so-called Kuznets curve, income inequality will initially rise with GDP per capita but then fall as countries get richer. For a long time, the history of the poor and rich countries seemed to confirm this relationship (Glaeser, 2005). Goldberg and Pavcnik (2007) showed that the exposure of developing countries to international markets as measured by the degree of trade protection, the share of imports and/or exports in GDP, the magnitude of foreign direct investment and exchange rate fluctuations increased inequality in the short and medium run, although the precise effect depends on country- and time-specific factors. They researched seven representative developing countries that had substantially reduced import tariff levels and non-tariff barriers to trade during the eighties and nineties. All these countries experienced an increase in wage dispersion between high and low skilled labor, coinciding with the trade reforms.

Goldberg and Pavcnik (2007) offered several explanations. First, the rise of China and other low-income developing countries (India, Indonesia, Pakistan, etc.) may have shifted the comparative advantage in middle-income countries from low skill to intermediate or high skill intensity and therefore increased the demand and wage for skilled labor at the expense of unskilled labor. Some of the middle-income countries started to outsource their production to the upcoming low-income developing countries, and this also raised the skill premium in the developing countries. Second, the globalization has fostered international capital inflows into the developing countries. Since the utilization of capital normally requires the use of a higher share of skilled labor, the demand for skilled workers increased as well. A similar mechanism is skill-biased technological change. This technological change may have taken the form of increased imports of machines, office equipment and other capital goods that are complementary to skilled labor. Liberalization may also have raised the demand for skilled labor, because it advantages companies that are operating more efficiently or closer to the technological frontier. Trade shifts resources from non-exporters to exporters, and there is ample empirical evidence that exporters tend to be more productive than non-exporters. Trade openness may also have induced an additional upgrading of these firms, which are partly passed on to skilled workers in the form of higher wages. Finally, some researches indicate that trade liberalization has increased the prices of consumption goods (such as food and beverages) that have a relatively large share in the consumption bundle of the poor and decreased the prices of goods that are consumed in greater proportion by the rich. The latter effect seems, however, to be relatively small compared to the effects on the wage dispersion between unskilled and skilled labor.

Recent trends in income inequality suggest that the Kuznets curve does not apply anymore to the richer countries. This can be illustrated by the example of the United States. Initially, the economic process in the United States was very much in line with the Kuznets curve. The share of national wealth earned by the top 1% rose from 15% in 1775 to 30% in 1855 and 45% in 1935. After 1935 inequality declined, but this process stopped at the end of the sixties. A similar pattern has been observed for the Gini index. After a decline between the thirties and the second half of the sixties, it substantially increased since 1975, partly as a result of economic factors (skill-based technological change, increased trade and globalization, the decline of unions) and partly as a result of political factors (less progressive taxation, lower minimum wages and unemployment benefits). Similar trends are visible for several European countries, where income inequality is also on the rise.

Effect of economic freedom on income inequality

Since Piketty's *Capital in the 21st Century* in 2014, scientific interest into the impact of income inequality on society has been on the rise. Stiglitz (2012) argued that unfair policies and manipulation of the market through the underlying inequality in political and economic power enabled the top 1% of the income distribution to receive a disproportionate share of economic growth in the United States for the last 30 years. This analysis is in line with Roine et al. (2009) who argued, using data from Atkinson and Piketty's World Top Income Database, that the high economic growth during the last decades has been mainly beneficial to rich income groups. The increase in GDP did not trickle down, something which holds equally for Anglo-Saxon and continental European countries. Yet in contrast to the Anglo-Saxon countries, increasing trade has not led to a further increase in the very top incomes in continental Europe within the population class of the richest 10%. According to Roine et al. (2009), this is due to strong labor market institutions and the equalizing role of the government.

These findings indicate that inequality is related to government institutions and therefore to (various dimensions of) economic freedom. Some previous studies showed that economic freedom decreases income inequality in the longer run. Scully (2002) estimated that the index of economic freedom has a small but significant negative impact on the Gini index. Also, Berggren (1999) found that sustained and gradual increases in economic freedom influence inequality measures negatively. He argued that one cannot rightly claim on theoretical grounds that higher levels of economic freedom go hand in hand with higher levels of income inequality. This relationship is unclear a priori; even when redistribution falls, if the poor take advantage of changes in other variables of economic freedom (such as the protection of property rights or increased trade liberalization) more so than the rich, inequality may decrease (Gwartney et al., 1996; De Vanssay and Spindler, 1994). Hence, the freedom–inequality relationship should be empirically tested. Using four different variables for inequality, Berggren (1999) tested this hypothesis controlling for wealth and the illiteracy rate. In all regressions, he found that the lower the initial level of economic freedom and the higher the change in economic freedom, the lower the level of inequality at the end of the sample. Therefore, Berggren concluded that for the poor, the relatively strong income growth effect due to a positive change in economic freedom outweighs an increase in income inequality from lower redistributive policies. Berggren mentioned that trade liberalization and financial mobility drive these findings, suggesting that poor people are employed in industries that benefit more from free trade. A problem with Berggren's analysis is that he used data from 1975 to 1985. In this period, the economic context was different, especially, as explained by Piketty (2014), regarding inequality and the economic system. This diminishes the relevance of Berggren's article for the current state of the economy.

Bennett and Vedder (2013) looked at a more recent period. They found a non-linear, parabolic relationship between economic freedom and inequality, concluding that in the very long run (at least ten years), increases in economic freedom might have a negative effect on inequality. However, they also stated that this reduction in inequality falls in the same time period as the technology boom in the 1990s, and this could mean that this finding is related to exceptional circumstances. Apergis et al. (2014) studied economic freedom and income inequality through a panel error correction model of US data over the period 1981–2004. They found that economic freedom decreases inequality both in the short and in the long run. On the other hand, Bennett and Nikolaev (2017) found that economic freedom is related to higher levels of both net and gross Gini coefficients. Hall and Lawson (2014) made an overview of empirical studies using the Economic Freedom Index of the Fraser Institute. They concluded that the evidence from these studies indeed indicates that more economic freedom may come at a price of an increase in income inequality.

In the literature, researchers have usually focused on only one of the five dimensions of economic freedom or on the aggregate index (Berggren and Jordahl, 2006; Norberg, 2002; Jäntti and Jenkins, 2010; Berggren, 1999; Gwartney et al., 2004). However, it is likely that the various dimensions of economic freedom have different, and partly opposite, effects on income inequality. First, inequality may be negatively related to the size of government, of which tax income is a major indicator (Berggren and Jordahl, 2006). Traditionally, one of the major tasks of the government has been redistribution of income (Schwarze and Härpfer, 2002). Piketty (2014) stated that income inequality is mainly determined by tax policies. He argued that the progressivity of the tax system is an indicator of the general social morale of a society. It has an important signal function as to what is acceptable with respect to income inequality and therefore even affects income inequality before taxes (gross income inequality). Schneider (2012) argued that perceptions of the legitimacy of income inequality are important to their appreciation, which is reflected in the tax system (also Schmidt-Catran, 2014).

Second, Norberg (2002) argued that the free market system reduces inequality in the long run, because it protects the private property of all. A high quality of legal structure and security of property rights is particularly relevant for the poor, because in an economy that does not secure private property rights, they are much more vulnerable than are the rich and powerful. Lack of respect of private property rights limits economic opportunities and forces the poor to restrict their economic activities to the informal economy. Only the rich elite in such a context have the power and opportunities to initiate profitable, modern economic activities.

With respect to the relationship between access to sound money and inequality, the literature has indicated that inflation and inequality are positively related. The underlying reason is that low-income households use cash for a greater share of their purchases (Erosa and Ventura, 2002). The use of financial technologies that hedge against inflation is positively related to household wealth (Mulligan and Sala-i-martin, 2000). Attanasio et al. (1998) found that the use of an interest-bearing bank account is positively related to educational level and income. Inflation is therefore more costly for low-income households. Although Jäntti and Jenkins (2010) found no relationship between sound money and income inequality in the United Kingdom between 1961 and 1999, other research has confirmed the positive relationship between inflation and income inequality (Romer and Romer, 1998; Albanesi, 2002).

The literature has also related inequality to trade openness. Cornia (2004) argued that trade openness increased within-country inequality in developing countries. The World Bank (2006) also referred to various researches showing that trade liberalization has a positive influence on wage inequality. This is confirmed by an overview article by Goldberg and Pavcnik (2007) who showed that the exposure of developing countries to international markets has increased inequality in the short and medium term, although the precise effect depends on country- and time-specific factors (see earlier).

Finally, inequality may depend on the intensity of government regulation of financial, product and labor markets. Stiglitz (2012) and Piketty (2014) argued that business and labor regulations are necessary for assuring minimal standards of living through minimum wage and health regulations. Minimum wages and other labor market regulations, such as the right to be represented by unions, strengthen the bargaining power of employees, raising average wages. This enables a large part of the population to gather adequate savings to deal with economic shocks. Liberalization may also lead to unequal access to the financial market (World Bank, 2006). Fast liberalization and privatization allow powerful insiders to gain control over state banks (Stiglitz, 2002). Important product market institutions that provide opportunities to the poor are anti-trust legislation, good infrastructure and low transportation costs and supply of information (for example, by Internet connections in rural areas) (World Bank, 2006).

TABLE 7.2
Multiple regression analysis of net Gini coefficient[a]

	Fraser Institute	Heritage Foundation
Small government	0.22**	0.46***
Property rights	0.30	−0.46*
Sound money	−0.55***	−0.65*
Free trade	0.73**	1.03***
Freedom from regulation	0.86***	0.65***
N	203	250
R^2	0.87	0.89

[a] * p <0.05; ** p <0.01; *** p <0.001; heteroscedasticity adjusted standard errors. Controlled for various control variables. For more details, see Graafland and Lous (2018).

In order to test the relationship between the sub-dimensions of economic freedom and income inequality, Graafland and Lous (2018) used a cross-country panel analysis for a period from 1990 to 2014 for 21 Organisation for Economic Co-operation and Development (OECD) countries. For income inequality, data for the net Gini coefficient (e.g. based on net income, corrected for income taxes) from Solt's database were used. For economic freedom, data from the Fraser Institute and the Heritage Foundation were used. As control variables, they used several control variables that are often used in the literature (Leigh, 2006; Steijn and Lancee, 2011; Bergh and Bjørnskov, 2014; Barone and Mocetti, 2016). Based on the outcome of the Hausman test, they used a fixed effects model that controls for unobserved heterogeneity. Following Bennett and Nikolaev (2017), the economic freedom indicators were lagged five years to minimize endogeneity, thus limiting the risk of reverse causality to a minimum.

Column 1 in Table 7.2 shows that the net Gini coefficient is positively related to small government, trade freedom and freedom from regulation and negatively related to sound money as measured by the Fraser Institute. Only property rights is insignificant. For economic freedom data of the Heritage Foundation (column 2), similar results were found, except that the net Gini coefficient is now also negatively related to the protection of property rights. These findings support the idea that some free market institutions may have negative effects on income inequality, whereas others increase income inequality.

7.4 FREE MARKETS AND INCOME INEQUALITY BETWEEN COUNTRIES

According to Milanovic (2005), 70% of worldwide income inequality arises from income variation between countries and 30% from income inequality within countries. In order to determine the impact of international markets on equality, one should therefore not only look at income inequality measures for individual countries but also consider the convergence between countries.

Trends at a country level

Table 7.3 indicates that the expansion of international markets after the second world war has not contributed to more income equality between the richest and poorest countries.

TABLE 7.3
Recent trends in worldwide income ratios

	Annual growth rate national income per adult		Per adult national income	
	1950–1980[a]	1980–2016	2016[b]	Idem, US = 100%
World	2.7	1.2	16,100	32
European Union	3.5	1.0	31,400	62
United States and Canada	2.0	1.5	50,570	100
Latin America	2.6	0.3	15,400	30
China	2.6	6.4	14,000	28
India	1.7	3.3	7,000	14
Japan	5.3	1.2	31000	61
Africa	2.1	0.5	6600	13

[a] Based on World Inequality Report 2018, Table 2.2.4
[b] Purchasing Power Parity, World Income Report 2018, Table 2.2.2

This contradicts the expectations of economists such as Lucas (2000), who argued that the spread of technology will diminish income inequality between countries in the long run. The difference between Western countries and Africa and Latin America has grown during the last 70 years. For Japan and more recently India and China, the difference in income with Western countries declined.

National income per capita is about three times higher in North America than the global average. In China, per-adult income is slightly lower than the world average. China as a whole represents 19% of today's global income. This figure is higher than North America (17%) and the European Union (17%). This marks a sharp contrast with the situation in 1980. China's impressive real per-adult national income growth rate from 1980 to 2016 highly contributed to reducing between-country inequalities over the world. Another converging force lies in the reduction of income growth rates in Western Europe as compared to the previous decades. This deceleration in growth rates was due to the end of the "golden age" of growth in Western Europe but also due to the Great Recession in 2008, which led to a decade of lost growth in Europe. Indeed, per-adult income in Western Europe was in 2016 the same as ten years before, before the onset of the financial crisis.

Despite a reduction in inequality between countries, average national income inequalities remain strong among countries. This indicates that market forces alone will not be sufficient to bring about worldwide income equality.

Worldwide individual income distribution

In the previous section we referred to countries as units of analysis for measuring inequality between countries. However, if one is concerned about income equality between individuals, it seems more useful to consider indices that take the population sizes of various countries into account. Some countries in Asia, like China and India, that have seen a substantial rise in income levels are large and populous, while many of the countries that have stagnated are not.

In order to construct a world distribution of income index, Sala-i-Martin (2006) integrated the annual income distributions for 138 countries. He showed that the Gini coefficient of individual citizens globally remained more or less flat during the 1970s and that it followed a downward trend over the following two decades. Overall, the Gini declined by almost 4% since 1979. Other income inequality indices (Atkinson indices, the variance of the logarithm of income, the ratio of the average income of the top 20% of the distribution to the bottom 20% and the ratio of the top 10% to the bottom 10% of the distribution, the Mean Logarithmic Deviation and the Theil Index) showed a remarkably similar pattern of worldwide inequality over time. They remained more or less constant (or possibly increased) during the 1970s but declined substantially during the 1980s and 1990s. Sala-i-Martin also decomposed the decrease in worldwide inequality between individuals into a within-country and between-country component. The components reflect that within-country inequality increased over the sample period, whereas the between-country index declined. Since the latter effect was larger, the overall global income inequality declined.

7.5   INCOME INEQUALITY, TRUST AND HAPPINESS[3]

Hayek (1960) has argued that inequality is necessary for economic progress. Innovative products that raise the quality of life can only be produced at first in limited quantities and will therefore be too expensive to provide for more than the few. But by providing these products for the few, business gradually learns to make them much cheaper so that they become affordable for the great majority. Whereas the rich pay for experimentation, they fund entrepreneurs in finding ways to provide these luxuries to all. Although being an end in itself for reasons of fairness, income equality may therefore also have negative costs for society if it would hinder economic progress.

However, equality may also have positive consequences for society. In particular, we will argue and show in this section that equality may increase trust and life satisfaction.

Income inequality and generalized trust

Generalized trust is one of the measurable components of social cohesion (Helliwell and Putnam, 2004; Bjørnskov, 2005). Generalized trust entails trusting people you do not know personally (Berggren and Jordahl, 2006). If a certain group in a society is marginalized, this might make it feel less associated with the rest of the society and trust that society less. If the marginalization endures, this group might either opt for violent resistance or develop aggressive opportunistic behavior towards the rest of society, resulting in higher crime rates and deteriorating social trust generally. In the words of Caruso and Schneider (2011: S38): "poverty and income inequality would feed frustration, hatred and grievance which make political violence more likely". Thus, income inequality affects social cohesion and social trust within society as a whole.

A number of articles have been published on the link between income inequality and trust. Kawachi and Kennedy (1997) found a strong association between income inequality and the lack of social trust. Knack and Keefer (1997) and Zak and Knack (2001) provided further empirical evidence for this association, while Oishi et al. (2011) found that social trust is a robust mediator of the impact of income inequality on average life satisfaction. Elgar and Aitken (2011) also found a significant negative causal relationship between income inequality and trust and showed trust to be a significant mediator in the relationship between income inequality and homicide statistics across countries. Leigh (2006) claimed that on a regional level, ethnic heterogeneity appears to be of greater importance than income inequality in explaining trust. On a national level, however, he found a negative causal effect from inequality to trust. Steijn and Lancee (2011) have provided a thorough discussion of this relationship and the weaknesses of research on the topic. They argued that one must distinguish between inequality effects and wealth effects and must control for different impacts for high-income countries and other countries. Their analysis of income inequality in 20 countries led to the conclusion that once national wealth is controlled for, inequality no longer seems to explain trust. They stressed, however, that their sample only includes countries with very little inequality, and this may explain their results. Nor did Bergh and Bjørnskov (2014) find a causal relationship between inequality and trust, while they did find an opposite causal relationship. However, they do not use panel data. Barone and Mocetti (2016) used a panel regression, in which they exploited predicted exposure to technological change as an instrument for income inequality. They also considered the income shares of the top 10% and the top 1%, as well as intergenerational income mobility, in addition to the traditional Gini index. They found that inequality negatively affects generalized trust in developed countries, regardless of which measure is used.

Whether income inequality makes people less trusting may depend on how they perceive income inequality within their personal social context and social cognition. Graafland and Lous (2019) therefore conjecture that the relationship between income inequality and trust depends on how income inequality affects inequality of life satisfaction. If life satisfaction inequality is high, distrust is generated among the least happy. This will increase polarization and the risk of rebellion, thereby also affecting trust among the happier people. Thus, life satisfaction inequality may be an essential factor in the relationship between income inequality and trust. They test this hypothesis by panel analysis on 25 OECD countries in the period 1990–2014. The panel analysis showed that income inequality increases life satisfaction inequality and that both income inequality and life satisfaction inequality have a significant negative impact on generalized trust (see Table 7.4).

These results imply that policy options for increasing trust are not limited to countering income inequality. If there are other ways of influencing life satisfaction inequality directly that do not focus on income inequality, they will also be beneficial to trust. For example, policies that provide health care access to low-income families will raise the level of life satisfaction for them and provide them with more opportunities to participate fully in society, thereby reducing the frustration and disconnectedness of these population groups.

TABLE 7.4
Income inequality, life satisfaction inequality and trust[a]

	Life satisfaction inequality[b]	Generalized trust
Life satisfaction inequality$_{-1}$		−0.34**
Net Gini$_{-1}$	0.86***	−1.13**

[a] Unstandardized coefficients. ** p <0.01 *** p <0.001. Controlled for various control variables. For more details, see Graafland and Lous (2019).
[b] Measured by the standard deviation of average life satisfaction per country.

Income inequality and life satisfaction

While the debate on the magnitude and effects of income inequality in market economies has been going on for some decades (Berggren, 1999; Gwartney et al., 2004; Wilkinson and Pickett, 2010; Stiglitz, 2012; Piketty, 2014), its relationship to subjective well-being has only recently attracted serious attention from economists (Oshio and Kobayashi, 2010; Berg and Veenhoven, 2010; Verme, 2011; Hajdu and Hajdu, 2014). Most economic literature linking subjective well-being to national income inequality consists of case studies of specific countries (Oshio and Kobayashi, 2010; Hajdu and Hajdu, 2014; Zagorski et al., 2014). Only a few studies used a cross-country model, but in these studies the relationship between subjective well-being and income inequality is not the main focus (Berg and Ostry, 2011; OECD, 2012; Ostry et al., 2014). Initial studies into this relationship tended to look at happiness. More recent studies have focused on life satisfaction or a combination of well-being indicators (Verme, 2011; Hajdu and Hajdu, 2014; Zagorski et al., 2014). Although much of the literature on subjective well-being focused on happiness, which is associated with emotions and short-term satisfaction, for macroeconomic evaluations, life satisfaction is more interesting due to its evaluative and long-term nature.

Most studies have confirmed a negative relationship between income inequality and life satisfaction at the macroeconomic level. Oshio and Kobayashi (2010) concluded that national income inequality strongly decreases (average) happiness. In his broad overview study, Verme (2011) found that the significance of the relationship between inequality and life satisfaction depends on the indicator for inequality. After synchronizing different measures and research methods, he found that income inequality has a definite significant and negative impact on life satisfaction. Graafland and Lous (2018) found confirmation for a negative relationship between national income inequality and life satisfaction, in which income inequality functions as a mediator in the relationship between economic freedom and life satisfaction.

Besides research into the direct relationship between national income inequality and subjective well-being, a number of studies researched the relationship between income inequality and variables that are related to subjective well-being. Kahn et al. (2000) showed a link between income inequality and low maternal health. Sturm and Gresenz (2002) linked income inequality to chronic illnesses and mental ill health. In addition, income inequality has been shown to lower the quality of the social environment (Helliwell et al., 2009). This lower quality of the social environment manifests itself in crime statistics. For example, Elgar and Aitken (2011) concluded that income inequality correlates with higher homicide figures. Unfortunately, they did not examine the causality, making it impossible to draw definite conclusions. Oishi et al. (2011) claimed that the increased happiness associated with lower income inequality is explained by perceived fairness and general trust. Guimaraes and Sheedy (2012) linked distrust, resulting from power differences and differences in happiness, to a higher risk of social unrest, of which higher crime is one example. During the last decade, both the International Monetary Fund (IMF) (Berg and Ostry, 2011; Bastagli et al., 2012; Ostry et al., 2014) and the OECD (2012) have produced critical studies on the social impact of income inequality. It is clear from the literature that income inequality negatively affects variables closely related to social cohesion at the macro-level.

On the micro-level, a few studies have examined the relationship between life satisfaction and national income inequality. Whereas Schneider (2012) showed the importance of perceptions in evaluating income inequality (see also Bavetta et al., 2019), Helliwell et al. (2009) found that the social environment is much more important than income to subjective well-being, as well as comparison to reference groups (Budría and Ferrer-I-Carbonell, 2019). However, Zagorski et al. (2014) found no direct effect from the Gini coefficient on individual life satisfaction. Levin et al. (2011) also found no association of income inequality with individual life satisfaction, but they only looked at the impact of income inequality on the life satisfaction of adolescents, not a sample representative of the whole population of a country. Haller and Hadler (2006) found that life satisfaction is higher in countries with low inequality. However, they used data from only one wave of the World Values Studies. Finally, Fahey and Smyth (2004) did find some effect from income inequality on life satisfaction, but they suggested that this might have been influenced by the timing of the data they used. Thus, the literature suggests the existence of a negative relationship between income inequality and life satisfaction at the macro-level, but it does not offer conclusive empirical evidence to answer the question of how national income inequality relates to individual life satisfaction.

In a recent paper, Lous and Graafland (2021) investigated this relationship at the microeconomic level combining national indicators of income inequality with individual data of life satisfaction. Table 7.5 reports the regression results. The results in the first two columns show that income inequality is significantly negatively related to individual life satisfaction, independent which indicator of income inequality is used (net Gini coefficient or the share of national income earned by the top 1%). Life satisfaction increases significantly with personal income level, although the difference between the fourth and fifth (the reference quintile) income quintiles is not significant. Marriage, religiosity and Protestantism correlate significantly and positively with life satisfaction, whereas the coefficients for the other religious traditions do not show a significant relationship. Furthermore, unemployed people are less satisfied, while for age, the happiest are those under 25, followed by those who get to enjoy their pension, as well as those between 25 and 34, whose life satisfaction does not differ significantly from that of the reference group. The 45–54 age group are the least happy.

In order to test whether the negative relationship between life satisfaction and income inequality holds for all income groups or only from an exceptionally strong negative relationship with the lower group(s), Lous and Graafland (2021) also performed regressions with interaction dummies between the different income inequality indicators and (income) quintiles. The results are shown in the third and fourth columns of Table 7.5. For the Gini coefficient (column 1), the results show that all income quintiles experience a significant negative relationship between income inequality and life satisfaction. The relationship is, however, most negative for the lowest two quintiles, while it becomes less negative when personal income level increases. When the income share of the top 1% is used, the pattern does not change very much. These results mean that life satisfaction of the lowest income quintiles is most negatively related to income inequality. However, the negative relationship is not limited to the lowest-income groups.

TABLE 7.5
Income inequality and life satisfaction[a]

	(1)	(2)	(3)	(4)
	Net Gini	Top 1%	Net Gini	Top 1%
Income inequality (IncIneq)	−0.34**	−0.18**		
IncIneq * lowest income quintile			−0.35**	−0.20***
IncIneq * 2nd income quintile			−0.35**	−0.20***
IncIneq * 3rd income quintile			−0.33**	−0.18**
IncIneq * 4th income quintile			−0.30**	−0.14*
IncIneq * highest income quintile			−0.26*	−0.10
Macro controls				
GDP/capita	0.10	0.07	0.10	0.08
Political rights	−0.15*	−0.20	−0.15	−0.20*
Civil liberty	0.04	0.05	0.04	0.05
Inflation	−0.02**	−0.02**	−0.02**	−0.02*
Individual controls				
Lowest income quintile	−0.50***	−0.50***	−0.51***	−0.51***
2nd income quintile	−0.33***	−0.33***	−0.35***	−0.34***
3rd income quintile	−0.16***	−0.16***	−0.18***	−0.18***
4th income quintile	−0.04	−0.04	−0.06*	−0.06*
Married	0.17***	0.17***	0.18***	0.18***
Religiosity	0.09***	0.08***	0.09***	0.08***
Protestant	0.05*	0.05*	0.06*	0.05*
Catholic/orthodox	−0.03	−0.03	−0.03	−0.03
Muslim	−0.05	−0.05	−0.05	−0.06
Other religion	−0.01	−0.01	−0.01	−0.01
Unemployed	−0.27***	−0.27***	−0.27***	−0.27***
Male	−0.02	−0.02	−0.02	−0.02
Age (15–24)	0.16***	0.16***	0.17***	0.17***
(25–34)	0.02	0.02	0.02	0.02
(35–44)	−0.07*	−0.07*	−0.07*	−0.06*
(45–54)	−0.13***	−0.12***	−0.12***	−0.12***
(55–64)	−0.08***	−0.08***	−0.07***	−0.07***
Country dummies	Yes	Yes	Yes	yes
Time dummies	Yes	Yes	Yes	yes
R^2 overall	0.09	0.06	0.08	0.06

[a] *: p-value <0.05; **: p-value <0.01; ***: p-value <0.001. Robust standard errors. The reference group for income scale, religious affiliation, age and wave are the highest quintile, non-religious people, people >65 years. Controlled for time dummies per wave and country dummies. The sample consists of 138,193 observations from 39 countries. For more details, see Lous and Graafland (2021).

NOTES

1   Furthermore, note that income inequality only affects absolute poverty in medium-income countries. The reason that income inequality does not affect absolute poverty in poor countries is that if the average income is equal to the income level demarking absolute poverty, widening the income distribution does not really affect the share of people with an income below the absolute poverty line. How income inequality is affected by economic freedom will be studied in Section 7.3.

2   Part of this section was published in Graafland and Lous (2018).

3   Part of this section was published in Graafland and Lous (2019) and Lous and Graafland (2021).

Recommended literature

Graafland, J. and Lous, B. (2018) 'Economic freedom, income inequality and life satisfaction in OECD Countries', *Journal of Happiness Studies*, 19: 2071–2093.

Piketty, T. (2014) *Capital in the 21st Century*, London: Belknap/Harvard University Press.

Stiglitz, J. (2012) *The Price of Inequality*, London: W. W. Norton & Company.

Wilkinson, R. and Pickett, K. (2010) *The Spirit Level: Why Equality Is Better for Everyone*, London: Penguin Books.

Part III

Free markets, virtues and happiness

8

Virtue ethics and care ethics

Although utilitarianism, rights ethics and justice ethics apply different criteria to judge the value of market institutions, there are important similarities. In particular, both utilitarianism, rights ethics and the ethics of justice give ethical standards to judge the moral value of certain actions or institutions. The goal of these ethical theories is to identify and defend some fundamental principle (for example, utility or the categorical imperative) that can serve as the foundation for all morality.

However, one can question whether these principles will be able to move economic agents to specific acts that are required by the principle. The theories discussed in Parts I and II remain silent about the moral qualities of the agent that are required to perform good actions.[1] They give answer to the question 'What should I do?' while disregarding the question 'What kind of person should I be?' Even if principles would give us unambiguous advice, the motivational question remains: 'Why should I act in accordance with the principle?' Principles are distinct from the people who are to use them. There is a gap between the person and the principles or rules to be adopted and applied. If one disregards this gap, attempts to institutionalize ethical responsibility by appeal to a principle are likely to fail (Desjardins, 1984). Only if people learn to internalize these ethical principles by developing a good moral character can the principles function in daily reality. This is the subject of virtue ethics.

There are also economic reasons that stress the importance of individual qualities of agents to behave in an ethical way. On an individual level, economic agents may fail to see all relevant consequences of their acts, and their decisions may therefore result in consequences they do not like. On a social level, external effects may create prisoners' dilemmas that hamper an optimal social outcome if economic agents behave in an opportunistic self-interested way. Commitment both to inner values and to social values may help the individual to internalize these individual and social externalities. That requires the development of individual and social virtues. If we evaluate the market, we should therefore also consider its effects on virtues.

In this chapter we consider virtue ethics and the ethics of care. In Section 8.1 we first characterize virtue ethics. Then we discuss the virtue theories of Aristotle and Adam Smith in Sections 8.2 and 8.3, respectively. As most virtue ethics theories take their inspiration from Aristotle, his theory is a logical starting point for describing and explaining virtue ethics. However, as Aristotle's socioeconomic world was a very different one from ours, his framework and concerns can be difficult to grasp and apply in the modern world without either a major effort in translation or drastic simplification. Whereas Adam Smith was

DOI: 10.4324/9781003181835-11

working within the extended virtue ethical tradition that began with Plato and Aristotle and was particularly indebted to Aristotle, his virtue ethics is more familiar with modern economics (McCloskey, 2006), since he was also an enlightenment philosopher concerned with integrating that tradition with liberal individualism. What makes Smith particularly apt for application to economic life is that he himself saw and described the appearance of a commercial society characterized by an enormously increased division of labor, formal property rights and individual mobility. Section 8.4 describes recent theories of virtues of MacIntyre (1985), Bruni and Sugden (2013), and McCloskey (2006) that have been developed in the context of a modern market economy and are therefore even more directly applicable to the evaluation of current market institutions. Section 8.5 closes with the ethics of care, which has some similarities with virtue ethics, but has its own focus.

8.1   CHARACTERISTICS OF VIRTUES

Virtue ethics considers the cultivation of virtuous traits of character as the primary function of morality. Whereas utilitarianism and deontological theories provide general guides to actions, the aim of virtue ethics is that people cultivate a tendency to virtuous conduct. Acts are the results of the inner reality of persons. A virtuous action is an act performed by a virtuous person. When one strives for good acts, one should concentrate on being a good person. Virtue ethics asks what kind of person I ought to be. A good person is a person of character who exhibits several virtues in his behavior.

Virtues are character traits that are socially valued, such as patience, attentiveness, concern, humility, honesty, integrity, self-control and the like. Or, in the words of Bruni and Sugden (2013), virtues are acquired character traits or human dispositions that are judged to be good. Virtues go deeper than mere behavior and habits (although this may be important for their development), as they are constitutive of how a person perceives situations and reasons for actions. Virtues can be moral but also non-moral (Beauchamp, 1982). Admirable traits such as calmness and competitiveness are virtues and socially valued, but they are not moral virtues.

What is a moral virtue? Velasquez (1998) defines a (moral) virtue as an acquired disposition that is socially valued as part of the character of a morally good human being exhibited in the person's habitual behavior. This definition has several elements.

- Disposition: A virtue is a tendency. For example, we could say that a person possesses the virtue of honesty if he or she is not inclined to lie, steal, cheat, deceive or break promises.
- Acquired: A moral virtue is praiseworthy in part because it is an achievement. According to Aristotle, virtues are learned through a tedious process of trial and error. We are not born virtuous, but must be trained so that virtuous activity becomes habitual, just as we must be trained in other skills. Its development requires effort. For example, the virtue of courage or temperance is only acquired after training oneself or being trained by others, especially during one's youth, by a good upbringing by parents and education at school. The ends of activities are what people are after, but in order to obtain them, they need to practice and solidify habits of conduct (Burbidge, 2016). Everybody should try to develop virtues so that they become second nature.

- Socially valued: A third element inherent in the definition of virtue is the notion of a moral standard or code against which behavior can (and should) be measured. This is in line with the definition of virtues by Webster (1989) as "conformity of one's life and conduct to moral and ethical principles".
- Morally good human: An action obtains its moral merit if it is done from a good motive. The reason why the person acted is crucial: persons who act in a virtuous way but intensely dislike considering the interests of others should be judged deficient in virtue. A morally well-constituted individual cultivates virtues not as rules of thumb for moral action, but because of the kind of person she is or wants to be. The habitual performance of virtuous acts can eventually instill a disposition to choose them in harmony and with pleasure, resulting in the ability to act from intrinsic motivation. In contrast to Kant's philosophy, virtue ethics implies that acting out of duty is not sufficient. Being moved by natural sympathy, rather than obligation, is clearly virtuous, yet it has no clear moral place in Kant's philosophy.
- Person's habitual behavior: The possession of a virtue is supposed to generate an identifiable pattern of virtuous behavior. If so, virtue ethics helps us understand how people get from knowing what is right to doing the right thing (Heath, 2014). A virtuous disposition does not exclude that a person will make faults in extreme circumstances: none of us is unfailingly good. One deed of anger does not make a virtuous person nasty.

Vices

The acquirement of virtues is necessary because every person has a natural tendency to do wrong (vices). If one is optimistic about the natural capacity of human beings to do well, there is no need for the struggle to become virtuous. Virtue ethics assumes that human beings do not have a spontaneous will to be good, neither to themselves nor to others. Any person is open to evil seductions, and succumbing to these seductions makes that person or other people unhappy. The evil caused by vices tends to escalate and can destroy one's life and that of others and turn harmony into chaos, fighting, quarrels and war. Human beings are, however, not powerless. They can take up the challenge and fight back, be alert when seductions occur and develop good habits that regulate their behavior.

In Western literature, seven core vices – natural tendencies to do wrong – are distinguished (Kinneging, 1998). This list of seven main vices had a long history (Linssen, 2019). Over time, changes occurred in the composition of the list. The most influential list came from Gregory the Great (540–604). But it was not until the thirteenth century that the list of seven main vices really took off. The two that received the most attention were greed and haughtiness. A well-known painting in which the seven vices are depicted is attributed to Hieronymus Bosch (1450–1516).

The list that slowly but surely came to dominate consisted of the following vices. (1) Haughtiness is a misplaced self-confidence that denies one's own weakness and vulnerability. Related vices are pride, arrogance, conceitedness and self-complacency. (2) Greed is excessive wanting to obtain property and is related to holding on to property (avarice or austerity). It is a preoccupation with making money or an extreme reluctance to part with it. Everything is counted in terms of money. Greed also induces other types of non-honorable behavior, like flattery (in order to earn money), theft, fraud, extortion and blackmail, and it only values things insofar as they generate money. (3) Voluptuousness is unlimited sexual lust. Potential adverse effects caused by sexual misconduct are unwanted pregnancies, sexual diseases, assault, rape, unfaithfulness, quarrels, divorces, loneliness and seclusion. (4) Anger (and related vices like rancor, resentment and wrath) has many faces. It can be expressed if a person fires up in an instant. A furious person who has lost his mind can be very dangerous and can inflict great violence on other persons. Anger can also remain hidden in the form of rancor and resentment that slowly poisons the social relationship. It may arise if one feels that others unjustly harm one or if one feels insulted, humiliated or despised. Although one cannot blame such a person for being angry, such anger becomes a vice if it is disproportional to the harm suffered. (5) Gluttony is voracious use of food and drink. Although this vice seems less important than the other vices, it may cause great harm to the bodily and spiritual health. Instead of being in control of one's own body, the body will control the mind when it gets used to huge amounts of food and/or drink. (6) Envy (jealousy) is the displeasure about the success or happiness of others. It is related to malicious pleasure in the misfortunes of others. Envy is not only engendered by material things. It can be caused by many other attributes or qualities of other people, like beauty, power, virtues, love, status, education, etc. Envy only arises if the envying person compares herself or himself with another person of which she or he is jealous. (7) Indolence means that a person experiences a kind of emptiness. She is not interested in anything and lacks the capacity to rejoice, to be sad or angry. Related terms are inertness, laziness, slovenliness and apathy. This apathy may not only concern others but may also affect the interest in one's own life, which can express itself by slovenliness. These seven vices were perceived to be the 'mothers' of other vices. For example, cruelty, unfaithfulness and snobbery are vices too, but they are 'daughters' of the seven classical vices. For example, unfaithfulness may be caused by greed.

8.2   THE VIRTUE ETHICS OF ARISTOTLE

The source of the ethics of virtues is to be found in the classical Hellenistic tradition represented by Plato and Aristotle. According to Aristotle, ethics is the study of how to live well as an individual, whereas politics is the study of how to live well as a community. Both topics can only be studied within the context of society. In contrast to Plato, who argued that the standards for goodness are transcendental, Aristotle followed an inductive approach. His biological studies made him believe that any being has a certain end. This end is immanently present in the being.

Aristotle uses the word 'telos' to refer to the end or good toward which a thing is moving. "If there is some end of everything that is pursued in action, this will be the good pursued in action. . . . An end pursued in itself, we say, is more complete than an end pursued because of something else" (Aristotle, *Ethica Nicomachea*: 33). For human beings, the 'telos' is well-being or happiness (*eudaimonia*). "Now happiness more than anything else seems unconditionally complete, since we always choose it because of itself, never because of something else" (Aristotle, *Ethica Nicomachea*: 34). It is intrinsically good.

In Aristotle's view, a human being is happy if she or he performs activities of the soul that express excellence or virtue. Only if a good person performs actions in accordance with standards of excellence will she or he become happy. For example, a harpist will be happy if she plays excellently. The word for virtue in Greek is 'arete', a word that is close in meaning to 'goodness' or 'excellence'. The virtue of a human is a state that makes a human being good and makes her perform her function well. Happiness is not a quality of the character itself.

Aristotle distinguishes between two sorts of virtues: the virtues of thought and the virtues of character. The virtues of thought are the practical and theoretical intellect that arises from teaching and experience (Aristotle, *Ethica Nicomachea*: 55). Practical intellect is about the praxis: How should I act in concrete situations in a way that contributes to a successful life? The theoretical intellect is not related to the praxis. It is the intelligence that is required to distinguish between true and false to obtain scientific knowledge.

The virtues of character are the ethical virtues. Aristotle argues that virtues arise as a result of habit: we become just by doing just actions, temperate by doing temperate actions, brave by doing brave actions.[2] Hence, we must display the right activities, because differences in these imply corresponding differences in the qualities of character. This generates an interesting spiral: good actions generate a good character, and a good character makes it easier to do good actions. This also implies that human beings are responsible for their character. Hence, if one obtains, after a long series of bad actions, a bad character and therefore becomes insensitive or ignorant of what is good, one is still responsible for one's bad actions (Aristotle, *Ethica Nicomachea*: 91, 94). The importance of habit formation further implies that one cannot change overnight from a bad person into a good person. As one's character changes only slowly, it is not possible to stop being bad. Although one initially has a choice between doing good or bad actions, once one is used to doing bad actions, it is not possible not to be a bad person anymore, according to Aristotle.

Aristotle mentions several virtues of character. The common characteristic of the virtues of character is that they keep a middle ground between the vice of going too far and the vice of not going far enough in one's actions (see Table 8.1). In each situation one must take stock of what is required. The mean is what an intelligent person would find reasonable. The quality of character tends to be ruined by excess or deficiency.

Regarding feelings, courage is the virtue that holds the middle ground between the vice of cowardice and the vice of recklessness in case of danger or war. To be courageous is to have an appropriate recognition of danger and risk and to be willing to confront that danger

TABLE 8.1
Virtues of character as a middle ground of vices[a]

	Vice (shortage)	*Virtue (middle ground)*	*Vice (excess)*
Feelings			
Daring	Cowardice	Courage	Recklessness
Pleasure	Austerity	Temperance	Gluttony
Anger	Inertness	Self-possession	Anger
Emotions	Malicious pleasure at the misfortunes of others	Indignation	Envy
Praxis			
Giving	Avarice	Generosity	Extravagance
Status	Humility	High-spiritedness	Haughtiness
Exchange	Injustice	Justice	Injustice

[a] Aristotle describes some other virtues, as well as variants of some of the virtues.

and risk (Brennan and Jaworski, 2016). If someone is afraid of everything, she or he becomes cowardly, but if one is afraid of nothing at all, she or he becomes rash. Temperance is the middle ground with respect to the feelings of pleasure of taste that human beings share with animals. Temperance holds the middle ground between the vice of austerity and the vice of gluttony. People of temperance enjoy the right things and take the right quantity. When they lack some food or drink, they do not get dissatisfied, or at least not more than is appropriate. Only temperate people have the ability to become happy, because the longing for pleasure is insatiable. Therefore, our desires must be tempered and be low in number and consistent with reason. Self-possession is the mean between inertness and anger or quick temper. Indignation concerns our feelings with respect to the pleasure and pain of other people. People who are justly indignant take offense at the undeserved success or undeserved pain of other people. People who are envious take offense at any success of other people. Malicious people chuckle over the undeserved pain of other people.

Regarding praxis, generosity is the mean between avarice and extravagance. Avaricious persons devote too much attention to their property. On the other hand, extravagant people squander their property. Generous persons do not give with aversion. They give with pleasure the right amount to the right people. They will also not be inclined to acquire property in an unjust way, because they are not so much concerned with getting rich. On the other hand, generous persons will not waste their property either, because they want to use it to serve other persons. Because of their generous attitude, generous people will not easily become rich (Aristotle, *Ethica Nicomachea*: 114). Avaricious persons take what they can get – more than is appropriate. In order to earn money, they are even prepared to lose a good reputation. Although extravagant people are less depraved than avaricious persons, they, too, run a risk of becoming corrupt. As they like to spend too much, they often need more money than they can earn in an honest way. With respect to prestige, the mean is high-spiritedness or appropriate proudness, whereas the excess is haughtiness and the deficiency is humility. In this respect, the virtue ethics of Aristotle differs from Christian ethics, which views humility as a virtue. The virtue of justice is the middle ground between suffering injustice from and doing injustice to another person. Justice means respecting equality. Aristotle distinguishes between two concepts of equality: proportional equality (distributive justice) and arithmetical equality according to which the value of an effort and the compensation for this effort should be exactly equal (compensatory or retributive justice). In the case of distributions, justice is a virtue that induces a just person not to take too much for himself and not to leave too little for others (Aristotle, *Ethica Nicomachea*: 159). In cases of transactions, justice is an attitude of paying the price that is exactly equal to the value of the good. An unjust person willingly causes harm to another person.

Aristotle's virtue ethics versus utilitarianism

Although Aristotle's ethics focuses on virtues, it is, in some respects, reminiscent of utilitarianism, because it is consequentialist in nature, as virtues are considered to be essential to bring about the human good. The utilitarian standard approves of those acquired desires because it promotes the general happiness. Only when virtues would become injurious to the general happiness will utilitarianism disclaim its acquirement. For example, self-sacrifice by a hero deserves admiration if it contributes to the overall happiness by benefiting others. If not, it deserves no more admiration than the ascetic mounted on his pillar: He may be an astonishing proof of what men can do, but is not an example of what they should do, according to utilitarianism (Mill, 1871, 2:16).

Another similarity with utilitarianism is that Aristotle defines the good as 'happiness'. Also the utilitarianist John Stuart Mill (1871) believed that happiness and virtue are closely connected. In his view, virtue is an ingredient of happiness. Those who desire virtue for its own sake desire it because of the enjoyable experience of being virtuous or acting virtuously.

However, there are also several differences between utilitarianism and the virtue ethics of Aristotle. First, Aristotle does not have a principle that requires maximizing utility.

Second, he does not regard human happiness as consisting of the satisfaction of desires, as some forms of utility theory (the formal theory of well-being) do. Rather, he interprets happiness as an objective end that follows from the nature of humans and their ontological structure. Since all living beings strive after pleasure, Aristotle believed that the highest end of human beings is a kind of pleasure. Pleasure is so naturally connected to the emotions and desires of people that it cannot be wrong, as anti-hedonists sometimes argue. Pleasure is, however, not limited to bodily pleasure from sex, food and drink (which are only temporary in nature, as long as one is hungry or thirsty) but also comprises more enduring pleasures from activities like studying, writing or playing music. In Aristotle's view, the latter are more honorable and good, whereas the other types of desire – money, profit, victories and status and the bodily pleasures – are good as such, but only if one wants them in a moderate degree (Aristotle, *Ethica Nicomachea*: 218). Only vicious people who act unreasonably go too far in striving after this type of pleasure. Hence, in contrast to economists who assume individual sovereignty and reject any normative judgment about the value of various preferences of individuals, Aristotle stressed a certain hierarchy in different types of pleasures. The good that humans seek is therefore not singular or commensurable, but plural. Because the essence of the human being consists of activities of the soul that obey reason (logos) – reason clearly distinguishes mankind from other beings – understanding is the highest good. In contrast to other types of pleasures, knowledge is durable and creates independency. Even if the circumstances are unfavorable and make it impossible to have everything that contributes to happiness (like a noble descent, good friends, wealth, children, health, beauty and power), the virtue of thought makes a person independent, because intelligent persons find their own value in themselves.

Another difference between the virtue theory of Aristotle and utilitarianism is that Aristotle stresses the intention of acts (although in a different way as Kant does, see Section 8.1). An act is only virtuous if the acting person has a certain steady inner attitude when acting. In particular, one must know what one does and must deliberately choose for what one does and choose the act because of the act itself. An act is therefore only just if it is performed by a just person (Aristotle, *Ethica Nicomachea*: 61). In contrast, utilitarianism only considers the consequences of the act. Given the outcome of the act, the intention of the act does not matter.

A fourth difference between utilitarianism and the virtue ethics of Aristotle is a stronger focus on communal relationships. The framework of reference of Aristotle's virtue ethics is the continuity of the community, which exists at different levels within all functioning human groups. When Aristotle touched on a question of economy, he therefore aimed at developing its relationship to society as a whole. At the family level, the community consists of the household (oikos). The final goal of household management is not only to secure the material well-being and continuity of the household but also to contribute to the wider community. Together the households form the community of the village (polis), whereas the state is the complete association of several villages. While both the individual household and the larger political orders aim at some good, the association that is the most sovereign of all and embraces all the other aims is the state. "It is by nature a thing prior to the household and to each of us individually, for the whole must be prior to the part" (Aristotle, *Politics*, book I.2: 1253a20). The management of the household (oikonomia) is subjected to the politics and should serve the good life of the community. Anything that is needed to continue and maintain the community, including its self-sufficiency, is intrinsically right. Also wealth is a means, necessary for the maintenance of the household and the wider community. Exchange, facilitated by the use of money as a medium of exchange, is sometimes necessary to satisfy the natural requirement of self-sufficiency. But trade is only right when it contributes to the community's self-sufficiency by correcting shortages and surpluses and is done from a virtuous attitude, expressing itself in a behavior of retributive justice (paying just prices) and distributive justice (taking a proportional share in the burdens of the community and sharing mutually in the benefits of the community). Usury and profit-making are not according to nature, because they happen at the expense of others and distort the community (Neusner, 1990).

Private property rights and virtues

Notwithstanding the priority of the community, Aristotle still prefers a system of private property rather than a system of common property, because private property rights prevent several vices. First, people are less inclined to take care of and develop the common property than their own private business. A system of common property would lead to laziness and disinclination to work, since each seeks to shift his work on to others. Aristotle thus endorses the utilitarian argument that private property is more productive than common property. Second, a community of goods is the root of social unrest and quarrelling. According to Aristotle, we see far more disputes between those who own and share property in common than we do among separate holders of possession. Because if they are unequal in their effort, "charges will inevitably be brought against those who enjoy or take a lot without doing much work by those who do more work but take less" (Aristotle, *Politics*, book II, 1263). Private property will not lead to those charges. Third, private property contributes to the virtue of liberality. It gives great pleasure to help and to do favor to others, and this happens when property is private. Where would be the possibility of sharing with others if no one possessed anything? A final reason to defend private property is that to regard something as one's own generates a lot of pleasure on its own.

Virtue ethics and sustainability: an extension of Aristotle's framework

Jordan and Kristjánsson (2017) argued that Aristotle's virtue ethics also provides a framework to address questions of how to live and flourish within a more sustainable world. Indeed, virtue ethics is well placed to consider sustainability as a way of life. Many of the principles considered integral to sustainability, such as temperance, self-command, benevolence and justice, are already considered virtues and promoted in virtue ethics. Also prudence or practical wisdom is essential when it comes to adjudicating the novel and complex ('wicked') problems presented by (lack of) sustainability.

Additionally, Jordan and Kristjánsson (2017) extended the Aristotelian virtue ethics with a new virtue that deals explicitly with the human relationship with nature, which they called 'harmony with nature'. This kind of virtue includes wondering at and rejoicing in nature, being anxious to preserve nature and not assuming one can always put a price on everything in the natural world. Wonder of the natural world is associated with feelings of aesthetic appreciation and delight and involves a sense of humility, e.g. of being part of the ecosystem that is larger than the self. It requires an understanding that nature is inextricably linked to society as a whole. In the Aristotelian framework that views virtues as the middle ground between the vice of going too far and the vice of not going far enough, harmony with nature can be interpreted as the virtuous mean between the deficient vice of a mechanistic, instrumental, non-ecological worldview and an excessive vice of a mindset of romantic aestheticism towards nature. Living according to this virtue will contribute to a sustainable development and ultimately to human flourishing.

8.3   THE VIRTUE ETHICS OF ADAM SMITH

Among economists, Adam Smith is widely viewed as the defender of an amoral, if not antimoral, economics in which individuals' pursuit of their private self-interest is converted by an 'invisible hand' into shared economic prosperity (see Chapter 1). This is often justified by reference to a select few quotations from *The Wealth of Nations*.

However, Adam Smith was not only an economist but also a philosopher. Besides *The Wealth of Nations* (WN), he wrote *The Theory of Moral Sentiments* (TMS). TMS is an impressive book that gives a brilliant account of the moral sentiments of people. Whereas in WN Smith seemed to argue that man is largely driven by self-interest, in TMS Adam Smith observed that people sympathize with other people. This divergence in views has become known as *Das Smith Problem* (Etzioni, 1988).

TMS is about two core concepts, propriety and sympathy, that provide the keys to, respectively, two questions: (1) What is proper behavior? and (2) What does proper behavior accomplish? The first question is a moral question that we will discuss in this section. The second question is a social-psychological question that we discuss in Chapter 9 where we discuss Smith's worldview. Often the borderline between moral concepts and social-psychological concepts is not very clear in TMS, because Adam Smith grounds his ethical theory on the psychosocial nature of man. Smith understands morality as something that is intrinsic to the human nature, a sense of propriety that is established by the phenomenon of sympathy. Mutual sympathy is a natural urge of human beings to relate their behavior and thought to others in order to gain praiseworthiness. By looking to themselves from the perspective of others, they develop an intersubjective set of moral values, virtues and norms: "It is thus that the general rules of morality are formed. They are ultimately founded upon experience of what, in particular instances, our moral faculties, our natural sense of merit and propriety, approve, or disapprove of" (Smith, 1759: 224).

Virtues

In contrast to what one would have expected, Smith is not a utilitarian who used a utilitarian concept of morality when he discusses propriety as a moral standard, but rather a virtue ethicist. In many cases, proper behavior refers to virtuous behavior in TMS. Smith argued that we approve of another man's feelings not as something useful, but as right (Smith, 1991 [1759]: 21).

In part VI of TMS Smith presents a systematic overview of his virtue ethics. He distinguishes four main virtues: prudence, self-command, benevolence and justice. The virtues of prudence are reminiscent of Aristotle's virtues of practical intellect, whereas the virtue of self-command links to Aristotle's virtues of temperance and courage. However, Smith's account of the virtues of justice and benevolence is quite different from Aristotle's virtues of justice and generosity. We first discuss the virtues of prudence and self-command. We next describe Smith's view of the virtues of benevolence and justice.

Prudence and self-command

The virtue of *prudence* aims at the pursuit of self-interest. The title of section I of part VI of the TMS (*Of the character of the individual so far as it affects his own happiness*) reflects the connection between self-interest and prudence. Prudence is superior reasoning and understanding by which one is capable of discerning the remote consequences of all one's actions (Smith, 1991 [1759]: 271). Or, in Smith's words, prudence is 'the careful and laborious and circumspect state of mind, ever watchful and ever attentive to the most distant consequence of every action . . . to procure the greatest goods and to keep off the greatest evils' (Smith, 1991 [1759]: 434). We can interpret prudence as the central virtue of economic man assumed in neoclassical economics, the *homo economicus* that is rational and self-interested.

The notion of prudence goes back to the Stoic philosopher Epicurus (a Greek philosopher living from 341 to 270 BC). According to Epicurus, the only purpose of the human being is happiness. Just like Jeremy Bentham, he defines happiness as the enjoyment of pleasure and the avoidance of pain. But Epicurus knows that after every indulgence in pleasure follows a double painful experience. Therefore, reason or prudence must guide our search for happiness. Reason teaches us that real happiness is fostered by an uninterrupted reflective life (Störig, 1990). According to Epicurus, prudence is the source of other virtues, like temperance, self-command, courage and justice. He argued that temperance is nothing but prudence with regard to pleasure. Fortitude enables us to do those things that prudence – good judgment – would advise in order to avoid greater evil. And justice is no more than discrete and prudent conduct with regard to our neighbors.

As already stated, Smith relates prudence to the character of the individual, so far as it affects her own happiness. As one grows up, one soon learns that some care and foresight are necessary for providing the means of procuring pleasure and avoiding pain. According to Smith, the happiness of a person depends on the fulfillment of three basic needs: health, fortune and status. In order to obtain these goals, the prudent man improves his skills, values assiduity and industry in his work and exercises soberness and parsimony in his expenditure. The prudent person always studies seriously and earnestly to understand things. She is cautious and does not expose her health, fortune or reputation to any sort of hazard. People who live in this way will, according to Smith, be contented with their situation, which, by continual though small accumulations, is growing better every day. The *homo economicus* is not avaricious. Rather, she or he walks the middle way between avarice and extravagance. As she or he grows richer, she or he is enabled gradually to relax, both in the rigor of soberness and in the severity of its application. From producer she or he gradually changes into consumer (Van Leeuwen, 1984).

The *homo economicus* combines prudence with self-command by which one is able to abstain from present pleasures or to endure present pain in order to obtain greater pleasures or to avoid a greater pain in some future time. Without self-command a person is not able to act in accordance with the rule of prudence. Both qualities are highly regarded in society and have a beauty in themselves, according to Smith, because few possess these qualities.

> Although the prudent man is in most cases motivated by the pursuit of his own interest, we not only approve in some measure of the conduct of the homo economicus, but also admire it and think it worthy of a considerable degree of applause.
>
> (Smith, 1991 [1759]: 273)

In this way, Smith has raised prudence to the highest virtue of the *homo economicus*. Together with self-command it comprises several lower virtues such as alertness, cautiousness, temperance, firmness, industry, entrepreneurship and efficiency.

Benevolence

Whereas prudence affects one's own happiness, the virtue of *benevolence* affects the happiness of other people, just as the subtitle of section II of part VI of TMS reflects (*Of the character of the individual, so far as it can affect the happiness of other people*). The virtue of prudence has priority over the virtue of benevolence: "Every man is, no doubt, by nature, first and principally recommended to his own care, and as he is fitter to take care of himself than of any other person, it is fit and right that it should be so" (Smith, 1991 [1759]: 119).

Adam Smith distinguished between several degrees of benevolence. After the care for oneself, one is naturally most concerned with the happiness of one's own family: children, parents, brothers and sisters are the objects of the warmest affections. People are more benevolent to their family than to strangers because they sympathize with them. A person simply knows his own family better than other people and how their feelings are affected by changing circumstances. Therefore, one's sympathy with them is more precise and determinate than it can be with the greater part of other people. It approaches nearer, in short, to what he feels for himself.

Next, Smith mentioned friends, colleagues and people living in the same neighborhood. Smith explained this affection as nothing but habitual sympathy for the sake of convenience and accommodation. There is a great deal of mutuality or reciprocity in this kind of relation. We are particularly beneficent to those whose beneficence we have ourselves already experienced. Third comes the benevolence to the persons who receive our benevolent attention by their great fortunate position. We are fascinated by their greatness and respect them for their fortune.

Finally comes the benevolence to the greatly unfortunate, the poor and the wretched. It is the effect of the sympathy which we feel with the misery and resentment of those sensible human beings whose happiness is disturbed by their malice. This kind of benevolence is closely related to the concept of universal benevolence that is the subject of the last part of section II of part VI in TMS. Indeed, the good will is not bounded to people living in our neighborhood or country, but may embrace the whole universe. We cannot think of any innocent person or child whose misery we would not desire to be lifted. Still, this kind of noble and generous benevolence plays a relatively small role according to Adam Smith.

Because of the imperfection of men, they are unable to act according to the motive of universal benevolence. As Smith states:

> The care of the universal happiness of all rational and sensible being, is the business of God and not of man. To man is allocated a much humbler department . . . the care of his own happiness, that of his family, his friends, his country."
>
> (Smith, 1991 [1759]: 348)

Justice

Of more importance in Smith's account of the virtues is the virtue *of justice*. Smith described justice as a sacred regard not to hurt or disturb in any respect the happiness of our neighbor (Smith, 1991 [1759]: 319). People feel themselves to be under a stricter obligation to act according to justice than to be benevolent. Smith defended the priority of justice over benevolence by explaining that society cannot subsist if people are unjust and ready to hurt and injure each other. If benevolence does not exist, society may subsist, though maybe not in the most comfortable state. If mutual love and affection are lacking, society will not be dissolved. But if injury begins and mutual resentment grows, a society will break down and its different members will be dissipated by the violence of their discordant affections.

In order to enforce the observation of justice, nature has provided people with a strong sense of shame and horror when they are found to violate the laws of justice. This is a much surer way of safeguarding the association of mankind than feelings of benevolence. As Smith stated:

> Men, though naturally sympathetic, feel so little for another with whom they have no particular connection, in comparison of what they feel for themselves . . . they have it so much in their power to hurt him and so many temptations to do so, that if this principle (of justice) did not stand up within them in his defense, they would like wild beasts, be at all times ready to fly upon him.
>
> (Smith, 1991 [1759]: 125)

Corruption of morality and utility

According to Smith's virtue ethics, only the intention of actions should be judged as proper or improper, because the consequences of the actions are not only dependent on the intention of the actor but are also determined by luck or fortune. We should not blame a person who intends to do well, but whose actions turn out to be harmful for others because of intervening influences beyond his control. "Everybody agrees to the general maxim, that as the event does not depend on the agent, it ought to have no influence upon our sentiments, with regard to the merit or propriety of his conduct" (Smith, 1991 [1759]: 152).[3]

Still, Smith acknowledged an irregularity or corruption in our moral judgments in the sense that in reality we also tend to praise or blame people for the unintended consequences of their choices. People tend to develop sentiments of gratitude towards persons from whom they receive benefits and sentiments of resentment towards persons who harm them, even if these persons did not intend these favorable or harmful consequences. Whereas Smith convicted this way of judging, he also gave a utilitarian defense of this human inclination. In particular, he argued that nature has implanted this irregularity in the human breast in order to foster the happiness and perfection of mankind: if we would only reward good intentions or punish bad intentions and disregard the consequences of actions, we would easily make judgment errors because we cannot look into the hearts of people. If the intention of actions would be the sole criterion for judging the moral value of the action, every court of jurisdiction would become an inquisition. Another reason for this corruption of moral sentiments is that the irregularity of sentiments contributes to economic welfare. Man was made for action and to promote by the exertion of his faculties such changes in the external circumstances as may seem most favorable to the happiness of all. Thus, utility considerations affect the judgment of the propriety of the actions of others.

Besides, Smith acknowledged another corruption of the human capacity to judge the propriety of actions or feelings of other persons, namely that mankind is disposed to sympathize more with the rich than with the poor. Smith explained the usefulness of this corruption by arguing that it provides an important motive to pursue riches and avoid poverty. Rich people enjoy their riches, not because of the high consumption level, but because they feel that their riches naturally draw upon them the attention of the world and that other persons are disposed to sympathize with them. The disposition to admire the rich and the powerful and to despise or, at least to neglect, persons of poor and mean condition, is, according to Smith, the greatest and most universal cause of the corruption of our moral sentiments. We see frequently that the respectful attention of the world is more directed towards the rich and the great than towards the wise, the virtuous and the humble. The vanity of the former is much more admired than the real and solid merit of the latter. However, again Adam Smith defended this corruption of the moral sentiments by utilitarian considerations. Although this corruption of moral sentiments is strictly wrong from a virtue point of view, Nature has implanted this corruption in the human breast with the purpose to increase human happiness. It uses this corruption of moral sentiments in order to stimulate mankind to exploit their talents. It motivates man to cultivate the land, to build houses and cities, to improve the sciences and arts that improve and beautify human life. Moreover, this disposition of mankind to sympathize with the passions of the rich and the powerful grounds the order of society and distinction of ranks. The order of society is not dependent on the virtuousness of people, but on the plain difference of fortune.

Summary

The virtue ethics of Adam Smith is rather complex because it combines deontological ethics and virtue ethics with utilitarianism. First, just as Kant, Smith attaches a high value to the intentions of actions, which is reminiscent to the Kantian idea of the categorical imperative. Second, Smith's exposition of virtue ethics shows similarities to the virtue ethics of Aristotle and communitarianism (discussed in Chapter 11). On the other hand, Smith also defended divergences from a '*Gesinnungsethic*' and virtue ethics by applying utilitarian considerations: the corruption of the moral sentiments has positive consequences for society's welfare and contributes to its overall happiness in the long run.

8.4   MODERN VIRTUE ETHICS: MACINTYRE, BRUNI AND SUGDEN, McCLOSKEY

In this section we discuss three modern theories of virtues that present opposing views of the role of virtues in a market society. First, we will discuss MacIntyre's virtue ethics that centers on the concept of practices. We confront this view with Bruni and Sugden, who defend a market-oriented virtue ethics. Lastly, we describe virtue ethics of McCloskey.

Virtue ethics of MacIntyre

In a famous book, *After Virtue, A Study in Moral Theory*, Alisdair MacIntyre (1985) built on the ideas of Aristotle and gave an original view on virtues. MacIntyre approaches virtue theory by using a few technical terms, the most important of which are 'practice' and 'internal good'. Our various social roles involve practices in business and other types of organizations (chess, physics, medicine, etc.). MacIntyre defines a practice as any complex form of socially established cooperative human activity through which goods internal to that form of activity are realized in the course of trying to achieve those standards of excellence, which are appropriate to that activity. Goods internal to these practices cannot be obtained but by participating in the practice. For example, an internal good of doctors in hospitals is a good medical diagnosis. Goods external to the practice are goods that can be obtained independent from the practice, like prestige among colleagues, financial rewards, job security and the like. These goods are external because they may be achieved by many alternative ways not related to the practice and are objects of competition.

But what does this have to do with the concept of virtue? MacIntyre gives the following definition of a virtue. A virtue is an acquired human quality, the possession and exercise of which tends to enable us to achieve those goods that are internal to practices, such as playing chess or teaching at school, that have internal rules of the game and internal standards of doing well, of 'excellence' (MacIntyre, 1985: 191). Each practice has a history that sustains a tradition and requires the participants to cultivate certain virtues. In relation to a given domain, an acquired character trait is a virtue to the extent that the person who possesses it is thereby better able to contribute to the ends of that domain. Virtuous people are oriented towards their various activities in ways that respect the intrinsic ends of the domains to which those activities belong. Practices cannot flourish in societies in which the required virtues (such as truthfulness, justice, and courage) are absent.

Box 8.1   MacIntyre's virtue theory and cosmetic surgery

In this box, we illustrate MacIntyre's virtue ethics with cosmetic surgery. For the practice of cosmetic surgery, several virtues are required, which can be illustrated by the example of Suzanne Noel, a famous female cosmetic surgeon (Davis, 2000). A first characteristic is dedication. Suzanne Noel excelled in her medical studies. She gained much experience in operating on wounded soldiers during the First World War. She became particularly interested in cosmetic surgery when one of her first facelift operations on a woman, who was not able to earn her own living, was so successful that the patient was immediately able to find a job. After this experience, Noel decided to make cosmetic surgery her vocation. In 1928 she was awarded for being a doctor of unusual skill. Another virtue is courage. She started her experiments by pinching the skin of her own face to see what effect she could get. She was forced to practice surgery in her home, as female surgeons were not admitted to hospitals. At a time when women were struggling to gain acceptance in the medical profession, Noel won considerable recognition in her work: Noel was the world's first female cosmetic plastic surgeon. A third virtue is transparency and honesty. Noel wrote a widely read book about cosmetic surgery, and physicians from all over the world visited her to observe her work. She traveled extensively and demonstrated her surgical techniques. Her book showed that she wanted to help colleagues to perform operations in such a way that the best possible result would be achieved. Her goal was to teach rather to stake out her own field. She also provides photographs of her own less-than-satisfactory results and was ready to admit that her work was experimental without quite knowing what she was getting. She thus shows the virtue of modesty about one's own accomplishments. A fourth virtue is care for the patients. Noel saw her vocation as a way to help women to support themselves. Her patients came to her because they were afraid of losing their jobs as their faces begin to show the first signs of age. Noel was a feminist and a strong advocate of women's right to work. She perceived cosmetic surgery as a matter of being able to choose one's own destiny. Her concern for the patients' well-being extended beyond the actual surgery and included advice that served the patient's return to home. A final virtue is respect for the client. The patient is present in her book as an active and knowledgeable participant in the surgery. Noel makes use of the patient's ideas of how the operation should be done. She never belittled nervous patients and acknowledged that patients may be often in a better position to decide whether an operation is necessary. This shows that she was averse to haughtiness. For Noel, patients were individuals with different needs and desires.

MacIntyre distinguished practices from institutions. Chess, physics and medicine are practices; chess clubs, laboratories and hospitals are institutions. They are characteristically concerned with external goods. They are involved in acquiring money and other material goods, and they distribute money, power and status as rewards. Institutions are necessary to sustain practices, but can also corrupt the ideals and creativity of the practices due to the acquisitiveness and competitiveness of institutions. Without virtues, practices cannot resist this corrupting power of institutions. Whereas the possession of the virtues is necessary to achieve internal goods, it may actually hinder people in achieving external goods.

Besides practices, MacIntyre also relates the notion of virtues to the good of the person. A person may participate in various practices and therefore needs an overriding concept of the good of a whole personal human life. In order to define this overriding concept of the good life, MacIntyre introduces a concept of the individual person whose unity resides in the unity of a narrative, which links birth to life to death as a narrative links beginning to middle to end. To be the subject of a narrative that runs from one's birth to one's death is to be accountable for the actions and experiences that compose a narratable life. The unity of a narratable life requires a unity in character that creates the personal identity. Without this continuity in the personal life, the actions of a person will look like a train of events that lacks intelligibility. To ask 'What is good for me?' is to ask how best I might live out that unity and bring it to completion. The virtues therefore are not only dispositions which will sustain practices and enable us to achieve the goods internal to practices but will also help us in the search for identity required to live out the unity of our life.

Box 8.2   Application of MacIntyre's virtue theory to banking

Graafland and Van de Ven (2011) applied MacIntyre's theory to the practice of banking. To identify the internal goods in the practice of banking and the virtues that financial professionals need to produce them, they studied codes of ethics and mission statements of financial institutions. From the mission statements of ten banks that belong to the biggest investment banks in the world, Graafland and Van de Ven conclude that the mission of banks is to serve the interests of customers by providing them with relevant financial products at competitive prices. An important internal good that banks claim they want to provide can therefore be defined as offering customers financial products that optimally meet their needs at competitive prices. Some of the mission statements (Goldman Sachs, Deutsche Bank) also explicitly mention service to shareholder interests as a mission. However, shareholder value is not specific to the practice of banking. Hence, we should classify this as an external good to banking.

To realize the internal goods, bankers need several virtues that are considered essential to providing good financial services to the customers. A review of the codes of conduct showed that the virtue of honesty (integrity) in particular (and the related virtues of transparency and openness) is generally perceived to be important for bankers. Deutsche Bank, for example, tells us on its corporate website that integrity and honesty are instrumental in gaining and keeping the trust of its stakeholders.

A second set of virtues that are typical of the banks that Graafland and Van de Ven investigated relates to due care for consumer interests. Examples are servitude, responsibility and (long-term) commitment. For example, the RABO bank ensures that it will create customer value by "providing those financial services considered best and most appropriate by our clients, ensuring the continuity of those services, with a view to the long-term interests of the client and by demonstrating our commitment to our clients and their environment, in ways that help them achieve both their personal, social, and economic ambitions". Although the virtue of due care is closely connected to the virtue of honesty, it presupposes a further responsibility of banks toward their clients. Whereas honesty and transparency are obvious moral duties of any contract, they assume that buyer and seller meet each other as equals in an agreement and are equally skilled to evaluate the quality of a product. This assumption is based on classical laissez-faire ideology that stresses 'caveat emptor' (let the buyer take care of himself). By contrast, the due care theory argues that sellers and buyers often do not meet as equals and that sellers that are in a more advantaged position have a duty to take special care of the buyer's interest in the design of the product and the instructions of how to use it (Velasquez, 1998). This is particularly relevant in the case of financial products that typically cover a long period of time (mortgages) and therefore involve complex intertemporal considerations most ordinary people are not well capable of assessing. This means that a supplier is morally negligent when others are harmed by a product in a way that the supplier could possibly have foreseen or prevented. A third set of virtues that are often mentioned in the business principles of banks concerns quality or accuracy. The Deutsche Bank states: "As a German global brand, a desire for accuracy, thoroughness and quality runs through our organization. We understand issues in depth. This is why we keep things simple and clear". Société Générale links quality to appropriate training and development of their employees: "We need to ensure continual management quality, capitalising on the expertise we possess today in order to maintain it into the future and guarantee our clients the same level of service". The virtues of quality and accuracy can be connected to the phenomenon of risk taking, in the sense that an accurate banker will only deal with products of which she or he has a thorough understanding of the risks involved. Professional bankers will aim to improve fortune by real skill in trade or profession and not by excessive risk taking. If they enter into new projects or enterprises, they are likely to be well-concerted and well-prepared. This link between accurateness and risk taking is nicely illustrated by J.P. Morgan & Co's statement that "To build a fortress balance sheet, we must thoroughly understand all our assets and liabilities".

Bruni and Sugden on market virtues

In a recent interesting article, Bruni and Sugden (2013) defended a view on virtue ethics that is quite opposite to MacIntyre's theory. They argued that character traits that best equip individuals to be successful in markets are not necessarily corrosive of the virtues that MacIntyre stressed. According to Bruni and Sugden, the virtues that are necessary to flourish in the marketplace are grounded on ideas of reciprocity and mutual benefit and include, for example, enterprise and alertness, respect for the tastes of one's trading partners, acceptance of competition and self-help.

MacIntyre's theory has strong undertones of Aristotelian hostility to markets, as he suggests that the corrupting tendencies of the market can be contained only to the extent that individuals are motivated by the internal ends of practices. An intrinsically motivated person does an activity for its inherent satisfaction rather than for external rewards. This would suggest an ideal of an economy in which everyone's actions and efforts are coordinated to realize gains from trade but in which no one is actually motivated to seek those gains. According to Bruni and Sugden, this ideal is profoundly unrealistic and excludes all ordinary market activities. It may actually lead to abuse of the virtuous person, since a person with such an intrinsic motivation would have a lower reservation wage for working as one that is only motivated by external goods. Intrinsic motivation might also insulate people from pressures to respond to the interests of the people to whom their services are being provided.

Bruni and Sugden argued that if we are to reconcile the ideas of virtue and authenticity with real economic life, we need a way of understanding market relationships that acknowledges that gains from trade are not realized because individuals seek them out. They link this idea to Smith's virtue of prudence that is associated with the pursuit of long-term self-interest. In their view, the purpose (telos) of markets is mutual benefit or gains from trade through voluntary transactions. Such transactions are morally valuable because individuals want to make them – they satisfy their preferences, create wealth and allow them a form of freedom. They therefore propose to treat mutual benefit as the telos of the market.

The compatibility of self-interested behavior and mutual benefit can be illustrated by a famous text in WN:

> It is not from the benevolence of the butcher, the brewer, or the baker, that we expect our dinner, but from their regard to their own interest. We address ourselves, not to their humanity but to their self-love, and never talk to them of our own necessities but of their advantages. Nobody but a beggar chuses to depend chiefly upon the benevolence of his fellow citizens.
>
> (Smith, 2000 [1776]: I.ii.2)

In this chapter, Smith argued that labor division is a major source of wealth, because it allows a dramatic increase in labor productivity. However, the division of labor makes people highly dependent on each other. If you specialize in one product, you need others for all the other products that one needs in life. Smith argued that it is in vain to expect this assistance from the benevolence of others. People are only benevolent to their family and friends, but much less so towards strangers. It would be much too uncertain to trust the benevolence of other people to help us meet our needs. Nobody but a beggar chooses to depend chiefly upon the benevolence of his fellow citizens. So what motivates people to assist others in fulfilling their needs? The answer that Smith gave is self-interest. The fact that we expect to receive a good bread from the baker at a fair price is not because we think that the baker wants to help us. No, just because the baker wants to earn an income for himself, he takes care that he produces good bread at a reasonable price, and that is how we will be served. When we buy bread, we gain utility from the bread and the baker receives utility from the money. Both the demand for and the supply of bread is motivated by self-interest, although the outcome of the transaction is mutual gain.

The function of market virtues is, according to Bruni and Sugden, to make an individual better able to contribute to the creation of mutual benefits through market transactions. For a virtuous market participant, mutual benefit is not just a fortunate by-product of the individual pursuit of self-interest: he or she intends that transactions with others be mutually beneficial. Bruni and Sugden provide the following list of such market virtues. First, universality – the disposition to make mutually beneficial transactions with others on terms of equality, whoever those others may be. This virtue promotes the widest possible network of mutually beneficial transactions as it opposes favoritism, familiarity, patronage and protectionism that create market barriers. Universality enables us to satisfy our economic needs in the marketplace with independence and self-respect. Second, enterprise and alertness in seeking out mutual benefit. Discovering and anticipating what other people want and are willing to pay for it is a crucial component of successful entrepreneurship. It requires empathy and imagination. The virtue of alertness also applies to the demand side of the market: consumers should be inclined to shop around, to compare prices and to experiment with new products and new suppliers to find the best opportunities for mutual benefit. Third, one is more likely to succeed in making mutually beneficial transactions if one is disposed to respect the preferences of potential trading partners and producing what customers want to buy. Fourth, efficient market operation requires the virtue of accepting competition. A virtuous trader will not obstruct competitors from pursuing mutual benefit in their transactions with clients and thus not seek to protect one's own business by barriers to entry or make agreements with other traders on the same side of the market to restrict supply or demand. Another virtue that befits the market context is the virtue of self-help. Within the practice of a market, the wants and aspirations of individuals are relevant to others only in so far as they can offer something that others are willing to accept in return. Thus, one should accept that others are merely motivated by the satisfaction of their own wants and that this is the only way to provide you with opportunities for self-realization. This attitude requires, furthermore, that people do not envy other people's gains. Instead, market participants should take pleasure in other people's gains, particularly those that have been created in transactions in which they were involved themselves. Finally, as market transactions often involve luck, one should not always expect to be rewarded according to one's deserts and not resent other people's undeserved rewards.

Remarkably, Bruni and Sugden seem to reject corporate social responsibility as a market virtue. Being concerned about externalities resulting from one's activities is not the business of individual market parties: the telos of the market is mutual benefit among the transaction parties, not mutual benefit among everyone in a society. It is the responsibility of governments to regulate markets in order to prevent or reduce externalities.

Finally, although Bruni and Sugden claim that their theory of virtue ethics is more realistic than the theory of MacIntyre, it is still a normative theory that prescribes an ideal that is by no means always realized in unruly reality. For example, where there is market concentration and inequality in market power, the creation of joint benefits is jeopardized. Trade barriers may weaken the respect for other market parties and competitors and reduce the motivation to innovate.

Bourgeois virtues: McCloskey

McCloskey's philosophy can be characterized as a libertarian version of Aristotelianism (McCloskey, 2006: 297). In a trilogy, McCloskey (2006, 2010, 2016) reflects on the question why Western countries are so rich. She argued that the enrichment of the world since 1800 (by a factor ranging from 30 to 100) cannot be explained by material matters or institutions, but rather by the rise of the ideology of European liberalism. An institution, such as the protection of property rights, works well not merely because of good rules, but mainly of the good ethics of the people. If a substantial minority of the people does not have the right kind of ethics, a country will be stuck by a badly functioning economy. The great wealth of the modern world is due to a skill in supplying without force or fraud what people are willing to buy. It is based on liberty for ordinary people and dignity for them, that means, on equality of respect and equality before the law. McCloskey claims that bourgeois life[4] has not excluded virtues. In fact, it often has nourished them. Besides the leading bourgeois virtue of prudence, actual businesspeople exhibited other virtues like love, justice, courage, hope, faith and temperance.

In her scheme of virtues, McCloskey combined three Christian virtues (love, hope, faith) and four classical virtues (courage, temperance, prudence, justice). Love refers to the commitment of the will to the true good of another. It is a disinterested concern for the well-being or flourishing of the person who is loved. Bourgeois love includes caring for employees, colleagues, customers and fellow citizens and to wish well of humankind. The virtue of faith integrates the known and the unknown into a living whole. It includes having faith in others and loyalty. Faith is a virtue, because it is a kind of spiritual courage, a willed steadfastness against contrary moods. Faith is also about identity, i.e. to see one's labor as a glorious calling. Hope is, in contrast to faith, forward-looking. It is related to imagination and optimism. It sees the future as something other than stagnation. It infuses the day's work with a purpose. It is the virtue of the energetic entrepreneur who seeks a future, difficult, but attainable good.

The other four virtues in the scheme of McCloskey mimic the virtues in Aristotle's scheme. Courage is associated with daring, steadfastness, endurance and autonomy. Courage overcomes the fear of change, is courteous to new ideas and resists despairing pessimism. Temperance is about individual balance and restraint, chastity and sobriety. Temperance induces people to save and accumulate, to educate oneself, but also to resist the temptation to cheat. McCloskey also reckons humility to the virtue of temperance. To be humble is to temper one's passions in pursuing goods difficult to achieve. It includes having a decent respect for the opinions of others and a selfless respect for reality. For a business person, humility implies listening closely to what customers want. Justice is about social balance and honesty. Justice insists on private property honestly acquired, to honor labor and pay willingly for good work, to break down privilege and to view other's success without envy. Prudence is about good judgment or practical wisdom, know-how, foresight, self-interest and rationality. It includes the alertness of business people to opportunities to buy low and sell high.

The system of seven virtues proposed by McCloskey is supported by psychological research by Peterson and Seligman (2004) (see also Dahlsgard et al., 2005). Examining philosophical and religious traditions in China (Confucianism and Taoism), South Asia (Buddhism and Hinduism) and the West (Athenian philosophy, Judaism, Christianity and Islam), they found a surprising amount of similarity across cultures that strongly indicates a historical and cross-cultural convergence of six core virtues: courage, justice, temperance, wisdom (prudence), humanity (love) and transcendence. They number them as six rather than seven (as McCloskey does), because they lump hope and faith together in one virtue named transcendence (defined as strengths that forge connections to the larger universe and thereby provide meaning; examples include gratitude, hope and spirituality).

In business practice, the bourgeois virtues, derivable from the seven core virtues, include enterprise, adaptability, imagination, optimism, integrity, prudence, thrift, trustworthiness, humor, affection, self-possession, consideration, responsibility, solicitude, patience, toleration, peaceability, civility, neighborliness, reputability, dependability and impartiality. Even love plays a role in business partnerships. A business contract cannot govern every detail of the relationship's functioning. A lack of commitment would undermine the self-giving required to establish the mutual benefits that cannot be included in the set of legally enforceable promises.

8.5   CARE ETHICS

As discussed in Section 8.2, one of the defining characteristics of the virtue ethics of Aristotle is its focus on communal relationships. The acknowledgement that people are part of a community and live in a web of relationships is most prominent in the so-called ethics of care. Concrete communities and communal relationships have a fundamental value that should be preserved and maintained. This implies that special relationships of loving and caring in concrete communities may override the ethical norm of impartiality that is characteristic for liberal theories like utilitarianism, rights and justice. Whereas utilitarianism counts the welfare of all individuals together, rights ethics and Kantianism imply that all people have basic rights and should be treated as an end in themselves. Also the ethical theory of justice argues that equals should be treated as equals, although it leaves some room for deciding who is equal and who is not. All these theories prescribe that we should have a neutral attitude towards other people. In reality, people often feel more responsible for particular persons, such as relatives, friends or one's employees, than for strangers. For example, a parent has more responsibility towards his or her own children than to the children of somebody else. Also, when we look to other cultures, we see that communities play a much more central role than individual liberty and equality. Utilitarianism and the ethics of duties, rights and justice, with their stress on equality, disregard these specific moral requirements that are related to our special and personal relationships with other people.

The ethics of care defines these moral requirements as follows (Velasquez, 1998):

1 We should preserve the concrete and valuable relationships we have with specific persons. Valuable relationships are relationships that exhibit virtues of compassion, concern, love, friendship and loyalty.
2 We should exercise special care for those who are vulnerable and dependent on our care.

Care ethics has a feminist background. Like virtue ethicists, care ethicists stress the importance of social virtues like caring, loving, trusting, gentleness and the like. By making room for an ethics of love and trust, the ethics of care gives an account of human bonding and recognizes that trust is a necessary condition for relationships of obligation.

Tensions with rights and justice theories

Another defining element of care ethics is that it stresses that many relations lack three central features as understood by Kantian and social contract theory: many relations are (1) not chosen, but given; (2) intimate rather than impersonal; and (3) between unequals rather than between equals. For example, parents do not choose their children (although they can choose to have children or not), and the relationship between parents and children is one of unequal power. Care ethicists therefore reject contractarian models which view people as autonomous and equal agents. The contractarian model fails to see that parents (or, for example, health professionals) should see their responsibilities to their children (or patients) not in terms of contracts, but rather in terms of care, needs and love.

Rather than universal principles prescribing general rules of moral duty, care responsibilities are developed and sustained in contextual-dependent relationships between concrete persons on the basis of needs arising from human vulnerability. The ethics of care is therefore sometimes criticized for possible degeneration into unjust favoritism that conflicts with the demands of justice. For example, whereas in Asian countries appointing family members in important business positions because of close family relations is acceptable, these practices are generally rejected in Western countries because it conflicts with fair opportunities. Alternatively stated, the ethics of care sets other standards for defining equality than utilitarianism and the ethics of justice: whereas the ethics of justice considers personal relationships to be an irrelevant criterion for distinguishing different applicants, it is not according to the ethics of care. There is no fixed rule how to solve such conflicts between justice and care ethics. If the injustice is very small, the obligation to care for close relations should dominate. But if the injustice is substantial, an impartial judgment is more suitable. It also depends on the culture and the context of the decision or institution which degree of favoritism is acceptable.

Another tension between the ethics of care and the theories described in Parts I and II is that the ethics of care may easily become paternalistic, whereas the other theories stress individual autonomy. Paternalism can be defined as the limitation of the autonomy of a person, in which the person who limits the autonomy of another appeals exclusively to grounds of protection for the person whose autonomy is limited (Beauchamp, 1982). Since the ethics of care is especially concerned with relationships of dependency and vulnerability, there is some danger that the care may become paternalistic. For example, family companies sometimes have a hierarchal and paternalistic decision structure, in which employees have little access to strategic background information and democratic structures are weak. Often this paternalistic structure goes together with an attitude of good care for the workers, showing itself in good pension arrangements, lifetime employment and high salaries, which can be interpreted as a kind of profit sharing. In return, employees are expected to be loyal to the family and committed to the company. Anti-paternalistic philosophers would reject such paternalism, because it violates individual rights and unduly restricts free choice. They find any paternalistic power of the state or any class of individuals in a position of authority unacceptable, because the rightful authority resides in the individual who is being controlled.

NOTES

1   It should be acknowledged that Rawls (1999a) does pay attention to the personal dimension of ethical behavior. In particular, he assumes that when his principles of justice are satisfied in a certain society, people will also develop a corresponding sense of justice because they realize that the principles contribute to their good. Thus, the principles of justice will create a stable situation in the sense that once they are respected in the real society, people will continue to adhere to them. Rawls thinks that the motivation to act in accordance with the utilitarian principle is too weak because this principle requires that persons be perfectly able to identify and intrinsically value the interests of other people.

2   Besides education, habit formation and natural inclination, Aristotle also acknowledges the value of the external pressure from a good and reasonable government law to induce people to good behavior.

3   Also Hume, in his *A Treatise of Human Nature*, argued that when we praise any actions, we regard only the motives that produced them. The external performance has no merit. Hume thinks virtues are motivational structures that can be inferred from the person's actions, whose presence produces a pleasing sentiment of approbation in an impartial spectator (Beauchamp, 1982).

4   By bourgeoisie, McCloskey means the middle class of entrepreneurs and merchants, big or small in their capital.

Recommended literature

Aristotle, *Ethica Nicomachea*, Groningen: Historische Uitgeverij.

Bruni, L. and Sugden, R. (2013) 'Reclaiming virtue ethics for economics', *Journal of Economic Perspectives*, 27: 141–164.

Jordan, K. and Kristjánsson, K. (2017) 'Sustainability, virtue ethics, and the virtue of harmony with nature', *Environmental Education Research*, 23(9): 1205–1229.

MacIntyre, A. (1985) *After Virtue: A Study in Moral Theory*, London: Duckworth.

McCloskey, D.N. (2006) *Bourgeois Virtues: Ethics for an Age of Commerce*, Chicago: The University of Chicago Press.

Smith, Adam (1759) *The Theory of Moral Sentiments*, New York: Prometheus Books.

9

Adam Smith on markets, virtues and happiness

In the literature on the relationships between market institutions, virtues, and human happiness, two debates have attracted the attention of philosophers and economists. First, there is a long and ongoing dispute over whether free market institutions encourage or discourage civic virtues (Fourcade and Healy, 2007). Civic virtues can be defined as "those social norms, ethical commitments, and other-regarding preferences that facilitate the workings of the institutions advocated by liberals" (Bowles, 2011: 50). Civic virtues, or 'bourgeois' virtues, do not include so-called 'higher virtues', such as beneficence and magnanimity (Herzog, 2011), but virtues that are commonly held to be among the cultural foundations of a well-functioning liberal order, such as voluntarily paying taxes and contributing to public goods, respect for private property, honesty and fair treatment. For most of the eighteenth century, market relations were assumed to make people more cordial. As Montesquieu states: "wherever there is commerce, manners are gentle" (Cited in Hirschman, 1982: 1464). Today, Deidre McCloskey (2006) is one of the best-known defenders of this so-called doux commerce thesis that commerce fosters the civic virtues. She argues that free markets nurture several bourgeois virtues, such as integrity, honesty, trustworthiness, enterprise, respect, modesty and responsibility. The antithesis to the doux commerce thesis is the so-called self-destruction thesis, which states that free market institutions favor a cultural learning process that is inimical to the virtues needed for liberal institutions to function well (Bowles, 2011). Markets will crowd out traditional institutions that sustain the civic virtues, such as family life and religious communities, while endorsing the pursuit of self-interest. The lack of virtues caused by market operation may subsequently lead to a call for even more market operation if policy makers believe that markets economize on virtues. This may induce self-enforcing dynamics towards fewer virtues and more market operation.

The second debate that is related to, but has to be distinguished from, the debate between defenders of the doux commerce and self-destruction thesis concerns the effect of virtues on human or societal happiness. In classical virtue ethics, virtues enable people to become happy. In Aristotle's view, a human being becomes happy if she or he performs activities of the soul that express excellence or virtue. In contrast, Mandeville argued in his *Fable of the Bees* that the practice of private virtues leads to societal disaster and therefore, ultimately, to human unhappiness, because without vices a nation will not prosper. In his view, private vices, like pride and vanity, have built more hospitals than all the virtues put together.

DOI: 10.4324/9781003181835-12

In this chapter, we focus on the founding father of economics, Adam Smith. In these two debates, it seems that Adam Smith would largely side with the view that free market institutions encourage civic virtues and that civic virtues increase human happiness. In his *Lectures on Jurisprudence* (§ 17) (Smith, 1896 [1763]) he states: "whenever commerce is introduced into any country, probity and punctuality always accompany it. . . . Of all the nations of Europe, the Dutch, the most commercial, are the most faithful to their word". This quote indicates that Smith supported the doux commerce thesis. However, closer inspection shows that Smith was also aware that market institutions can have destructive effects on virtues.

Furthermore, as a virtue ethicist, Adam Smith believed that virtues enhance human and societal happiness. He wholeheartedly disagreed with Mandeville's *Fable of the Bees*, where Mandeville argued that the practice of private virtues leads to societal disaster (Sedláček, 2011). For example, in his *Theory of Moral Sentiments* (TMS), Smith stated that

> By acting according to the dictates of our moral faculties, we necessarily pursue the most effectual means for promoting the happiness of mankind, and may therefore be said, in some sense, to co-operate with the Deity, and to advance as far as in our power the plan of Providence.
>
> (TMS, III.5.7)

Smith believed that it is not great fortunes that make people truly happy in the first place, but rather simpler pleasures such as the knowledge that one has acted virtuously (Rasmussen, 2006). People are so constituted that they take pleasure in knowing that they have acted in a praiseworthy manner. However, in his *Wealth of Nations* (WN), Smith seems to defend the self-interest principle as a basic driver of societal well-being. According to Pabst (2011), Smith hovers halfway between Mandeville's claim that private vice leads to public benefits and the claim that virtuous practices of civil life are indispensable for public happiness. This calls into question to what extent Adam Smith embraced the view that virtues are really necessary to establish a happy and flourishing society.

In what follows, we will first describe Hirschman's seminal paper on four theses in the debate on the effects of commerce on virtues. Then we describe Smith's position in this debate. In the third section, we reflect on the second question and present Mandeville's view and confront it with Smith's ideas. In the conclusion, we construct an overall picture of Smith's views on the relationship between free market economy, virtues and societal flourishing.

9.1   THE DOUX COMMERCE AND SELF-DESTRUCTION THESIS

In a seminal paper, Albert Hirschman (1982) distinguished four alternative theses to describe how virtues have been affected by the introduction of the market economy to the Western economies.

First, the doux commerce thesis states that commerce has a favorable impact on the manners of men. As Montesquieu states: 'wherever there is commerce, manners are gentle (moeurs douces)' (cited in Hirschman, 1982: 1464). Recent authors that have defended the doux commerce hypothesis are, for example, Florida (2002) and McCloskey (2006), who predict that the market will make people more virtuous in the long run, because the wealth generated by the market will make people less greedy. This resembles Keynes's view, who wrote in his essay *Economic Possibilities for Our Grandchildren* (1930: 372) that after 100 years of economic growth, scarcity would be definitely solved. We would then become "free, therefore, to return to some of the most sure and certain principles of religion and traditional virtue – that avarice is a vice ... and the love of money is detestable" (Keynes, 1930: 372). This thought is in line with the writings of classical authors like David Hume (who considered wealth to be a friend of virtue) and Montesquieu, famously quoted by Hirschman (see earlier).

Second, the self-destruction thesis states that the market undermines the virtues that are essential for the good functioning of the market. The processes of capitalism themselves destroy the ability of individuals to live a good life and the sustainability of capitalism itself. Authors supporting the self-destruction thesis are, for example, Hirsch (1977), MacIntyre (1985), Putnam (2000) and Layard (2003).[1] Hirsch (1977) argued that the social morality that underpins the operation of markets has been a legacy of the pre-capitalist and pre-industrial past. This legacy has diminished with time due to the emphasis on self-interest, as well as to the greater mobility and anonymity of industrial society. As a result, habits based on communal attitudes and objectives have lost out. This undermining left a vacuum in social organization. MacIntyre (1985) characterizes 'external goods', such as fame, power or profit, as objects of competition, in contrast to 'internal goods', which are derived from practices. He argues that much modern industrial productive and service work is so organized as to exclude the features distinctive to a practice. According to MacIntyre, "We should expect that, if in a particular society the pursuit of external goods were to become dominant, the concept of virtues might suffer first attrition and then perhaps something near total effacement" (MacIntyre, 1985: 196). This is the so-called crowding-out effect (see more on crowding effects in Chapter 10). Putnam (2000) shows in his book *Bowling Alone* that many forms of community life have declined enormously over the second half of the twentieth century and that people have become increasingly disconnected from one another. As a result, civic virtues like trustfulness, mutual respect and civic-mindedness have crowded out. He mentions four factors that have contributed to this development: longer working hours, rampant suburban sprawls, television and increasing dominance of orientation on the self. According to Layard (2003), flexibility and geographical mobility, often defended by economists because they facilitate economic efficiency, increase family break-up and criminality and decrease mutual trust and therefore trustfulness.

A third thesis is what Hirschman names the feudal shackles thesis. Here the real grudge against capitalism is its weakness to break down the traditional pre-capitalistic social relations. The penetration of the market economy has been too partial and half-hearted and therefore left several elements of the previous social order intact. Aristocratic and military classes retain considerable power and influence in modern societies, such as, Latin America. These elements are feudal shackles or ballast. The United States has largely escaped from these feudal remnants. It has never been in the grip of ancient regimes. Because of the absence of a feudal background, the United States was able to experience a vigorous capitalist development. Thus arose the idea that America is exceptionally fortunate among the nations because of its peculiar historical background. Hirschman (1982: 1479) cites de Tocqueville: "The great advantage of the Americans is that they have come to democracy without having to endure democratic revolutions; and that they are born equal, instead of becoming so".

However, the absence of the feudal remnants seems to be a mixed blessing. Being deprived of authentic conservative traditions, the United States lacks the social and ideological diversity stemming from these traditions, including its socialist reactions. This lack of diversity stimulates the tendency toward a tyranny of the majority and toward pragmatic policies. For example, lacking the socialist challenging of the old regime, the welfare schemes (as introduced during the New Deal reforms) were never truly consolidated as an integral part of the economic order and remained vulnerable. This is what Hirschman mentions in the feudal blessings thesis, as it implies that a feudal background is a favorable factor for subsequent democratic-capitalist development.

Although these different theses give very different and excluding views on the relationship between capitalism and virtues, Hirschman believed all of them are relevant. The moral basis of a capitalistic society is constantly depleted (self-destruction thesis) and replenished (doux commerce thesis). Likewise, pre-capitalist forms and values both hamper the full development of capitalism (feudal shackles thesis) and bequeath something precious to it (feudal blessings thesis). The balance between these forces is likely to be different in each historical situation.

9.2   SMITH ON THE EFFECTS OF MARKETS ON VIRTUES

Smith's support of doux commerce thesis

Smith is often classified as one of the authors who support the doux commerce thesis. The texts of Adam Smith that are most often cited to show his support of the doux commerce thesis stem from *Lectures* (Smith, 1896 [1763]): "Whenever commerce is introduced into any country, probity and punctuality always accompany it. . . . Of all nations in Europe, the Dutch, the most commercial, are the most faithful to their word" (Lectures, II.II.17); "When people seldom deal with one another, we find that they are somewhat disposed to cheat, because they can gain more by a smart trick than they can lose by the injury which it does their character" (Lectures, II.II.17). The reason that commerce fosters the virtues of probity, punctuality and faithfulness is that it is a matter of prudence. Cheating one's trading partners generates more loss than profit in the long term. Therefore it is not surprising that Smith also mentions the virtues of sincerity and honesty in his description of the qualities of the prudent man (TMS, VI.i.8).

Besides *Lectures*, the WN also provides evidence that Smith supported the doux commerce thesis. For example, Smith argues that lack of competition through exclusive privileges stimulates the vice of envy: "The exclusive privileges of those East India companies, their great riches, the great favour and protection that these have procured them from their respective governments, have excited much envy against them" (WN, IV.i.33). According to Smith, mercantilist trade policies, which assumed that national interest consists of beggaring one's neighbors, have become the most fertile source of discord and animosity instead of forming bonds of union and friendship, which commerce can accomplish (WN, IV.iii.c.9). Second, tax regulations invite transgressions of the law: "An injudicious tax offers a great temptation to smuggling . . . from being at first, perhaps, rather imprudent than criminal, he at last too often becomes one of the hardiest and most determined violators of the laws of society" (WN, V.ii.k.64). In this quote, Smith criticizes harsh penalties for tax evasion by smugglers: the penalties entirely ruin them and worsen the situation.

In *The Theory of Moral Sentiments* we find hardly any direct evidence that supports Smith's positive view on the relationship between free markets and civic virtues. We could only find one citation wherein Smith states: "The most vulgar education teaches us to act, upon all important occasions, with some sort of impartiality between ourselves and others, and even the ordinary commerce of the world is capable of adjusting our active principles to some degree of propriety" (TMS, III.3.7). Here Smith states that ordinary commerce helps us to some degree to act in a proper way, that is, with some impartiality between ourselves and others. This links to a more general point in the TMS that people need others in order to develop a moral sense that requires impartiality (TMS III.i.5). Without the presence of others, people are too often at risk of being deformed by their self-love. As family and friends are too close to develop moral impartiality, allowing us to indulge too much in our selfish passions (Paganelli, 2010), we need to interact with strangers in order to develop virtues. The kind of society that is most favorable to moral development is therefore a market society, because in the marketplace we are constantly interacting with people we do not know.

Box 9.1   Smith's support of doux commerce thesis: some other citations[a]

The habit of sauntering ... which is necessarily acquired by every country workman who is obliged to change his work, renders him almost always *slothful and lazy* and incapable of any vigorous application. (WN I.1)

Certainty of being able to exchange ... encourages every man ... to *bring to perfection* whatever talent or genius he may possess. (WN I.2)

The strict *frugality* and *parsimonious attention* of the poor as naturally establish themselves in that of the free man. ... When wages are high, accordingly, we shall always find the workmen more active, *diligent*, and expeditious, than where they are low. ... A poor independent workman will generally be more *industriousness* than even a journeyman who works by the piece. (WN I.8)

The late multiplication of banking companies ... obliges all of them to be more *circumspect* in their conduct ... to guard themselves against those malicious runs, which the rivalship of so many competitors is always ready to bring upon them. ... This free competition too obliges all bankers to be more *liberal* in their dealing with their customers, lest their rivals should carry them away. In general, if any branch or trade, or any division of labour, be advantageous to the public, the freer and more general the competition, it will always be the more so. (WN II.2)

This capital has been silently and gradually accumulated by the private *frugality* and good conduct of individuals, by their universal, continual, and uninterrupted effort to better their own condition. It is this effort, protected by law and allowed by liberty to exert itself in the manner that is most advantageous, which has maintained the progress towards opulence. (WN II.3)

This regulation, instead of preventing, has been found from experience to increase the evil of *usury*. (WN II.4)

All these trades should be free, though this freedom may be abused. ... The cheapness of wine seems to be a cause, not of drunkenness, but of *sobriety*. ... People are seldom guilty of *excess* in what is their daily fare. Nobody affects the character of *liberality* and good fellowship, by being profuse of a liquor which is as cheap as small beer ... where wine is dear and a rarity, drunkenness is a common *vice*. (WN IV.4)

[T]he mean *rapacity*, the <u>monopolizing</u> spirit of merchants and manufacturers, who neither are, nor ought to be, the rulers of mankind . . . commerce, which ought naturally to be, among nations, as among individuals, a bond of *union* and *friendship* has become the most fertile source of *discord and animosity*. (WN IV.4)

To become co-partners instead of <u>competitors</u> . . . the farmers are generally the most opulent people. Their wealth would alone excite the public indignation, and the *vanity* which almost always accompanies such upstart fortunes, the foolish *ostentation* with which they commonly display that wealth, excites that indignation still more. (WN V.2)

It is <u>commerce </u>that introduces *probity* and *punctuality*. (Lectures II.II.16)

Whenever <u>dealings</u> are frequent, a man does not expect to gain so much by any once contract, as by *probity and punctuality* in the whole, and a *prudent* dealer, who is sensible of his real interest, would rather choose to lose what he has a right to, than give any ground for suspicion. . . . When the greater part of people are merchants, they always bring probity and punctuality into fashion, and these, therefore, are the principle virtues of a commercial society. (Lectures II.II.17)

---

^a Words in italics refer to virtues (vices); underlined words refer to instances of free market economies.

Smith on self-destructive forces

The texts cited in the preceding section make one inclined to put Adam Smith firmly among the authors that support the doux commerce thesis. However, then we disregard that Adam Smith often had multiple perspectives. This is also the case when studying his view of the influence of free market economies on virtues. While unambiguously endorsing commercial society, Smith was acutely aware of the possible ethical shortcomings of commercial society and carefully read and responded to Rousseau's powerful critiques of its inequality, inauthenticity and materialism (Rasmussen, 2008; Hanley, 2008). For example, he recognized that the high degree of labor division that markets allow could rob workers of their intelligence and spirit:

> The man whose whole life is spent in performing a few simple operations . . . has no occasion to exert his understanding, or to exercise his invention in finding our expedients to removing difficulties. . . . He, naturally, therefore loses the habit of such exertion, and generally becomes as stupid and ignorant as it is possible for human creature to become.
>
> (WN, book V, chapter 1, part III)

Box 9.2   Link with Marxian theory on alienation

Smith's view that assembly lines could rob workers of their intelligence and spirit links to Marx's theory of alienation. Marx held that humanity requires free labor (Lyon, 1979). The human being is a *homo faber*, a creating being. Humans develop and construct their own world by labor. However, in the capitalistic production process, the labor becomes disconnected from its creativity because of the subjection of labor to capital and the capitalistic way of organizing the production process through labor division and specialization. The mechanization reduces workers to mechanical ciphers and creates a sense of isolation, self-estrangement and powerlessness (Blaug, 1978). As a result, the laborer does not enjoy his activity anymore and labor loses its specific human character. Labor becomes merely an extension piece of the machine, and the product of labor becomes a fetish, something that is independent from the laborer and demanded and traded by independent forces that dominate market transactions. The relationship between the laborer and his product is dissolved, as well as the relationship with his co-producers, the nature and his own material and cultural needs (Verkuyl, 1982). This leads to a loss of identity. Alienation is the source of other vices such as greed, egoism and avarice, and lack of respect for other people and mental degradation of the working class increase.

Box 9.3 presents various other quotes from WN, *Lectures* and TMS that illustrate the complexity and ambiguity of Smith's view regarding the doux commerce–self-destruction debate. In the first quote Smith argues that whereas the commercial benefits of free labor encourage the virtue of diligence, they might also create an imbalance by providing incentives to work so hard that they ruin the workman's health and constitution. Although Smith does not explicitly refer to it, this text seems to point out that commercial benefits may fuel the vice of imprudence. The second quote counterbalances Smith's characterization of the Dutch as the most faithful. In this text, Smith contrasts France and England as nations consisting in a great measure of proprietors and cultivators of land, with Holland and Hamburg composed chiefly of merchants and manufacturers. Whereas proprietors and cultivators can be enriched by industry, merchants and manufacturers can grow rich only through parsimony and privation. Then Smith argues that these different circumstances are likely to reflect the common character of the people and connects commerce to narrowness, meanness, a selfish disposition and an aversion to all social pleasure and enjoyment. In contrast, he characterizes the common character in France and England as kind, liberal and frank. In *Lectures*, Smith argues that commerce has another bad effect in that it sinks the courage of mankind and increases effeminacy and dastardliness, because labor division leads to a situation in which every one's thoughts are employed about one particular thing. The last quote from TMS is not an example of support for the self-destruction thesis, as Smith does not refer to market operation in this text. However, if one applies this text to the context of modern commercial societies, where free markets have created a situation where people live in ease, it is easy to see a link between free market economies and the crowding out of the virtue of self-command.

Box 9.3   Smith's support of the self-destruction thesis[a]

Workmen, on the contrary, when they are <u>liberally paid by the piece</u>, are very apt to *over-work* themselves, and to ruin their health and constitution. (WN I.8)

In those of the former kind (proprietors and cultivators), *liberality, frankness and good fellowship*, naturally make a part of that common character. In the latter (merchants, artificers and manufacturers) *narrowness, meanness, and a selfish disposition, averse to all social pleasure and enjoyment.* (IV.9)

Another bad effect of commerce is that it sinks the *courage* of mankind, and tends to extinguish martial spirit . . . by having their minds constantly employed on the arts of luxury, they grow *effeminate* and *dastardly*. . . . The minds of men are contracted, and rendered incapable of elevation. Education is despised, or at least neglected, and *heroic spirit* is almost utterly extinguished. (Lectures II.II.17)

He may have lived too much in ease and tranquility. . . . Hardships, dangers, injuries, misfortunes, are the only masters under whom we can learn the exercise of this virtue . . . *self command.* (TMS III.3)

---

[a] Words in italics refer to virtues (vices); underlined words refer to instances of free market economies.

Overall, Adam Smith seemed to have believed that a market society enforces human virtues. However, in several places we find examples where he qualifies some of the positive effects of market society on virtues and highlights the other side of the coin that commerce may crowd out virtues.

9.3 VIRTUES AND HAPPINESS: ON THE WORLDVIEW OF ADAM SMITH

As a virtue ethicist, one would expect that Smith, like Aristotle, perceived that virtues foster human happiness. As noted earlier, Smith explicitly distanced himself from Mandeville in his *Theory of Moral Sentiments*. Mandeville had argued in his famous allegory, *The Fable of the Bees,* that the hive prospered under egotism but flagged under moral restraint. The widespread egotism does not lead to economic disaster. On the contrary, only when some bees pray to the god Jupiter and complain about the mean behavior of other bees do things go wrong. By divine intervention, the bees turn away from their vicious practices and deceit. All bees become honest and start to live soberly. The cafés are closed, and the demand for luxury products declines. The economy and cultural activities go down. Mandeville concludes that without vices, the nation will not live in splendor and magnificence. People who are satisfied with enough and do not feel they are subject to scarcity sabotage the economy and human progress. His argument can be summarized by the slogan 'Private vices, public benefits'. In his view, pride and vanity have built more hospitals than all the virtues put together.[2]

Smith's view on the role of virtues is much more complex. As already discussed in Chapter 1, Smith also stressed the favorable outcomes of the pursuit of self-interest in his WN. But in his TMS, his virtue ethics dominate. In this section we describe the tension in these views. First, we sketch Smith's descriptive view on the human being as is expressed in the TMS. Then we discuss his view on the function of virtues in society. Next, we contrast this with the invisible hand theory that he uses both in WN and TMS. We conclude with a discussion on how the tension in Smith's view can be interpreted.

Adam Smith on sympathy

In this section we first discuss Smith's view on human nature as laid down in TMS. This book is about two questions: (1) What is proper behavior? and (2) What does proper behavior accomplish? The first question is a moral question that we described in Chapter 8, Section 3. The second question is an analytical and social-psychological question on which we will focus now.

The core concept in Smith's view on human beings is sympathy. For Smith, sympathy is the central sentiment regulating relationships with other people. Smith explains this concept in the first part of TMS. Already in the first sentence of TMS, Smith starts with a thought about sympathy:

> How selfish so ever man may be supposed, there are evidently some principles in his nature, which interest him in the fortune of others, and render their happiness necessary to him, though he derives nothing from it, except the pleasure of seeing it.
>
> (Smith, 1991 [1759]: I.1)

Smith defines sympathy as our fellow feeling with any passion whatever.[3] For example, when we see an innocent person being tortured, we feel pity and compassion, and we tremble at the thought of what she or he feels. This sentiment is felt so instantaneously that it is evident that it cannot be derived from self-interested considerations, according to Smith.

Since sympathy is a fellow feeling with the passions of another, the question arises how we obtain access to the passions of others. For this, Smith refers to the human capacity to place oneself by imagination in the situation of others. As we have no immediate experience of what other persons feel, we can form no idea of their passions but by conceiving what we ourselves would feel if we were in the same situation as they are. Sympathy therefore results from the imagination placing you in the situation of others (empathy). It is only by the imagination that we can form any concept of what the other person experiences. As long as we do not place ourselves in the position of the other person, our senses will not inform us of what the other person feels. Only at the thought of his or her situation does an analogous emotion springs up in the mind of the spectator.

In Smith's theory, sympathy does not only mean feeling affection for the pleasant aspects of the character of another person or having warm feelings of humanity. Sympathy can also generate unpleasant feelings, like anger, fear or hate, for example, if one sympathizes with a person who is tortured. Still, sympathy has always one pleasant aspect, because sympathizing with the feelings of another person implies that we approve of his passions as suitable. To approve of the passions of another as suitable is the same thing as to observe that we entirely sympathize with them. Each person judges the propriety or impropriety of the affections of other men by their concord or dissonance with his or her own affections. If we do not approve of the passions of others and consider their behavior improper, we will not sympathize with them. For example, we do not sympathize with a person who laughs loud and heartily at a joke that we consider to be offensive.

The natural inclination to sympathize with other people contributes to the harmony of society, because sympathy is a reciprocal relationship. Whereas person A places herself in the situation of person B, person B tries to place herself in the situation of person A. As a result, they will understand each other's position more clearly. The background of Smith's view is his deistic theology of providence. In the deistic view, nature or God has, as a good clockmaker, provided the human being with several sentiments that enforce harmony between men and secure the happiness and perfection of the species.[4] According to Smith, people are often not rational. The rationality of man therefore cannot secure the harmony of society. Only nature or God himself has the wisdom to take care that human beings realize happiness and perfection (Berns and van Stratum, 1986). According to Smith, the author of nature has therefore not entrusted human reason, but instead endowed humans with more immediate instincts to foster human happiness (Smith, 1991 [1759]: II.2). This immediate instinct is sympathy. Sympathy is a working cause (causa efficiens) that contributes to the final cause of happiness and perfection of individuals and humanity.[5]

The ability to place oneself by imagination in the position of others also provides harmony in a different way. One of the basic needs of human beings is to gain status. Everyone likes it if other people sympathize with them. Mutual sympathy gives much pleasure: "Nothing pleases us more than to observe in other men a fellow-feeling with all the emotions of our own breast; nor are we ever so much shocked as by the appearance of the contrary" (Smith, 1991 [1759]: I.1). One way of obtaining the sympathy of others is to do things that other people approve of. This natural inclination to be admired by other people is another provision of the nature to induce people to cooperate and foster harmony. As Smith states: "Nature, when she formed man for society, endowed him with an original desire to please, and an original aversion to offend his brethren. She taught him to feel pleasure in their favorable, and pain in their unfavorable regard" (Smith, 1991 [1759]: III, 2). And somewhere else he states:

> The all-wise Author of Nature has, in this manner, taught man to respect the sentiments and judgments of his brethren, to be more or less pleased when they approve of his conduct, and to be more or less hurt when they disapprove of it.
>
> (Smith, 1991 [1759]: III. 2)

It is clear that this wish for social acceptance also fosters harmony in society, as it stimulates each person to do what other people regard as good and respectable.

Box 9.4 Empathy and trade

The capacity to place oneself by imagination in the situation of others' needs is also often practiced in the economy. In *The Wealth of Nations* (WN), Smith explains the welfare by the division of labor. In Chapter II of Book I of the WN, Smith notes, however, that this division of labor, from which so many advantages are derived, is not the effect of any human wisdom, which foresees and intends welfare. Rather, it is the consequence of a certain propensity in human nature, namely the propensity to truck, barter and exchange one thing for another. In the very same section Smith illustrates his argument with what has become a well-known passage in WN: "It is not from the benevolence of the butcher, the baker and the brewer that we expect our dinner, but from their regard for their own self-interest. We address ourselves, not to their humanity but to their self-love, and never talk to them of our own necessities but of their advantages" (Smith, 2000 [1776]: I.2). Economists normally refer to this quote to argue that Smith explains economic behavior by the self-interest of people and that the invisible hand transmutes selfish actions into wealth for others. Indeed, the self-interest of the baker is maximally served if he considers the needs of his customers as much as possible. But the example also illustrates the importance of human capacity to imagine how other people think and feel. The trucking disposition, which gives occasion to the division of labor, reflects the human capacity to place oneself in the position of the trading partner. Realizing that most people act out of self-interest, they will use arguments in the bargain that appeal to the self-interest of the other.

But how can one know what others think about oneself? Smith's answer to this question is again the human capacity to place oneself by imagination in the position of others. In particular, if a person places herself by imagination in the position of another person, she can also imagine how the other thinks about her. For example, if I beat a child and another person sees this happening, I can imagine what this other person will think of me. We consider how our acts must appear to others by considering how they would appear to us when in their situation. We suppose ourselves the spectators of our own behavior and endeavor to imagine what effect it would, in this light, produce upon us. The other person functions as a mirror or looking glass by which we can, in some measure, scrutinize the propriety of our own conduct (Smith, 1991 [1759]: III.2). It is by this mirror that we are capable of moral self-criticism. When I judge my own conduct in this way, by imagining how others would judge it, I divide myself, as it were, into two persons. The first is the spectator, who examines and judges the conduct by placing himself in the position of other people. The second is the agent, the person whom I properly call myself, and whose conduct is to be judged.

Box 9.5 Mutual sympathy and the search for richness

For Smith, mutual sympathy is also the main motive for the search of richness. As discussed in Chapter 8, Smith believes that people tend to sympathize more with the rich than with the poor and humble. It is chiefly from this regard to the sentiments of others that people pursue riches and avoid poverty. The rich man glories in his riches because he feels that they naturally draw upon him the attention of others and that they are disposed to go along with him in all those emotions with which the advantages of his richness inspires him. It is not the supply of the necessities of nature that motivates one to work hard, because the wages of the meanest laborer can supply these things. No, the motivation is to be notified by others, to get attention and the sympathy of others and approval of one's own sentiments:

> From whence, then, arises that emulation which runs through all the different ranks of men, and what are the advantages that we propose by that great purpose of human life which we call bettering our condition? To be observed, to be attended to, to be taken notice of with sympathy, complacency and approbation, are all the advantages which we can propose to derive from it.

> (Smith, 1991 [1759]: I.3)

And somewhere else Smith states:

> The desire of becoming the proper object of this respect, of deserving and obtaining this credit and rank among our equals is, perhaps, the strongest of all our desires, and our anxiety to obtain the advantages of fortune is accordingly much more excited and irritated by this desire, than by that of supplying all the necessities and conveniences of the body, which are always very easily supplied.
>
> (Smith, 1991 [1759]: VI.1)

Morality and the impartial spectator

Until this point, the theory of Adam Smith gives a plausible account of how people correct their own behavior by reflecting on the perceptions of other people. However, our behavior is not always monitored by other people, nor do we always take the judgments of other people seriously. As Smith himself states: "We can be more indifferent about the applause, and, in some measure, despise the censure of the world" (Smith, 1991 [1759]: III.1). If the opinions of others do not offer a secure basis of what we ought to do, what does? According to Smith, nature also provided for this:

> Nature, when she formed man for society, endowed him with an original desire to please ... his brethren.... But this desire of the approbation (by his brethren) ... would not alone have rendered him fit for that society for which he was made. Nature, accordingly, has endowed him, not only with a desire for being approved of, but with a desire for being what ought to be approved of; or for being what he himself approves of in other men.
>
> (Smith, 1991 [1759]: III.2)

But how can one know what ought to be approved of? The key to the answer to this question is Smith's idea of the impartial spectator. The idea of the 'impartial spectator' starts with the notion that it is easier to sympathize with the passions of other spectators – the general audience – than with the passion of persons who are directly involved in a certain event, because the general audience judges the situation from a more distant and impartial point of view than the person directly involved. The sympathy of the audience is therefore the more general standard for judging the propriety of the feelings of the persons directly involved. In the last edition of TMS Smith links this idea of the impartial spectator to the subjective moral conscience of persons. The impartial spectator is interiorized within the human being, an 'imagined man within the breast'. This is illustrated by the following quote:

> The all-wise Author of Nature has ... made man ... the immediate judge of mankind ... and appointed him ... to superintend the behavior of his brethren.... But though man has, in this manner, been rendered the immediate judge of mankind, he has been rendered so only in the first instance; and an appeal lies from his sentence to a much higher tribunal, to the tribunal of their *own consciences*, to that of the supposed impartial and well-informed spectator, to that of the man within the breast, the great judge and arbiter of their conduct.
>
> (Smith, 1991 [1759]: III.2)

Where at first it seemed that Adam Smith divided a person into two persons, the spectator and the agent, the spectator becomes a super-ego who decides independently between the agent and the other people with whom the agent lives. This super-ego is the inner person in us, who really longs to be praiseworthy. It is the vice-agent of God, the Author of Nature. In this way, according to Smith, the Author of Nature has tried to foster the happiness of the people that He intended to realize when He created them.

Relationship between virtues and happiness

As Smith believed that God, as creator and provident sustainer of the world, has implanted several types of virtues in the human breast to foster human happiness, one can understand that he wholeheartedly disagreed with De Mandeville. Smith considers human and societal happiness to depend on both economic and social virtues. In the WN, he focused particularly on material welfare and argues that economic virtues, such as industry, frugality and attention, contribute to business success at the micro-level and macro-opulence (see Box 9.6 citations [2], [7] and [10]). The economic vices of imprudence, prodigality, indulgence and avidity have an opposite effect and harm the public interest (citations [5], [6], [7], [9], [10]). Also social virtues, such as humanity, increases the productivity of labor (citation [1]), whereas social vices, such as jealousy and deceitfulness, are economically harmful to society (citations [3], [4], [8]; see also citation [11] from *Lectures*).

Box 9.6   Virtues increase (vices decrease) societal flourishing[a]

Wealth of Nations

---

1   If masters would always listen to the dictates of *reason* and *humanity*, they have frequently occasion rather to moderate, than to animate the application of many of their workmen . . . as to be able to work constantly, not only preserves his <u>health</u> the longest, but . . . executes the greatest <u>quantity of work</u>. (I.8)

2   It seldom happens that <u>great fortunes</u> are made . . ., but in consequence of a long life of *industry, frugality and attention*. (I.10.1)

3   The *jealousy* of strangers . . . reduce the whole manufacture into a sort of slavery to themselves, and raise the price of their labour above what is due. (I.10.2)

4   The interest of the dealers . . . is always in some respects different from, and even opposite to, that of the <u>public</u>. . . . It comes from an order of men, whose interest is never exactly the same with that of the public, who have generally an interest to *deceive* and even to *oppress* the public, and who accordingly have, upon many occasions, both deceived and oppressed it. (I.11.3; IV.4)

5   So far at it (money) is employed in the first way (consumption by *idle* people), it promotes *prodigality*, increases expence and consumption without increasing production . . . and is in every respect <u>hurtful to the society</u>. (II.2)

6   But the bank of England <u>paid very dearly</u>, not only for its own *imprudence*, but for the much greater *imprudence* of almost all Scotch banks. (II.2)

7   Every *prodigal* appears to be a public enemy, and every *frugal* man a <u>public benefactor</u>. (II.3)

8   If those two countries, however, were to consider their real interest, without either mercantile *jealousy* or national *animosity*, the commerce of France might be more <u>advantageous</u>. (IV.4)

9   The *avidity* of our great manufacturers, however, has in some cases extended these exemptions . . . sell their own goods as dear as possible . . . buy the work of the poor spinners as cheap as possible . . . keep down the wages of their own weavers . . . by no means for the <u>benefit of the workman</u>. (IV.8)

Wealth of Nations

10   It is the *sober* and *industrious* poor who . . . principally supply the demand for useful labour. . . . The
dissolute and disorderly might continue to *indulge* themselves . . . their children perishing from neglect . . .
the example of that bad conduct common corrupts their morals; so that, instead of being useful to society by
their industry, they become <u>public nuisances</u> by their *vices* and *disorders*. (V.2)

Lectures

11   All *jealousies* therefore between different nations, and *prejudices* of this kind, are extremely <u>hurtful to</u>
<u>commerce</u>, and limit <u>public opulence</u>. (II.I.11)

Theory of Moral Sentiments

12   In all the middling and inferior professions, real and solid professional abilities, joint to *prudent, just,*
firm, and temperate conduct, can very seldom fail of <u>success</u> . . . honesty is the best policy, holds, in such
situations, almost always perfectly true. (I.III.3)

13   Where the necessary assistance is reciprocally afforded from *love, from gratitude, from friendship and esteem,*
the <u>society flourishes and is happy</u>. (II.II.3)

14   *Beneficence*, therefore, is less essential to the <u>existence of society</u> than justice. Society may subsist, though
not in the most comfortable state, without beneficence; but the prevalence of *injustice* must utterly destroy
it. . . . Justice, on the contrary, is the main pillar that upholds the whole edifice. If it is removed, the great, the
immense fabric of human society, that fabric which to raise and support seems in this world, if I may say so,
to have been the peculiar and darling care of Nature, must in a moment crumble into atoms. (II.II.3)

15   It is reason, principle, *conscience*, the inhabitant of the breast, the man within, the great judge and arbiter
or our conduct. It is he who, whenever we are about to act to as to affect the happiness of others, calls to us.
. . . The poor man must neither defraud nor steal from the rich. . . . The *man within* . . . upon the tolerable
observation of which depend the <u>whole security and peace of human society</u>. (III.3)

16   What is the reward most proper for encouraging *industry, prudence, and circumspection*? <u>Success in every</u>
<u>sort of business</u>. (III.3)

17   But upon the tolerable observance of these duties (of *justice, of truth, of chastity, of fidelity*) depends the very
<u>existence of human society</u>, which would crumble into nothing if mankind were not generally impressed
with a reverence for those important rules of conduct. (III.5)

18   The *prudent, the equitable, the active, resolute, sober* character promises <u>prosperity and satisfaction</u>, both to
the person himself and to every on connected with him. The *rash, the insolent, the slothful, effeminate, and*
voluptuous, on the contrary, forebodes <u>ruin</u> to the individual, and <u>misfortune</u> to all who have any thing to do
with him. . . . What institution of government could tend so much to promote the <u>happiness of mankind</u> as
the general prevalence of wisdom and virtue? All government is but an imperfect remedy for the deficiency
of these. . . . On the contrary, what civil policy can be so <u>ruinous and destructive</u> as the *vices* of men. (IV.2)

19   The qualities most <u>useful to ourselves</u> are, first of all, *superior reason* and *understanding*. . . ; and secondly,
self-command. (IV.2)

20   The care of the health, of the fortune, of the rank and reputation of the individual, the objects upon which
his <u>comfort and happiness</u> in this life are supposed principally to depend, is considered the proper business
of that virtue which are commonly called *prudence*. The methods of improving our fortune, which it
principally recommends us, are those which expose to no loss of hazard: real knowledge and skill in our
trade or profession, *assiduity and industry* in the exercise of it, *frugality*, and even some degree of *parsimony*,
in all our expenses . . . always *sincere* . . . never tells any thing but the truth. . . . is very capable to friendship
. . . sober esteem of *modesty, discretion*, and good conduct . . . *temperance* . . . *industry* . . . *frugality*. (VI.I)

ª Words in italics refer to virtues (vices); underlined words refer to instances of societal flourishing.

The importance of economic virtues for material aspects of human and societal flourishing is also firmly established in TMS. Economic virtues – prudence, self-command,

assiduity, industry, frugality, circumspection and parsimony – produce comfort and happiness, whereas economic vices – rashness, insolence, slothfulness, effeminacy and voluptuousness – ruin the individual and cause misfortune to all others who are affected by his or her behavior (citations [12], [16], [18], [19], [20]). But in TMS Smith enlarges the scope of virtues that enhance societal flourishing by stressing the importance of non-economic virtues, such as love, gratitude, respectfulness and justice (citations [13], [17]). In particular, the virtue of justice is, for Adam Smith, the safeguard of the security and peace of human society.

Self-interest and societal flourishing: the invisible hand

Although the evidence in the preceding section illustrates that Smith disagrees with Mandeville's 'private vices, public benefits', this evidence is not unambiguous. In WN and *Lectures* there are also texts that indicate that Smith relativized the dependency of human happiness on virtues and argued for a morally neutral relationship between virtues and societal flourishing. Although these citations are not as numerous, they are very well known and have therefore led many to believe that for Adam Smith, morality is not that important for the human flourishing potential of free market economies.

For evidence from WN, I refer to the two most well-known quotes about the butcher, brewer and the baker and the invisible hand. In a market economy with specialization, it is in vain to expect deliverance of the goods that one needs from the benevolence of others. People are only benevolent to their family and friends, but much less so towards strangers. It would be too risky to trust the benevolence of other people to meet one's needs. Only self-interest motivates people to assist others in fulfilling their needs, which is illustrated by the famous citation of the butcher, brewer and baker (see Box 9.7, citation [1]). Both the demand for and the supply of bread are motivated by self-interest, although the outcome of the transaction is mutual gain. Citation [2] refers to Smith's argument that money facilitates the exchange of goods in the market and then connects this to the opportunity to be mutually serviceable to each other. Although the outcome of the self-interested actions of traders is that they serve the interest of others, it is not their intention to do so, and hence it has no relationship with the virtue of benevolence.[6] In WN Smith mostly understands self-interest in a morally neutral sense. Self-interest can motivate people to virtuous actions, but also motivate people to vicious actions, as Smith described in I.11.3 and IV.4 in WN (see citation [4]) where he argued that the self-interest of merchants and manufacturers leads them to deceive their clients and harm the public interest.

The irrelevance of virtues for material welfare in a market context is more explicitly stated by Adam Smith in book IV of WN (citation [3]). Here Smith argues that individuals are continually looking for ways to employ capital and employment that are personally most advantageous to them. As by an invisible hand, the profit-driven behavior of businesspersons increases the wealth of nations, which is in the interest of society.[7] The superfluity of virtues appears particularly in the second part of the quote that states that businesspersons who intend to promote the interest of society (which could be classified as a virtue) actually less effectually promote society's interest than those who merely aim to increase their own profits. This comes very close to Mandeville's view that virtues are harmful to society.

Box 9.7   Free market economies increase societal flourishing in a morally neutral or vicious way[a]

Wealth of Nations

1   It is not from the *benevolence* of the butcher, the brewer, or the baker, that we expect our <u>dinner</u> . . . from a regard to his own interest, the making of bows and arrows grows to be a chief business. (I.2)

2   No exchange can be made between them . . . and they are all of them thus mutually less *serviceable to one another*. (I.4)

3   He intends only his own gain, and he is in this, as in many other cases, led by an invisible hand to promote an end which was no part of his intention. . . . By pursuing his *own interest* he frequently promotes <u>that of the society</u> more effectually than when he really intends to promote it. I have never known much good done by those who affected to trade for the public good. (IV.2)

Lectures

4   <u>The division of labour</u> . . . we cannot imagine this to be an effect of human *prudence* . . . it flows from a direct propensity in human nature for one man to barter with another . . . works on the *self love* of his fellows. (II.II.5)

5   We may observe that those principles of the human mind which are most <u>beneficial to society</u>, are by no means marked by nature as the most honourable . . . that principle in the mind which prompts to truck, barter, and exchange, though it is the great foundation of arts, commerce, and the division of labour, yet it is not marked with anything amiable. . . . To perform anything, or to give anything without a reward, is always *generous* and *noble*, but to barter one thing for another is *mean*. (II.II.16)

Theory of Moral Sentiments

6   It is to no purpose that the *proud* and *unfeeling* landlord . . . without a thought for the wants of his brethren . . . all of whom thus derive from his luxury and caprice that share of the necessaries of life which they would in vain have expected from his *humanity or his justice* . . . in spite of their *natural selfishness and rapacity*, though they mean only their own conveniency, though the sole end . . . be the gratification of their own *vain* and *insatiable* desires, they divide with the poor the produce of all their improvements. They are led by an **invisible hand** to make nearly the same distribution of the necessaries of life which would have been made had the earth been divided into equal portions among all its inhabitants; and thus, without intending it, without knowing it, advance the <u>interest of the society</u>. (IV.2)

7   When providence divided the earth among a few lordly masters, it neither forgot nor abandoned those who seemed to have been left out in the partition. . . . In what constitutes the real <u>happiness of human life</u>, they are in no respect inferior to those who would seem so much above them. In ease of body and peace of mind, all the different ranks of life are nearly upon a level. (IV.2)

---

[a] Words in italics refer to virtues (vices); underlined words refer to instances of societal flourishing.

Further evidence is provided by two quotes from the *Lectures* on labor division that is, according to Smith, so crucial for generating societal wealth. In these texts, Smith argues that labor division does not stem from noble motives, but from mean motives that induce people to exchange things rather than performing anything without reward. Therefore, he concludes that those principles of the human mind that are most beneficial to society are by no means marked by nature as the most honorable.

Even TMS, wherein Smith explicitly criticized Mandeville's view, provides evidence that Smith was ambiguous in his own view on the importance of virtues in creating societal benefits. This is apparent from the (only) citation in TMS that refers to the invisible hand, where Smith describes the motives of the landlord (see citations [6] and [7]). The landlord aims at great richness and therefore hires people to labor on his lands to produce food. It is not for the wants of his fellowmen that he does so, but for his own desires. But since the capacity of his own stomach is very small in proportion to his production, he brings most of the produce to the market. As if he is led by an invisible hand, he thus contributes to the supply of food that meets people's basic needs. In this way, the landlord contributes to human flourishing in society without intending it. His vices – Smith mentions proudness, unfeelingness, natural selfishness and rapacity – rather than his virtues (humanity and justice) make the landlord serve the interest of society, which is basically the same idea that Mandeville defended. The seventh citation in Box 9.7 shows that Adam Smith believed that the vices of the landlord do not only increase the overall interest of society but even lead to equality in happiness. Once the basic needs of poor people are met, due to the invisible hand, there is almost no difference in real happiness between rich and poor people.

Das Smith problem

The ambiguity in Smith's views in WN and TMS has puzzled many scientists and raised the question of how to interpret it. In WN Adam Smith observed that people are strongly driven by self-interest, whereas according to TMS, people also obtain pleasure from seeing the happiness of other people. They feel sympathy for those people whose feelings they approve of. This divergence in views has become known as *Das Smith Problem* (Etzioni, 1988). How should we interpret the relationship between both books?

On the one hand, one could argue that Adam Smith does not reject self-interest as the most basic motive for explaining human behavior in TMS, because the sentiment of mutual sympathy stressed by Smith serves the self-interested goal of attaining a high social status. Also sympathy towards others can be interpreted as a sentiment that contributes to one's own happiness, because sympathy produces joy. Therefore, Sen (1977) classifies this sentiment still as self-interested in an important sense. For one is oneself pleased with the other's pleasure and pained by the other's pain. Thus, the pursuit of one's own utility may be helped by a sympathetic action.[8]

Second, Smith's understanding of self-interest has strong moral undertones and refers to a proper care of the self. This is the virtue of prudence (see Chapter 8). It is more something like a proper care of the self that can be universalized rather than a kind of selfishness. Examples are industry and frugality, which are motivated by self-interest but are also virtues that have a positive influence on the economy. As discussed earlier, Box 9.6 gives many examples of how, according to Smith, these virtues are good for society.

Third, when Smith argues that the pursuit of one's own interest is beneficial to society, he implicitly assumes that the self-interested businessperson respects and is bounded by important moral requirements (particularly concerning justice). Smith did not defend an unfettered pursuit of self-interest, let alone that greed is good. Also in WN he criticizes entrepreneurs who want to serve their own interest by monopolies and deceive others for that reason.

Box 9.8   Mode of ethical values in three domains[a]

The idea that ethical values are dependent on the context or domain has been system-ized by Van Staveren. She distinguished three domains:

Domain	Market	Government	Household
Value of the:	Individual	Public	Community
Core value:	Self-esteem	Rights	Relationship
Virtue:	Prudence	Propriety, justice	Benevolence, love
Signals:	Price	Votes	Symbols
Social mechanism:	Exchange	Distribution	Gift

---

[a] Modified from Van Staveren (2001).

A fourth explanation is that the Das Smith problem has to do with the scope of both books. WN is about the economic domain. In this book, Smith particularly stresses the economic virtues that are aligned with self-interest. But TMS is about personal human rela-tions. In the social domain, social virtues are more important, and consequently Smith paid more attention to this kind of virtue. This is similar to the distinction of three spheres by Van Staveren (2001) (see Box 9.8): the market, whose virtue is prudence; the home, whose virtue is love; and the government, whose virtue is justice. Each domain or sphere has its own mode of ethical values, feeling, reasoning and action.

A plausible interpretation is therefore that Smith's economic analysis in WN rested to a substantial extent on his social analysis in TMS. Whereas Smith perceived man as a moral being, he also considered that he is motivated by the pursuit of self-interest in many arenas in life, and in particular in the economic domain. This was already illustrated by Box 9.4 and Box 9.5 on the links between the human capability to place oneself in the position of others and the human propensity to truck and barter, and the link between mutual sympathy and the search for richness. This shows that the promotion of self-interest is part of the search for approval or sympathy from others and, thus, subject to the values and norms of the com-munity. Furthermore, both books refer to an invisible hand that causes harmony between individuals. Still, the accents are different. Whereas WN focuses on the market mechanism as a mechanism that causes harmony between self-interested individual actions, TMS more explicitly stresses the sympathy mechanism through which the invisible hand fosters social harmony. One should therefore read WN with TMS in mind. Together these books explain why Smith was optimistic about the possibility of attaining a harmonious society.

9.4   OVERVIEW

The relationships between free market economy, virtues and societal flourishing discussed so far imply four possible types of market societies (see Table 9.1). In the flourishing virtuous market society, the free market economy encourages virtues (discourages vices), whereas

TABLE 9.1
Four types of market societies

Societal flourishing increased by	Free market system encourages:	
	Virtues	Vices
Virtues	1 Flourishing virtuous	2 Stagnating vicious
Vices	3 Stagnating virtuous	4 Flourishing vicious

virtues increase (vices decrease) societal flourishing. In the stagnating vicious market society, free market economies stimulate vices, and vices have a destructive effect on societal flourishing. In the stagnating virtuous market society, markets encourage the virtues, but the virtues have a destructive effect on societal flourishing. Finally, in the flourishing vicious market society, the free market economy also stimulates vices, but vices have a positive rather than a negative effect on societal flourishing (Mandeville's hive model). Based on the previous sections, we now can determine Smith's view on which type of society is likely to result from a free market system.

Up to now, we have used qualitative methods to analyze Smith's views on the relationship between market economy, virtues and happiness. Graafland and Wells (2020) gave a more systematic overview by applying a semantic-network approach (Alfano et al., 2018) that uses digital research and visualization techniques to Smith's WN (2000 [1776]) to examine quantitatively what he said. They collected 448 quotes from WN on the relationship between free markets, virtues and human flourishing. By counting the frequency of Smith's references to the relationships between markets, virtues and happiness, a more accurate picture is obtained. Graafland and Wells limited their analysis to the text of WN because this is the book that inspired many economists to believe that Smith had a Mandevillian view on morality.

The virtues were grouped into six clusters: prudence, temperance, industriousness, courage, justice and love (benevolence). For each set of virtues, the nature of their relationship with a free market economy and with societal flourishing were researched. Table 9.2 and Figure 9.1 summarize the quantitative outcomes and show how, according to Smith, the introduction of a market economy affects societal flourishing via virtues and vices.

The first conclusion we can derive from these findings is that in an overwhelming majority (over 90%) of citations, Smith associates virtues positively with societal flourishing (or vices with societal failure). This contrasts directly and emphatically with the Mandevillian hive thesis. For example, Smith makes a mere four references to the idea that the vice of intemperance can drive public prosperity, six references to selfishness and unkindness (vices that correspond to the virtue of benevolence) driving prosperity and only one reference to injustice doing so. Thus, while it is true that Smith made a few remarks consistent with the hive thesis, including several famous ones always quoted, he had far more to say about the opposite thesis that societal flourishing relies on the presence of individual virtues.

Whether Smith supported the stagnation vicious market view or the flourishing virtues market view is more ambiguous. In the majority of cases (about 60%) he associates free markets positively with virtues, and in 40% he associates free markets with vices. Table 9.2 shows that Smith was particularly concerned about the vulnerability of the virtues

TABLE 9.2
Quantitative outcomes per type of virtue

Free market encourages:

	Temperance	Industrious	Prudence	Justice	Benevolence	Courage	Total
Positively	23	27	31	18	19	2	120
Negatively	24	4	23	5	28	4	88
	47	31	54	23	47	6	208

Virtues affect societal flourishing

	Temperance	Industrious	Prudence	Justice	Benevolence	Courage	Total
Positively	83	24	49	26	34	5	221
Negatively	4	2	5	1	6	1	19
	87	26	54	27	40	6	240

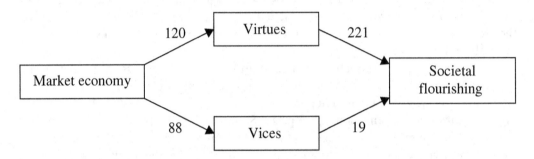

FIGURE 9.1   Markets, virtues and societal flourishing: overview of results

of temperance, prudence and benevolence under free market conditions. At the aggregate level, adding up Smith's references suggests he acknowledged both doux commerce and self-destruction mechanisms.

NOTES

1   Another proponent is Richard Sennett (see e.g. Sennett 2000).
2   George Blewhitt, the author of a pamphlet against the 1723 edition of Mandeville, argued that Mandeville's argument was flawed. In response to Mandeville's argument that universal honesty would put locksmiths out of work, he protested: "The change [to an honest way of life] must necessarily be supposed to be gradual; and then it will appear still plainer that there would arise a succession of new trades . . . in proportion as the trades in providing against roguery grew useless and wore off" (cited by McCloskey, 2006: 460). This reflects the belief of economists that workers will not become permanently idle if they are dismissed, as they would in the long run find alternative employment.
3   In *An International Reader's Dictionary*, sympathy is defined as sharing the feelings of another, e.g. be glad when she or he is glad, sad when she or he is sad, etc.
4   The deistic view was popular in the eighteenth century. Newton, for example, explained the regular motions of the planets and moons by the divine ordinances of an omniscient and omnipotent being. Smith was a fervent admirer of Newton. However, he is more hesitant about the concept of God, which he names with terms as Author of Nature, Wisdom of Nature, Nature or God. In the final print of the TMS, his deistic worldview falls into the background. Still, the idea that the working causes that explain human behavior work together to contribute to a final cause (as expressed by the metaphor of the invisible hand) is everywhere present in his books (Kerkhof, 1986).

5 This is a teleological view of reality. Teleology means that one explains reality by the final ends of things – the so-called final causes – and not by the factors that cause them – the so-called working causes (Störig, 1990).

6 However, one could consider that virtues arise as a result of habit formation. The extrinsic motive of self-interest may slowly crowd in and become internalized in the attitudes of individuals. Macneil (1986) argued that relationships with others that were entered into as means to an economic ends become transformed into ends in themselves (intrinsic motive). If the baker develops the habit of putting himself in the position of the client in order to judge if the bread he sells serves the client's interest, the baker trains a predisposition of considering others' interest, which may result, in time, in a genuine attitude of serviceability.

7 The Smithian argument about the merits of self-interest can also be defended by another important notion concerning the informational role of self-interest. Self-interested behavior does not only give everyone the role of protecting and pursuing his own interest but allocates this role to the person that is best known with these interests, namely the person himself. If another person or the government would pursue your interest, they will do a worse job than if you would look after your own interest yourself. The person who knows an individual best is the individual herself, and this signaling function may well be lost if, rather than acting from personal self-interest, one pursues other goals (Sen, 1984).

8 Sen illustrates this notion with the following example. If the knowledge of torture of others makes you sick, it is a case of sympathy. Suppose now that the knowledge of torture of others does not make you feel personally worse off, but you still think it is wrong and that it is your duty to do something to stop it. Then the person is not motivated by self-interest, but by duty.

Recommended literature

Bowles, S. (2011) 'Is liberal society a parasite on tradition?', *Philosophy & Public Affairs*, 39(1): 46–81.

Fourcade, M. and Healy, K. (2007) 'Moral views of market society', *Annual Review of Sociology*, 33: 285–311.

Hirschman, A.O. (1982) 'Rival interpretations of market society: Civilizing, destructive or feeble?', *Journal of Economic Literature*, XX: 1463–1484.

Kerkhof, B. (1986) 'Systemen zijn als machines. Een opmerkelijke theorie over theorieën', in G. Berns (ed.) *Adam Smith. Ethiek, Politiek en Economie*, Tilburg: Tilburg University Press, 61–89.

Mandeville, B. (1714) *The fable of the bees: Or, private vices, publick benefits.* www.xs4all. nl/~maartens/philosophy/mandeville/fable_of_bees.html.

Sedláček, T. (2011) *Economics of Good and Evil: The Quest for Economic Meaning from Gilgamesh to Wall Street*, New York: Oxford University Press.

Smith, A. (1759) *The Theory of Moral Sentiments*, New York: Prometheus Books.

Smith, A. (1776) *Inquiry into the Nature and Causes of the Wealth of Nations*, New York: Prometheus Books.

Smith, A. (1896 [1763]) *Lectures on Justice, Policy, Revenue and Arms*, Oxford: Clarendon Press.

10

Markets, virtues and happiness

Empirical research

In the business and management literature, there has been a resurgence of interest in virtues (Moore and Beadle, 2006; Wright and Goodstein, 2007; Bright et al., 2014; Ferrero and Sison, 2014). In economics, literature on virtues is scarce. Traditionally, in economics the basic components that account for individual behavior are preferences, possibilities and beliefs. If at all, virtues are implicitly covered. For example, Bowles (2016) uses the word 'social preferences' to refer to motives that are closely related to virtues, such as altruism, intrinsic pleasure in helping others, aversion to inequity and ethical commitments. But social preferences are not limited to virtues, because they may also refer to the warm glow of doing well rather than a genuine concern for the good. Some research in economics also explicitly refers to virtues (Bruni and Sugden, 2013; Burbidge, 2016). Arrow (1972: 345, 356) already argued that "the presence of what are in a slightly old-fashioned terminology called virtues in fact plays a significant role in the operation of the economic system". Likewise, Sen (1977: 332) assents to a statement of Leif Johansen that no society would be viable without the upholding of social norms and rules of conduct, where he explicitly refers to the virtue of honesty. To run a society entirely on incentives to personal gain is pretty much a hopeless task (Solomon, 1992). In a dynamic economy relying on innovation, transaction partners often cannot write down *ex ante* what they exactly expect from each other in each contingency (Bovenberg, 2002). In order to cooperate, trading parties must trust each other, so that both will share the benefits from these investments. Frank (2004) gives several examples of how integrity contributes to profitable business opportunities and wealth. Opportunistic behavior will render this kind of cooperation impossible. Kay (1993) names contracts based on social norms and trust relational contracts. The terms of the relationship are not written down, and often cannot be precisely articulated. Therefore, the contract cannot be enforced by law, but depends on trust between the parties. In economic theory, social norms and trust that sustain relational contracts is labeled social capital, i.e. "features of social organization, such as networks, norms, and trust that facilitate coordination and cooperation for mutual benefit" (Putnam, 1993: 2). Virtues like honesty, loyalty, trustfulness and justice facilitate social capital, and hence efficient coordination, if individual and common goals are not perfectly aligned and if markets and government regulations are imperfect.

In this chapter, we present an overview of recent economic research into the role of virtues in the economic domain. Section 1 sheds light on the debate on doux commerce

DOI: 10.4324/9781003181835-13

versus self-destruction by an overview of the literature on the empirical effects of market institutions on various virtues. Next, we discuss game theory that provides insight into the effects of social preferences that are closely aligned with virtues in the economic domain and consider some recent experimental research on the behavioral effects of different types of social preferences on social outcomes. Third, we present some recent research on the impact of civic virtues on happiness, based on data from the World Values Survey. In the last section we describe some researches that show that the influence of free markets on happiness might be conditional on virtues.

10.1   MARKETS AND VIRTUES: DOUX COMMERCE OR SELF-DESTRUCTION?

In this section, we present literature that sheds light on the impact of market operation on virtues. As a reference, we selected the six types of virtues that were distinguished in the analysis of Smith's views on the doux commerce and self-destruction theses in Chapter 9, Section 9.4 (temperance, industriousness, prudence, justice, love and courage). There are several reasons for favoring Adam Smith's system in contrast to the more famous classical Aristotelian approach. Although Smith was working within the extended virtue ethical tradition of Aristotle, his concerns are much more familiar with modern economics (McCloskey, 2006).

Methodological challenges

Before discussing the relationship between markets and the virtues, we first highlight some methodological challenges in researching this relationship (Graafland, 2010a). Empirical research into the effects of market institutions on the various virtues is relatively scarce. This has to do with the fact that this link is, for several reasons, hardly measurable.

First, analyzing this impact is hindered by the fact that virtues concern inner attitudes or character traits that are not directly observable. Empirical observations often only relate to behavioral patterns. Behavioral changes do not necessarily indicate changes in character traits, since other, external forces may be at work. For instance, an increase in consumption does not necessarily imply that people have become more intemperate. Similarly, if the market provides more incentives to working, one cannot derive the conclusion that it stimulates diligence. The rise in labor hours may be caused by economic incentives without changing the characters of individuals.

Another problematic issue concerns the development of virtues over time. Since virtues are a result of habit formation, changes in virtues typically take a long time. In order to identify the impact of market institutions, one therefore needs a long time series, which are often lacking. Experimental research is generally ill suited to such analysis. Since experiments focus on how a particular factor affects human choice behavior during the short time interval of the experiment, the link with character formation remains uncertain.

One possible way of escaping these two problems is to assume that external factors will affect characters in the long run through changing behavioral patterns. As argued in Chapter 8, virtues arise as a result of habit formation. They are learned and become internalized through the regular repetition of certain (good) actions and thinking, often originally motivated by extrinsic motives. Extrinsic motives will therefore slowly crowd in and become internalized. Competition may encourage or discourage the development of virtues unconsciously by likewise operating on habit formation: different external motives may result in different behavioral patterns that then slowly crowd in into inner attitudes. For instance, Macneil (1986) argues that relations with others that were entered into as means to economic ends become transformed into ends in themselves. Sharing in so-called relational contracts thus results, in time, in full-blown social solidarity. Where we interpret the outcomes of experimental research in terms of changes in virtues, we thus implicitly assume that behavioral patterns influence virtues, but one should be aware that this need not be true in all cases.

Another complication of analyzing the causal influence of market institutions on virtues is the possible interaction between virtues. In everyday moral life, virtues are often mixed together. Virtues can enforce each other, but also oppose each other, can combine into new virtues,[1] provide dilemmas because of their incommensurability and context dependency and are also context dependent in their effect on happiness. It is the details that count in virtue ethics, and there are many context-specific details that are more or less significant in particular situations (Solomon, 1992).[2]

Another issue that is not yet solved concerns the debate on situationism (Alzola, 2012). Virtue ethics presumes that dispositions generate an identifiable pattern of virtuous behavior and lead to cross-situational consistency in people's behavior (Kamtekar, 2004). However, individual differences in behavior may arise from a combination of dispositional differences and differences related to how a particular situation is framed (Henrich et al., 2004). A recurrent finding of social psychologists over the past 50 years has been that situational factors can more powerfully affect behavior than the dispositions traditionally posited by virtue theory. For example, in experiments with brightly lit rooms, less than half of the players cheated, whereas when the room was slightly less well lit, more than half did (ceteris paribus the chance that one's cheating could be observed) (Kaminski et al., 2013). This would suggest that we tend to overestimate the role of moral dispositions as causes of behavior (Heath, 2014). On the other hand, research by Falk et al. (2018) showed that preferences regarding patience, trust, risk, altruism and positive reciprocity across and within countries are related to behavior and economic outcomes and that the heterogeneity in these preferences is at least partly systematic and linked to both individual-level characteristics and aggregate cultural or biogeographic endowments. Furthermore, experiments have also shown that the adverse effects of incentives on social behavior can persist long after the incentive was removed (Bowles, 2016). This indicates that the effects of preferences go beyond situational cues.

Temperance

Temperance is the disposition to restrain and moderate one's impulsive and inappropriate appetites. Producers under competition have an obvious interest in competing with each other to meet customers' wants and in promoting additional consumption. Competition in products pushes companies to engage in continuous product development, model changes and planned obsolescence, as these serve the output of the company. Capitalism therefore fosters a tendency to excessive consumption as an inherent part of the system (Moore, 2005). Business management can never rest content with the secure knowledge that enough is enough. In order to secure the demand for their products, firms seek to influence market demand through their sales strategies, like advertising. Because of its manipulative power, it seduces consumers to more consumption. According to Waide (1987), the most important theme of the cumulative effects of thousands and thousands of advertisements is that you are what you own. The not very surprising result is that people neglect non-market methods of satisfying their desires, which discourages non-market cultivation of their virtues. Group pressure makes other people into enforcers so that there are penalties for not going along with the popular currents induced by advertising.

Value studies indicate, however, that the current trend is no longer towards more materialism, but towards lifestyle values (Inglehart, 2000). The shift in values is driven by the affluence in modern society, which allows giving higher priority to the quality of life than to economic growth. However, if we look to actual consumption patterns, it is difficult to discern substantial changes towards more temperance. Frey et al. (2005) estimate that an abundance of television watching leads to a lack of self-control and balance, presumably because those watching television more frequently see a lot more advertisements than others. One very visible form of overconsumption is obesity, which has severe negative consequences on national health, causing diabetes, heart problems and some forms of cancer.

Temperance is related to Hirsch's theory of positional goods (see Chapter 4). Hirsch develops the thesis that as the economy grows, the demand shifts from private goods to positional goods. Empirical research has abundantly confirmed the importance of relative consumption (see e.g. Solnick and Hemenway, 1998; Alpizar et al., 2005; Carlsson et al., 2007). Positional considerations appear particularly important for visible goods but relatively unimportant for invisible ones, like vacation time. This social mirror of consumption works like a ratchet and rises notch by notch (cf. Schor, 1997). According to Hirsch, economic growth will therefore intensify what he terms positional competition, i.e. competition for a higher place within some hierarchy that yields gains for some only by dint of losses for others.

According to Schwartz (2004), concern for status is nothing new, but nonetheless he believes that the problem is more acute now than in the past because of the plethora of choices that the market offers. With the explosion of telecommunications – TV, movies, the Internet, social media – almost everyone has access to information about almost everyone else. Using data from the World Values Survey, Bruni and Stanca (2006) found that the effect of income on both life and financial satisfaction is significantly smaller for heavy television viewers. One reason is possibly that when watching television, people are overwhelmed by images of people wealthier than they are. This contributes to shifting up the benchmark for people's positional concerns. Also Layard (2005) reports that television viewing is negatively related to perceived relative income and happiness, whereas Frey et al. (2005) estimate that television consumption leads to higher material aspirations.

Another way of overstretching the consumer's capacity of consumption is the choice overload that the market provides. The supermarket economy provides consumers with abundant choices. Psychological research shows, however, that the large array of options reduces rather than increases satisfaction from consumption (Carmon et al., 2003; Schwartz, 2004). Iyengar and Lepper (2000) found that an extensive array of options can at first seem highly appealing to consumers, yet can reduce their subsequent motivation to purchase this product. In another experiment, they found that people perform better in a limited-choice context than in an abundant-choice context. One of the explanations is that the experience of opportunity costs of the option that consumers finally select increases the more alternatives there are from which to choose. The existence of multiple alternatives in a marketplace makes it easy to imagine alternatives that do not exist by combining the attractive features of the ones that do exist. The more options are available, the less satisfying each of them is. Another explanation is offered by Carmon et al. (2003). In five experiments, they found that consumers become attached to the choice options during the deliberation process before choosing among them, i.e. they develop a sense of pre-factual possession of the choice options they deliberate. Once they select an option, they can no longer think of themselves as potentially owning the non-chosen options. This induces a feeling of loss and post-choice discomfort. As they state (2003: 28): "choosing feels like losing". This also contributes to dissatisfaction and continuous striving at more consumption in order to diminish the discomfort.

Industriousness

Industriousness concerns the honoring of work, being diligent and committed to the requirements of one's work. There is a general agreement that markets foster industry and inventiveness (Maitland, 1997). Markets stimulate virtues like diligence, punctuality, entrepreneurship and the intrinsic motivation to work (Kreps, 1997). Being one's own boss makes one work harder than salaried employment (McCloskey, 2006).

Goette and Lienhard (2006) found in experiments that working under piece rates, as opposed to fixed wages, increases performance. Piece rates not only directly increased performance relative to fixed wages by increasing effort but also had an endogenous effect: piece-rate workers raised their productivity in each period (perhaps reflecting an increased incentive to learn). While those working under piece rates generally reported feeling more restless than those under fixed wages, they also reported feeling more focused on their work and having more fun. So competition can lead to meritocracy that induces industriousness. Also Frey (1998) argues that the market may generate positive effects on intrinsic motivations to work. An example of such a 'crowding-in' effect is the motivating power of a good salary. The efficient wage theory predicts and empirics show that higher pay tends to result in higher productivity, partly because of the higher motivation of workers. Job experiences can also improve the personal efficacy outside the job (spillover effect). Longitudinal empirical studies show that job position has causal effects on individual psychological functioning and affects personal values and leisure time preferences. Workers whose jobs become more passive also become passive in their leisure and political participation.

The downside of the incentive effects of competition is, however, that markets induce too much working effort and make people overzealous (see Section 4.4). An over-exercised virtue of industriousness can crowd out the other virtues, leading to people living to work instead of working to live. The greater the degree of market competition to which worker-entrepreneurs are exposed, the more they will be judged purely on the basis of the market value of what they produce, and the more relentlessly they must compete with every other worker in this field and treat every project as crucial for their identity, as well as their career. Managers have an obvious interest in encouraging this in order to get as much work as possible out of workers: in increasingly competitive circumstances that incentive increases as the labor regulations restricting them decrease (cf. Schor, 1993). Workers subject to such competition are subject to a relentless and self-perpetuating anxiety and restlessness, which undermines the peace of mind required for the exercise of prudence and temperance. They may find themselves working many hours per week at the expense of the other important commitments in their lives, such as family relationships and long-term health,[3] for a financial reward that, if they thought about it, they would realize they don't really need.

Prudence

Prudence is the virtue of practical wisdom, of calculating efficient means to secure one's more important commitments and interests. It is often argued that the discipline imposed by competition on the market instills a sense of realism regarding the feasibility and value of one's goals and the means by which they may be achieved. Because market transactions are voluntary, competition imposes a discipline on the reasoning of individual agents by requiring them to evaluate the true worth of their activities and products from the perspective of those others with whom they hope to transact and comparing themselves with their competitors. McCloskey (2006) argues that the market teaches humility in the sense of selfless respect for reality. In addition markets train agents to discipline their unruly present-oriented passions, since they are responsible for managing themselves and their resources over time. Through commerce one thus learns to deliberate objectively and to exercise self-command over oneself – to be prudent.

But overly successful market players may stop paying proper attention to the market and consider themselves the best judge of their capacities and plans, thus converting humility into arrogance. In markets, as in races, 'winners' receive a great deal of praise, which can reinforce one's own self-confidence about one's judgment. We are all familiar with stories of chief executive officers (CEOs) lionized by the press for their earlier achievements who came to believe that praise too much and neglected the information available to them about their current performance and capacities. Competitive success itself can thus distort or short-circuit that aspect of prudence, which requires continual attention to the critical reflective analysis of one's rational capacities (Wells and Graafland, 2012).

Markets may also increase economic rationality by making products more comparable. Bowles (1998) remarks that markets increase commensurability because they favor thinking of goods both abstractly and more comparatively as representing more or less market value. Markets are thus powerful simplifiers, allowing radical reductions in the complexity with which one typically views an assortment of disparate goods. However, from a virtue point of view, such a simplification may also reduce a wider sense of wisdom. Aristotle made a sharp distinction between the higher and lower types of pleasure. The use of money tends to reduce all concrete qualities to mere quantities. All qualitative differences are expressed in terms of 'how much?' (Gay, 2003). It has the effect of stripping the world of color, taste and texture. In a money economy, everything looks like a commodity.

Furthermore, market operation may reduce the rationality of economic actors by stimulating a narrow and short-term focus on one's immediate circumstances in opposition to what true prudence requires. For example, although the evidence is contended, several empirical studies suggest that competition in the stock market induces a short-termist orientation in company managers because of impatient capital seeking immediate high returns (e.g. Laverty, 1996; Segelod, 2000; Rappaport, 2005; Graafland, 2016).[4] The argument goes that since any company's stocks are easily substituted for others, managers feel a strong pressure to satisfy shareholder expectations, even if they seem unreasonable.

A final reason why markets may reduce rationality is through the abundance of choices that it creates (already discussed under the heading of the virtue of temperance) that may overwhelm and thus reduce prudent deliberation (see e.g. Shafir and Tversky, 1992). The emotional cost of making trade-offs does more than just diminish our sense of satisfaction with a decision (Schwartz, 2004: 131). It also reduces the quality of decisions by narrowing people's focus and creating confusion due to the heavier psychological demand and the resultant decrements in self-regulation and willpower (Mick et al., 2004). Baumeister and Vohs (2003) performed experiments that show that going through a decision-making process reduces persistence in finishing one's task. This also suggests a reduction in prudence as understood by Aristotle, since Aristotle considers that a rational person not only knows what should be done in a concrete situation but also actually does what he should do (EN 1152a8).

Courage

Since market transactions require mutual consent, a market-based economy teaches self-attribution and perceived self-determination (Kreps, 1997). People who develop self-confidence as a result of numerous transactions on the free market are also more inclined to take risks. From these arguments, it is likely that free markets will stimulate courage.

However, under certain conditions the free market may also elicit fear. If the competition is very fierce and the stakes are very high, people will be under constant danger of losing a lot. The globalization of free markets has made jobs more insecure. Most Americans are well aware that the industrial-era model of secure jobs with good wages has given way to a more cost-conscious and global competitive workplace marked by stagnant wages and growing threats of having jobs outsourced abroad (Pew Research Center, 2006).

Very strong competition and economic incentives may also induce recklessness. For example, according to Rezaee (2005), economic pressure and incentives to meet Wall Street forecasts are the fundamental motives for publicly traded companies to engage in financial statement fraud. Since the costs of corporate fraud can be very significant, these activities are very risky. Grant and Visconti (2006) show that a striking feature of the major companies involved with accounting scandals, like Enron, WorldCom, Ahold and Parmalat, was their reckless and flawed strategy, including over-reliance on acquisition-led growth, misguided vertical integration, penetration in sectors with limited globalization potential and diversification in the absence of synergies. Also the credit crisis indicated that financial markets free of government regulation (of the banking and housing market) may result in too risky investment patterns. By packaging and selling mortgage loans for the sub-prime segment to investors around the world, information about the risks of the underlying loans was lost. In addition, rating agencies made too optimistic assumptions about the performance of these securities. Because of the competition between these agencies, they gave double-A ratings to almost junk bonds. Furthermore, the market incentives from high bonuses pushed portfolio managers to invest too many funds in risky assets. This indicates a link between market incentives and the crowding out of the virtue of courage.

Justice

Justice includes several various dimensions. One of them is the virtue of honesty. Since trustfulness is related to trust, we also discuss some literature on trust.

In commercial societies where buyers and sellers are free to switch to other partners, establishing a reputation for honesty is certainly the best policy. Members of commercial societies therefore have an interest in honesty: there is a competitive advantage to interacting with honest merchants and thus for being seen as honest oneself.

A free market system may also foster trust and social capital because of institutions that back the market system. Most important is the rule of law. The institutions of law and order detect and punish people who break contracts, steal or do other such non-cooperative things. If these institutions work well, then people will have reason to believe that the chance people have to get away with this kind of behavior is small. Hence, people will have good reason to refrain from untruthful behavior and, as a result, most people will believe that most people can be trusted. Research by Knack and Keefer (1997), Zak and Knack (2001), Berggren and Jordahl (2006) and Graafland and Compen (2015) confirms that the quality of the legal structure and the protection of property rights positively affect trust. Market participation will enforce this effect: if one repeatedly makes deals with other people that turn out to meet expectations, one may develop a trustworthy outlook on other people as a matter of habit and unreflected internalization. On the basis of experiments in 15 small-scale societies, Henrich et al. (2001) found that in countries where payoffs to cooperation and market integration are large, the offers in an (anonymous) ultimate game are greater. They explain this finding by the fact that the more frequently people experience market transactions, the more they will also experience abstract sharing principles of fairness. Also access to sound money may foster trust, because a stable value of money will be conducive to engaging in voluntary transactions.

However, honesty can be undermined by the effects of increasing competition. First, players in the market may change constantly so that information quickly becomes outdated and long-term horizons collapse. The short-term focus induced by competition can crowd out people's long-term commitments (Sennet, 2000). If people are highly mobile, they invest less in local amenities and social capital (Glaeser and DiPasquale, 1999). Also Putnam (2000) considers mobility a cause of erosion of social bonds. People trust each other more if fewer people are moving house and if the community is more homogenous (Knack and Keefer, 1997; Zak and Knack, 2001; Berggren and Jordahl, 2006).

Second, Shleifer (2004) argues that fierce competition may promote corruption. If a government official takes money in exchange for reducing taxes or tariffs that the briber owes to the government, corruption reduces the production costs of the briber and gives him a competitive advantage. Other things being equal, a firm that is burdened by ethical scruples is presumably at a competitive disadvantage in the marketplace compared with a rival not laboring under such a burden (Maitland, 1997). Likewise, competition between rating agencies appears to have induced a softening of professional standards ('rating inflation') because of the clear financial incentive rating agencies have to keep their paying customers happy by giving them somewhat higher ratings than objectively warranted (Skreta and Veldkam, 2009). Another example is accounting scandals (see also the discussion on courage earlier). Rezaee (2005) and Choo and Tan (2007) found that the most fundamental factor of this kind of fraud is economic incentives. Without creative accounting, the costs of capital might have been too high for them to survive. Choo and Tan (2007: 209) quote Messner and Rosenfeld who observe that "given the strong, relentless pressure for everyone to succeed, understood in terms of an inherently elusive monetary goal, people formulate wants and desires that are difficult, if not impossible, to satisfy within the confines of legally permissible behavior". The root cause of corporate scandals was not many executives suddenly deciding to be crooks, but rather lay with the competitive system in which they were working (Grant and Visconti, 2006).

Furthermore, free market institutions may decrease trust by fostering income inequality (Graafland and Compen, 2015; see also Chapter 7). The negative relationship between income inequality and trust has also been found at the micro-level. For example, Bloom (1999) showed that wage dispersion in baseball teams has a negative impact on the performance of both players and teams because it instills feelings of inequity, promotes dissatisfaction and therefore undermines cooperation. Similar results are found by Bloom and Michel (2002) and Wade et al. (2006). A public policy that is committed to promoting social capital should therefore address the presence of grave inequalities.

Love (benevolence)

The market allows self-interested behavior as long as one respects the negative rights to freedom of others. When individualism spreads around, love (altruism, benevolence and generosity) may come under pressure. Also competition puts pressure on the virtue of love. Competition leads to a struggle for survival. It teaches men to think of each other as competitors (Knight, 1925) who intend to gain market share by beating you.

Furthermore, the literature on intrinsic motivation provides considerable empirical evidence that market operations crowd out contributions to public good (Bowles and Polania-Reyes, 2012; Bowles, 2016; Abatayo and Lynham, 2016; Moros et al., 2019). For example, there are a number of studies that show that price incentives harm the intrinsic motivation to contribute to a social good. In particular, paying someone to perform a task that she or he might willingly have done without pay may undermine their motivation. In a well-known research by Titmuss (1970), it was found that the market allocation system for blood in the United States proved less efficient than the gift allocation system in England. In terms of price per unit of blood to the patient, the market system was 5 to 15 times more costly than the voluntary system in Britain, whereas the risks for the patients of disease and death because of contaminated blood were substantially greater. Individuals who give blood for altruistic reasons may suffer a utility loss when blood is priced. The reason might be that the price incentive is perceived to be coercive, thereby reducing self-determination and the freedom to act. Besides, price incentives may frame choice behavior in terms of the self-interest rather than the responsibility for the common good. The monetary incentive provided by the market may thus crowd out the intrinsic motivation to help other people. In the extreme case, the use of the price mechanism could destroy intrinsic motivation totally, and when the use of price incentives is unable to produce any supply of blood donation at all, the net impact may be negative. The undermining effect is maintained even if the monetary incentive is stopped (Gneezy and Rustichini, 2000). Crowding out intrinsic motivation by price incentives holds for a wide variety of other areas of economy and society, as well as for many different countries and time periods and in different research environments (Frey and Jegen, 2001).[5]

There is, however, also research that shows that competition may crowd in (enforce) intrinsic motivations. For example, Graafland (2020b) found that the intensity of (technological) competition stimulates the intrinsic motivation of companies to engage in corporate social responsibility. A possible explanation for this difference in findings is that rewarding socially desirable behavior is more likely to be perceived as supportive and increasing self-determination in a business context than in the context of a private household. Companies that face severe competition may not be able to survive if costly investments in corporate social responsibility are not rewarded by market parties, whereas financial rewarding of household contributions to the common good, such as blood donation, will only have a negligible effect on the continuity of their way of life.

Conclusion

Table 10.1 presents an overview of the preceding discussion and compares it with Smith's view as measured by the semantic network data-mining approach in Section 9.4. Two conclusions stand out. First, there seems to be a fairly good fit between Smith's views and the indications provided by the literature review. Whereas Smith firmly believed in the positive effects of commercial society on the virtue of industriousness, he was concerned about the vulnerability of the virtues of temperance, prudence and benevolence under free market conditions. Compared with the qualitative tendencies from current literature, these concerns are still relevant for today's economy.

Second, based on this overview, the verdict on the doux commerce thesis is ambiguous. Whereas we find indications of a positive influence of free market operation on the virtue of industriousness and a negative influence on the virtue of temperance and benevolence, the effects on the other three virtues in our framework (prudence, justice and courage) are ambivalent. This indicates that the impact of market operation on virtues is too diverse to take sides in the debate about the doux commerce or self-destruction thesis.

TABLE 10.1
Impact of market operation on virtues

	Number of citations in Wealth of Nations		Qualitative indications from current literature
	Positive	Negative	
Temperance	23	24	Market operation crowds out temperance.
Industriousness	27	4	Market operation fosters industriousness.
Prudence	31	23	The net effect of market operation on prudence is ambiguous.
Courage	2	4	Market operation stimulates courage. Fierce competition may encourage fear as well as recklessness.
Justice	18	5	A good legal system and security of property rights stimulates trustfulness; fierce competition stimulates fraud.
Love	19	28	Market operation discourages generosity through crowding out by monetary incentives.
Total	120	88	

10.2 THE IMPORTANCE OF VIRTUES: RESULTS FROM GAME THEORY AND EXPERIMENTAL ECONOMICS

Virtues and social outcomes in game theory

In game theory various types of games have been developed that provide theoretical insight into the effects of social preferences and beliefs on the efficiency of the outcome. Table 10.2 provides an overview of five types of games that have often been researched (Henrich et al., 2004; Bowles, 2016). Next, we shortly discuss each of them.

The prisoner's dilemma, the public goods game and the dictator game are non-sequential games. The public goods game is a prisoner's dilemma game (see later) with more than two players. An individual may choose to bear a cost in order to take an action that furthers some public good. Examples are payment of taxes, limiting carbon footprint, upholding social norms and maintaining public safety (for example during COVID 19 crisis). If the cost to each individual in contributing is greater than the benefit she personally will receive, not contributing at all is the individually payoff-maximizing choice, no matter what the other citizens do. From a social point of view, the best outcome is that everyone contributes, because then everyone would be better off. The dictator game only involves a proposer's division between herself and another player. The recipient cannot respond to the proposer's decision. Since the dictator game only involves one player actually choosing a strategy, it cannot really be classified as sequential. Self-interested proposers will allocate nothing to the recipient.

The ultimatum game and trust game are sequential games. A game is sequential if one player performs her or his actions after another player. In a sequential game, the second mover can reciprocate the first player's move. This disciplines the first mover. Besides preferences, the beliefs of the first player about the preferences of the second player also affect the

TABLE 10.2
Overview of well-known games[a]

Game	Definition of the game	Predictions with rational and self-regarding players
Prisoner's dilemma	Two players, each of whom can either cooperate or defect.	Each player defects.
Public goods	N players simultaneously decide about their contribution to a public good.	Each player contributes nothing.
Dictator	A proposer dictates a division of a fixed sum of money between the proposer and a responder. The responder cannot reject.	The proposer does not share.
Ultimatum	A proposer offers x. If responder rejects x, both earn zero; if x is accepted, the proposer earns S – x and the responder earns x.	Proposer offers $x = \varepsilon$, where ε is the smallest money unit. Any $x > 0$ is accepted by responder.
Trust	Investor has endowment S and makes a transfer y between 0 and S to the trustee. Trustee receives 3y and can send back any x between 0 and 3y.	Trustee repays nothing and investor invests nothing.

[a] Adapted from Bowles (2016)

outcome. In the ultimatum game, a proposer can divide a fixed amount of money between herself and a responder. The responder can accept the offer or reject it, in which case neither player earns anything. This opens the possibility of negative reciprocity. In theory, self-interested responders will accept any positive offer, and proposers anticipating this will offer the smallest amount possible. In the trust game, trustees may express positive reciprocity by repaying an investor who has exhibited trust in the trustee (Camerer and Fehr, 2004). Self-interested trustees will keep everything and repay nothing. Self-interested investors who anticipate this would transfer nothing. If they expect the trustee to reciprocate, the trustor will contribute more.

How virtues affect the outcomes of a game can be illustrated by the prisoner's dilemma. The metaphor of the prisoner's dilemma is based on the following story credited to Albert Tucker. Two prisoners are arrested and put in separate cells. The sheriff presents the following alternatives. If either A or B confesses that A and B committed the crime, the confessor gets a sentence of one year in jail, the other one five years. If both confess, each will be convicted, but can expect a lighter sentence of three years. If neither confesses, the outcome is a short two-year sentence for each.

Table 10.3 shows the possible outcomes of the game. Each partner has the choice of confessing or not confessing, and the payoff to each strategy depends on what the other party chooses to do. Both prisoner A and B are uncertain about what the other will do. Independent of what B chooses, A is better off if she confesses. In particular, if B confesses, confessing yields three years in jail to A, whereas not confessing results in five years in jail. If B does not confess, confessing then means one year in jail for A, whereas not confessing results in two years in jail for A and likewise for B. As a result, both go to jail for three years. This is not optimal for them, because if both would not confess, they would both spend fewer years in jail. It is, in fact, Pareto-efficient for them if both would not confess. This Pareto improvement results from an externality. In particular, the choice of A does not only affect her own term of imprisonment but also the number of years that B will spend in jail. Likewise, the choice of B influences the number of years that A will have to be in jail. Even if both prisoners agreed to a policy of not confessing before being imprisoned, this policy will not come about if both are self-interested. It will be in the interest of each to break with the policy (Sen, 1967).

Despite the fanciful nature of the example, the prisoner's dilemma is a real problem with daily applications in business and society as a whole. The potential disastrous result that uncoordinated choices of rational actors have has been coined the tragedy of the commons. The so-called commons existed as pieces of land during the sixteenth century that were accessible to all members of the community and could be used for the grazing of cattle, the cutting of peat, the collection of wood and small agriculture. The essence of the commons was that every member had a right to use these grounds to provide themselves with the

TABLE 10.3
The prisoner's dilemma

	Prisoner A confesses	*Prisoner A does not confess*
Prisoner B confesses	A and B both 3 years in jail	A 5 years, B one year in jail
Prisoner B does not confess	A 1 year, B 5 years in jail	A and B both 2 years in jail

necessary goods rather than a right to possess. One could not use these sources for trading and profit making. The commons functioned well as long as there was enough land for everybody. However, when land became scarce, each peasant had an incentive to make more use of the commons. This resulted in an overburdening of the ground. In the end, the common ground became fully exhausted and useless for all.

How do virtues affect the outcomes in the prisoner's dilemma game? First, the virtue of altruism tends to raise the probability of an efficient outcome. If the prisoners in the prisoner's dilemma of Table 10.3 cared about the sentence of the other criminal, they would prefer not to confess and end up in the optimal quadrant. Suppose that the prisoners attach an intrinsic value with weight v to the other's payoff and a weight $(1 - v)$ to their own payoff. If $v = 0.35$, prisoner A will choose not to confess if she trusts B not to confess too (and vice versa). However, she will still choose to confess (and vice versa) if she does not trust B. Hence, the choice becomes dependent on the expectation about the behavior of others and therefore on trust. If trust is lacking, the social efficient solution will only be selected if the prisoners are highly altruistic: if each does not trust the other to cooperate, v must be 0.5 to arrive at the cooperative outcome. If, on the other hand, each expects the other to cooperate and attaches a weight more than 0.25 to the other's payoff, she will herself cooperate. Hence, the less trust there is, the more altruism is required to yield cooperation (Collard, 1978).

Trust reflects the belief that others are just and trustworthy and is therefore related to the virtue of justice. Also reciprocity is related to the virtue of justice. This particularly holds for so-called compensatory justice, which concerns the justice of restoring to a person what he has done wrong or good to you (Velasquez, 1998). The principle 'an eye for an eye, a tooth for a tooth' is the prototypical example of negative reciprocity. Reciprocal motives manifest themselves not only in people's refusal to cooperate with others who are being uncooperative but also in their willingness to sacrifice to hurt others who are being unfair (Rabin, 1993, 1998). In the ultimatum game, negative reciprocity improves cooperation. The more responders are willing to negatively reciprocate small offers of the proposers, sacrificing their own money to punish a proposer who has been unfair, the more proposers are induced to contribute (Camerer and Fehr, 2004). In the trust game, positive reciprocity improves the social outcome. Positive reciprocity is the impulse or the desire to be kind to those who have been kind to us. If the trustor believes that the trustee is willing to positively reciprocate the offer of the proposer, the proposer is encouraged to share a larger part of the endowment. This trust in the trustee leads to a mutual gain for both the trustor and the trustee. Besides trustfulness and reciprocity, distributive justice also may foster a more cooperative outcome. An example is the so-called third-party punishment game. In this game the dictator game is extended with a third player who can at some cost assign punishment to the dictator for unfair behavior. A self-interested third party will never punish. The stronger the third player is intrinsically motivated to share, the more the dictator is disciplined to comply with the sharing norm.

Although game theory does not explicitly model the effects of individual virtues such as prudence, temperance and courage, it could be argued that these dispositions are also likely to improve cooperation. For example, Fehr and Leibbrandt (2011) implemented a public goods game and an experimental measure of impatience and found that players with both greater patience (prudence) and greater cooperativeness were more inclined to contribute to the public good. When it comes to courage, Nooteboom (2017) argued that in a situation of uncertainty it requires courage to trust others. In deciding to trust others, not only people's beliefs about others but also their attitudes towards uncertainty matter, because the decision to trust involves making oneself vulnerable to the trustworthiness of another, which is ambiguous. Hence, the more a person dislikes ambiguity, the less attractive she will find it to trust another person. Furthermore, temperance may support the ability to withstand the inclination to allocate endowments only to oneself in the dictator and ultimatum game and foster positive reciprocity in the trust game.

Virtues and welfare-enhancing behavior in experimental economics

In experimental economics, it is now an established outcome that people exhibit substantially different degrees of social preferences, with a substantial portion of people showing pro-social behavior that cannot be explained by the selfishness axiom (Fehr and Fischbacher, 2002; Henrich et al., 2004). For example, when the prisoner's game is played, between 40% and 60% of the players cooperate rather than defect, the latter being the theoretical prediction for selfish people.

In this section, we are particularly interested in how virtue-related preferences and beliefs affect social outcomes. Next we give a snapshot of researches that support the thesis that preferences can be related to individual virtues (prudence, temperance and courage) and social virtues (justice and altruism) and foster cooperation, without the pretention to give a complete overview of the rapidly expanding literature.

Mischel et al. (1989) performed the most widely known experiment regarding delay gratification, the so-called marshmallow experiment. The children who delayed gratification more had, as teenagers, greater social competence, self-assurance and self-worth and were rated by their parents as more mature, better able to cope with stress, more likely to plan ahead and more likely to use reasoning. Patience in gratification, which can be interpreted as prudence and temperance, is thus associated with better mental health and likely also better economic outcomes. Curry et al. (2008) found that more impatient individuals contribute less to the public good than do patient ones. Fehr and Leibbrandt (2011) estimated that those who exhibited less impatient behavior in an experiment were in the field less likely to overexploit the common-pool resource. Noussair et al. (2014) constructed an experiment that distinguishes prudent from imprudent and temperate from intemperate behavior. They correlated individuals' prudence and temperance levels to their demographic profiles and their financial decisions outside the experiment and observed that prudence is positively correlated with saving, as predicted by precautionary saving theory. Temperance is negatively correlated with the riskiness of portfolio choices. Kocher et al. (2017) researched the relationship between self-control and cooperation. The self-control problem is often perceived as an intrapersonal conflict between better judgment and temptation and therefore links to prudence as well as to temperance. They found a strong association between self-control and cooperation. Taken together, the existing literature on cooperation and time preferences would be consistent with the notion that self-control benefits cooperation.

Defining courage as "mental or moral strength to withstand danger, fear or difficulty" (Merriam Webster), we assume it can be related to risk aversion. Kocher et al. (2017) found that, controlling for self-control levels, a higher level of risk aversion is associated with lower levels of contributions because more risk-averse individuals are more likely to avoid incurring the costs of self-control to behave cooperatively. Li et al. (2019) researched the effect of risk aversion on trust, controlling for beliefs. Their experiments showed that people's ambiguous attitudes and beliefs both matter for their trust decisions and that people who are more ambiguity-averse are less inclined to trust others in a trust game.

Besides individual virtues, several types of preferences that can be related to social virtues have been extensively researched, such as reciprocity (e.g. Ashraf et al., 2006; Ambrus and Pathak, 2011; Regner, 2018; Yamakawa et al., 2016), honesty (Abeler et al., 2019) and altruism (e.g. Maggian and Villeval, 2016; Hernandez-Lagos et al., 2017; Engler et al., 2018; Alempaki et al., 2019). In many experiments, reciprocity has beneficial effects. Evidence from public goods experiments shows that most participants are conditional cooperators, i.e. their contributions to the public good are positively correlated with their ex ante beliefs about the average group contribution or with the actual contributions made by the same (Chaudhuri, 2011). Fehr and Gächter (2000) showed that in a repeated public goods game, average contributions decline over time. This indicates that because of the presence of selfish subjects, the reciprocal subjects gradually notice that they are matched with free riders and refuse to be taken advantage of by them. If a punishment opportunity is introduced, cooperators are willing to punish the free riders, and this induces the free riders to increase cooperation.[6] The presence of reciprocal players encourages selfish players to contribute to the public good (Camerer and Fehr, 2006, Ambrus and Pathak, 2011). A minority of other-regarding individuals can thus generate a cooperative aggregate outcome. Conversely, a minority of self-regarding individuals can trigger a non-cooperative aggregate outcome because selfish players can influence future contributions of reciprocal players. As a result, it is worthwhile for them to contribute more of their endowment to the public good at the beginning of the game. In equilibrium, reciprocal players correctly anticipate these high contribution levels in early periods, which induces them to also contribute. Ashraf et al. (2006) found that in a trust game, the amount sent by the trustor was related to beliefs of trustworthiness (defined as the amount returned by the trustee) and to the willingness to be kind to others (altruism).

Regarding altruism, the experimental literature distinguishes unconditional from conditional other-regarding preferences (Sobel, 2005; Engler et al., 2018). An example of the first class is Maggian and Villeval (2016), who estimated that lying by children is driven mainly by selfish motives and envy. Children with stronger social preferences are less prone to deception. Another example is Kuhn and Uler (2019), who constructed a "personal responsibility index" derived from a series of survey questions eliciting information on subjects' concern for their contribution to externalities – such as engaging in recycling. They found that individuals with a high personal responsibility index increase their carbon-offset purchases as their own environmental damage increases. Furthermore, Hernandez-Lagos et al. (2017) performed an experiment with relative performance incentives in indefinitely repeated settings and estimated that other-regarding individuals internalize the externality they impose on others, without engaging in long-term strategic behavior.

In conditional other-regarding models, the response of a second mover in a two-stage game depends on the perceived altruism of the first mover. For example, Alempaki et al. (2019) researched the response to unkind behavior. They found evidence that individuals engage in deception to reciprocate unkind behavior: The smaller the payoff received in the first stage of a dictator game, the higher the lying rate. Intention-based reciprocity largely drives behavior, as individuals use deception to punish unkind behavior and truth-telling to reward kind behavior. Oliveira et al. (2015) researched the effects of selfish behavior on group behavior in a public good provision. They first identified experimental participants' social preferences. Next, they systematically assigned individuals to homogeneous or heterogeneous groups to examine the impact of 'bad apples' on cooperation and efficiency. They found that groups with more selfish types achieve lower levels of efficiency for two reasons. Not only do selfish players contribute less, but they also induce lower contributions from the conditional cooperators, and this effect increases with the number of selfish players.

From this overview, we derive a basic and simple conclusion that, although not surprising, has not often been explicitly stated, namely, that preferences and beliefs that are fostered by the virtuous development of people stimulate cooperation and, in many instances (although not all), lead to Pareto-efficient outcomes.

10.3   VIRTUES AND HAPPINESS

Whereas Smith was ambivalent with regard to the effects of commerce on virtues, he was quite unambiguous in his rejection of Mandeville's thesis that virtues destroy the economy and societal flourishing. In this section, we consider whether Smith's view in this regard is still supported by modern research. We focus particularly on the role of civic virtues, including generalized trust (trusting most people you do not know). Although strictly speaking generalized trust is not a civic virtue, it reveals how individuals perceive the civic virtuousness of other individuals, including virtues such as trustfulness, integrity, honesty, reliability and justice. If many individuals in a society are trustful, members of that society are more likely to trust other people. Moreover, Nooteboom (2017) argues that trust also reflects virtuousness in the trustor, as in a situation of uncertainty, it requires courage to trust others. Indeed, generalized trust has also been called moralistic trust (Uslaner, 2002). It is moral because it follows from the moral dictate that people should be trustworthy and that people should trust each other. Therefore, one could interpret generalized trust as an indicator of civic virtuousness, as it meets the definition of a civic virtue proposed by Bowles (2011) (e.g. a social norm that facilitates the workings of the institutions advocated by liberals; see Chapter 9).

The literature has argued and shown that trust is important in explaining life satisfaction (Helliwell, 2003; Helliwell, 2006; Bjørnskov et al., 2007; Bjørnskov et al., 2010; Oishi et al., 2011; Graafland and Compen, 2015). Trust is a precondition for social order and social cohesion, without which many forms of social interaction are much more difficult (Helliwell and Putnam, 2004). People benefit from living in an environment where other people can be trusted. Helliwell and Barrington-Leigh (2010) explored the determinants of the respondents' sense of belonging to their communities and found that measures of trust explain the extent to which one feels a strong sense of belonging, which in turn increases subjective well-being. Trust reduces information and transaction costs and thus lowers the complexity and uncertainty of decision-making in everyday life. Furthermore, trust is likely to increase health because individuals will be less healthy the greater the lack of social cohesion in a country. Empirical research by Berggren and Jordahl (2006) and Jen et al. (2010) supported a positive relation between trust and health indicators. Since life satisfaction has been found to be positively associated with income and health (Helliwell et al., 2016), one would expect that trust increases life satisfaction. Furthermore, trust is often associated

TABLE 10.4
Estimated effects of civic virtues on individual life satisfaction[a]

	Life satisfaction
Honesty	0.05***
Generalized trust	0.04***

[a] Significance: * $p < 0.05$ ** $p < 0.01$ *** $p < 0.001$. Controlled for various control variables.

with other beneficial outcomes that increase life satisfaction, such as a reduction in violent crimes (Bjørnskov et al., 2007).

Whereas most previous research based their conclusions on cross-country data, there is still a lack of micro-evidence linking life satisfaction to generalized trust or other civic virtues. In order to fill this gap, we test the impact of civic virtues and trust on life satisfaction using the micro-data of individuals from five waves of the World and European Value Studies between 1990 and 2014. The dataset consists of 247,992 individuals from 83 countries. In order to measure civic virtues, we used two indicators from the illegal–dishonesty domain of the Morally Debatable Behaviors Scale (Katz et al., 1994) on the extent to which respondents believe cheating on taxes or someone accepting a bribe in the course of their duties is justifiable. Generalized trust is measured by the (binary) response to the question "In general, do you think most people can be trusted?" – a standard approach in the literature (Özcan and Bjørnskov, 2011). Life satisfaction is measured by the survey question from the World and European Value Studies on life satisfaction ("How satisfied are you with your life?").

The estimation results of the regression analysis are reported in Table 10.4. The estimation results support Smith's view that civic virtues increase life satisfaction, as both honesty and generalized trust are significantly positively related to life satisfaction.

10.4 VIRTUES AS MODERATORS BETWEEN FREE MARKETS AND WELL-BEING[7]

Whereas Chapter 4 and the previous sections in this chapter discussed the isolated influences of market institutions and virtues on aspects of happiness or well-being, recent studies have considered that the influence of institutions may be contingent on virtues. The central thesis that underlies this mechanism is that free market institutions contribute to well-being in so far as the key market actors practice moral virtues.

We present five studies that provide some support for this thesis. In these studies, virtues are measured by long-term orientation (as a proxy for temperance and prudence), trust (as a proxy of justice and honesty) and intrinsic motivation to take responsibility for the environment (as a proxy of altruism). Aspects of well-being are measured by the human development index, the Organisation for Economic Co-operation and Development (OECD) Better Life Index (BLI) and the environmental performance of companies

Long-term orientation

Well-being is not only likely to depend on market institutions like economic freedom (see Chapter 4) but (among other factors) also on virtues or culture. As culture is a very broad concept, we focus on one specific element of culture, namely long-term orientation. Long-term or future orientation can be defined as "the degree to which individuals in organizations or societies engage in future-oriented behaviors such as planning, investing in the future, and delaying individual or collective gratification" (House et al., 2004: 12). Long-term orientation is related to various types of virtues, such as self-command, temperance, patience, perseverance and foresight (prudence). People living in countries that are not long-term oriented like to enjoy the moment, but might be incapable of seeing the incompatibility of their current behavior with their long-term goals. In contrast, long-term–oriented people have a strong capacity for maintaining self-control and prepare for the future in order to reach their long-term goals. For example, by putting more effort in working now to advance their career and long-term economic prosperity, they can enjoy more consumption and leisure in the future. Long-term orientation is likely to encourage saving and technological development (Chen, 2013; Galor and Özak, 2016) and is therefore likely to be related to higher levels of long-term economic prosperity. Bukowski and Rudnicki (2019) have shown that long-term orientation is a strong cultural predictor of the intensity of national innovation. The rise in savings and economic prosperity will lead to improved quality of housing and an increase in the number of jobs created.

Long-term orientation has also been linked to non-material aspects of the human condition (House et al., 2004), such as health and education. As long-term–oriented people are able to delay gratification and are able to plan for the future, they are also more likely to invest in their (psychological) health and education that create more favorable future prospects. Chen (2013) found a positive relationship between health and language structures that associate the future and the present (an indicator of long-term orientation). Figlio et al. (2016) estimated that students from countries with long-term–oriented attitudes perform better than students from cultures that do not emphasize the importance of delayed gratification. Moreover, parents from long-term–oriented cultures are more likely to secure better educational opportunities for their children. Higher levels of education, in turn, encourage civic participation. Through the effects on education, health, income and jobs, long-term orientation will also positively affect life satisfaction. Furthermore, long-term orientation will help people to maintain a proper work–life balance. People that lack a sufficient work–life balance may suffer from negative consequences for their well-being, and these consequences are likely to become more pressing and manifest in the long run. Long-term–oriented people will be more able to anticipate and take more account of the negative long-term consequences of an improper work–life balance and adjust their behavior accordingly.

The literature has also argued that a long time horizon will foster the implementation of environmental policies by companies. The reason is that environmental investments cost money in the short term (Brammer and Millington, 2008), whereas the benefits from engaging in environmental responsibility are mainly realized in the long run (Mallin et al., 2013; Rehbein et al., 2013; Graafland, 2016). Developing business opportunities to meet consumers' increasing demand for environmentally friendly products often takes a long time (Dijk et al., 2013). Hence, the benefits from such investments in lowering production costs and augmenting the environmental quality of products mainly exist in the future. A company with an excessive focus on short-term results will reckon with a lower net discounted value from investments in environmental improvements than a company that takes account of long-term results, and will therefore be less inclined to invest in such measures. Finally, long-term orientation is also likely to improve health and safety, since it encourages people and business to focus on long-term gains and creates more awareness of the importance of a safety culture in companies. Empirical research by Reader et al. (2015) supported this positive relationship.

In this section, we assume that for these reasons the relationship between economic freedom and quality of life is likely to be moderated by long-term orientation. Moderated models explain when a given relationship occurs by explaining that its strength depends on the level of some other (moderating) variables (Preacher et al., 2007). The intuition of the moderation argument is that economic freedom is not a sufficient condition for stimulating behavior that increases well-being, because that also depends on how people make use of their freedom. If people and companies exhibit virtues that stimulate and enable them to engage in future-oriented behaviors such as planning, investing in the future and delaying individual or collective gratification, they will use the freedom that economic freedom institutions allow to make investments that stimulate their welfare in the long term. For organizations this means sacrificing current profit for future development and sustainability, and for people this translates into a propensity to save and invest for the future. Economic freedom without a long-term perspective is less likely to lead to higher levels of well-being that demand long-term investments. Instant gratification limits people in many facets of their well-being, because they lack the motivation to invest in goods and services that only pay off in the long run, such as investment in health, education, housing and environment.

Moderation also implies that the influence of the moderator on the dependent variable is contingent on the independent variable. The same can be said of long-term orientation and economic freedom. When there is no economic freedom, long-term–oriented people will not invest to meet their long-term needs, as the government is assumed to take responsibility for human well-being in society, including education, health and material welfare. Moreover, long-term–oriented people living in countries with low levels of economic freedom may fear that the state will expropriate their property such that they underinvest in satisfying their long-term needs. Hence, whereas under the first set of conditions – economic freedom without long-term orientation – economic actors will be disinclined to engage in practices that will pay out only in the long term, under the second set – long-term orientation without economic freedom – they would perhaps have a stronger inclination to do so, but in practice trust that the government takes responsibility rather than taking personal responsibility for their long-term interests. Based on these arguments, we surmise that the effect of economic freedom on well-being is positively moderated by long-term orientation.

This hypothesis was tested in three researches with different data (Graafland, 2019b). In the first research, the dependent variables are the 11 dimensions of the OECD BLI. The data are available for the years 2011–2017 and 37 countries. For economic freedom, the Economic Freedom of the World Index (EFWI) of the Fraser Institute was used. Long-term or future orientation has been taken from the GLOBE project that measured long-term orientation for 61 societies (on a scale ranging from 1 to 7) through a survey measurement (House et al., 2004).[8]

Table 10.5 reports the results of the multiple regression analysis. Economic freedom is significantly and positively related to most indicators of the BLI except community and work–life balance. Furthermore, the findings support the interaction effect between economic freedom (EF) and long-term orientation (LTO) for income, community, health, life satisfaction, safety and work–life balance. It is noticeable that in four out of five cases of insignificant interaction effect (jobs, education, environment and civic engagement), a

TABLE 10.5
Estimation results of the OECD Better Life Index

	Housing	Income	Jobs	Community	Education	Environment
EF	0.47***	0.57***	0.58***	0.16	0.37***	0.25***
LTO	−0.03	0.14	0.41***	−0.16	0.31***	0.18**
EF * LTO	−0.00	0.27***	−0.02	0.20**	0.00	−0.02
R²	0.73	0.77	0.74	0.60	0.92	0.73

	Civic engaging	Health	Life satisfaction	Safety	Work–life balance	
EF	0.29***	0.18**	0.21***	0.21***	−0.55***	
LTO	0.42**	−0.41***	0.01	−0.03	−0.45***	
EF * LTO	−0.10	0.31***	0.14**	0.11**	0.17**	
R²	0.67	0.72	0.83	0.89	0.70	

[a] EF: Economic freedom. LTO: Long-term orientation. Standardized coefficients. Significance: * $p < 0.05$, ** $p < 0.01$, *** $p < 0.001$. For more details, see Graafland (2019b).

significant positive effect for the linear influence of long-term orientation on the respective well-being indicator is found. Only for housing does no significant positive relation with long-term orientation or its interaction with economic freedom exist.

In another study, the effect of the interaction between EF and LTO has been studied in an analysis of corporate social responsibility (CSR) by companies (Graafland and Noorderhaven, 2020), using ASSET4 data for a sample of 3,045 companies from 34 countries for 2005–2014. Time orientation plays an important role in CSR (Graafland, 2016). Graafland and Noorderhaven argue that whether market incentives stimulate CSR crucially depends on the perception of time. The time horizon applied in the calculation of costs and benefits of CSR is influenced by a firm's environment. The longer the time horizon of the society, the more stakeholders of companies will value long-term benefits of voluntary CSR initiatives, e.g. in terms of quality of stakeholder relations (Rehbein et al., 2013). And if consumers and other stakeholders care about the quality of life of future generations, they are more likely to protest against unsustainable business practices and are more willing to punish irresponsible behavior (King, 2008). LTO in the national environment can press managers to engage in CSR practices that will pay out only in the future. This suggests that a high level of EF is associated with a high level of CSR, provided that the firm operates in a society that takes a long-term perspective. Vice versa, LTO stimulates CSR, especially if firms have the freedom to decide about their level of CSR. Firms within a particular society may also differ in their time orientation (Souder and Bromiley, 2012), and the extent to which this is the case may also have an effect on CSR. The longer the time horizon of the firm, the more it will take into account the long-term benefits of CSR. And just like with societal-level LTO, the extent to which an orientation on the future leads to extra CSR efforts will depend also on the level of CSR forced by government regulation (reflecting the level of economic freedom). This suggests an interactive effect on CSR of economic freedom from both society-level and company-level long-term orientation.

The estimation results of Graafland and Noorderhaven (2020) are summarized in Table 10.6. The societal level measure was retrieved from Hofstede's database. For measuring the LTO of the company, Graafland and Noorderhaven followed Souder and Bromiley

TABLE 10.6

Estimation results of CSR[a]

Economic freedom (EF)	−0.11 (0.000)
Society's long-term orientation (LTO$_s$)	0.02 (0.844)
Interaction term EF * LTO$_s$	0.13 (0.005)
Company's long-term orientation (LTO$_c$)	−0.02 (0.056)
Interaction term EF * LTO$_c$	0.04 (0.008)

[a] Standardized coefficients; p-values are reported between parentheses. Number of firms = 3,045; Number of countries = 34; Number of years: 10; Number of industries: 54. Number of observations = 19,167. For the estimation results of the control variables, see Graafland and Noorderhaven (2020).

(2012), who defined it as the ratio between capital expenditure and depreciation expense. Table 10.6 shows that EF has a negative effect on CSR, but no main effect of LTO is found, either at the level of the society or that of the company. Both the interaction term of EF and society-level LTO and the interaction term of EF and company-level LTO are significantly positively related to CSR. At the societal level LTO may affect the CSR policy of a firm through the pressure exerted by various groups of stakeholders, like influence groups and consumers. At the company level LTO can have a more direct influence on the level of CSR, through the values and beliefs of decision-makers in the firm.

These results have implications for managers and policy makers. Although LTO at the level of the society cannot be influenced, LTO at the level of the firm can be to a certain extent. For instance, policy makers can prescribe corporate governance arrangements that encourage managers to focus more on long-term effects of their decisions. Likewise, top management teams and boards of directors can also implement policies (e.g. regarding rewards) that put more emphasis on the longer term. The analysis of Graafland and Noorderhaven shows, however, that in terms of stimulating CSR, this will only be effective in environments where firms have sufficient economic freedom, a factor that can be influenced by policy makers at the level of the society.

Trust

As discussed in Section 10.1, the economic importance of generalized trust (e.g. trusting most people you do not know) for economic growth has been established by empirical research (Knack and Keefer, 1997; Berggren and Jordahl, 2006; Bjørnskov, 2012; Algan and Cahuc, 2014). As trust has also been shown to be positively related to education (Papagapitos and Riley, 2009; Bjørnskov, 2012) and health (Jen et al., 2010; Berggren and Jordahl, 2006; Rostila, 2007), it is likely that it correlates with human development as well. This is confirmed by Özcan and Bjørnskov (2011), who found that trust is positively related to the human development index.

In this section, we contend that the effect of economic freedom on human development is dependent on generalized trust. For example, experimental research by McCannon et al. (2018) showed a significant interaction effect between trust and contract enforcement in fostering contract formation. Also, the literature on interorganizational governance has shown that legal contracts and so-called relational governance (which includes trust) act in a complementary fashion (Arranz and Arroyabe, 2012; Poppo and Zenger,

2002). When contract enforcement is greater, people are more likely to enter into an agreement, and this probability increases when people exhibit high rather than low levels of trust. These findings indicate that trust and contract enforcement are complements rather than substitutes. In this section, we build on this new avenue of research and will argue that the effects of economic freedom on human development is likely to be contingent on generalized trust.

Trust can be defined as a psychological state comprising the intention to accept vulnerability based on positive expectations of the intentions or behavior of another person (Rousseau et al., 1998). Generalized trust indicates an inclusive and tolerant approach to the population at large and is considered to be at the heart of social capital. Generalized trust fosters so-called bridging social capital, which refers to the connections between dissimilar people (Jen et al., 2010). Trust is an important factor for well-functioning cooperative relationships (Gächter et al., 2004; Balliet and Van Lange, 2013) and is the glue in building and maintaining longer-term relationships between buyers and sellers (Weitz and Bradford, 1999). In an economically free society, there are potentially more opportunities for commerce. Globalization through freeing markets from trade limitations provides more chances of economic interactions with more distant players (Tabellini, 2008). But the extent to which people or companies make use of these potential opportunities is dependent on trust. In order to benefit from these opportunities, it is important that people have generalized trust in distant trade partners (Alesina and Giuliano, 2015). Trust will safeguard against hazards poorly protected by the contract and help overcome the adaptive limits of contracts (Poppo and Zenger, 2002). It lowers bargaining, monitoring and policing costs, thereby increasing economic efficiency and stimulating collective investments in innovation, education and health. In the absence of trust, transaction costs may become very high and many opportunities for mutually beneficial cooperation may be foregone.

This complementary relationship may also function in reverse in the sense that formal contracts complement generalized trust. High trust can lead to 'blind faith' that exposes the trusting party to malfeasance of the contract partner. In that case, formal contracts could counter the breach of trust, because they specify a clear scope of the alliance activities, regulate the basic behaviors of partner firms and specify severe punishments for opportunistic behaviors (Jiang et al., 2013). Therefore, we expect that there will be some complementary or synergistic effect when both economic freedom and generalized trust are high. This implies that the positive effects of economic freedom on human development are likely to be stronger when people trust each other. If there is no trust, an economy relies better on government regulation. Fukuyama (1995) postulates that people who do not trust each other only cooperate under a system of formal rules. Therefore, it might be beneficial to set up a system of formal regulatory rules (i.e. less economic freedom) when economic activity is inert to increases in freedom.

However, institutions and trust can also function as substitutes (Knack and Keefer, 1997; Ahlerup et al., 2009; Poppo and Zenger, 2002; Masten and Prüfer, 2014; Jiang et al., 2013). When pro-social behaviors are not prevalent and generalized trust is low, economic agents can rely on formal contract arrangements to facilitate trade (McCannon et al., 2018). By comparison with other allocation mechanisms (for example, gift exchange or central planning), markets may function tolerably well in the absence of trust. A well-ordered legal system that protects property and contract rights increases the cost of opportunistic behavior, hence assuring people that self-interested trade partners are not likely to exploit them. The advantages of free market institutions then substitute for the benefits of trust (Bowles, 2011) and economize on virtues, such as honesty (Hayek, 1948). By defining and enforcing property rights, economic freedom thus obviates the need for trust. This substitution relationship may also function in reverse: by reducing transaction costs, generalized trust may replace 'contracts with handshakes'. If one party trusts the other, there is simply little need for contractually specifying actions (Poppo and Zenger, 2002). This leads to an alternative hypothesis in which the strength of the effect of economic freedom on human development is negatively related to generalized trust: if generalized trust is low, there is more need of free market institutions, whereas if trust is high, there is less need for free market institutions. Hence an increase in economic freedom will have a stronger effect on human development if generalized trust is low. If generalized trust is high, it substitutes for economic freedom, and an increase in economic freedom will only have minor effects on human development.

One could also argue that the relationship between economic freedom and human development is independent from generalized trust. This possibility arises if generalized trust not only increases the efficiency of market operation but also fosters the efficiency of government intervention and regulations. In a more trustworthy country, government members are also more likely to be trustworthy and less inclined to abuse their position for personal benefit (Cruz-García and Peiró-Palomino, 2019), and this increases the efficiency of government actions. Moreover, if trust is high, citizens are more likely to comply with tax regulations, because they believe that others will also do so (Rothstein, 2000). The implementation costs of government policies and regulations are lower where trust is high, as there is no need to create and maintain complex systems of supervision. An example is given by Putnam (1993), who described a nationwide institutional reform in Italy at the beginning of the 1970s that established regional governments across the country. Although the institutions were virtually equal in terms of setup, the efficiency of these government institutions differed vastly between different regions. The regions endowed with high levels of social capital had superior outcomes regarding all kinds of government services (job training centers, daycare structures), investment and environmental standards compared with those without it. Hence, generalized trust not only enhances the efficiency of free markets but also the efficiency of government actions and regulations. As a result, the effect of an increase in economic freedom (e.g. reduction in government intervention) on human development might be independent of the level of trust.

In order to test the model, Graafland (2020a) created a sample of 29 OECD countries covering the period from 1990 to 2015. He used the human development index of the United Nations Development Programme and EFWI of the Fraser Institute. For general trust, he used the well-known trust data of the World Value Survey (WVS) and European Value Survey (EVS) and measured generalized trust as the share of respondents in each country answering yes to the question "In general, do you think most people can be trusted?" which is a standard approach in the literature.

Table 10.7 shows that economic freedom is significantly and positively related to the HDI, as well as to its three underlying components: income, education and life expectancy. This is in line with the analysis in Section 4.4. The interaction term of economic freedom and trust is positive and significant. This finding supports the hypothesis that the influence of economic freedom on the HDI is contingent on trust.

TABLE 10.7
Estimation results of the human development index (HDI)[a]

	HDI	Income	Education	Life expectancy
Economic freedom	0.44***	0.28***	0.42***	0.43***
Generalized trust	−0.02	−0.00	−0.09**	0.12
Economic freedom * and generalized trust	0.22**	0.14**	0.26**	0.13**
R² (overall)	0.73	0.39	0.44	0.61

[a] Robust standard errors. Fixed effects. Significance: * $p < 0.05$, ** $p < 0.01$, *** $p < 0.001$. Number of observations: 91. Number of countries: 29. For more details, see Graafland (2020a).

Intrinsic motivation

Whether free market capitalism is compatible with or harmful to environmental sustainability is strongly debated. Various authors argue that capitalism may inhibit corporate environmental performance, because private industry will invest in the most profitable technologies, which leads to a focus on the cheapest rather than the most environmentally responsible processes (Williamson et al., 2006; Bell, 2015). Other authors argue that economic freedom in markets and competition stimulate corporate environmental performance (CEP) (Baughn et al., 2007; Jackson and Apostolakou, 2010; Kinderman, 2012; Hartmann and Uhlenbruck, 2015), and businesses has expressed its interest in adopting a more extensive CEP approach conditional upon receiving greater freedom from the state (Kinderman, 2008). Jackson and Apostolakou (2010) argue and found that firms in liberal market economies outstrip firms in coordinated market economies, because their voluntary CEP initiatives substitute for the lack of government interventions. Kinderman (2012) stated that during the period of rapid deregulation and liberalization in the UK (a typical liberal market economy), CEP not only developed and thrived but even managed to outperform the previous economic model in terms of corporate accountability and corporate standards.

However, when researchers only focus on institutional factors, there is insufficient consideration for differences in CEP at the individual company level. Although some companies have incorporated CEP in their business model, it is not standard business practice. There is a flavor of social desirability in the belief that alleviating regulatory constraints from firms increases their contribution to society and the environment in terms of resources and efforts. But corporations have more options. Various authors argue that capitalism may inhibit rather than encourage improving environmental performance, since private industry will mostly invest in technologies that it expects to be profitable (Bell, 2015).

In a recent paper, Graafland and Gerlagh (2019) postulate that internal motivations of managers are fundamental for the company's engagement in CEP in a free market system. Motivation (i.e. the reason upon which one acts) is an important antecedent to behavior (Treviño et al., 2006). The literature on motives for CEP distinguishes between extrinsic and intrinsic motives (Muller and Kolk, 2010; Rode et al., 2015; Abatayo and Lynham, 2016). An extrinsic motive encourages CEP because of its instrumental value for other goals, such as financial performance or the company's reputation. Intrinsically motivated CEP perceives environmental responsibility as an end in itself that requires no separate reward (Vollan, 2008). Intrinsic motivation may stem from personal satisfaction of engaging in CEP when executives enjoy helping others (Rabin, 1998) or enjoy a 'warm glow' from contributing to a public good. But intrinsic motivation may also stem from a genuine concern for the environment and a sense of obligation to contribute to society and the welfare of future generations (Lindenberg, 2001). The goal is then to act appropriately. Managers feel that they are responsible to prevent the negative impacts of their companies on the natural environment (Bansal and Roth, 2000).

Graafland and Gerlagh (2019) expected that economic freedom will hardly encourage companies to increase their engagement in CEP if they are not intrinsically motivated to take responsibility for the environment. That is, the positive relationship between economic freedom and CEP is conditional on intrinsic environmental motivation. Since environmental policies may require costly investments, companies will be less motivated by the extrinsic profit motive to make investments in CEP. If companies are motivated by the business case, they will adopt CEP only insofar as it can be aligned with narrow strategic interests (Marens, 2008). These companies will be tempted to use ceremonial instead of substantive CEP policies in order to gain social legitimacy without incurring the costs of substantive CEP policies. CEP is ceremonial if companies decouple policies from implementation and/ or impacts (Jamali, 2010; Okhmatovskiy and David, 2012).

But if the management of a company is intrinsically motivated to improve environmental performance, economic freedom enables the managers to implement environmental policies that improve environmental outcomes, such as participation in environmental networks, even if these are costly and not profitable. Indeed, firms whose managers are highly intrinsically motivated to CEP are likely to apply broad and effective programs if external conditions allow them to (Muller and Kolk, 2010). If companies have little freedom to determine their own policies, internal motivations will have a lesser effect on environmental performance. Under these conditions, internally motivated companies would perhaps have a stronger inclination to do so, but in practice focus on complying with the interventions and standards prescribed by the government (Jackson and Apostolakou, 2010).

In order to test the moderation hypothesis, data for CEP were generated through a large online survey in 2011 that targeted small and medium-sized enterprises (SMEs) operating in 12 countries from different European regions. CEP is measured by the reduction in energy consumption, waste disposal and water consumption. Intrinsic motivation was measured by two survey questions. The first question measures moral motivation by asking the respondent to state his or her view on the extent to which the company's engagement in CEP is motivated by the company's responsibility for the environment and society. The second survey question measures personal satisfaction by inquiring to what extent personal satisfaction of the people in the enterprise is a motive to engage in environmental responsibility. Graafland and Gerlagh controlled for extrinsic motivation, which was measured by three survey questions on long-term financial benefits, reduction in reputational risks and customer demand as motives for engaging in CEP.

Table 10.8 reports the estimation results. The estimation results show that the interaction term of economic freedom and intrinsic motivation increases participation in environmental networks. Participation in environmental networks is measured by participation in CEP networks in the supply chain (Pirsch et al., 2006; Bos-Brouwers, 2010), partnerships with professional training institutes in order to anticipate the technological evolution of products or services (Bos-Brouwers, 2010), participation in local CEP initiatives of governments or social organizations (Barth and Wolff, 2009) and dialogue with societal organizations and

TABLE 10.8

Estimation results of environmental performance[a]

Dependent variable	Environmental networks	Environmental outcomes
Economic Freedom × Intrinsic motivation	0.037*	0.018
Economic Freedom × Extrinsic motivation	0.013	0.015
Intrinsic motivation	0.333***	0.039
Extrinsic motivation	0.076	−0.021
Economic freedom	−0.031	0.073**
Environmental networks		0.151***

[a] Standardized (beta) coefficients. Robust standard errors clustered by country. Standard errors between brackets. * p <0.05 ** p <0.01 *** p <0.001. All models use control variables and have N = 4,338. For the estimation results of the control variables, see Graafland and Gerlagh (2019).

TABLE 10.9

Estimated effect of difference in economic freedom on environmental performance[a]

Intrinsic motivation of companies (X)		
X = Lowest in Sample	X = Sample Average	X = Highest in sample
−0.15	0.27	0.69

[a] $a_1 (EF_{UK} - EF_{It}) + a_2 (EF_{UK} - EF_{It}) * X$. a_1 and a_2 denote the total effects of economic freedom (EF) and the interaction term of economic freedom and intrinsic motivation, EF_{UK} (standardized) economic freedom of UK, EF_{It} (standardized) economic freedom in Italy and X (standardized) intrinsic motive.

local communities (Hall et al., 2015). There is no significant positive effect of the interaction term of economic freedom and extrinsic motivation. The importance of intrinsic motivation vis-à-vis extrinsic motivation is further stressed by comparing the direct effects of intrinsic and extrinsic motivation on environmental networks. The last row shows that firms' participation in environmental networks has a significant positive effect on environmental outcomes in terms of increases or decreases of energy use, water use and waste disposal.

Based on the estimation results, Graafland and Gerlagh (2019) calculated the differential effects between Italy (lowest economic freedom) and the UK (highest economic freedom) for a firm with average, low and high intrinsic motivation. Table 10.9 shows that a rise in economic freedom induces companies with low intrinsic motivation to worsen environmental outcomes, whereas companies with high intrinsic motivation use the extra economic freedom to better their contribution to the environment. The table unambiguously shows the importance of the interaction between intrinsic motivation and economic freedom for environmental outcomes. The average effect of economic freedom is positive, though.

Conclusion

This section illustrates the general idea that the success of free markets depends on the economic agents' virtues: societies with free market economies can flourish in so far as key market actors act virtuously.

This also has implications for managers and policy makers. Although culture at the level of the society cannot easily be influenced, at the level of the firm, it can be to a certain extent. The lesson for management is that it is important to stimulate an ethical culture that encourages moral sensitivity and awareness. This has implications for recruitment policies and the socialization and training programs at the company level. At the institutional level, intrinsic motivation can be fostered by calls for socially responsible behavior in important business publications and curricula in business schools and by dialogues with unions, employees, community groups and other stakeholders; it appears that companies then better appreciate the concerns of these other actors (Campbell, 2007).

Policy makers can prescribe corporate governance arrangements that encourage managers to focus more on long-term effects of their decisions. Furthermore, countries with high economic freedom and low trust should pay more attention to the development of virtues in business life. If individuals are intrinsically motivated to have concern for others' well-being, then they are less inclined to make use of opportunities to break agreements and benefit financially. If policy makers liberalize their economy in a situation of low trust, institutional misalignments emerge. The improved formal framework will then not generate the economic benefits that people expect from them, as a lack of cultural values might hamper entrepreneurial actions. Virtuousness in economic actors is therefore an important condition for societal acceptance of free markets. If companies cannot be trusted, society expects that more negative externalities will result from free market operations, and support for free market operations decreases. If citizens come to expect higher risks and costs because companies develop unfair practices by abusing information asymmetry, citizens will support (more) government regulation (Aghion et al., 2010; Djankov et al., 2003; Glaeser and Shleifer, 2003; Pinotti, 2012).

NOTES

1 McCloskey (2006: 361) gives the following examples: love and faith yield loyalty; courage and prudence yield enterprise.
2 Another problem concerns the embedment of virtues in the culture of a community. Whereas communities are collectives, virtues are characteristics of individual persons. However, both are highly intertwined. As Solomon (1992) argues: what is best in us – our virtues – are in turn defined by the larger community. Market operation may influence the community by affecting the character traits of (groups of) individuals, but communities may also resist these influences if certain values are strongly anchored in a culture. Some sub-communities, such as that of the Quakers, are hardly influenced by the commercial values of the market economy. In my analysis, I will abstract from this kind of interactions between virtues and cultures.
3 If people are under great pressure to be too industriousness, they may 'burn out'. There is a wealth of literature discussing how work intensity and duration affect workers' stress, long-term health and life and relationships outside work. For example, Major et al. (2002) found 'work overload' (job intensity) and organizational expectations for time spent at work directly related to reported work–family conflicts and psychological distress, with implications for long-term mental health and hence future industriousness. White et al. (2003) found that 'high performance work practices', employed by firms to raise commitment and productivity through, for example, performance-related pay and appraisal systems, are associated with increased work–family life conflicts.
4 For example, Rappaport notes that while the average holding period for stocks until the mid-1960s was about seven years, it is now less than a year in professionally managed funds (Rappaport, 2005).
5 It should be noted that government regulation may also crowd out intrinsic motivations. This is supported by Graafland and Bovenberg (2020), who found that government regulation of environmental performance of companies crowds out their intrinsic motivation towards corporate environmental responsibility.
6 Other mechanisms that cause increases in cooperation are communication, expressions of approval or social exclusion, giving advice and assortative matching of like-minded participants (Chaudhuri, 2011). Communication allows conditional cooperators to coordinate on the cooperative outcome, and it may also create a sense of group identity (Camerer and Fehr. 2004).
7 Some parts of this section were published in Graafland (2019b), Graafland (2020a), and Graafland and Gerlagh (2019).

8   The GLOBE methodology distinguishes societal practices ('as is') from societal values ('should be'). Practices capture the tangible attributes of culture (e.g. current policies and practices), and values reflect the intangible attributes (e.g. cultural norms and values). Since we are interested in the effects of long-term orientation, we used the GLOBE's practices of long-term orientation. Our choice is validated by a correlation analysis relating GLOBE practices and GLOBE values to three indices of long-term orientation based on language structure, developed by Chen (2013). Chen (2013) found that languages that grammatically associate the future and the present foster future-oriented behavior. Future orientation as measured by GLOBE practices correlates more to the three measures for future orientation developed by Chen (2013) than the measures based on the GLOBE values.

Recommended literature

Bowles, S. (2016) *The Moral Economy: Why Good Incentives Are No Substitute for Good Citizens*, New Haven: Yale University Press.

Bowles, S. and Polania-Reyes, S. (2012) 'Economic incentives and social preferences: Substitutes or complements?', *Journal of Economic Literature*, 50: 368–425.

Frey, B. (1998) *Not Just for the Money, an Economic Theory of Personal Motivation*, Cheltenham: Edward Elgar.

Henrich, J., Boyd, R., Bowles, S., Camerer, C., Fehr, E. and Gintis, H. (eds.) (2004). *Foundations of Human Sociality: Economic Experiments and Ethnographic Evidence from Fifteen Small-scale Societies*, Oxford: Oxford University Press.

Sennet, R. (2000) *The Corrosion of Character*, trans. M. Blok, Amsterdam: Byblos.

Part IV

Consolidation and integration

11

Liberalism and communitarianism

In Parts I and II we have discussed utilitarianism and the various kinds of deontological ethics (duty, rights and justice). Although these theories apply different criteria to judge the value of market institutions, there are important similarities. In particular, in utilitarianism, duty ethics, rights ethics and (some forms) of the ethics of justice, the autonomy of the individual is an important cornerstone for the evaluative analysis. For example, as we have seen in Chapter 2, utilitarianism is based on the aggregation of individual utilities that, in the case of the formal variant of welfarism, is defined as the satisfaction of individually determined preferences (individual sovereignty). Also Kant stresses the autonomy and rationality of the individual. The individualistic base of the rights ethics, like the entitlement theory of Nozick, hardly needs explaining, since the most basic right is the right to individual freedom. Even the theory of justice, like that of Rawls, can be termed individualistic. Although Rawls's theory of justice calls for substantial redistribution of wealth and power, it does so in the name of providing citizens with the means to plan and implement their own views of the good with little concern with communal values over and above their own desires and needs (Anderson, 1998). Because of the individualistic basis of these ethical theories, they can all be classified as belonging to the liberal tradition.

Since the early 1980s a distinguished group of philosophers and political theorists have been working in a tradition of thought that has come to be called the communitarian tradition. These thinkers are critical about the individualistic basis in the liberal tradition. According to communitarianism, liberalism has an impoverished view of the self, because it rests on an attenuated view of the self as an unencumbered self, a self not defined in terms of its relationships to others. People define themselves in terms of ancestry, religion, language, history, values, customs and institutions (Huntington, 1997). Their relations are shaped to a significant extent by their place in various social structures. The influence of parents, the situation within the community and the religious morals of that community form the basis of human behavior, not rational choice. The unencumbered self is not just a fiction but also an incoherent idea. To become the sort of mature, reflective thinker that Rawls assumes in the original position assumes a preexisting social environment. People are who they are because of the culture and social environment they have been nurtured in. Moreover, liberal values, such as freedom and individual rights, presuppose some normative community-related obligations, like an obligation to belong to and help sustain society and a genuine acceptance of the legitimacy and need for binding legal and political authority over individuals (Johnson, 2001). Rawls's social contract would only work when its contractors are committed from the beginning to interpersonal values that express their pre-contractual

DOI: 10.4324/9781003181835-15

relationships. The demands of the Rawlsian rules of justice may not be fulfilled in practice in the absence of preexisting communal solidarity and social identity. Whereas the liberal tradition comprises utilitarianism, the ethics of duty, rights ethics and the ethics of justice, the communitarian tradition is much more present in virtue ethics and the ethics of care. Both virtue ethics and the ethics of care stress community relations and social norms developed within communities.

In this chapter, we characterize liberalism and communitarianism as overarching philosophical approaches of the ethical standards discussed in Parts I and II and Part III, respectively. Then we describe an intermediate position, the so-called I & we paradigm.

11.1   LIBERALISM: UTILITARIANISM, RIGHTS AND JUSTICE ETHICS

Liberalism rests on two pillars: individual freedom and rationalism. The liberal tradition trusts the rationality of the individual person. The individual person and his preferences take priority over the communion with other persons and communal values. These individual preferences are the final ground for judging the optimality of a decision or social norm (Van Erp, 1994). Communal relationships, regulations and institutions only have value inasmuch as individuals prefer these relationships as an end in themselves or because they depend on these institutions for realizing their own interests. This is the core assumption of contract theory on which liberal theories are based.

It should be noted that liberal ethical theories do not imply moral egoism. One should make a distinction between self-interest and selfishness (egoism). In the liberal theory, the public good is best served if people act out of enlightened self-interest or self-interest rightly understood. When people are allowed to operate within a system that respects their individual rights and to pursue the 'good life' in their own individual ways, they can, out of self-interest, be expected to respect and help maintain the political-economic order that guarantees them these rights and liberties, and in so doing they are helping to promote the rights and liberties of all others to achieve a good life for themselves (Madison, 1998).

In order to channel this self-interest in socially beneficial directions, the liberal philosophers especially stress the importance of institutional arrangements (such as a democratic polity and a market economy), which guarantee that all members of a civil society reciprocally recognize the right to the pursuit of one's own self-interest. This requires constitutional arrangements that prevent people from making short-sighted, socially harmful choices. The liberal theory argues that the civil society (including the civil market economy) will emerge spontaneously, sustained by means of free agreement among the members of the society. It is a self-generating system, an unintended outcome of actions on the part of a myriad of individuals pursuing their own self-interest within an institutional context, of which the rules have been deliberately designed by themselves by a social contract.

In liberal theory, institutions are much more important than virtues for the functioning of the civil society. One does not have to be a good virtuous person in the moralistic sense of the term in order to be a good citizen. The civil market economy is not just an immensely effective way of creating wealth; it is also the best means for generating socially ethical behavior, according to liberal philosophers. As Novak (1982) argues, in order to succeed in business, one must face remarkable moral responsibilities. In particular, in order to be successful in a market economy, one has to cooperate with others. The cooperation of others is most likely to be secured when one respects the right of these others to pursue their own interests. The chief characteristic of a civil market economy based on calculated personal interest is therefore that of reciprocity and mutual respect. One can even argue that a civil market economy is better characterized by enlightened cooperation than by competition. There is no call for devotion to the community as a whole or self-sacrifice. In a market economy, one helps the other by helping oneself. People do not have to act out of benevolence in order to be good citizens. It is enlightened self-interest, not communitarian solidarity, which produces the best of all possible worlds. The state should therefore be ordered so that individuals enjoy the maximum freedom (Madison, 1998).

In liberalism, the principal rationality of all individuals guarantees the universality of the civil values of freedom and individuality. Although the individual decides to which values she or he commits, the relationship with the community is considered immediately when she or he determines the appropriateness of social customs and norms. For example, in the theory of Kant the human being will of her own accord conclude the categorical imperative as an implication of her rationality. This means that each person recognizes the human dignity of each other. In the utilitarian version of the liberal theory, the relationship between the individual and the community is even more pronounced in the sense that any limitation of individual freedom is acceptable if it raises the utility of all. This implies that individuals judge the appropriateness of their acts in light of the preferences of all other people (Graafland, 2002).

11.2 COMMUNITARIANISM: VIRTUE ETHICS AND CARE ETHICS

Communitarian philosophers like Michael Sandel, Charles Taylor and Alasdair MacIntyre (1985) stress the social nature of the human being. This line of thought goes back to Aristotle, Hegel and Hume. Communitarianism is a post-modern philosophical position in the sense that it stresses an organic view of community in ethics and political philosophy. With post-modern epistemology and language theory, it shares a communal approach of reality (Murphy and McClendon, 1989). For example, post-modern epistemology argues for the community dependency of knowledge. This view is holistic in the sense that a paradigm – the constellation of beliefs, presumptions, heuristics and values that tie together the theoretical efforts of practitioners of some discipline – is accepted or rejected as a whole. The scientific community makes such decisions on the basis of maxims such as the injunctions to seek simplicity and empirical fit. Similarly, post-modern philosophy of language claims that all language is to be understood in terms of the social world, with its linguistic and other conventions, in which it plays a role. Private languages are in general impossible. The language must be public from the start.

The communitarian philosophy stresses that the community is logically prior to the individual. The neoclassical notion of free-standing individuals is replaced by the concept of persons as members of communities that to a significant degree shape individual decisions. What 'community' means varies from political state to smaller communities, including the family as a basic communal unit. Communities (such as ethnic groups and peer groups at work and neighborhood groups) are the prime decision-making units. Decisions of the kind economists routinely study – what people buy, how much they invest, how hard they work and so on – largely reflect their community. Language, capabilities and preferences are learned from other people. The individual does not create her autonomy and rationality by herself, but receives them from her community and tradition. Since there are limita-tions to the rationality of the individual person, people need the help of other people to develop their preferences and cognitive methods. Social norms can be interpreted as the accumulated wisdom of previous generations. Moreover, as socioeconomic studies show, people act not only on the basis of logical reasoning and empirical facts but also mostly on non-rational factors as commitments to values and emotions. Thus, if one asks for the reason why individuals prefer this or that product, why they expect some events to be more likely than others, the answers are to be found to a significant extent in differences among the social collectivities to which they belong. Even whether or not people sense they have a choice to make – the attribution of choice – is itself to a large extent socially and culturally shaped. Hence, follows the argument that macro-behavior is not a simple aggregation of micro-behavior, but the result of all interdependent interactions between people.

The collective works, in part, via internalization. Although individuals may sometimes be aware of the influence of the community on their decisions, they normally do not realize that other parts of the social realm shape what they see, the sources of communication they choose to expose themselves to, the way they interpret what they have heard and the conclu-sions they draw. Thus, collectivities work on individual decision-making in ways individu-als are not aware of and are unable to control.

Also much of what one ought to do is determined by the community. The validation of values and norms and the definition of the good life depend on the particular community to which a person belongs. One of Hume's premises is that what we morally ought to do is what the institution of morality determines we ought to do and that the rules in the institution of morality are a consensual, social matter. The moral rules are not merely the formulation of what individuals feel; they are the product of a cultural and community's determination of its moral interests. Understanding moral rules therefore requires an understanding of the community's history and a sense of communal life.

One of the hallmarks of communitarianism is the notion that whether moral rules serve the community well or ill is a critical factor in their acceptability. The optimality of a certain policy or decision should not be evaluated in terms of individual preferences, but in terms of the common good, because the common good provides a necessary condition for the devel-opment of the individual capacities. Only if the communal relationships are good and if the individual can experience herself as a member of the community can the individual attain a good life, because only in such communities do people find the psychic and social support that is required to sustain decisions free of pressures from the authorities, demagogues or mass media (Etzioni, 1988). Individuals who are cut off and isolated are much more unable to act freely than individuals who have comprehensive and stable relationships. The latter group is much more able to make sensible choices, to render judgment and to be free from persuasion. This explains why the communitarian theory stresses other values and norms than the liberal theory. In liberalism, personal autonomy, self-command, prudence and individual development are admired. In contrast, communitarian philosophers are more concerned about values and virtues that enhance communal relationships and relations of care. Social virtues like altruism, trust and commitment to common goals can sustain the cooperative behavior of individuals. Reciprocity is not enough, because this may result in both positive equilibriums of agents rewarding each other and in negative equilibriums of agents punishing each other. The communitarian ethics that stress the normative value of good relations can help select the positive equilibriums. According to communitarian philosophers, it is not the calculated self-interest behind a veil of ignorance and the wish to ensure one against the consequences of bad luck that motivates the compliance with elementary civil duties. What is required is a communal ethos, based on a sense of common history and positive identification with the community and fellow citizens (VandeVelde, 2001). In a slogan: socioeconomic science shows us how humans act, and communitarianism shows us how we should act (Anderson, 1998).

Another aspect of communitarianism is that it accepts pluralism (VandeVelde, 2001). In liberalism, the universality of values follows from the assumption of the principal rationality of the human being. However, in practice appeals to universal principles are uncommon. Rather, the normal situation is that people appeal to a highly diverse and plural set of practices, rules and conceptions of the good. The rules are formulated, shaped and reshaped by the moral practices, codes and communal judgments in everyday communal life. Communitarians accept this pluralism and tend to tolerate many different viewpoints (Beauchamp, 1982). The definition of the good life is related to communities and traditions. As these vary significantly, there is no universal definition of the good life. The traditional liberal values of freedom and individuality are not truly universal values. They are not only strictly Western in origin; they are also incompatible with the traditional values of non-Western cultures which are much more communal in nature, like the Latin American, the African, the Islamic, the Hindu, the Orthodox, the Buddhist and the Japanese civilizations. The world is, in short, divided between a Western civilization and many non-Western civilizations. Some authors, like Francis Fukuyama, assumed that the end of the Cold War meant the end of significant conflicts and the emergence of one relatively harmonious model. As Fukuyama argued: 'the end of history as such, that is, the endpoint of mankind's ideological evolution and the universalization of Western liberal democracy as the final form of human government' (Cited in Huntington, 1997: 31). Other authors believe, however, that the West's universalistic pretensions increasingly bring it into conflicts with other civilizations, most seriously with Islam (Huntington, 1997). And although the West is and will remain the most dominant civilization, its power may relatively decline in the future.

Communitarianism, virtue ethics and care ethics

Communitarianism reminds us of the many premises of virtue ethics and care ethics described in Chapter 8. For example, we saw that Aristotle places the community first. Another similarity with virtue ethics is that communitarians stress the importance of social virtues that serve the community, which are also of central importance in Aristotle's virtue ethics. Third, communitarianism and virtue ethics also subscribe to the importance of proper motives. Indeed, some recent communitarian theorists, like MacIntyre, are manifestly Aristotelian. However, virtue ethics cannot be completely identified with communitarian ethics. The virtue ethics of Bruni and Sudgen, for example, also stress individual virtues that enable individuals to realize the personal good. More generally, the focus and the framework of virtue ethics are different from that of communitarianism. Whereas in communitarianism the community–individual relationship is the central issue, virtue ethics is about developing good character traits (instead of developing principles, as in consequential and deontological ethical theory). Virtue ethics is therefore less vulnerable to certain criticisms of over-accenting the role of community (as, for example, expressed by Sen (1998), see later) than communitarianism. Notwithstanding the many similarities,

Beauchamp (1982) therefore classifies virtue ethics and communitarian theories as two separate strands of ethics.

The relationship between communitarianism and care ethics is, however, tighter, because relationships in communities constitute the focal point of care ethics. Care ethicists and communitarians share many viewpoints and, thus, similar types of criticism. Beauchamp therefore classifies the ethics of care as a class or extension of communitarian ethics. The close relationship between care ethics and communitarians is also indicated by the fact that care ethicists defend communitarian ideas. Baier, for example, a well-known care ethicist, credits Hume's ethics for stressing (Baier, 1987):

- That morality is not a matter of obedience to a universal law or consulting some book of rules, but of cultivating the character traits (virtues) which give a person consciousness of integrity and at the same time make that person good company to other persons.
- That moral rules are not determined by human reason, valid for all people at all times and places, but authored by custom and tradition. These rules, such as property rights, are not universal, but vary from community to community.
- The centrality of family love. Socially destructive conflicts over scarce goods can only be prevented if persons have learned, in the family, the advantages that can come from self-control and from cooperation. Were there no minimally sociable human passions such as love between man and woman, love of parents for their children, love of friends, sisters and brothers, the virtue of justice could not develop.
- No special centrality to relationships between (autonomous) equals. As Hume's analysis of social cooperation starts with the family, relations between unequals rather than between equals are necessarily at the center of his ethics.

Criticism

In his *Romanes Lecture* Sen (1998) criticizes several of the communitarian premises. First, he doubts the claim that identities and relationships are not a matter of choice, but rather given. According to communitarianism, a person's identity is something he or she detects, rather than determined by own choice. Sen doubts that people really have no substantial choice between alternative identifications. Although he acknowledges that there are limits to what we can choose to identify with, he defends the claim that the room for choices can be quite substantial. Communities do not incorporate one uniquely defined set of attitudes and beliefs, but often contain considerable internal variations. An adult and competent person is therefore confronted with alternative value systems and has to develop the ability to compare them and to question his own background.

From a moral perspective, Sen criticizes communitarianism for its tendency to defend conservatism. The belief that individuals do not have the capacity to choose independently from the community by use of reasoning may easily give way to uncritical acceptance of conformist behavior. Such conformism may have conservative implications and protect old customs and practices from intelligent scrutiny. Denial of the individual independent choice may demolish the responsibility to consider and assess how one should think and what one should identify with.

Another moral problem with over-accenting communal values is that within-group solidarity may go hand in hand with between-group discord, as we know all too well from nationalistic violence. The importance of nationality cannot be denied, but in a globalizing world, we have to take note of forms of solidarity across borders. The identity of being a human being is perhaps our most basic identity. Our practical interactions across borders will have to lead to norms or rules that are not derived from the intranational norms.

A third moral problem is that group identities can also tyrannize by eliminating the claims of other identities that we should accept and respect. There are many different maps of partitioning people. A person can simultaneously have the identity of being African, a woman, a feminist, bisexual, a teacher, a gardener, a Christian, a lover of poems, etc. There may well be conflicting demands arising from these different identities and affiliations. This calls for reasoning on the varying priorities of the respective identities. To deny this kind of plurality in identities can be a source of repression.

11.3   I & WE PARADIGM

There can be little doubt that communities and cultures to which persons belong have a major influence on the way they see a situation and value different solutions. The view of individuals merely as self-concerned atomistic beings is unrealistic. On the other hand, the criticism of Sen is also persuasive: individuals do have the ability of reasoning and making choices that is, to a certain degree, independent from their community. We therefore propose an intermediate position, where basic cultural attitudes do influence individuals' decisions and reasoning but do not fully determine them.

In this respect, it is important to realize that liberalism and communitarianism are not mutually exclusive (Boettke, 1998). On the one hand, liberalism is a political philosophy based on a sociological understanding of human agency. It is far from the atomistic doctrine which it is often accused of being. Within a liberal society, communitarian values of family, virtue, duty and social consciousness can be adopted. Novak (1982) even argues that real community among people is served if the individuality of persons is respected. The community should not impose communion on individuals. Respecting the individuality of people makes communal life more active, intense, voluntary and multiple.

On the other hand, communitarianism presupposes certain basic liberal values that govern the discourse about values, e.g. respect for personhood and the community of discourse. In any properly drawn communitarian ethic, there is no ineliminable conflict between the autonomy of persons and the authority of a moral community. Any worthy community values the singularity and inviolability of each person. Autonomous agents may freely choose to submit to the decisions of the larger community. Moreover, in order to prevent circumstances in which the community tyrannizes certain individuals, a communitarian ethic should build in some protections for individuality, for example, by protecting individual rights (Beauchamp, 1982).

Etzioni (1988) also combines both perspectives when he proposes an 'I & we' paradigm. A deterministic view that holds individual behavior as being entirely determined by others is just as erroneous as the concept of man as isolated and independent. Economic behavior is neither purely determined by the collective nor purely the result of independent decisions of rational individuals. Rather, it is the interdependent action of individuals in their social relations (Van Staveren, 2001). Furthermore, while a sense of community will always be a major ally of liberal values such as justice, justice cannot alone rely on that. Social interaction inescapably involves people who are not closely tied by bonds of affection of partnership (Sen, 1998). Justice has to go beyond the domain of communal affection.

Recommended literature

Beauchamp, T.L. (1982) *Philosophical Ethics, an Introduction to Moral Philosophy*, New York: McGraw-Hill Inc.
Etzioni, A. (1988) *The Moral Dimension: Towards a New Economics*, New York, The Free Press.
Huntington, S.P. (1997) *The Clash of Civilizations and the Remaking of World Order*, London and New York: Touchstone Books.
Novak, M. (1982) *The Spirit of Democratic Capitalism*, New York: Simon and Schuster.
Sen, A. (1998) *Reason before Identity*, The Romanes Lecture for 1998, Oxford: Oxford University Press.

12

The morality of free markets

Integration and application

In Parts I to III we considered free market institutions from the perspectives of utilitarianism, deontological ethics (rights and justice) and virtue ethics. In this chapter we connect the three perspectives and develop an integrated view on free market operation. This view is necessarily generic. Application to concrete market policies in particular sectors demands an accurate analysis of the specific context. An example is economic policy that aims at more market operation in a particular economic sector. According to Armstrong and Sappington (2006), even a comparatively simple choice between regulated monopoly and unregulated competition

> 'can be intricate and complex in practice. The decision to introduce competition into an industry is only the beginning of a journey down a long and winding road that can present many obstacles and detours. The best route from monopoly to competition can differ substantially in different settings. Therefore, there is no single set of directions that can guide the challenging journey from monopoly to competition in all settings.'
>
> (Armstrong and Sappington, 2006: 326)

Armstrong and Sappington conclude that in practice the question is not whether liberalization policies per se are desirable or undesirable, but which benefits and costs specific liberalization policies generate. There is a wide variety of liberalization policies, and the merits of the different policies vary considerably.

Concrete application of various ethical standards to evaluate alternative economic policies often leads to different conclusions. The different approaches can make one think that ethical theories are so diverse that it is almost impossible to arrive at unambiguous conclusions in concrete cases. Notwithstanding the call for morality in economics and business, this may easily give ground to skepticism. Although the consequential theory of utilitarianism and the deontological ethical theories of duties, rights and justice have a common base in the liberal approach, these theories apply very different criteria to evaluate the moral value of a certain institution, act or rule. It is therefore not surprising that these theories can provide conflicting judgments in concrete cases. The complexity even increases if one takes account of community considerations stressed by virtue ethics and ethics of care. In such cases, the question arises which theory should prevail. Unfortunately, there is no overarching ethical theory that determines the priority of the various ethical theories. In case

DOI: 10.4324/9781003181835-16

of conflicting outcomes, this means that a final judgment must include an account of the priority of the different moral standards used.

Whereas most policy questions on market operation focus on how markets should be organized (including to what extent government should intervene to correct for market imperfections), we have not yet paid attention to some more fundamental debates that discuss whether markets should be allowed at all for certain types of goods or services. Examples of goods or services that are topics of discussion in this debate are markets for human organs, sex, airport queues and pregnancy surrogacy. The moral criticisms on these 'noxious' markets stem from consequentialist, deontological and virtue ethics. For this reason, we discuss the ins and outs of this debate on what goods and services should not be bought or sold on a market in this chapter, which integrates the various ethical perspectives (rather than in the previous parts of the book).

The purpose of this chapter is therefore threefold. First, we compare the outcomes of Parts I to III and derive an integrated evaluation of free market institutions from a moral point of view. Second, we describe moral arguments pro and contra noxious markets. Third, we present a practical method and case study for applying ethics to concrete economic policies and will provide some heuristics to apply the different ethical theories of utilitarianism, duties, rights, justice, virtue and care ethics if these alternative theories point at different conclusions in concrete cases to determine the hierarchy between the various ethical standards.

12.1 OVERVIEW OF ANALYSIS OF FREE MARKETS FROM DIFFERENT ETHICAL STANDARDS

Table 12.1 presents the most important findings of Chapters 4, 7 and 10. A comparison of the findings provides a rather coherent picture.

From the utilitarian perspective, the free market system is partly positively evaluated. In particular, the sub-dimension of the rule of law (protection of property rights) is important, because it fosters life satisfaction. However, small government tends to reduce life satisfaction. Economic freedom is also found to correlate positively with other dimensions of quality of life (housing, jobs, community, education, civic engagement, environment and safety). Only work–life balance is negatively related to economic freedom. Testing the predictive power of the free market perspective of the neoliberal school, the perfect market perspective of the neoclassical school and the welfare-state perspective of the Keynesian school on market institutions, we find that a strong state is necessary to reduce market imperfections and to make the market economy subservient to human development.

From a rights and justice perspective, the verdict about the free market system is also ambiguous. The rights and justice ethics legitimate free market institutions because of the respect of negative rights to freedom and because of the capitalist principle of justice (rendering each his or her due). Furthermore, the share of people living in absolute poverty is negatively related to economic freedom (particularly the rule of law and freedom to trade), which suggests that the free market system increases the respect of the positive right to subsistence. Hence, if one cares about the poor, one should accept the market economy as an important and useful instrument to improve their situation. Without economic growth, it will be impossible to improve the welfare of the poor. The ambiguity of the free market system is most clear from the effects on income inequality. Income inequality increases

TABLE 12.1
Overview of empirical research

Section	Happiness (Chapter 4)
4.3	Rule of law and sound money are positively and small government negatively related to happiness
4.4/10.4	Economic freedom is positively related to quality of life, except work–life balance
4.5	A perfect market perspective better explains human development than a free market or welfare-state perspective
	Justice (Chapter 7)
7.2	Rule of law and free trade are positively related to respect of positive rights by reducing absolute poverty
7.3	Fiscal freedom, free trade and freedom from regulation are positively and rule of law and sound money negatively related to income inequality
7.5	Income inequality is positively related to inequality in life satisfaction and negatively related to generalized trust
7.5	Income inequality is negatively related to life satisfaction, mostly for low-income groups
	Virtues (Chapter 10)
10.1	Market operation fosters industriousness and courage, crowds out temperance and generosity and has an ambivalent effect on prudence and justice
10.2	Prudence and temperance improve health and economic outcomes; courage, self-control, justice and altruism foster cooperation
10.3	Trust and civic virtues are positively related to life satisfaction
10.4	The positive influence of economic freedom on quality of life and corporate environmental responsibility increases with long-term orientation
	The positive influence of economic freedom on human development increases with generalized trust
	The positive influence of economic freedom on corporate environmental responsibility increases with intrinsic motivation

with tax freedom, trade freedom and freedom from regulation, whereas it decreases with the rule of law and sound money. Income inequality harms egalitarian justice, as it increases inequality in life satisfaction. Besides, it also has a depressing impact on life satisfaction, particularly of the low-income groups. The expansion of free international markets has not contributed to more income equality between the richest and poorest countries. But for some highly populated countries (Japan, China, India), the difference in income with Western countries declined. As a result, income inequality between individual citizens globally followed a downward trend over the last two decades. Within-country inequality increased; fostering justice and human happiness thus require income redistribution by the government and government interventions that fight market imperfections.

Also the virtue ethics partially legitimates the free market system. Whereas free market institutions foster diligence and courage, they have ambivalent effects on prudence and justice and tend to crowd out temperance and benevolence. We also find ambiguous effects on trust: whereas the rule of law increases trust, small government decreases trust by raising income inequality. Next, there is much evidence that virtues improve economic outcomes and happiness. Finally, we find that virtues that foster long-term orientation, trust and intrinsic motivation to corporate environmental responsibility moderate the influence of free market institutions on well-being. This suggests that the free market system will only lead to human flourishing if key actors in the economy are virtuous (e.g. can be trusted and have a long-term orientation). By appealing to self-interest, the social virtues can be compromised by crowding out intrinsic motivations. As markets are imperfect, virtues such as integrity are of great importance for the trust required for economic welfare and happiness.

12.2   MORAL EVALUATION OF 'NOXIOUS' MARKETS

In our discussion of the morality of (free) market institutions, we have until now particularly focused on the 'how' question: How should we organize markets? What kind of market institutions are best? How much should governments intervene in and regulate the market? Yet in the academic literature, there is also an important debate on the 'what' question: What sort of things should not become commodities (anything with a price tag that could be exchanged on a market), i.e. not put for sale on markets? Some types of markets trade in contested commodities that generate an intuitive disgust. These markets are sometimes called 'noxious' markets. This raises the question of what moral problems arise if we commodify certain things.

Brennan and Jaworski (2016) distinguished seven kinds of moral objections to the commodification of certain goods or services:

1   Disutility because of harm to others. For example, a market for selling pit bulls may cause harm to innocent neighbors, because pit bulls are very dangerous.
2   Disutility because of bounded rationality. For example, markets for certain food items or drugs induce people to make self-destructive choices.
3   Rights violations. Examples are markets in stolen goods, child porn or slaves that violate people's rights.
4   Justice violations because of exploitation of the vulnerable. For example, markets in human organs may allow the rich to take advantage of the poor. The rich, who already have so much more than the poor, get yet further advantages (namely in health) over them through allowing these markets.
5   Justice violations because of misallocation. For example, line-standing services or paying for access to excellent universities are inegalitarian because rich people can afford these, but the poor often cannot.
6   Crowding out of virtues. For example, as the primary motivation in business is to make money, markets may create a culture of greed, which leads to lying and cheating, and this corruption may spread to all who enter the market.
7   Semiotic objections, because of stimulating the wrong attitudes. For example, organ sale or pregnancy surrogacy may communicate the idea that the human body is a mere commodity and thus fail to show proper reverence.[1] Anderson (1993) argued that people value different goods in different ways, and constraints are needed to secure a robust differentiation in spheres that enables people to express different types of valuations.[2] If prostitution detaches intimacy from sex, widespread use of prostitutes might cause us not to see sex as intimate at all.

The first two objections can be classified as utilitarian objections, the next three are deonto-logical criticisms and the last two objects best fit with virtue ethics.

Brennan and Jaworski (2016) argued, however, that the moral criticisms of noxious mar-kets are not inherent to markets. They stem either from the principle of wrongful possession of some things or from incidental limits to the market. The principle of wrongful possession means that it is wrong to possess certain things, period. Examples are slaves and porno-graphic images of young children. If it is morally wrong to possess a thing, then it is also morally wrong to buy or sell this thing. It is the existence of child pornography and not the selling of child pornography that introduces the wrongness, although a market for child pornography may amplify the wrongness by increasing the number of children who are harmed. Reversely, Brennan and Jaworski (2016) perceived that if it is morally right to have certain things or to do things for free, then you should also be allowed to buy or sell these things for money.

Incidental limits concern cases where things should not be commodified because of spe-cial circumstances. There is no inherent limit to markets for these things. For example, Brennan and Jaworski (2016) argued that a market for sex is not inherently wrong, but only in certain situations. For example, a married man should not buy sex from a prostitute without his spouse's permission. In their view, the problem is not prostitution, but cheat-ing on his spouse. Furthermore, whether market transactions signal disrespect varies from culture to culture. In some cultures, paying your own wife for sex did not carry a stigma of being impersonal. In the view of Brennan and Jaworski, a thoroughly commodified mar-riage could be as healthy as a typical marriage. Moreover, even if the very best kind of sex is intimate and loving, this does not imply, according to Brennan and Jaworski, that it is wrong to engage in non-intimate sex.

Incidental limits to the market can be diminished by changing the market architecture (the manner of exchange). For example, if one is worried that desperately poor people will be taken advantage of in organ markets because they have no other options than selling their organ, one could fix that by a legal requirement that sellers should have a certain mini-mum income. Alternatively, if sellers do not fully understand the harm they might cause themselves, the law could require them to pass certain tests before they may sell their organ. In the view of Brennan and Jaworski, it is therefore not the 'what' but only the 'how' ques-tion that is relevant if there are incidental limits to the market.

Whatever one's moral position, it is clear that noxious markets create moral dilemmas. Even if one accepts some of the anti-commodification criticisms categorized earlier, not allowing noxious markets may generate high costs. For example, if one perceives that organ markets show disrespect for the body or cause exploitation, a dilemma may arise if organ markets would appear to prevent thousands of deaths per year.

12.3   APPLYING ECONOMIC ETHICS TO MARKET INSTITUTIONS: A PRACTICAL APPROACH

Although the summarizing conclusions in Section 12.1 and the underlying analysis in Parts I to III provide some help in the ethical evaluation of free market institutions in gen-eral, they do not give sufficient guidance for evaluating concrete policy proposals concern-ing economic institutions. In the economic policy making process, politicians have to face all kinds of moral dilemmas. A moral dilemma arises if two moral standards are conflicting (see Chapter 1). What method can be applied to arrive at a responsible decision when one faces such a difficult dilemma?

The literature presents several practical methods to handle moral dilemmas. Examples are the eight-step plan of Treviño and Nelson (2004) and the method of Van Luijk (1993). Next we present a seven-step method that combines several elements of these methods:

1 Gather the background facts of the decision problem. How did the situation occur?
2 Identify the options.
3 Identify the affected parties.
4 Identify the consequences of each option for each of the affected parties.
5 Identify the moral standards that are met or violated by the options or their consequences.
6 If various moral standards are involved and the different options cannot be completely ordered, determine the hierarchy of moral standards that should prevail and identify the option that optimally meets this hierarchy.
7 Check the outcome:
   a   Think again creatively about potential options that could possibly meet the conflicting standards involved.
   b   Check your intuition. The emphasis in the preceding steps has been on a highly rational fact-gathering and evaluation process. But that does not ensure that you derive a conclusion that fits your intuition. If you feel uncomfortable about the final selected option, give the preceding steps more thought and try to identify which step causes the problem.
   c   Use the model of the methodological assumption to determine whether the outcome is defendable to others (see later).

Clarification of step 6: a rule of thumb for weighing moral standards

Step six demands a weighing of moral standards involved. The various liberal and communitarian ethical theories apply different criteria to evaluate the moral value of a certain institution, act or rule. If there is a dominant alternative that satisfies all the criteria (utilitarianism, duties, rights and justice, and virtues and care), the differences need not be a problem to identify a dominant ordering of a set of alternative options. An example is accounting fraud by large companies. From a utilitarian point of view, providing false information about the financial accounts induced shareholders to supply financial resources to companies that did not use these resources in an efficient way. When the fraud comes out, the trust in the capital market declines, with negative consequences for almost all shareholders. Besides the utilitarian objection that the accounting fraud causes harm to the overall welfare of the economy, the illegal accounting activities can also be convicted from other moral points of view. From a duty ethics perspective, accounting fraud is condemned because the company's stakeholders are merely used as instruments and not as ends in themselves. Financial misinformation is not universalizable: fraudulent managers that try to enrich themselves would not like to be financially harmed by others who deceive them. From a rights ethics point of view, by lying about the real financial strength of the company, managers do not respect the right to freedom and information of their shareholders. From a justice point of view, the practices violate the capitalist criterion of justice (i.e. benefits be distributed according to the value of the contribution the company makes), since shareholders then paid too much for their stocks. Also from a virtue point of view the attempts to enrich oneself at the expense of other stakeholders of the company can be condemned as greedy and showing a bad example to other managers. In this case we thus see that the various ethical theories unambiguously point into the same direction, namely that fraud in accounting practices is wrong.

The scope for dominant ordering is substantially expanded in situations of incomplete information. Moral arguments are often subject to informational limitations that rule out the use of one criterion or another (Sen, 1981). The informational limitation can be intrinsic to the type of criterion used (like the problems involved with making interpersonal comparisons of utility in utilitarianism) or it can be case-specific. Sen illustrates this point by the decision how to allocate a flute between three boys, A, B and C. Suppose there are three alternative scenarios. In the first scenario, it is known that A plays the flute better and with more pleasure than B and C. The decision-maker knows nothing else about the three boys and therefore decides to give the flute to A, in conformity with utilitarianism. In the second scenario, the decision-maker knows that B is much more deprived than the other two boys and has very few toys and that he is much less happy than the other two. Nothing else is known, and the decision-maker gives the flute to B on grounds of egalitarian considerations like the difference principle. In the third scenario, it is only known that boy C has made the flute with his own labor from a bamboo belonging to no one. In this case, the decision-maker gives the flute to C on libertarian grounds, acknowledging the right to what one has produced. In each case, the decision-maker may feel that an unambiguously correct decision has been made. This is, however, only due to the presence of some information and the absence of other information. If the decision-maker knew that A would get more joy out of the flute, B is most deprived and C made the flute, the decision would be much more complex.

Indeed, there are many cases where the various ethical theories provide conflicting judgments. Ethical theory does not provide us with an unambiguous hierarchy of principles. There is no objective or even intersubjective answer to the question of which moral standard should precede others. In such cases, the question arises which theory should prevail. The answer to this question is not completely objective and independent from one's view. Persons who are committed to one of the ethical theories will select the outcome resulting from applying the standard required by their theory. For example, utilitarians will prefer the utilitarian standard of maximizing overall utility and defend the thesis that other ethical standards can be grounded on the utilitarian principle. A good example is Mill (1871). He states that virtues deserve admiration insofar as they contribute to the overall happiness. Mill also argues that Kant's categorical imperative only has meaning if the sense put upon it must be that we ought to shape our conduct by a rule that all rational beings might adopt with benefit to their collective interest. Similarly, Mill believes that a right to something and the standards of justice are only valid because rights and the rules of justice concern the most important conditions for our security and thus for our well-being. It is their observance that alone preserves peace among human beings. Finally, with respect to distributive justice, Mill thinks that justice requires equality except when inequality is more beneficial overall. Where the maxims of justice harm the general happiness, they are overridden by the principle of utilitarianism. Summarizing, in Mill's view, the basic reason society ought to respect various ethical standards is therefore general utility. There is so much disagreement about the concept of justice or other ethical standards, that any choice between them must be arbitrary. In his view, social utility alone can decide what is right or wrong (Mill, 1871: Section 5:30).

However, as shown in Parts I to III, there are many good reasons to argue that utilitarianism or one of the other theories are inadequate on their own. In many cases, so many aspects must be taken into account that it remains difficult to arrive at an unambiguous judgment. How, then, do we come to a conclusion?

If there is neither a complete ordering of alternatives nor a lack of information, one should balance different ethical criteria by specifying a weighting procedure for different criteria (Sen, 1981). The literature provides several examples. Often the various alternative criteria are weighted in lexicographic form with no trade-offs. An example is the serial order of the three principles of justice of Rawls (1999a), with the first principle used first, then the second principle and finally the difference principle if there are any choices left to make (see Chapter 6).

A second example of a lexicographic weighting procedure is the well-known rule of thumb that perfect duties and correlated rights have greater weight than justice and that justice has greater weight than utilitarian standards (Velasquez, 1998). The reason is that moral duties and rights identify areas of the individual life in which other people may not interfere, even if this would create higher benefits from a welfare perspective. We cannot sacrifice individuals and minorities to the common good when to do so would be to abuse their human rights to life and liberty. Similarly, maximization of the aggregate social welfare by measures that are perceived as highly unjust is also generally considered unacceptable. Standards of justice have therefore generally a higher priority than maximizing aggregate welfare. However, these relations hold only in general. If a certain action, policy or institution generates very high social benefits, utilitarian arguments may override arguments of duties, rights or justice. This is particularly true for imperfect duties. Likewise, if duties or correlating rights are conflicting, one should take into account the importance of the consequences of the act, policy or institution when evaluating which duty is the actual duty that outweighs other prima facie obligations. Likewise, a high degree of injustice may provide arguments to justify limited infringements on individual property rights.

A third example of a lexicographic weighting is the rule of thumb that not harming others or the prevention of harm to others has priority over doing well to others. In particular, this rule proposes the following priority (Jeurissen, 2000):

1 One should not cause any harm
2 One should prevent that other people cause harm
3 One should oppose existing harm
4 One should foster the good.

This principle gives more weight to harm than to benefits. This has several relations with the various ethical theories. For example, for the theory of utilitarianism, it implies that disutilities carry greater moral weight than utilities. For the ethics of duties, one could derive that the duty not to harm others (in most cases, a perfect duty) normally overrides the duty to help others (in most cases, an imperfect duty).

A fourth way of weighting is to consider the certainty of the moral conclusions. Suppose that in the example of Sen, it is sure that C has made the flute but that A probably derives more pleasure from it. In that case, one would like to give the libertarian argument a higher weight than the utilitarian argument because of the higher degree of certainty. This is one of the arguments why rights normally receive a higher weight than consequences. The prediction of consequences is often more surrounded by uncertainty than the violation of rights.

The four weighting schemes discussed here do not take into account possible conflicts between liberal and communitarian ethics. How can we integrate virtue ethics and the ethics of care in the weighting scheme? A morality based on virtues cannot easily be squeezed into a morality of rules, because the frameworks differ. Human warmth and friendliness, for example, cannot be prescribed by rules of behavior. However, one can argue that virtue ethics in most cases complement liberal ethics because virtues enable people to do what the moral principles of the liberal ethical theories require. The virtue of justice, for example, makes people more inclined to apply the principles of justice. Likewise, generous or altruistic people will be inclined to take into account the consequences of actions or institutions for other people which will enhance the application of utilitarianism. In most cases, an ethics of virtue will therefore not conflict with liberal theories of ethics. Integration of the ethics of care is more problematic, because the ethics of care reject the type of impartiality demanded by the liberal ethical theories. It sets other standards for defining equality than utilitarianism and the ethics of justice because of its focus on personal and valuable relationships.

An attempt to weight Western liberal theories and (Asian) communitarian ethical theories is the integrated social contract theory developed by Donaldson and Dunfee (1999). Traditional applications of the contract theory, like the theory of Rawls, usually derive ethical norms deductively from general macro-statements. Donaldson and Dunfee argue that such a deductive approach should be combined with an inductive micro-approach that recognizes the pluralism in values and norms in reality. Local communities have a space of freedom to determine ethical norms by arranging social contracts that apply on the local level. The only limitation is that these local norms should conform to some fundamental principles (so-called hypernorms in the terminology used by Donaldson and Dunfee). Donaldson and Dunfee propose the following procedure to apply their integrated social contract theory. We should first identify the communities that are involved in the decision and identify the norms that are authentic for the community. For example, in the Asian culture, the trading partner should be trusted on his word. The enforcement of regulations to control the word of the producer goes against this cultural norm. In contrast, in Western countries, companies should prove what they say. The next step in the decision model of Donaldson and Dunfee is to test the norm against the fundamental principles, which include the procedural norms of voice (the right to protest) and exit (the opportunity to leave the community) and substantive norms like the right to private property and respect for humanity. If the norm or policy does not break any fundamental hypernorm, applying some practical considerations should solve the conflict in cultural norms. Note that the theory of Donaldson and Dunfee (1999) clearly gives priority to the fundamental rights of freedom and private property compared to local communitarian standards. In this sense, it is still Western in nature.

Combining these various weighting schemes, we propose the following scheme: If there are several conflicting ethical criteria and if it is impossible to select a dominant alternative, one should normally take the following steps when evaluating the moral value of a set of alternatives:

1 Reject those alternatives that substantially conflict with perfect duties and correlating human rights. Besides the negative rights defended by libertarianism and the basic liberty rights stressed by Rawls (1999a), also the (positive) right to a minimum standard of living must be respected. In case of conflicting perfect duties or human rights, one must intuit as best as one can which potential duty has the greater weight in the case of two conflicting obligations (the all things considered duty).
2 Of the remaining alternatives, reject those alternatives that are contrary to authentic cultural norms. For example, one should reject those alternatives that substantially violate the principle of capitalist justice, the principle of fair equality of opportunity or the principle of socialist justice or that discourage the development of virtues. The importance of these standards may vary among different cultures.
3 Of the remaining alternatives, select the alternative that maximizes some concept of overall well-being. The exact type of well-being to be maximized again depends on cultural norms and the context of the decision. It may be based on the difference principle of Rawls (i.e. maximize the primary social goods of the least advantaged) or utilitarianism. In maximizing overall well-being, one should give more weight to preventing harm than to generating benefits. The weight should also be related to the certainty of the arguments or consequences.

Finally, it should be stressed that this decision tree is just a proposal and hence open to criticism. As already stated, there is no objective ranking of the priority of different ethical standards. The preference for one or another ethical theory is partly a personal matter. For example, proponents of utilitarianism will skip step 1 and 2 and directly apply utilitarianism in step 3. Moreover, the relevance of different ethical standards is also dependent on the specific situation. For instance, for discussions about social assistance, the right to a minimum standard of living and distributive justice according to needs is more important than for discussions about the fairness of bonuses or the financing of pre-retirement schemes for which the libertarian principle or capitalist justice is more apt. The decision-making model presented here therefore does not only offer a concrete method of deriving responsible solutions but also wants to stimulate readers to become aware of their own position and of the reasons why they would like to divert from the three steps proposed earlier.

Clarification of step 7c

For the final choice Manenschijn (1982) proposes that, after one has identified the most preferable option after going through steps 1–7b, the choice is methodologically tested by confronting it with contraindications. That means the conclusion is put forward as a provisional claim that can be contested by others (often informed by practical experience). Often this confrontation takes place by exchanging viewpoints with other people. But if communication with others is not possible, one can also try to reconstruct the debate by putting oneself in the position of others through imagination. One should try to develop the strongest contra-arguments, both those that relate to relevant facts (about the consequences of the option) and those that relate to the principles. The advantage of confronting the provisional claim with the strongest contra-argument is that if the provisional claim remains standing, one can disregard other, weaker, contra-arguments. If the contra-argument proves, however, to be more convincing than the provisional claim, one should adapt the initial claim accordingly.

12.4   CASE STUDY

This section presents a case study to illustrate the operation of the seven-step method presented in Section 12.3. The case concerns replacing a progressive income tax bracket system with a flat income tax system. This policy has been implemented in several East European countries and has also been discussed in some Western European countries. This policy leads to a reduction in the marginal income tax rate, which is one of the elements of the first sub-index of economic freedom (small government). Hence, it can be interpreted as an institutional change that increases economic freedom.

Step 1: Background information

A flat tax system is a system that annually taxes an income base with one fixed tariff (de Kam and Ros, 2006a). In contrast, the tax bracket system applies different and rising tax rates as income increases (in steps). Most Western European countries use a tax bracket system. However, the popularity of the flat tax system has increased. For example, East European countries like Estonia, Latvia, Lithuania, Russia, Slovakia, Serbia, Georgia and Romania introduced a flat income tax system during the last 12 years.

Also in the Netherlands, various options of flat income taxes have been discussed in policy circles. In 2001, the scientific bureau of the Christian Democratic Party (CDA) published a report presenting a flat tax system with a 35% tax rate. In 2005 the Conservative Liberal party (VVD) proposed a flat income tax. Economists like Bovenberg and Teulings (2006) developed a flat income tax system with a tax rate of 38%. In 2008, former Prime Minister Balkenende expressed serious interest in a similar proposal.

Step 2: Identify the options

Normally, a flat tax system is perceived as a tax system that combines a broad tax base with a low tax rate. This kind of tax system particularly benefits the rich income groups and hardly corrects the primary income distribution. There are, however, many alternative flat tax systems, and the implications for the net income distribution crucially depend on the specific characteristics of the system. Table 12.2 presents two concrete proposals for the Netherlands.

In the first alternative, the current tax brackets are replaced by one tax bracket. Incomes are taxed at a rate of 37.5%. In the second alternative, the tax credit is raised by 1,400 euro. This is financed by increasing the tax rate from 37.5% to 43.5%. The capital tax system and the structure of tax exemptions are not changed.

TABLE 12.2
Two examples of a flat tax system for the Netherlands

Old tax bracket system in 2006		Two alternative flat tax systems (Jacobs et al., 2006)		
Tax credit	1,900[a]	Tax credit	1,900	3,300
Tax rates	Income bracket starting at:[a]	Tax rate	37.5%	43.5%
34.15%	0			
41.45 %	17,000			
42 %	30,600			
52 %	52,200			

[a]Thousands of euros.

Step 3: Identify the affected parties

Replacing a tax bracket system with a flat tax system affects all income earners. Economic analyses often distinguish between various household types, such as single persons, bread-winners, two-earner households, recipients of unemployment assistance and the retired elderly. Micro-simulations are used to determine the income effects of various income groups within these household types. In our analysis, we distinguish low, medium, high and top income groups.

Step 4: Identify the consequences of each option for each of the affected parties

The possible (dis)advantages of the flat tax system are summarized in Table 12.3.

The first advantage is that opportunities of tax-saving constructions diminish (Bovenberg and Teulings, 2006). Since the rich have more means to hire tax experts, the simplification of the tax system benefits the low- and medium-income groups. However, this advantage is particularly relevant if tax exemptions are cancelled. In the two proposals under review, the

TABLE 12.3
Advantages and disadvantages of a flat tax system

Advantages	Disadvantages
Rich benefit less from tax saving constructions	More unequal income distribution
More labor market participation	Less labor supply
Government is more predictable	Less possibilities for fine-tuning of income distribution by government
Less fiscal arbitrage and tax fraud	
Simplification and lower administrative costs for employers	
More transparency for citizens	

TABLE 12.4
Income effects of a flat tax system[a]

Household types	Income group	Flat tax 37.5%	Flat tax 43.5%
Single employees	Low	−2.5	−1.5
	Medium	−0,5	−2.25
	High	3.25	−1.75
	Very high	?	?
Breadwinners	Low	−2	−1.5
	Medium	−0.5	−2
	High	4.25	−0.75
	Very high	?	?
Two-earner households	Low	−2	1.25
	Medium	−2	1.25
	High	0.25	−1.25
	Very high	?	?
Unemployment assistance	Low	−3.75	1.25
	Medium	−1.5	−2.25
Retired	Low	−3.5	−1.5
	Medium	−1.5	−4

[a] Percentage of growth compared to current tax system.
Source: Jacobs et al. (2006), Tables 5.1 and 5.2

tax base is not changed. Also the argument that a flat tax system reduces the opportunities of tax fraud is only relevant if the number of tax exemptions is decreased. It is the complexity of the tax exemptions, not the difference in tax rates, that elicits tax fraud.

One of the disadvantages of the flat tax system is that it directly benefits the higher-income groups. However, as already stated, the precise income effects depend on the exact specification of the tax system. This is illustrated by Table 12.4.

The table shows that the income effects are highly diverse. Nevertheless, there are some general tendencies. First, in both flat tax systems, retired persons face a reduction in income. Second, the highest-income groups benefit. Unfortunately, we could only get indirect information about the income effects of the highest-income groups. de Kam and Pen (2006) show, for example, that the income of top managers like the chief executive officer (CEO) of Shell will increase by 8% in alternative 1. Finally, an important difference between proposal one and two is that the least advantaged groups benefit more from alternative two due to the increase in the tax credit.

The income effects presented in Table 12.4 do not take into account the economic behavioral effects of replacing a tax bracket system with a flat tax system. It is often assumed that a flat tax system encourages labor supply because the marginal tax rate declines. The impact on labor supply depends, however, on the exact profile of the marginal tax structure. Using the MIMIC model (Graafland et al., 2001) Jacobs et al. (2006) estimate that the first variant decreases the participation rate of women, because the new tax rate of 37.5% is higher

TABLE 12.5
Economic effects of a flat tax system[a]

	Flat tax 37.5%	Flat tax 43.5%
Theil coefficient	6.50	−3.00
Marginal tax rate (absolute change)	−3.0	0.25
Participation rate of women	−1.75	1.50
Labor supply in hours	1.00	−0.25
Breadwinners	1.25	0.00
Two-earner	0.00	−0.25
Single person	1.00	−1.00
Share high skilled in labor supply	0.75	0.00
Employment	1.50	−0.25
Low skilled	−2.00	−0.50
High skilled	2.50	−0.25
Unemployment rate	0.00	0.00

[a] Percentage of growth compared to current tax system.
Source: Jacobs et al. (2006), Table 5.3

than the current tax rate of the first tax bracket (34.15%, see Table 12.4). The total supply of labor hours increases, however, because the marginal tax rate for most other income groups declines. Also the investment in human capital through education improves. The second variant causes a decline in the total supply of labor hours. Labor supply research shows that part-time and low-income workers respond relatively more to financial incentives than do high-income groups. For these groups, the marginal income tax rate increases, causing negative substitution effects. Although the marginal income tax rate declines for high-income groups, these groups are rather insensitive to economic incentives and therefore hardly raise their labor effort. However, the participation rate increases because the additional tax credit in this proposal only applies to those receiving an income from working. This encourages non-working people to accept a small part-time job.

This illustrates the lessons from optimal tax literature that show that the optimal tax structure depends on four factors (Jacobs et al., 2006: 94): (1) the income inequality before taxation, (2) the society's aversion to income inequality, (3) the impact of monetary incentives on labor supply and (4) the density of the income distribution. If a society is averse to income inequality, the optimal marginal tax structure will have a U-shape: low-income groups will receive high income tax credits and pay low taxes. In order to collect sufficient taxes, the medium- and high-income groups will have to pay substantially more taxes, and this requires that the marginal tax rate between low- and medium-income groups be relatively high (A in Figure 12.1). However, for medium-income groups high marginal tax rates have a large disincentive effect on labor supply, explaining why marginal tax rates should be lower for medium-income groups than for the lowest-income groups (B in Figure 12.1). The labor supply of high-income groups is less sensitive to economic incentives. Hence, for high-income groups marginal tax rates have to increase again in order to realize additional income redistribution (C in Figure 12.1). These lessons imply that a flat tax system will not be efficient in general.

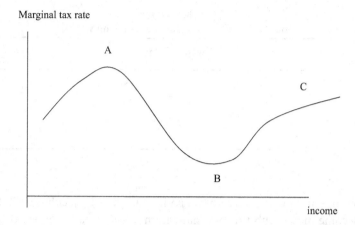

FIGURE 12.1 Optimal marginal tax structure according to optimal tax literature

A third advantage mentioned by proponents of a flat tax system is a more reliable government. If the tax system only consists of a tax credit and one tax rate, the government has fewer opportunities for intervening in the market and therefore becomes more predictable. This advantage has the obvious disadvantage that the simplified tax structure leaves the government with fewer possibilities to correct income distribution. The debate about incomes of top executives shows that the government also runs a risk of losing credibility if it cannot intervene when top executives earn exorbitant salaries according to a majority of citizens.

Another advantage of the flat income tax is a reduction of opportunities of tax arbitrage. If different tax bases (for example, of labor income and capital income) are taxed by significantly different tax rates, people will try to reallocate income towards the tax base with the lowest tax rate. Jacobs et al. (2006) argue, however, that a flat tax system is not necessary to reduce tax arbitrage. One can also redefine tax bases in a way that precludes or hinders tax arbitrage, for example, by sampling all types of income in one base (without using one tariff) (de Kam and Ros, 2006b).

Other advantages of the flat tax system are a reduction in administrative costs of employers and more transparency for the citizen (Bovenberg and Teulings, 2006). This contributes to the flexibility of the labor market. de Kam and Ros (2006b) doubt, however, the empirical relevance of these effects, since other parts of the social security system still require that companies provide the type of information that a flat tax system would save.

Step 5: Identify the moral standards that are met or violated by the options or their consequences

Table 12.6 presents an overview of the values that are involved with the two variants.

First, one can doubt whether the two flat tax systems really improve happiness or welfare. The theoretical analysis of Jacobs et al. (2006) indicates that a simple flat tax system is less efficient than a tax bracket system that takes into account that the incentive effects of taxes vary for different income groups. If one also considers the negative external effects

TABLE 12.6
Qualitative effects of a flat tax system on values

	Flat tax 37.5%	Flat tax 43.5%
Utility/welfare	−	−
Egalitarian justice	−	+
Capitalistic justice	+	−
Virtues	?	0

of positional competition (which are not taken into account by Jacobs et al.), the efficiency effects even become more doubtful. Internalization of the negative externalities caused by positional competition and habit formation requires tax rates of 50% or more. Furthermore, the efficiency gains from less tax arbitrage, tax fraud and administration costs and from more transparency remain modest as long as the tax base is not substantial broadened and simplified. Therefore, the overall impact on welfare is likely to be relatively small.

The potential negative effect on happiness is also indicated by the empirical research of Graafland and Compen (2015), reviewed in Chapter 4. They found that small government reduces life satisfaction. As replacing the progressive tax bracket system with a flat tax system reduces marginal income tax rates, which is one element of the size of the government as measured by the Fraser Institute and Heritage Foundation, this policy will diminish life satisfaction. This negative effect is also implied by research by Graafland and Lous (2018) and Lous and Graafland (2021), reviewed in Chapter 7. Graafland and Lous (2018) found that fiscal freedom (that includes low marginal income tax rates) increases income inequality, whereas Lous and Graafland (2021) showed that income inequality diminishes life satisfaction.

The second standard that we consider is egalitarian distributive justice. The first proposal decreases income of all low-income groups, whereas the higher-income groups all benefit from this tax proposal. The Theil coefficient – an aggregate standard for income inequality – increases by 6.5%. In the second variant inequality decreases: the Theil coefficient declines with 3% because the low-income groups benefit from the higher tax credit. From this we conclude that the first variant is rejected and the second accepted from the perspective of egalitarian justice.

A reverse evaluation is obtained when applying capitalistic justice. Whereas the first variant increases the link between net income and gross income (which can be interpreted as an indicator of the marginal productivity) by lowering marginal tax rates, the second variant increases the marginal tax rate on average. Even a flat tax system is not completely just from a strict capitalistic justice point of view, because it still implies that the rich pay more taxes than the poor. From a capitalistic point of view, this is only fair if the rich would also benefit more from public expenditures than the poor (which they probably do, but the extent is uncertain).

The final standard that we apply is virtue ethics. de Kam and Pen (2006) argue that the large increase in incomes of very high-income groups will elicit negative effects on the tax morality because people will consider these effects to be unfair. On the other hand, the flat income tax may encourage the virtue of diligence, because it creates an incentive to work more and invest in human capital. It is not possible to determine empirically the net effects of both variants on various virtues or to derive an overall judgment. The effects of the second variant are probably too marginal to expect any substantial impact on virtues.

Step 6: If various moral standards are involved and the different options cannot be completely ordered, determine the hierarchy of the moral standards that should prevail and identify the option that optimally meets this hierarchy

In order to derive a final evaluation, we will have to weigh the various moral standards of Table 12.6. Whereas the effects on welfare and virtues are ambiguous, the first proposal scores better in terms of capitalistic justice and the second proposal in terms of egalitarian justice. This renders a complete ordering impossible. A final judgment therefore requires a hierarchy between, in this case, egalitarian and capitalistic justice. Figure 12.2 represents the choice process implied by the rule of thumb proposed in Section 12.3. First, in all cases – the current tax system, proposal 1 and proposal 2 – no perfect duties and basic rights are violated. That implies that all three tax systems pass the first test. In the second test all variants that cause a severe violation of socialist justice, the principle of rendering each his or her due, equality of opportunities or encouragement of vices are rejected. Again, there is no ground to reject any of the three tax systems. Although the old tax system and proposal 2 confront citizens with a higher (marginal) tax burden, the violation of their property rights is too limited to reject these alternatives on grounds of the second test.

That implies that the choice should be determined in the last test of the rule of thumb. In this test, proposal 1 is rejected because it worsens the position of all low-income groups and increases income inequality. The decision between the old system and proposal 2 is less obvious. Whereas proposal 2 benefits the low-income groups among two-earner households and recipients of unemployment assistance, it reduces the income of other low-income groups (see Table 12.4). Considering that Rawls defines the least advantaged as a broad group (30% lowest-income group), this test is therefore more or less neutral between the old bracket income tax system and proposal 2, if one opts for the difference principle. Overall, proposal 2 increases income equality, however. When one opts for utilitarianism, the bracket income tax system is preferable, as the increase in income inequality might reduce overall happiness.

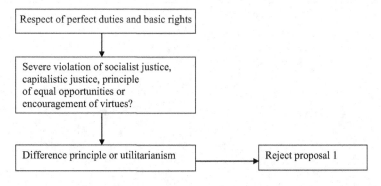

FIGURE 12.2 Application of the rule of thumb

Step 7: Check the outcome once again

The evaluation of the flat income tax system is just a finger exercise that illustrates the application of the seven-step model presented in Section 12.3. Based on the theoretical analysis of Jacobs et al. (2006), we expect that proposal 2 is not the most optimal tax system. For example, a tax system with two brackets that progressively tax higher-income groups (as proposed by Kam and Pen, 2006) is probably both more efficient and just. This is actually what happened in the Netherlands in 2019, when the Dutch government replaced the former tax bracket system with a simplified tax bracket system with only two brackets. One can think of innumerable other variants of tax systems that vary in terms of tax credit, number of tax brackets, the length of tax brackets and the tariffs per tax bracket. Furthermore, one should also consider changes in the tax base, which we left out in this section for purposes of clarity. It is up to the creativity of policy makers to construe attractive alternatives and to evaluate them on the basis of moral standards that have been described in this book.

NOTES

1   More specifically, Brennan and Jaworski (2016) distinguish three types of semiotic objections: (1) Things that have intrinsic value are regarded on the market as having merely instrumental value; (2) Market transactions signal disrespect for the object in question; and (3) Market transactions cause estrangement by making things that belong to personal relationships inherently impersonal.
2   This point relates to the issue of incommensurability in Chapter 3 and the distinction of spheres in Chapter 8.

Recommended literature

Brennan, J. and Jaworski, P.M. (2016) *Markets without Limits: Moral Virtues and Commercial Interests*, London and New York: Routledge.
Donaldson, T. and Dunfee, T.W. (1999) *Ties that Bind*, Boston: Harvard Business School Press.
Rawls, J. (1999a) *A Theory of Justice*, Revised edition, Boston: Harvard University Press.
Sen, A. (1981) 'Ethical issues in income distribution: national and international', in: S. Grassman and E. Lundberg (eds.) *The World Economic Order: Past and Prospects*, London: Macmillan, 464–494.
Velasquez, M.G. (1998) *Business Ethics: Concepts and Cases*, Fourth edition, Upper Saddle River, NJ: Prentice Hall.

References

Abatayo, A.L. and Lynham, J. (2016) 'Endogenous vs. exogenous regulations in the commons', *Journal of Environmental Economics and Management*, 76: 51–66.

Abeler, J., Nosenzo, D. and Raymond, C. (2019) 'Preferences for truth-telling', *Econometrica*, 87(4): 1115–1153.

Achterhuis, H. (1988) *Het Rijk van de Schaarste van Hobbes tot Foucault*, Fifth edition, Amsterdam: Ambo.

Aghion, P., Algan, Y., Cahuc, P. and Shleifer, A. (2010) 'Regulation and distrust', *Quarterly Journal of Economics*, 125: 1015–1049.

Ahlerup, P., Olsson, O. and Yanagizawa, D. (2009) 'Social capital vs institutions in the growth process', *European Journal of Political Economy*, 25(1): 1–14.

Aixalá, J. and Fabro, G. (2009) 'Economic freedom, civil liberties, political rights and growth: A causality analysis', *Spanish Economic Review*, 11(3): 165–178.

Albanesi, S. (2002) 'Inflation and inequality', *Centre for Economic Policy Research*, Discussion Paper No. 3470.

Alempaki, D., Doğan, G. and Saccardo, S. (2019) 'Deception and reciprocity', *Experimental Economics*, 22: 980–1001.

Alesina, A. and Giuliano, P. (2015) 'Culture and institutions', *Journal of Economic Literature*, 53(4): 898–944.

Alessie, R. and Kapteyn, A. (1991) 'Habit formation, interdependent preferences and demographic effects in the almost ideal demand system', *The Economic Journal*, 101: 404–419.

Alfano, M., Higgins, A. and Levernier, J. (2018) 'Identifying virtues and values through obituary data-mining', *The Journal of Value Inquiry*, 52(1): 59–79.

Algan, Y. and Cahuc, P. (2014) 'Trust, growth, and well-being: New evidence and policy implications', in: P. Aghion and S.N. Durlauf (eds.) *Handbook of Economic Growth, Volume 2A*, Amsterdam and San Diego: Elsevier, 49–120.

Alpizar, F., Carsson, F. and Johansson-Stenman, O. (2005) 'How much do we care about absolute versus relative income consumption?', *Journal of Economic Behaviour & Organization*, 56: 405–421.

Alzola, M. (2012) 'The possibility of virtue', *Business Ethics Quarterly*, 22(2): 377–404.

Ambrus, A. and Pathak, P. (2011) 'Cooperation over finite horizons: A theory and experiments', *Journal of Public Economics*, 95: 500–512.

Anderson, D.M. (1998) 'Communitarian approaches to the economy', in: H. Giersch (ed.) *Merits and Limits of Markets*, Berlin: Springer-Verlag, 29–52.

Anderson, E. (1993) *Value in Ethics and Economics*, Cambridge, MA and London: Harvard University Press.

Apergis, N., Dincer, O. and Payne, J. (2014) 'Economic freedom and income inequality revisited: Evidence from a panel error correction model', *Contemporary Economic Policy*, 32(1): 67–75.

Arikan, G. (2011) 'Economic individualism and government spending', *World Values Research*, 4(3): 73–95.

Aristotle, *Ethica Nicomachea*, Groningen: Historische Uitgeverij.

Aristotle, *Politics*, book I and II, Oxford: Clarendon Press.

Armstrong, M. and Sappington, D.E.M. (2006) 'Regulation, competition, and liberalization', *Journal of Economic Literature*, XLIV: 325–366.

Arneson, R.J. (2002) 'Why justice requires transfers to offset income and wealth inequalities', *Social Philosophy and Policy Foundation*, 19: 172–200.

Arneson, R.J. (2007) 'Luck egalitarianism and prioritarianism', *Ethics*, 110: 339–349.

Arranz, N. and de Arroyabe, J.C.F. (2012) 'Effect of formal contracts, relational norms and trust on performance of joint research and development projects', *British Journal of Management*, 23: 575–588.

Arrow, K. (1972) 'Gifts and exchange', *Philosophy and Public Affairs*, I: 343–362.

Ashraf, N., Bohnet, I. and Piankov, N. (2006) 'Decomposing trust and trustworthiness', *Experimental Economics*, 9(3): 193–208.

Attanasio, O., Guiso, L. and Jappelli, T. (1998) *The Demand for Money, Financial Innovation, and the Welfare Cost of Inflation: An Analysis with Households' Data*. National Bureau of Economic Research, No. w6593. https://www.nber.org/papers/w6593

Azman-Saini, W.N.W., Baharumshah, A.Z. and Law, S.H. (2010) 'Foreign direct investment, economic freedom and economic growth: International evidence', *Economic Modelling*, 27(5): 1079–1089.

Baier, A. (1987) 'Hume, the women's moral theorist?', in: E. Kittay and D. Meyers (eds.) *Women and Moral Theory*, Totowa, NJ: Rowman & Littlefield, 37–55.

Baldwin, R.E. (1992) 'Are economists' traditional trade policy views still valid?', *Journal of Economic Literature*, 30(2): 804–829.

Balestra, C., Boarini, R. and Tosetto, E. (2018) 'What matters most to people? Evidence from the OECD Better Life Index users' responses', *Social Indicators Research*, 136: 907–930.

Balliet, D. and van Lange, P.A. (2013) 'Trust, conflict, and cooperation: A meta-analysis', *Psychological Bulletin*, 139(5): 1090–1112.

Bansal, P. and Roth, K. (2000) 'Why companies go green: A model of ecological responsiveness', *Academy of Management Journal*, 43(4): 717–736.

Barone, G. and Mocetti, S. (2016) 'Inequality and trust: New evidence from panel data', *Economic Inquiry*, 54(2): 794–809.

Barth, R. and Wolff, F. (2009) *Corporate Social Responsibility in Europe: Rhetoric and Realities*, Cheltenham: Edward Elgar Publishing Ltd.

Barton, A. and Grüne-Yanoff, T. (2015) 'From libertarian paternalism to "nudging – and beyond"', *Review of Philosophy and Psychology*, 6: 341–359.

Bastagli, F., Coady, D. and Gupta, S. (2012) *Income Inequality and Fiscal Policy*. IMF Staff Discussion Note, SDN/12/08, International Monetary Fund.

Baughn, C.C., Bodie, N.L. and McIntosh, J.C. (2007) 'Corporate social and environmental responsibility in Asian countries and other geographical regions', *Corporate Social Responsibility and Environmental Management*, 14: 189–205.

Baumeister, R. and Vohs, K. (2003) 'Willpower, choice and self-control', in: G. Loewenstein and D. Read (eds.) *Time and Decision: Economic and Psychological Perspectives on Intertemporal Choice*, New York: Russell Sage Foundation.

Bavetta, S., Li Donni, P. and Marino, M. (2019) 'An empirical analysis of the determinants of perceived inequality', *Review of Income and Wealth*, 65(2): 264–293.

Beauchamp, T.L. (1982) *Philosophical Ethics, an Introduction to Moral Philosophy*, New York: McGraw-Hill Inc.

Bell, K. (2015) 'Can the capitalist economic system deliver environmental justice?', *Environmental Research Letters*, 10: 125017.

Bennett, D.L., Faria, H.J., Gwartney, J.D. and Morales, D.R. (2017) 'Economic institutions and comparative economic development: A post-colonial perspective', *World Development*, 96: 503–519.

Bennett, D.L. and Nikolaev, B. (2017) On the ambiguous economic freedom-inequality relationship. *Empirical Economics*, 53: 717–754.

Bennett, D.L., Nikolaev, B. and Aidt, T.S. (2016) 'Institutions and well-being', *European Journal of Political Economy*, 45: 1–10.

Bennett, D.L. and Vedder, R. (2013) 'A dynamic analysis of economic freedom and income inequality in the 50 US States: Empirical evidence of a parabolic relationship', *Journal of Regional Analysis & Policy*, 43(1): 42–55.

Benz, M. and Frey, B.S. (2003) *The Value of Autonomy: Evidence from the Self-employed in 23 Countries*. Working Paper 173. Institute for Empirical Research in Economics, University of Zurich.

Benzeval, M. and Judge, K. (2001) 'Income and health: The time dimension', *Social Science and Medicine*, 52(9): 1371–1390.

Berg, A. and Ostry, J. (2011) *Inequality and Unsustainable Growth: Two Sides of the Same Coin?* IMF Staff Discussion Note, SDN/11/08. https://www.imf.org/en/Publications/Staff-Discussion-Notes/Issues/2016/12/31/Inequality-and-Unsustainable-Growth-Two-Sides-of-the-Same-Coin-24686

Berg, M. and Veenhoven, R. (2010) 'Income inequality and happiness in 119 nations', in: B. Greve (ed.) *Social Policy and Happiness in Europe*, Cheltenham: Edgar Elgar, 174–194.

Berggren, N. (1999) 'Economic freedom and equality: Friends or foes?', *Public Choice*, 100(3–4): 203–223.

Berggren, N. and Bjørnskov, C. (2019) 'Regulation and government debt', *Public Choice*, 178(1–2): 153–178.

Berggren, N. and Jordahl, H. (2006) 'Free to trust: Economic freedom and social capital', *Kyklos*, 59: 141–169.

Bergh, A. and Bjørnskov, C. (2014) 'Trust, welfare states and income equality: Sorting out the causality', *European Journal of Political Economy*, 35: 183–199.

Berns, E.E. and van Stratum, R. (1986) 'De plaats van de economie in Adam Smith's "Moral Philosophy"', in: G. Berns (ed.) *Adam Smith. Ethiek, Politiek en Economie*, Tilburg: Tilburg University Press, 176–203.

Bjørnskov, C. (2005) *The Determinants of Trust*. http://ssrn.com/abstract=900183

Bjørnskov, C. (2012) 'How does social trust affect economic growth?', *Southern Economic Journal*, 78(4): 1346–1368.

Bjørnskov, C., Dreher, A. and Fischer, J.A.V. (2007) 'The bigger the better? Evidence of the effect of government size on life satisfaction around the world', *Public Choice*, 130: 267–292.

Bjørnskov, C., Dreher, A. and Fischer, J.A.V. (2010) 'Formal institutions and subjective well-being: Revisiting the cross-country evidence', *European Journal of Political Economy*, 26: 419–430.

Bjørnskov, C. and Foss, N.J. (2008) 'Economic freedom and entrepreneurial activity: Some cross country evidence', *Public Choice*, 134(3): 307–328.

Blanchard, O.S. and Fischer, S. (1992) *NBER Macroeconomics Annual 1991*, Vol. 6, Cambridge, MA: MIT Press.

Blanchflower, D.G., Oswald, A.J. and Garrett, M.D. (1990) 'Insider power in wage determination', *Economica*, 57(226): 143–170.

Blaug, M. (1978) *Economic Theory in Retrospect*, Third edition, Cambridge: Cambridge University Press.

Block, J.H., Millán, A., Millán, J.M. and Moritz, A. (2018) *Entrepreneurship and Work-life Balance*. https://papers.ssrn.com/sol3/papers.cfm?abstract_id=3148885

Bloom, M. (1999) 'The performance effects of pay dispersion on individuals and organizations', *The Academy of Management Journal*, 42: 25–45.

Bloom, M. and Michel, J.G. (2002) 'The relationships among organizational context, pay dispersion and managerial turnover', *Academy of Management Journal*, 45: 33–42.

Blume, L. and Voigt, S. (2006) 'The economic effects of human rights', *Kyklos*, 60(4): 509–538.

Boettke, P.J. (1998) 'Rational choice and human agency in economics and sociology: Exploring the Weber-Austrian connection', in: H. Giersch (ed.) *Merits and Limits of Markets*, Berlin: Springer-Verlag, 53–80.

Bos-Brouwers, H. (2010) 'Corporate sustainability and innovation in SMEs: Evidence of themes and activities in practice', *Business Strategy and the Environment*, 19: 417–435.

Bosma, J. (2013) *The Duty to Assist the Poor and the Extent of Its Demands*, Dissertation Tilburg University.

Bovenberg, A.L. (2002) 'Norms, values and technological change', *De Economist*, 150: 521–553.

Bovenberg, A.L. and Teuling, C.N. (2006) 'Vlaktaks: haken en ogen', in: C.A. de Kam and A.P. Ros (eds.) *De Vlaktaks. Naar een Inkomstenbelasting met een Uniform Tarief?*, Willem Drees Stichting voor Openbare Financiën, Den Haag: Van Deventer.

Bowles, S. (1998) 'Endogenous preferences: The cultural consequences of markets and other economic institutions', *Journal of Economic Literature*, XXXVI: 75–111.

Bowles, S. (2011) 'Is liberal society a parasite on tradition?', *Philosophy & Public Affairs*, 39(1): 46–81.

Bowles, S. (2016) *The Moral Economy: Why Good Incentives Are no Substitute for Good Citizens*, New Haven: Yale University Press.

Bowles, S. and Polania-Reyes, S. (2012) 'Economic incentives and social preferences: Substitutes or complements?', *Journal of Economic Literature*, 50: 368–425.

Boyer, G.R. (1995) 'Anglo-Saxon model a fatality, or will contrasting national trajectories persist?', *British Journal of Industrial Relations*, 33(4): 545–556.

Boyer, G.R. and Smith, R.S. (2001) 'The development of the neoclassical tradition in labor economics', *Industrial and Labor Relations Review*, 54(2): 199–223.

Bozeman, B. (2007) *Public Values and Public Interest: Counterbalancing Economic Individualism*, Washington, DC: Georgetown University Press.

Brammer, S. and Millington, A. (2008) 'Does it pay to be different? An analysis of the relationship between corporate social and financial performance', *Strategic Management Journal*, 29(12): 1325–1343.

Bréban, L. (2014) 'Smith on happiness: Towards a gravitational theory', *The European Journal of the History of Economic Thought*, 21(3): 359–391.

Brekke, K.A. and Howarth, R.B. (2002) *Status, Growth and the Environment; Goods as Symbols in Applied Welfare Economics*, Cheltenham: Edward Elgar.

Brennan, J. and Jaworski, P.M. (2016) *Markets without Limits: Moral Virtues and Commercial Interests*, London and New York: Routledge.

Bright, D., Winn, B. and Kanov, J. (2014) 'Reconsidering virtue: Differences of perspective in virtue ethics and the positive social sciences', *Journal of Business Ethics*, 119(4): 445–460.

Brink, D.O. (1996) 'Moral conflict and its structure', in: H.E. Mason (ed.) *Moral Dilemmas and Moral Theory*, Oxford and New York: Oxford University Press, 102–126.

Brue, S.L. and Grant, R.R. (2007) *The Evolution of Economic Thought*, Mason: Thomson.

Brundtland Commission (1987) *Our Common Future*, Oxford and New York: Oxford University Press.

Bruni, L. and Stanca, L. (2006) 'Income aspirations, television and happiness: Evidence from the World Values Studies', *Kyklos*, 59: 209–225.

Bruni, L. and Sugden, R. (2013) 'Reclaiming virtue ethics for economics', *Journal of Economic Perspectives*, 27: 141–164.

Budría, S. and Ferrer-I-Carbonell, A. (2019) 'Life satisfaction, income comparisons and individual traits', *Review of Income and Wealth*, 65(2): 337–358.

Bukowski, A. and Rudnicki, S. (2019) 'Not only individualism: The effects of long-term orientation and other cultural variables on national innovation success', *Cross-Cultural Research*, 53(2): 119–162.

Burbidge, D. (2016) 'Space for virtue in the economics of Kenneth J. Arrow, Amartya Sen and Elinor Ostrom', *Journal of Economic Methodology*, 23(4): 396–412.

Camerer, C.F. and Fehr, E. (2004) 'Measuring social norms and preferences using experimental games: A guide for social scientists', in: Henrich et al. (eds.) *Foundations of Human Sociality: Economic Experiments and Ethnographic Evidence from Fifteen Small-scale Societies*, Oxford: Oxford University Press, 55–95.

Camerer, C.F. and Fehr, E. (2006) 'When does "economic man" dominate social behavior?', *Science*, 311: 47–52.

Campbell, J.L. (2007) 'Why would corporations behave in socially responsible ways? An institutional theory of corporate social responsibility', *Academy of Management Review*, 32: 946–967.

Campbell, N.D., Jauregui, A. and Heriot, K.C. (2008) 'Housing prices and economic freedom', *The Journal of Private Enterprise*, 23(2): 1–17.

Carlsson, F., Johansson-Stenman, O.L.O.F. and Martinsson, P. (2007) 'Do you enjoy having more than others? Survey evidence of positional goods', *Economica*, 74(296): 586–598.

Carmon, Z., Wertenbroch, K. and Zeelenberg, M. (2003) 'Option attachment: When deliberating makes choosing feel like losing', *Journal of Consumer Research*, 30: 15–29.

Caruso, R. and Schneider, F. (2011) 'The socio-economic determinants of terrorism and political violence in Western Europe (1994–2007)', *European Journal of Political Economy*, 27: S37–S49.

Chang, H.J. (2014) *Economics: The User's Guide*, London: Penguin Books.

Chaudhuri, A. (2011) 'Sustaining cooperation in laboratory public goods experiments: A selective survey of the literature', *Experimental Economics*, 14: 47–83.

Chen, M.C. (2013) 'The effect of language on economic behavior: Evidence from savings rates, health behaviors, and retirement assets', *American Economic Review*, 103(2): 690–731.

Choo, F. and Tan, K. (2007) 'An American dream theory of corporate executive fraud', *Accounting Forum*, 31: 203–215.

Christman, J. (1998) 'Property rights', in: *Encyclopedia of Applied Ethics*, Vol. 3, San Diego: Academic Press, 683–692.

Chryssides, G. and Kaler, J.H. (1993) *An Introduction to Business Ethics*, London: Chapman & Hall.

Claassen, R.J.G. (2004) *Het Eeuwig Tekort. Een Filosofie van de Schaarste*, Amsterdam: AMBO.

Clark, A.E. (1999) 'Are wages habit-forming? Evidence from micro data', *Journal of Economic Behavior & Organization*, 39: 179–200.

Collard, D. (1978) *Altruism & Economy: A Study in Non-Selfish Economics*, Oxford: Martin Robertson.

Conlisk, J. (1996) 'Why bounded rationality?', *Journal of Economic Literature*, XXXIV: 669–700.

Cornia, G.A. (ed.) (2004) *Inequality, Growth and Poverty in an Era of Liberalization and Globalization*, Oxford: Oxford University Press.

CPB (1992) *Scanning the Future: A Long-term Scenario Study of the World Economy 1990–2015*, The Hague: Sdu Publishers.

Crisp, R. (ed.) (1998) J.S. Mill, *Utilitarianism*, Oxford: Oxford University Press.

Crisp, R. (2003) 'Equality, priority and compassion', *Ethics*, 113: 745–763.

Cros, J. (1950) Le *"Néo-libéralisme" et la Révision du Libéralisme. Thèse Droit*, Toulouse: Imprimerie Moderne.

Cruz-Garcíal, P. and Peiró-Palomino, J. (2019) 'Informal, formal institutions and credit: Complements or substitutes?', *Journal of Institutional Economics*, 15(4): 649–671.

Curry, O.S., Price, M.E. and Price, J.G. (2008) 'Patience is a virtue: Cooperative people have lower discount rates', *Personality and Individual Differences*, 44: 780–785.

Dahlsgard, K., Peterson, C. and Seligman, M. (2005) 'Shared virtue: The convergence of valued human strengths across culture and history', *Review of General Psychology*, 9(1): 202–213.

Dawson, J.W. (1998) 'Institutions, investment, and growth: New cross-country and panel data evidence', *Economic Inquiry*, 36: 603–619.

Davis, K. (2000) *Cosmetic Surgery in a Different Voice: The Case of Madame Noël*. www.let. uu.nl/~kathy.davis/personal/cosmetic_surgery.html (assessed June 2004).

Deaton, A. (2008) 'Income, aging, health and wellbeing around the world: Evidence from the Gallup World Poll', *Journal of Economic Perspectives*, 22(2): 53–72.

De Beer, P. and den Hoed, P. (2004) *Wat gij niet wilt dat u geschiedt . . .*, Amsterdam: Amsterdam University Press Salome.

De Haan, J., Lundström, S. and Sturm, J.E. (2006) 'Market-oriented policies and economic growth: A critical survey', *Journal of Economic Surveys*, 20(2): 157–192.

Desjardins, J.R. (1984) 'Virtues and business ethics', in: M. Hoffman (ed.) *Corporate Governance and Institutionalized Ethics*, Lexington: D.C. Heath & Co.

De Vanssay, X. and Spindler, Z. (1994) 'Freedom and growth: Do constitutions matter?', *Public Choice*, 78(3–4): 359–372.

Diener, E. and Suh, E.M. (1997) 'Measuring quality of life: Economic, social, and subjective indicators', *Social Indicators Research*, 40(1–2): 189–216.

Diener, E. and Suh, E.M. (2002) *Culture and Subjective Well-being*, Cambridge, MA: MIT Press.

Dijk, M., Orsato, R.J. and Kemp, R. (2013) 'The emergence of an electric mobility trajectory', *Energy Policy*, 52(1): 135–145.

Di Tella, R. and MacCulloch, R.J. (2010) 'Happiness adaptation to income beyond "basic needs"', in: E. Diener, J. Helliwell and D. Kahneman (eds.) *International Differences in Well-Being*, New York: Oxford University Press, 217–247.

Di Tella, R., MacCulloch, R.J. and Oswald, A.J. (2001) 'Preferences over inflation and unemployment: Evidence from surveys of happiness', *American Economic Review*, 91: 335–341.

Di Tella, R., MacCulloch, R.J. and Oswald, A.J. (2003) 'The macroeconomics of happiness', *The Review of Economics and Statistics*, 85: 809–827.

Djankov, S., Glaeser, E., La Porta, R., Lopez-de-Silanes, F. and Shleifer, A. (2003) 'The new comparative economics', *Journal of Comparative Economics*, 31(4): 595–619.

Donagan, A. (1996) 'Moral dilemmas, genuine and spurious: A comparative anatomy', in: H.E. Mason (ed.) *Moral Dilemmas and Moral Theory*, Oxford and New York: Oxford University Press, 11–22.

Donaldson, T. and Dunfee, T.W. (1999) *Ties that Bind*, Boston: Harvard Business School Press.

Doucouliagos, C. (2005) 'Publication bias in the economic freedom and economic growth literature', *Journal of Economic Surveys*, 19(3): 367–387.

Dubbink, W. (2005) 'Democracy and the legitimacy of private discretion in public issues', *Business Ethics Quarterly*, XV(1): 37–66.

Durand, M. (2015) 'The OECD better life initiative: How' life? and the measurement of well-being', *Review of Income and Wealth*, 61(1): 4–17.

Easterlin, R.A. (1974) 'Does economic growth improve the human lot?', in: P. David and M. Reder (eds.) *Nations and Households in Economic Growth: Essays in Honor of Moses Abramowitz*, New York: Academic Press, 89–125.

Easterlin, R.A., McVey, L.A., Sawangfa, O., Switek, M.S. and Zweig, J.S. (2011) *The Happiness-income Paradox Revisited*. IZA Discussion Paper Series, No 5799. http://ftp.iza.org/dp5799. pdf.

Elgar, F. and Aitken, N. (2011) 'Income inequality, trust and homicide in 33 countries', *European Journal of Public Health*, 21(2): 241–246.

Engler, Y., Kerschbamer, R. and Page, L. (2018) 'Why did he do that? Using counterfactuals to study the effect of intentions in extensive form games', *Experimental Economics*, 21: 1–26.

Erosa, A. and Ventura, G. (2002) 'On inflation as a regressive consumption tax', *Journal of Monetary Economics*, 49(4): 761–795.

Etzioni, A. (1988) *The Moral Dimension: Towards a New Economics*, New York: The Free Press.

Evan, W.M. and Freeman, R.E. (1988) 'A stakeholder theory of the modern corporation: Kantian capitalism', in: T.L. Beauchamp and N. Bowie (eds.) *Ethical Theory and Business*, Englewood Cliffs: Prentice Hall, 75–84.

Fahey, T. and Smyth, E. (2004) 'Do subjective indicators measure welfare? Evidence from 33 European societies', *European Societies*, 6(1): 5–27.

Falk, A., Becker, A., Dohmen, T., Enke, B., Huffman, D. and Sunde, U. (2018) 'Global evidence on economic preferences', *The Quarterly Journal of Economics*, 133(4): 1645–1692.

Farhadi, M., Islam, M.R. and Moslehi, S. (2015) 'Economic freedom and productivity growth in resource-rich economies', *World Development*, 72: 109–126.

Fehr, E. and Fischbacher, U. (2002) 'Why social preferences matter – The impact of non-selfish motives on competition, cooperation and incentives', *The Economic Journal*, 112: C1–C33.

Fehr, E. and Gächter, S. (2000) 'Cooperation and punishment in public goods experiments', *American Economic Review*, 90: 980–994.

Fehr, E. and Leibbrandt, A. (2011) 'A field study on cooperativeness and impatience in the tragedy of the commons', *Journal of Public Economics*, 95: 1144–1155.

Feldmann, H. (2017) 'Economic freedom and human capital investment', *Journal of Institutional Economics*, 13(2): 421–445.

Ferrero, I. and Sison, A.J.G. (2014) 'A quantitative analysis of authors, schools and themes in virtue ethics articles in business ethics and management journals (1980–2011)', *Business Ethics: A European Review*, 23(4): 375–400.

Figlio, D., Giuliano, P., Özek, U. and Sapienza, P. (2016) *Long-term Orientation and Educational Performance*. NBER Working Paper 22541. www.nber.org/papers/w22541

Fischer, C.S. (2008) 'What wealth-happiness paradox? A short note on the American case', *Journal of Happiness Studies*, 9: 219–226.

Flanagan, R.J. (1988) 'Unemployment as a hiring problem', *OECD Economics Studies*, 11: 123–154.

Florida, R. (2002) *The Rise of the Creative Class: And How It's Transforming Work, Leisure, Community and Everyday Life*, New York: Basic Books.

Fourcade, M. and Healy, K. (2007) 'Moral views of market society', *Annual Review of Sociology*, 33: 285–311.

Frank, R.H. (2004) *What Price the Moral High Ground*, Princeton: Princeton University Press.

Frey, B.S. (1998) *Not Just for the Money, an Economic Theory of Personal Motivation*, Cheltenham: Edward Elgar.

Frey, B.S., Benesch, C. and Stutzer, A. (2005) *Does Watching TV Make us Happy?* Institute for Empirical Research in Economics, Working Paper No. 241, University of Zurich.

Frey, B.S. and Jegen, R. (2001) 'Motivation crowding theory', *Journal of Economic Surveys*, 15: 589–611.

Frey, B.S. and Stutzer, A. (2000) 'Happiness, economy and institutions', *The Economic Journal*, 110: 918–938.

Friedman, M. (1953) *Essays in Positive Economics*, Chicago: University of Chicago Press.

Friedman, M. (1962) *Capitalism and Freedom*. Chicago: University of Chicago Press.

Friedman, M. (1970) 'The social responsibility of business is to increase its profits', *The New York Times Magazine*: 13 September.

Friedman, M. (1999) 'The business community's suicidal impulse', *Cato Policy Report*, 21(2): 7.

Frijters, P., Haisken-DeNew, J.P. and Shields, M.A. (2005) 'The causal effect of income on health: Evidence from German reunification', *Journal of Health Economics*, 24(5): 997–1017.

Fukuyama, F. (1995) *Trust: The Social Virtues and the Creation of Prosperity*, New York: The Free Press.

Gächter, S., Herrmann, B. and Thöni, C. (2004) 'Trust, voluntary cooperation, and socio-economic background: Survey and experimental evidence', *Journal of Economic Behavior & Organization*, 55: 505–531.

Galbraith, J.K. (1992) *The Culture of Contentment*, Boston: Houghton Mifflin Co.

Galor, O. and Özak, Ö. (2016) 'The agricultural origins of time preference', *American Economic Review*, 106(10): 3064–3103.

Gay, C.M. (2003) *Cash Values. Money and the Erosion of Meaning in Today's Society*, Grand Rapids: William B. Eerdmans Publishing Company.

Geesbergen, A. van, Graafland, J. and Hoogland, J. (2020) 'Tensions in the paradigm of environmental economics An analysis inspired by Dooyeweerd's philosophy', *Philosophia Reformata*, 85: 66–88.

Gehring, K. (2013) 'Who benefits from economic freedom? Unraveling the effect of economic freedom on subjective well-being', *World Development*, 50: 74–90.

Girard, R. (1961) *Mensonge Romantique et Vérité Romansesque*. Kampen: Kok.

Glaeser, E.L. (2005) *Inequality*. Harvard Institute of Economic Research, Discussion Paper 2078. https://scholar.harvard.edu/files/glaeser/files/inequality.pdf.

Glaeser, E.L. and DiPasquale, D. (1999) 'Incentives and social capital: Are homeowners better citizens?', *Journal of Urban Economics*, 45: 354–384.

Glaeser, E.L. and Shleifer, A. (2003) 'The rise of the regulatory state', *Journal of Economic Literature*, 41(2): 401–425.

Gneezy, U. and Rustichini, A. (2000) 'Pay enough, or don't pay at all', *Quarterly Journal of Economics*, 115: 791–810.

Goette, L. and Lienhard, M. (2006) *Productivity and Well-being Under Fixed Wages and Piece Rates*. www.isu.uzh.ch/emap/docs/2006/poek/LienhardGoette.pdf

Goldberg, P.K. and Pavcnik, N. (2007) 'Distributional effects of globalization in developing countries', *Journal of Economic Literature*, XLV: 39–82.

Goudzwaard, B. (1976) *Kapitalisme en Vooruitgang. Een Eigentijdse Maatschappijkritiek*, Assen and Amsterdam: Van Gorcum.

Goudzwaard, B. and de Lange, H. (1995) *Beyond Poverty and Affluence: Toward an Economy of Care*, Grand Rappids, MI: William B. Eerdmans Publishing Company.

Graafland, J.J. (ed.) (2002) *Economie en Ethiek Over ICT*, Budel: Damon.

Graafland, J.J. (2010a) 'Do markets crowd out virtues? An Aristotelian framework', *Journal of Business Ethics*, 91(1): 1–19.

Graafland, J.J. (2010b) *The Market, Happiness, and Solidarity: A Christian Perspective*, London: Routledge.

Graafland, J.J. (2016) 'Price competition, short-termism and environmental performance', *Journal of Cleaner Production*, 116: 125–134.

Graafland, J.J. (2017) 'Economic freedom, poverty and life satisfaction: An economic analysis', in: W.M. Speelman et al. (eds.) *Poverty as Problem and Poverty as Path*, Münster: AschendorffVerlag, 187–196.

Graafland, J.J. (2019a) 'Economic freedom and corporate environmental responsibility: The role of small government and freedom from government regulation', *Journal of Cleaner Production*, 218: 250–258.

Graafland, J.J. (2019b) 'When does economic freedom promote well being? On the moderating role of long-term orientation', *Social Indicators Research*, 149: 127–153.

Graafland, J.J. (2020a) 'Contingencies in the relationship between economic freedom and human development: The role of generalized trust', *Journal of Institutional Economics*, 16(3): 271–286.

Graafland, J.J. (2020b) 'Competition in technology and innovation, motivation crowding, and environmental policy', *Corporate Social Responsibility and Environmental Management*, 27: 137–145.

Graafland, J.J. and Bovenberg, L. (2020) 'Government regulation, business leaders' motivations and environmental performance of SMEs', *Journal of Environmental Planning and Management*, 63(8): 1335–1355.

Graafland, J.J. and Compen, B. (2015) 'Economic freedom and life satisfaction: Mediation by income per capita and generalized trust', *Journal of Happiness Studies*, 16(3): 789–810.

Graafland, J.J., de Mooy, R.A., Nibbelink, A.G.H. and Nieuwenhuis, A. (2001) *MIMICing Tax Policies and the Labor Market*, Amsterdam: North Holland.

Graafland, J.J. and Gerlagh, R. (2019) 'Economic freedom, internal motivation, and corporate environmental responsibility of SMEs', *Environmental and Resource Economics*, 74: 1101–1123.

Graafland, J.J. and Lous, B. (2018) 'Economic freedom, income inequality and life satisfaction in OECD Countries', *Journal of Happiness Studies*, 19: 2071–2093.

Graafland, J.J. and Lous, B. (2019) 'Income inequality, life satisfaction inequality and trust: A cross country panel analysis', *Journal of Happiness Studies*, 20(6): 1717–1737.

Graafland, J.J. and Noorderhaven, N. (2020) 'Culture and institutions: How economic freedom and long-term orientation interactively influence corporate social responsibility', *Journal of International Business Studies*, 51(6): 1034–1043.

Graafland, J.J. and Van de Ven, B.W. (2011) 'The credit crisis and the moral responsibility of professionals in finance', *Journal of Business Ethics*, 103(4): 605–619.

Graafland, J.J. and Verbruggen, H. (2021) 'Three different perspectives on "good" markets and government regulation: An empirical test', *Applied Research in Quality of Life*, https://doi.org/10.1007/s11482-021-09946-2.

Graafland, J.J. and Wells, T.R. (2020) 'In Adam Smith's own words: The role of virtues in the relationship between free market economies and societal flourishing, a semantic network data-mining approach', *Journal of Business Ethics*. https://doi.org/10.1007/s10551-020-04521-5.

Grant, R. and Visconti, M. (2006) 'The strategic background to corporate accounting scandals', *Long Range Planning*, 39: 361–383.

Greenwald, B. and Stiglitz, J.E. (1986) 'Externalities in economies with imperfect information and incomplete markets', *Quarterly Journal of Economics*, 101(2): 229–264.

Gropper, D.M., Lawson, R.A. and Thorne Jr., J.T. (2011) 'Economic freedom and happiness', *Cato Journal*, 31: 237–255.

Guest, D. (2002) 'Perspective on the study of work life balance', *Social Science Information*, 41(2): 255–279.

Guimaraes, B. and Sheedy, K.D. (2012) *A Model of Equilibrium Institutions*. CEPR Discussion Paper, No. DP8855. https://cepr.org/active/publications/discussion_papers/dp.php?dpno=8855.

Gwartney, J., Holcombe, R. and Lawson, R. (2004) 'Economic freedom, institutional quality, and cross-country differences in income and growth', *Cato Journal*, 24: 205–233.

Gwartney, J., Lawson, R. and Block, W. (1996) *Economic Freedom in the World, 1975–1995*, Vancouver: Fraser Institute.

Hafer, R.W. and Belasen, A.R. (2012) 'Well-being and economic freedom: Evidence from the states', *Intelligence*, 40(3): 306–316.

Hajdu, T. and Hajdu, G. (2014) 'Reduction of income inequality and subjective well-being in Europe', *Economics: The Open-Access, Open Assessment E-Journal*, 8: 2014–2035.

Hall, J.C. and Lawson, R.A. (2014) 'Economic freedom of the world: An accounting of the literature', *Contemporary Economic Policy*, 32: 1–19.

Hall, J.C., Sobel, R.S. and Crowley, G.R. (2010) 'Institutions, capital, and growth', *Southern Economic Journal*, 77(2): 385–405.

Hall, N., Lacey, J., Carr-Cornish, S. and Dowd, A. (2015) 'Social licence to operate: Understanding how a concept has been translated into practice in energy industries', *Journal of Cleaner Production*, 86: 301–310.

Hall, P.A. and Gingerich, D.W. (2009) 'Varieties of capitalism and institutional complementarities in the political economy', *British Journal of Political Science*, 39(3): 449–482.

Hall, P.A. and Soskice, D. (eds.) (2001) *Varieties of Capitalism*, Oxford: Oxford University Press.

Haller, M. and Hadler, M. (2006) 'How social relations and structures can produce happiness and unhappiness: An international comparative analysis', *Social Indicators Research*, 75: 169–216.

Hanley, R. (2008) 'Commerce and corruption: Rousseau's diagnosis and Adam Smith's cure', *European Journal of Political Theory*, 7(2): 137–158.

Hartmann, J. and Uhlenbruck, K. (2015) 'National institutional antecedents to corporate environmental performance', *Journal of World Business*, 50: 729–741.

Harvey, D. (2005) *A Brief History of Neoliberalism*, Oxford: Oxford University Press.

Hausman, D.M. (1992) *The Inexact and Separate Science of Economics*, Cambridge: Cambridge University Press.

Hausman, D.M. and McPherson, M.S. (1996) *Economic Analysis and Moral Philosophy*, Cambridge: Cambridge University Press.

Hayek, F.A. (1944) *The Road to Serfdom*, London: Routledge & Sons.

Hayek, F.A. (1948) *Individualism and Economic Order*, London: Routledge.

Hayek, F.A. (1960) *The Constitution of Liberty*, Chicago: The University of Chicago Press.

Hayek, F.A. (1976) *Law, Legislation and Liberty: A New Statement of the Principles of Justice and Political Economy*, Vol. 2, Londen: Routledge & Kegan Paul.

Hayek, F.A. (1979) *Law, Legislation and Liberty: A New Statement of the Principles of Justice and Political Economy*, Vol. 3, London: Routledge and Kegan Paul Ltd.

Heath, J. (2014) *Morality, Competition, and the Firm: The Market Failures Approach to Business Ethics*, Oxford: University Press Scholarship Online.

Heilbronner, R.J. (1986) *The Worldly Philosophers*, trans. J.E. Kuiper, Amsterdam: Maarten Muntinga.

Helliwell, J.F. (2003) 'How's life? Combining individual and national variables to explain subjective well being', *Economic Modelling*, 20: 331–360.

Helliwell, J.F. (2006) 'Well-being, social capital and public policy: What's new?', *The Economic Journal*, 116: C34–C45.

Helliwell, J.F. and Barrington-Leigh, C.P. (2010) *How Much Is Social Capital Worth?* NBER Working Paper Series, No. 16025. https://www.nber.org/system/files/working_papers/w16025/w16025.pdf.

Helliwell, J.F., Barrington-Leigh, C.P., Harris, A. and Huang, H. (2009) *International Evidence on the Social Context of Well-being*. NBER Working Paper Series, No. 14720, Cambridge, MA: National Bureau of Economic Research.

Helliwell, J.F. and Huang, H. (2008) 'How's your government? International evidence linking good government and well-being', *British Journal of Political Science*, 38: 595–619.

Helliwell, J.F., Layard, R. and Sachs, J. (eds.) (2016) *World Happiness Report 2016*. https://worldhappiness.report/ed/2016/

Helliwell, J.F. and Putnam, R.D. (2004) 'The social context of well-being', *Philosophical Transactions-royal Society of London Series B Biological Sciences*: 1435–1446.

Henrich, J., Boyd, R., Bowles, S., Camarer, C.F., Fehr, E., Gintis, H. and McElreath, R. (2004) 'Overview and synthesis', in: Henrich et al. (eds.) *Foundations of Human Sociality: Economic Experiments and Ethnographic Evidence from Fifteen Small-scale Societies*, Oxford: Oxford University Press, 8–54.

Henrich, J., Boyd, R., Bowles, S., Camerer, C.F., Gintis, H. and McElreath, R. (2001) 'Cooperation, reciprocity and punishment in fifteen small scale societies', *American Economic Review*, 91: 73–78.

Hernandez-Lagos, P., Minor, D. and Sisak, D. (2017) 'Do people who care about others cooperate more? Experimental evidence from relative incentive pay', *Experimental Economics*, 20: 809–835.

Herzog, L. (2011) 'Higher and lower virtues in commercial society: Adam Smith and motivation crowding out', *Politics, Philosophy and Economics*, 10(4): 370–395.

Hirsch, F. (1977) *Social Limits to Growth*, London: Routledge and Kegan Paul.

Hirschman, A.O. (1982) 'Rival interpretations of market society: Civilizing, destructive or feeble?', *Journal of Economic Literature*, XX: 1463–1484.

Hodgson, G.M. (2006) 'What are institutions?', *Journal of Economic Issues*, XL(1): 1–25.

House, R.J., Hanges, P.J., Javidan, M., Dorfman, P.W. and Gupta, V. (2004) *Culture, Leadership, and Organizations: The Globe Study of 62 Societies*, London: Sage Publications.

Huntington, S.P. (1997) *The Clash of Civilizations and the Remaking of World Order*, London and New York: Touchstone Books.

Hurley, J. (2000) 'An overview of the normative economics of the health sector', in: A.J. Culyer and J.P. Newhouse (eds.) *Handbook of Health Economics, Volume 1*, Amsterdam: North Holland, 56–118.

Inglehart, R. (2000) 'Globalization and postmodern values', *The Washington Quarterly*, 23: 215–228.

Iyengar, S.S. and Lepper, M.R. (2000) 'When choice is demotivating: Can one desire too much of a good thing?', *Journal of Personality and Social Psychology*, 79: 995–1006.

Jackson, G. and Apostolakou, A. (2010) 'Corporate social responsibility in Western Europe: An institutional mirror or substitute?', *Journal of Business Ethics*, 94: 371–394.

Jacobs, B., de Mooij, R.A. and Folmer, C. (2006) 'Vlaktaks en arbeidsparticipatie', in: C.A. de Kam and A.P. Ros (eds.) *De Vlaktaks. Naar een Inkomstenbelasting met een Uniform Tarief?*, Willem Drees Stichting voor Openbare Financiën, Den Haag: Van Deventer.

Jamali, D. (2010) 'MNCs and international accountability standards through an institutional lens: Evidence of symbolic conformity or decoupling', *Journal of Business Ethics*, 95: 617–640.

Jäntti, M. and Jenkins, S. (2010) 'The impact of macroeconomic conditions on income inequality', *Journal of Economic Inequality*, 8: 221–240.

Jen, M.H., Sund, E.R., Johnston, R. and Jones, K. (2010) 'Trustful societies, trustful individuals, and health: An analysis of self-rated health and social trust using the World Value Survey', *Health & Place*, 16: 1022–1029.

Jeurissen, R.J.M. (ed.) (2000) *Bedrijfsethiek: een Goede Zaak*, Van Gorcum: Assen.

Jiang, X., Li, M., Gao, S., Bao, Y. and Jiang, F. (2013) 'Managing knowledge leakage in strategic alliances: The effects of trust and formal contracts', *Industrial Marketing Management*, 42: 983–991.

Johnson, J.L. (2001) 'Immunity from the illegitimate focused attention of others: An explanation of our thinking and talking about privacy', in: A. Vedder (ed.) *Ethics and the Internet*, Antwerpen, Groningen and Oxford: Intersentia, 47–70.

Jordan, K. and Kristjánsson, K. (2017) 'Sustainability, virtue ethics, and the virtue of harmony with nature', *Environmental Education Research*, 23(9): 1205–1229.

Justesen, M.K. (2008) 'The effect of economic freedom on growth revisited: New evidence on causality from a panel of countries 1970–1999', *European Journal of Political Economy*, 24: 642–660.

Kahn, R.S., Wise, P.H., Kennedy, B.P. and Kawachi, I. (2000) 'State income inequality, household income, and maternal mental and physical health: Cross sectional national survey', *British Medical Journal*, 321: 1311–1315.

Kam, C.A. de and Pen, J. (2006) 'Fiscale vervlakking is goed voor de rijken', in: C.A. de Kam and A.P. Ros (eds.) *De Vlaktaks. Naar een Inkomstenbelasting met een Uniform Tarief?*, Willem Drees Stichting voor Openbare Financiën, Den Haag: Van Deventer.

Kam, C.A. de and Ros, A.P. (2006a) 'Een vlak tarief voor de polder?', in: C.A. de Kam and A.P. Ros (eds.) *De Vlaktaks. Naar een Inkomstenbelasting met een Uniform Tarief?*, Willem Drees Stichting voor Openbare Financiën, Den Haag: Van Deventer.

Kam, CA. de and Ros, A.P. (2006b) 'Vlaktaks: lessen voor politici', in: C.A. de Kam and A.P. Ros (eds.) *De Vlaktaks. Naar een Inkomstenbelasting met een Uniform Tarief?*, Willem Drees Stichting voor Openbare Financiën, Den Haag: Van Deventer.

Kaminski, J., Pitsch, A. and Tomasello, M. (2013) 'Dogs steal in the dark', *Animal Cognition*, 16: 385–394.

Kamtekar, R. (2004) 'Situationism and virtue ethics on the content of our character', *Ethics*, 114: 458–491.

Kant, I. (1997) *Grundlegung zur Metaphysik der Sitten*, trans. T. Mertens, Amsterdam: Boom.

Katz, R.D., Santman, J. and Lonero, P. (1994) 'Findings on the revised morally debatable behaviors scale', *The Journal of Psychology*, 128(1): 15–21.

Kawachi, I. and Kennedy, B.P. (1997) 'Health and social cohesion: Why care about income inequality?', *BMJ: British Medical Journal*, 314(7086): 1037.

Kay, J. (1993) *Foundations of Corporate Success*, Oxford: Oxford University Press.

Kenny, C. (1999) 'Does growth cause happiness, or does happiness cause growth?', *Kyklos*, 52: 3–26.

Keynes, J.M. (1930) *Economic Possibilities for Our Grandchildren*. In: Essays in Persuasion, (New York: Harcourt Brace, 1932), 358–373.

Keynes, J.M. (1936, 1973) *The General Theory of Employment, Interest and Money*, The Royal Economic Society, London: MacMillan Press.

Kinderman, D. (2008) *The Political Economy of Corporate Responsibility in Germany, 1995–2008*, Mario Einaudi Center for International Studies Working Paper No. 5–08. https://papers.ssrn.com/sol3/papers.cfm?abstract_id=2229690

Kinderman, D. (2012) 'Free us up so we can be responsible. The co-evolution of corporate social responsibility and neo-liberalism in the UK, 1977–2010', *Socio-Economic Review*, 10: 135–157.

King, B.G. (2008) 'A political mediation model of corporate response to social movement activism', *Administrative Science Quarterly*, 53: 395–421.

King, E.M., Montenegro, C.E. and Orazem, P.F. (2012) 'Economic freedom, human rights, and the returns to human capital: An evaluation of the Schultz hypothesis', *Economic Development and Cultural Change*, 61(1): 39–72.

Kinneging, A. (1998) 'De giftige bron', *NRC*, 5 September 1998: 17–18.

Klein, N. (2002) *No Logo*, Rotterdam: Lemniscaat.

Knack, S. and Keefer, P. (1997) 'Does social capital have an economic pay-off? A cross-country investigation', *The Quarterly Journal of Economics*, 112(4): 1251–1288.

Knight, F.H. (1925) 'Economic psychology and the value problem', *Quarterly Journal of Economics*, 34: 372–409.

Kocher, M.G., Martinsson, P., Myrseth, K.O.R. and Wollbrant, C.E. (2017) 'Strong, bold, and kind: Self-control and cooperation in social dilemmas', *Experimental Economics*, 20: 44–69.

Kostova, T. (1997) 'Country institutional profile: Concept and measurement', *Academy of Management Best Paper Proceedings*, 180–184.

Kouwenhoven, A. (1981) *Inleiding in de Economische Ethiek*, Nijkerk: Callenbach.

Kreps, D.M. (1997) 'The interaction between norms and economic incentives. Intrinsic motivation and extrinsic incentives', *American Economic Review*, 87: 359–364.

Kuhn, K. and Uler, N. (2019) 'Behavioral sources of the demand for carbon offsets: An experimental study', *Experimental Economics*, 22: 676–704.

Landes, D.S. (1998) *The Wealth and Poverty of Nations: Why Some Are So Rich and Some So Poor*, trans. A. Abeling and P. Verhagen, Utrecht: Het Spectrum.

Laverty, K.J. (1996) 'Economic "short-termism": The debate, the unresolved issues, and the implications for management practice and research', *Academy of Management Review*, 21: 825–860.

Layard, R. (2003) 'Happiness – Has social science a clue?', *Lionel Robbins Memorial Lectures 2002/3*, Centre for Economic Performance, London School of Economics and Political Science, London.

Layard, R. (2005) *Happiness: Lessons from a New Science*, New York: Penguin.

Leigh, A. (2006) 'Trust, inequality and ethnic heterogeneity', *Economic Record*, 82(258): 268–280.

Levin, K.A., Torsheim, T., Vollebergh, W., Richter, M., Davies, C., Schnohr, C., Due, P. and Currie, C. (2011) 'National income and income inequality, family affluence and life satisfaction among 13 year old boys and girls: A multilevel study in 35 countries', *Social Indicators Research*, 104: 179–194.

Lewis, S. (2003) 'The integration of paid work and the rest of life: Is post-industrial work the new leisure?', *Leisure Study*, 22(4): 343–355.

Li, C., Turmunkh, U. and Wakker, P. (2019) 'Trust as a decision under ambiguity', *Experimental Economics*, 22: 51–75.

Lindbeck, A. and Snower, D.J. (1986) 'Wage setting, unemployment and insider-outsider relations', *The American Economic Review, Paper and Proceedings*, 76: 235–239.

Lindbeck, A. and Snower, D.J. (1987) 'Efficiency wage versus insiders and outsider', *European Economic Review*, 31: 407–416.

Lindenberg, S. (2001) 'Intrinsic motivation in a new light', *Kyklos*, 54: 317–342.

Linssen, J. (2019) *Hebzucht. Een Filosofische Geschiedenis van de Inhaligheid*, Nijmegen: Vantilt.

Lous, B. and Graafland, J. (2021) 'Who becomes unhappy when income inequality increases? Interaction effects of micro income levels on the inequality-life satisfaction relationship', *Applied Research in Quality of Life*. https://doi.org/10.1007/s11482-020-09906-2.

Lucas, R.E., Jr. (2000) 'Some macroeconomics for the 21st century', *Journal of Economic Perspectives*, 14: 159–168.

Lyon, D. (1979) *Karl Marx. A christian application of his life and thought*, Oxford: Lion Publishing.

MacIntyre, A. (1985) *After Virtue: A Study in Moral Theory*, London: Duckworth.

MacLean, D. (1994) 'Cost-benefit analysis and procedural values', *Analyze & Kritik*, 16(2): 166–180.

Macneil, I. (1986) 'Exchange revisited: Individual utility and social solidarity', *Ethics*, 96: 567–593.

Madison, G.B. (1998) 'Self-interest, communalism, welfarism', in: H. Giersch (ed.) *Merits and Limits of Markets*, Berlin: Springer-Verlag, 3–27.

Maggian, V. and Villeval, M.C. (2016) 'Social preferences and lying aversion in children', *Experimental Economics*, 19: 663–685.

Maitland, I. (1997) 'Virtuous markets. The market as school of virtues', *Business Ethics Quarterly*, 7: 17–33.

Major, V.S., Klein, K.J. and Ehrhart, M.G. (2002) 'Work time, work interference with family and psychological distress', *Journal of Applied Psychology*, 87: 427–436.

Mallin, C., Michelon, G. and Raggi, D. (2013) 'Monitoring intensity and stakeholders' orientation: How does governance affect social and environmental disclosure?', *Journal of Business Ethics*, 114: 29–43.

Mandeville, B. (1714) *The Fable of the Bees: Or, Private Vices, Publick Benefits*. www.xs4all. nl/~maartens/philosophy/mandeville/fable_of_bees.html.

Manenschijn, G. (1982) *Eigenbelang en christelijke ethiek. Rechtvaardigheid in een door belangen bepaalde samenleving*, Baarn: Ten Have.

Marcus, R.B. (1996) 'More about moral dilemmas', in: H.E. Mason (ed.) *Moral Dilemmas and Moral Theory*, Oxford and New York: Oxford University Press, 23–35.

Marcuzzo, M.C. (2010) 'Whose welfare state? Beveridge versus Keynes', in: R.E. Backhouse and T. Nishizawa (eds.) *No Wealth But Life: Welfare Economics and the Welfare State in Britain, 1880–1945*, Cambridge: Cambridge University Press, 189–206.

Marens, R. (2008) 'Recovering the past: Reviving the legacy of the early scholars of corporate social responsibility', *Journal of Management History*, 14: 55–72.

Marshall, A. (1890) *Principles of Economics*, Eighth edition, London: Macmillan, 1920.

Masten, E. and Prüfer, J. (2014) 'On the evolution of collective enforcement institutions: Communities and courts', *The Journal of Legal Studies*, 43(2): 359–400.

Mayda, A. and Rodrik, D. (2005) 'Why are some people (and countries) more protectionist than others?', *European Economic Review*, 49: 1393–1430.

McCannon, B.C., Tokar Asaad, C. and Wilson, M. (2018) 'Contracts and trust: Complements or substitutes?', *Journal of Institutional Economics*, 14(5): 811–832.

McCloskey, D.N. (2006) *Bourgeois Virtues: Ethics for an Age of Commerce*, Chicago: The University of Chicago Press.

McCloskey, D.N. (2010) *Bourgeois Dignity: Why Economics Can't Explain the Modern World*, Chicago: The University of Chicago Press.

McCloskey, D.N. (2016) *Bourgeois Equality: How Ideas, Not Capital or Institutions, Enriched the World*, Chicago: The University of Chicago Press.

Mick, D.G., Broniarczyk, S.M. and Haidt, J. (2004) 'Choose, choose, choose, choose, choose, choose: Emerging and prospective research on the deleterious effects of living in consumer hyper choice', *Journal of Business Ethics*, 52: 207–211.

Milanovic, B. (2005) *Worlds Apart: Measuring Interregional and Global Inequality*, Princeton, NJ: Princeton University Press.

Mill, J.S. (1848/1994) *Principles of Political Economy*, Oxford: Oxford University Press.

Mill, J.S. (1871) *Utilitarianism*, Oxford: Oxford University Press.

Miller, T. and del Carmen Triana, M. (2009) 'Demographic diversity in the boardroom: Mediators of the board diversity – firm performance relationship', *Journal of Management Studies*, 46(5): 755–789.

Milligan, K., Moretti, E. and Oreopoulos, P. (2004) 'Does education improve citizenship? Evidence from the U.S. and the U.K.', *Journal of Public Economics*, 88: 1667–1695.

Mischel, W., Shoda, Y. and Rodriguez, M.L. (1989) 'Delay of gratification in children', *Science*, 244: 933–938.

Mizobuchi, H. (2014) 'Measuring world better life Frontier: A composite indicator for OECD Better Life Index', *Social Indicators Research*, 118: 987–1007.

Moore, G. (2005) 'Humanizing business: A modern virtue ethics approach', *Business Ethics Quarterly*, 15: 237–255.

Moore, G. and Beadle, R. (2006) 'In search of organizational virtue in business: Agents, goods, practices, institutions and environments', *Organization Studies*, 27: 369–389.

Moros, L., Vélez, M.A. and Corbera, E. (2019) 'Payments for ecosystem services and motivational crowding in Colombia's Amazon Piedmont', *Ecological Economics*, 156: 468–488.

Muller, A. and Kolk, A. (2010) 'Extrinsic and intrinsic drivers of corporate social performance: Evidence from Foreign and Domestic Firms in Mexico', *Journal of Management Studies*, 47: 1–26.

Mulligan, C.B. and Sala-i-martin, X. (2000) 'Extensive margins and the demand for money at low interest rates', *Journal of Political Economy*, 108(5): 961–991.

Murphy, L.B. (1998) 'Institutions and the demands of justice', *Philosophy and Public Affairs*, 27: 251–291.

Murphy, N. and McClendon, J.Wm. Jr. (1989) 'Distinguishing modern and postmodern theologies', *Modern Theology*, 5: 191–214.

Murphy, R.H. (2016) 'Economic freedom of North America at state borders', *Journal of Institutional Economics*, 12(4): 885–893.

Neusner, J. (1990) *The Economics of the Mishnah*, Chicago: University of Chicago Press.

Nikolaev, B. (2014) 'Economic freedom and quality of life: Evidence from the OECD's your Better Life Index', *Journal of Private Enterprise*, 29(3): 61–96.

Nikolaev, B. and Bennett, D.L. (2016) 'Give me liberty and give me control: Economic freedom, control perceptions and the paradox of choice', *European Journal of Political Economy*, 45: 39–52.

Nooteboom, B. (2017) *Vertrouwen. Opening naar een Veranderende Wereld*, Utrecht: Klement.

Norberg, J. (2002) *Till Världskapitalismens Försvar*, trans. B. de Koster, Antwerpen and Amsterdam: Houtekiet.

Noussair, C.N., Trautmann, S.T. and van de Kuilen, G. (2014) 'Higher order risk attitudes, demographics, and financial decisions', *Review of Economic Studies*, 81(1): 325–355.

Novak, M. (1982) *The Spirit of Democratic Capitalism*, New York, NY: Simon and Schuster.

Nozick, R. (1974) *Anarchy, State and Utopia*, New York: Basic Books.

Nussbaum, M. (2011) *Creating Capabilities*. http://apps.ufs.ac.za/media/dl/userfiles/documents/News/2012_12/2012_12_10_ Martha_Nussbaum_UFS_December_2012.pdf.

Nyström, K. (2008) 'The institutions of economic freedom and entrepreneurship: Evidence from panel data', *Public Choice*, 136(3–4): 269–282.

OECD (2000) 'Literacy in the information age', *Final Report of the International Adult Literacy Survey*, Paris: OECD.

OECD (2012) 'Reducing income inequality while boosting economic growth: Can it be done?', *Economic Policy Reforms 2012: Going for Growth*, OECD. https://www.oecd-ilibrary.org/economics/economic-policy-reforms-2012/reducing-income-inequality-while-boosting-economic-growth_growth-2012-47-en.

Oishi, S., Kesebir, S. and Diener, E. (2011) 'Income inequality and happiness', *Psychological Science*, 22(9): 1095–1100.

Okhmatovskiy, I. and David, R.J. (2012) 'Setting your own standards: Internal corporate governance codes as a response to institutional pressure', *Organization Science*, 23: 155–176.

Oliveira, A.C.M. de, Croson, R.T.A. and Eckel, C. (2015) 'One bad apple? Heterogeneity and information in public good provision', *Experimental Economics*, 18: 116–135.

Oosterhuis-Blok, M. (2020) *Marktwerking en Publieke Belangen. Een Analyse vanuit het Neoliberale Denken en de Beginselen van Subsidiariteit en Soevereiniteit in Eigen Kring*, Dissertation University of Kampen/Tilburg University.

Oshio, T. and Kobayashi, M. (2010) 'Income inequality, perceived happiness, and self-rated health: Evidence from nationwide surveys in Japan', *Social Science & Medicine*, 70: 1358–1366.

Ostry, J., Berg, A. and Tsangarides, C. (2014) *Redistribution, Inequality, and Growth*, IMF Staff Discussion Note SDN/14/02. https://www.imf.org/external/pubs/ft/sdn/2014/sdn1402.pdf.

Ott, J.C. (2010) 'Good governance and happiness in nations: Technical quality precedes democracy and quality beats size', *Journal of Happiness Studies*, 11: 353–368.

Ovaska, T. and Takashima, R. (2006) 'Economic policy and the level of self-perceived well-being: An international comparison', *Journal of Socio-Economics*, 35: 308–325.

Özcan, B. and Bjørnskov, C. (2011) 'Social trust and human development', *The Journal of Socio-Economics*, 40: 753–762.

Pabst, A. (2011) 'From civil to political economy: Adam Smith's theological debt', in: P. Oslington (ed.) *Adam Smith as Theologian*, London: Routledge, 106–124.

Paganelli, M.P. (2010) 'The moralizing distance in Adam Smith: The theory of moral sentiments as possible praise of commerce', *History of Political Economy*, 42(3): 425–441.

Papagapitos, A. and Riley, R. (2009) 'Social trust and human capital formation', *Economics Letters*, 102: 158–160.

Parfit, D. (1998) 'Equality and priority', in: A. Mason (ed.) *Ideals of Equality*, Oxford: Blackwell, 1–20.

Pearce, D.W. (2002) 'An intellectual history of environmental economics', *Annual Review of Energy and the Environment*, 27: 57–81.

Pearce, D.W. and Turner, R.K. (1990) *Economics of Natural Resources and the Environment*, Harlow: Pearson Education Ltd.

Peil, J. (1995) *Adam Smith en de Economische Wetenschap. Een Methodologische Herinterpretatie*, Tilburg: Tilburg University Press.

Peiró-Palomino, J. and Picazo-Tadeo, A.J. (2018) 'OECD: One or many? Ranking countries with a composite well-being indicator', *Social Indicators Research*, 139(3): 847–869.

Peterson, C. and Seligman, M.E.P. (2004) *Character Strengths and Virtues: A Handbook and Classification*, New York: Oxford University Press and Washington, DC: American Psychological Association.

Pew Research Center (2006) *Labour Day 2006*. http://pewresearch.org.

Pigou, A.C. (1932) *The Economics of Welfare*, Fourth edition, London: Macmillan.

Piketty, T. (2014) *Capital in the 21st Century*, London: Belknap/Harvard University Press.

Pinotti, P. (2012) 'Trust, regulation, and market failures', *The Review of Economics and Statistics*, 94(3): 650–658.

Pirsch, J., Gupta, S. and Landreth Grau, S. (2006) 'A framework for understanding corporate social responsibility programs as a continuum: An exploratory study', *Journal of Business Ethics*, 70: 125–140.

Pogge, T. (2001) 'Priorities of global justice', in: T. Pogge (ed.) *Global Justice*, Oxford: Blackwell Publishers, 6–23.

Poppo, L. and Zenger, T. (2002) 'Do formal contracts and relational governance function as substitutes or complements?', *Strategic Management Journal*, 23: 707–725.

Preacher, K.J., Rucker, D.D. and Hayes, A.F. (2007) 'Addressing moderated mediation hypotheses: Theory, methods, and prescriptions', *Multivariate Behavioral Research*, 42(1): 185–227.

Putnam, R.D. (1993) 'The prosperous community: Social capital and public fife', *The American Prospect*, 13: 35–42.

Putnam, R.D. (2000) *Bowling Alone: The Collapse and Revival of American Community*, New York: Simon and Schuster.

Rabin, M. (1993) 'Incorporating fairness into game theory and economics', *The American Economic Review*, 83(5): 1281–1302.

Rabin, M. (1998) 'Psychology and economics', *Journal of Economic Literature*, XXXVI: 11–46.

Railton, P. (1996) 'The diversity of moral dilemma', in: H.E. Mason (ed.) *Moral Dilemmas and Moral Theory*, Oxford and New York: Oxford University Press, 140–166.

Rappaport, A. (2005) 'The economics of short-term performance obsession', *Financial Analyst Journal*, 61: 65–79.

Rasmussen, D.C. (2006) 'Does "bettering our condition" really make us better off? Adam Smith on progress and happiness', *The American Political Science Review*, 100(3): 309–318.

Rasmussen, D.C. (2008) *The Problems and Promise of Commercial Society*, Pennsylvania: Penn State Press.

Rawls, J. (1999a) *A Theory of Justice*, Revised edition, Boston: Harvard University Press.

Rawls, J. (1999b) *The Law of Peoples: With 'The Idea of Public Reason Revisited'*, Boston: Harvard University Press.

Reader, T.W., Noort, M.C., Shorrock, S. and Kirwan, B. (2015) 'Safety sans frontières: An international safety culture model', *Risk Analysis*, 35(5): 770–789.

Regner, T. (2018) 'Reciprocity under moral wiggle room: Is it a preference or a constraint?', *Experimental Economics*, 21(4): 779–792.

Rehbein, K., Logsdon, J.M. and Van Buren III, H.J. (2013) 'Corporate responses to shareholder activists: Considering the dialogue alternative', *Journal of Business Ethics*, 112: 137–154.

Reynolds, J. and Renzulli, L.A. (2005) 'Economic freedom or self-imposed strife: Work – life conflict, gender, and self-employment', *Entrepreneurship*, 15: 33–60.

Rezaee, Z. (2005) 'Causes, consequences, and deterrence of financial statements fraud', *Critical Perspectives on Accounting*, 16: 277–298.

Robbins, L. (1935) *An Essay on the Nature and Significance of Economic Science*, Second edition, London: MacMillan and Co.

Rode, J., Gómez-Baggethun, E. and Krause, T. (2015) 'Motivation crowding by economic incentives in conservation policy: A review of the empirical evidence', *Ecological Economics*, 117: 270–282.

Rodrik, D. (2002) *Feasible Globalizations*, NBER Working Paper 9129. https://www.nber.org/system/files/working_papers/w9129/w9129.pdf.

Rodrik, D., Subramanian, A. and Trebbi, F. (2002) *Institutional Rule: The Primacy of Institutions Over Geography and Integration in Economic Development*, CEPR Discussion Paper Series 3643. https://cepr.org/active/publications/discussion_papers/dp.php?dpno=3643.

Roine, J., Vlachos, J. and Waldenström, D. (2009) 'The long-run determinants of inequality: What can we learn from top income data?', *Journal of Public Economics*, 93: 974–988.

Romer, C.D. and Romer, D.H. (1998) 'Monetary policy and the well-being of the poor', in: *Income Inequality: Issues and Policy Options*, Federal Reserve Bank of Kansas City. https://www.kansascityfed.org/research/jackson-hole-economic-symposium/income-inequality-issues-and-policy-options.

Rostila, M. (2007) 'Social capital and health in European welfare regimes: A multilevel approach', *Journal of European Social Policy*, 17: 223–239.

Rothstein, B. (2000) 'Trust, social dilemmas, and collective memories', *Journal of Theoretical Politics*, 12: 477–501.

Rousseau, D.M., Sitkin, S.B., Burt, R.S. and Camerer, C. (1998) 'Not so different after all: A cross-discipline view of trust', *Academy of Management Review*, 23(3): 393–404.

Ruseski, J.E. and Maresova, K. (2014) 'Economic freedom, sport policy, and individual participation in physical activity: An international comparison', *Contemporary Economic Policy*, 32(1): 42–55.

Ryan, A. (1993) 'Liberalism', in: R.E. Goodin and P. Pettit (eds.) *A Companion to Contemporary Political Philosophy*, Oxford: Blackwell, 291–311.

Sala-i-Martin, X. (2006) 'The world distribution of income: Falling poverty and convergence, period', *The Quarterly Journal of Economics*, 121: 351–398.

Sandel, M.J. (2020) *The Tyranny of Merit: What's Become of the Common Good?* London: Penguin Books.

Sandmo, A. (2011) *Economics Evolving: A History of Economic Thought*, Princeton and Oxford: Princeton University Press.

Scheffler, S. (1994) *The Rejection of Consequentialism*, Revised edition, Oxford: Clarendon Press.

Schmidt-Catran, A.W. (2014) 'Economic inequality and public demand for redistribution: Combining cross-sectional and longitudinal evidence', *Socio-Economic Review*, 14(1): 119–140.

Schneider, S. (2012) 'Income inequality and its consequences for life satisfaction: What role do social cognitions play?', *Social Indicators Research*, 106: 419–438.

Schofer, E. and Meyer, J.W. (2005) 'The worldwide expansion of higher education in the twentiesth century', *American Sociological Review*, 70(6): 898–920.

Schor, J.B. (1993) *The Overworked American: The Unexpected Decline of Leisure*, New York: Basic Books.

Schor, J.B. (1997) *Beyond an Economy of Work and Spend*, Tilburg: Tilburg University Press.

Schumpeter, J.A. (1976) *Capitalism, Socialism and Democracy*, Fifth edition, London and Boston: George Allen & Unwin.

Schwartz, B. (2004) *The Paradox of Choice*, New York: HarperCollins Publishers Inc.

Schwarze, J. and Härpfer, M. (2002) *Are People Inequality Averse, and Do they Prefer Redistribution by the State? Evidence from German Longitudinal Data on Life Satisfaction*. IZA Discussion Paper No. 403. https://www.iza.org/publications/dp/430/are-people-inequality-averse-and-do-they-prefer-redistribution-by-the-state-evidence-from-german-longitudinal-data-on-life-satisfaction.

Scully, G.W. (2002) 'Economic freedom, government policy and the trade-off between equity and economic growth', *Public Choice*, 113: 77–96.

Sedláček, T. (2011) *Economics of Good and Evil: The Quest for Economic Meaning from Gilgamesh to Wall Street*, New York: Oxford University Press.

Segelod, E. (2000) 'A comparison of managers' perceptions of short-termism in Sweden and the U.S.', *International Journal of Production Economics*, 63: 243–254.

Self, P. (1975) *Econocrats and the Policy Making Process: The Politics and Philosophy of Cost-benefit Analysis*, London and Basingstoke: The MacMillan Press LTD.

Selten, R. (1999) *What Is Bounded Rationality?* University of Bonn, SFB Discussion Paper B-454, Paper prepared for the Dahlem Conference 1999. Sonderforschungsbereich (SFB) 303 Working Paper No. B-454. https://papers.ssrn.com/sol3/papers.cfm?abstract_id=182776.

Sen, A. (1967) 'Isolation, assurance and the social rate of discount', *Quarterly Journal of Economics*, 81: 112–124.

Sen, A. (1977) 'Rational fools: A critique on the behavioral foundations of economic theory', *Philosophy and Public Affairs*, 6: 317–344.

Sen, A. (1981) 'Ethical issues in income distribution: national and international', in: S. Grassman and E. Lundberg (eds.) *The World Economic Order: Past and Prospects*, London: Macmillan, 464–494.

Sen, A. (1982) 'Approaches to the choice of discount rates for social benefit-cost analysis', in: R. Lind (ed.) *Discounting for Time and Tisk in Energy Policy*, Washington, DC: Resources for the Future, 325–353.

Sen, A. (1983) 'Poor, relatively speaking', *Oxford Economic Papers*, 35: 153–169.

Sen, A. (1984) *Resources, Values and Development*, Oxford: Blackwell.

Sen, A. (1987) *On Ethics and Economics*, Oxford: Blackwell.

Sen, A. (1998) *Reason before Identity*, The Romanes Lecture for 1998, Oxford: Oxford University Press.

Sennett, R. (2000) *The Corrosion of Character*, trans. M. Blok, Amsterdam: Byblos.

Shafir, E. and Tversky, A. (1992) 'Thinking through uncertainty: Nonconsequential reasoning and choice', *Cognitive Psychology*, 24(4): 449–474.

Shleifer, A. (2004) 'Does competition destroy ethical behavior?', *American Economic Review*, 94(2): 414–418.

Shue, H. (1996) *Basic Rights: Subsistence, Affluence and U.S. Foreign Policy*, Second edition, Princeton, NJ: Princeton University Press.

Singer, P. (1972) 'Famine, affluence and morality', *Philosophy and Public Affairs*, 3: 229–243.

Singer, P. (2009) *Animal Liberation*, New York: HarperCollins Publishers.

Skidelsky, R. and Skidelsky, E. (2012) *How Much Is Enough: The Love of Money, and the Case for the Good Life*, London: Allen Lane.

Skreta, V. and Veldkam, L. (2009) 'Ratings shopping and asset complexity: A theory of ratings inflation', *Journal of Monetary Economics*, 56(5): 678–695.

Smith, A. (1896 [1763]) *Lectures on Justice, Policy, Revenue and Arms*, Oxford: Clarendon Press.

Smith, A. (1991 [1759]) *The Theory of Moral Sentiments*, New York: Prometheus Books.

Smith, A. (2000 [1776]) *Inquiry into the Nature and Causes of the Wealth of Nations*, New York: Prometheus Books.

Sobel, J. (2005) 'Interdependent preferences and reciprocity', *Journal of Economic Literature*, XLIII (June): 392–436.

Solnick, S.J. and Hemenway, D. (1998) 'Is more always better?: A survey on positional concerns', *Journal of Economic Behavior & Organization*, 37(3): 373–383.

Solomon, R.C. (1992) 'Corporate roles, personal virtues: An Aristotelean approach to business ethics', *Business Ethics Quarterly*, 2: 317–339.

Souder, D. and Bromiley, P. (2012) 'Explaining temporal orientation: Evidence from the durability of firms' capital investments', *Strategic Management Journal*, 33: 550–569.

Spruk, R. and Kešeljević, A. (2018) 'Economic freedom and growth across German districts', *Journal of Institutional Economics*, 14(4): 739–765.

Steijn, S. and Lancee, B. (2011) *Does Income Inequality Negatively Affect General Trust? Examining Three Potential Problems with the Inequality/Trust Hypothesis*. Gini Discussion Papers. https://ideas.repec.org/p/aia/ginidp/20.html.

Stevenson, B. and Wolfers, J. (2008) 'Economic growth and subjective Well being, reassessing the Easterlin paradox', *Brookings Paper on Economic Activity*, 39(1), Spring: 1–102.

Stigler, G.J. (1971) 'The theory of economic regulation', *Bell Journal of Economics and Management Science*, 2: 3–21.

Stiglitz, J. (2002) *Globalization and Its Discontents*, New York: Norton & Company.

Stiglitz, J. (2012) *The Price of Inequality*, London: W. W. Norton & Company.

Stiglitz, J., Sen, A. and Fitoussi, J.P. (2009) *The Measurement of Economic Performance and Social Progress Revisited: Reflection and Overview*. Commission on the Measurement of Economic Performance and Social Progress, Paris, 1–65.

Störig, H.J. (1990) *Geschiedenis van de Filosofie 1*, Utrecht: het Spectrum.

Stroup, M.D. (2007) 'Economic freedom, democracy, and the quality of life', *World Development*, 35(1): 52–66.

Stroup, R.L. (2003) *Economic Freedom and Environmental Quality*. Proceedings, Federal Reserve Bank of Dallas, 73–90. https://www.dallasfed.org/~/media/documents/research/pubs/ftc/stroup.pdf.

Sturm, R. and Gresenz, C. (2002) 'Relations of income inequality and family income to chronic medical conditions and mental health disorders: National survey in USA', *British Medical Journal*, 324: 20–23.

Tabellini, G. (2008) 'The scope of cooperation: Values and incentives', *Quarterly Journal of Economics*, 123(3): 905–950.

Tabellini, G. (2010) 'Culture and institutions: Economic development in the regions of Europe', *Journal of the European Economic Association*, 8(4): 677–716.

Terjesen, S., Aguilera, R.V. and Lorenz, R. (2015) 'Legislating a woman's seat on the board: Institutional factors driving gender quotas for boards of directors', *Journal of Business Ethics*, 128: 233–251.

Thaler, R.H. and Sunstein, C.R. (2008) *Nudge. Improving Decisions about Health, Wealth, and Happiness*, London: Penguin Books.

Thorsen, D.E. (2009) *The Neoliberal Challenge: What Is Neoliberalism?* Oslo, University of Oslo, Department of Political Science. http://folk.uio.no/daget/neoliberalism2.pdf.

Tieleman, H.J. (1989) *De economie als bal-masqué. Over verborgen betekenissen in onze economische handel en wandel*. Utrechtse Theologische Reeks 7, Utrecht: Universiteit van Utrecht.

Tieleman, H.J. (1991) *In het Teken van de Economie. Over de Wisselwerking van Economie en Cultuur*, Baarn: AMBO.

Titmuss, R. (1970) *The Gift Relationship: From Human Blood to Social Policy*, London: Allen and Unwin.

Treviño, L.K. and Nelson, K.A. (2004) *Managing Business Ethics: Straight Talk about How to Do It Right*, Hoboken: John Wiley & Sons.

Treviño, L.K., Weaver, G.R. and Reynolds, S.J. (2006) 'Behavioral ethics in organizations: A review', *Journal of Management*, 32: 952–990.

Tsai, M.C. (2009) 'Market openness, transition economies and subjective wellbeing', *Journal of Happiness Studies*, 10: 523–539.

Uslaner, E.M. (2002) *The Moral Foundations of Trust*, Cambridge: Cambridge University Press.

Van de Klundert, T. (1999) 'Economic efficiency and ethics', *De Economist*, 147: 127–149.

Van de Klundert, T. (2005) *Vormen van Kapitalisme. Markten, Instituties en Macht*, Utrecht: Lemma.

VandeVelde, T. (2001) 'Charles Taylor en de discussie tussen liberalen en communautaristen', *Wijsgerig perspectief*, 41(3), Boom: 15–28.

Van Erp, H. (1994) *Het Politiek Belang. Over de Politieke Orde in een Pluralistische Samenleving*, Amsterdam: Boom.

Van Leeuwen, A.Th. (1984) *De Nacht van het Kapitaal. Door het oerwoud van de economie naar de bronnen van de burgerlijke religie*, Nijmegen: SUN.

Van Liedekerke, L. (2000) *Values in Economy and Economic*, Leuven: Catholic University of Leuven.

Van Luijk, H. (1993) *Om Redelijk Gewin. Oefeningen in Bedrijfsethiek*, Amsterdam: Boom.

Van Parijs, P. (2003) 'Difference principles', in: S. Freeman (ed.) *The Cambridge Companion to Rawls*, Cambridge: Cambridge University Press, 200–240.

Van Staveren, I. (2001) *The Values of Economics: An Aristotelian Perspective*, London and New York: Routledge.

Varian, H.R. (1974) 'Distributive justice, welfare economics, and the theory of fairness', *Philosophy and Public Affairs*, 4: 223–247.

Veenhoven, R. (2000) 'Freedom and happiness: A comparative study in forty-four nations in the early 1990s', in: E. Diener and E.M. Suh (eds.) *Culture and Subjective Well-being*, Cambridge, MA: MIT Press, 257–288.

Velasquez, M.G. (1998) *Business Ethics: Concepts and Cases*, Fourth edition, Upper Saddle River, NJ: Prentice Hall.

Ver Eecke, W. (1982) 'Ethics in economics: From classical economics to Neoliberalism', *Philosophy and Social Criticism*, 9: 145–168.

Verkuyl, J. (1982) *De kernbegrippen van het marxisme-leninisme*, Kampen: Kok.

Verme, P. (2011) 'Life satisfaction and income inequality', *Review of Income and Wealth*, 57(1): 111–137.

Voigt, S. and Kiwit, D. (1998) 'The role and evolution of beliefs, habit, moral norms and institutions', in: H. Giersch (ed.) *Merits and Limits of Markets*, Berlin: Springer-Verlag, 83–108.

Vollan, B. (2008) 'Socio-ecological explanations for crowding-out effects from economic field experiments in southern Africa', *Ecological Economics*, 67: 560–573.

Wade, J.B., O' Reilly, C.A. and Pollock, T.G. (2006) 'Overpaid CEO's and underpaid managers: Fairness and executive compensation', *Organization Science*, 17: 527–544.

Waide, J. (1987) 'The making of self and world in advertising', *Journal of Business Ethics*, 6: 73–79.

Webster. (1989) *Webster's Ninth New Collegiate Dictionary*, Springfield, MA: Merriam-Webster, Inc.

Weitz, B.A. and Bradford, K.D. (1999) 'Personal selling and sales management: A relationship marketing perspective', *Journal of the Academy of Marketing Science*, 27(2): 241–254.

Wells, T. and Graafland, J.J. (2012) 'Adam Smith's bourgeois virtues in competition', *Business Ethics Quarterly*, 22(2): 319–350.

White, M.D. (2004) 'Can homo economicus follow Kant's categorical imperative?', *Journal of Socio-Economics*, 33: 89–106.

White, M.D. (2007) 'A Kantian critique on antitrust: On morality and Microsoft', *Journal of Private Enterprise*, XXII(2): 161–190.

White, M.D., Hill, S., McGovern, P., Mills, C. and Smeaton, D. (2003) 'High-performance' management practices, working hours and work – Life balance', *British Journal of Industrial Relations*, 41(2): 175–195.

Wilkinson, R. and Pickett, K. (2010) *The Spirit Level: Why Equality Is Better for Everyone*, London: Penguin Books.

Williams, B. (1981) *Moral Luck: Philosophical Papers 1973–1980*, Cambridge: Cambridge University Press.

Williamson, D., Lynch-Wood, G. and Ramsay, J. (2006) 'Drivers of environmental behaviour in manufacturing SMEs and the implications for CSR', *Journal of Business Ethics*, 67: 317–330.

Winters, L.A., McCulloch, N. and McKay, A. (2004) 'Trade policy and poverty: The evidence so far', *Journal of Economic Literature*, XLII: 72–115.

Witt, M.A., Kabbach de Castro, L.R., Amaeshi, K., Mahroum, S., Bohle, D. and Saez, L. (2018) 'Mapping the business systems of 61 major economies: A taxonomy and implications for varieties of capitalism and business systems research', *Socio-Economic Review*, 16(1): 5–38.

World Bank (2006) *World Development Report 2006*, Washington, DC: World Bank.

Wright, T.A. and Goodstein, J. (2007) 'Character is not "dead" in management research: A review of individual character and organizational-level virtue', *Journal of Management*, 33(6): 928–958.

Yamakawa, T., Okano, Y. and Saijo, T. (2016) 'Detecting motives for cooperation in public goods Experiments', *Experimental Economics*, 19: 500–512.

Zagorski, K., Evans, M., Kelley, J. and Piotrowska, K. (2014) 'Does national income inequality affect individuals' quality of life in Europe? Inequality, happiness, finances, and health', *Social Indicators Research*, 117: 1089–1110.

Zak, P.J. and Knack, S. (2001) 'Trust and growth', *The Economic Journal*, 111: 295–321.

Index

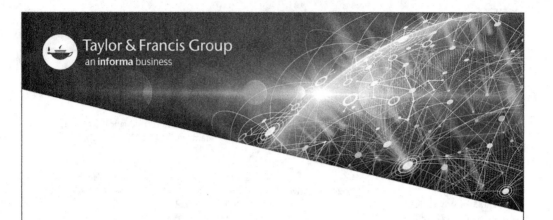

Printed in the United States
by Baker & Taylor Publisher Services